Promoting Social and Cultural Equity in the Tourism Sector

Priscila Cembranel
Universidade Sociedade Educacional de Santa Catarina, Brazil

Jakson Renner Rodrigues Soares
Universidad da Coruña, Spain

André Riani Costa Perinotto
Parnaíba Delta Federal University, Brazil

A volume in the Advances in Hospitality, Tourism, and the Services Industry (AHTSI) Book Series

Published in the United States of America by
IGI Global
Business Science Reference (an imprint of IGI Global)
701 E. Chocolate Avenue
Hershey PA, USA 17033
Tel: 717-533-8845
Fax: 717-533-8661
E-mail: cust@igi-global.com
Web site: http://www.igi-global.com

Library of Congress Cataloging-in-Publication Data

Names: Cembranel, Priscila, 1987- editor. | Soares, Jakson Renner Rodrigues, 1980- editor. | Perinotto, André, 1981- editor.
Title: Promoting social and cultural equity in the tourism sector / Priscila Cembranel, Jakson Renner Soares, and André Perinotto, editors.

Description: Hershey, PA : Business Science Reference, [2023] | Includes bibliographical references and index. | Summary: "This book provides empirical research on diversity and equity applied to tourism activity for those who wish to improve their understanding of the social, cultural, and legal issues regarding diversity applied to tourism experiences and land development"-- Provided by publisher.
Identifiers: LCCN 2022014011 (print) | LCCN 2022014012 (ebook) | ISBN 9781668441947 (hardcover) | ISBN 9781668441954 (paperback) | ISBN 9781668441961 (ebook)
Subjects: LCSH: Tourism. | Equality.
Classification: LCC G155.A1 P765 2023 (print) | LCC G155.A1 (ebook) | DDC 306.4/819--dc23/eng20220718
LC record available at https://lccn.loc.gov/2022014011
LC ebook record available at https://lccn.loc.gov/2022014012

This book is published in the IGI Global book series Advances in Hospitality, Tourism, and the Services Industry (AHTSI) (ISSN: 2475-6547; eISSN: 2475-6555)

British Cataloguing in Publication Data
A Cataloguing in Publication record for this book is available from the British Library.

For electronic access to this publication, please contact: eresources@igi-global.com.

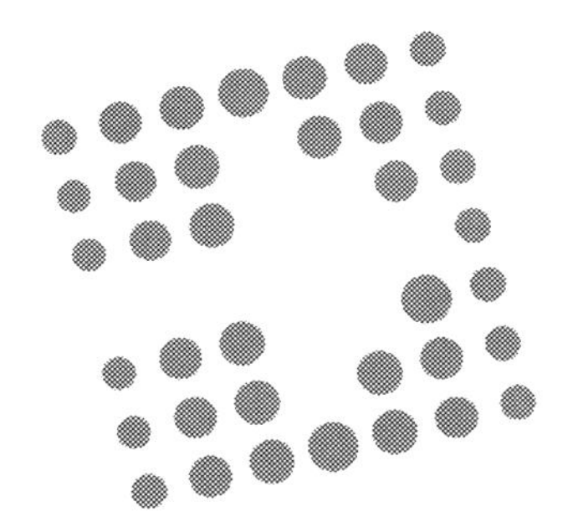

Advances in Hospitality, Tourism, and the Services Industry (AHTSI) Book Series

ISSN:2475-6547
EISSN:2475-6555

Editor-in-Chief: Maximiliano Korstanje University of Palermo, Argentina

MISSION

Globally, the hospitality, travel, tourism, and services industries generate a significant percentage of revenue and represent a large portion of the business world. Even in tough economic times, these industries thrive as individuals continue to spend on leisure and recreation activities as well as services.

The Advances in Hospitality, Tourism, and the Services Industry (AHTSI) book series offers diverse publications relating to the management, promotion, and profitability of the leisure, recreation, and services industries. Highlighting current research pertaining to various topics within the realm of hospitality, travel, tourism, and services management, the titles found within the AHTSI book series are pertinent to the research and professional needs of managers, business practitioners, researchers, and upper-level students studying in the field.

COVERAGE

- Sustainable Tourism
- Tourism and the Environment
- International Tourism
- Destination Marketing and Management
- Casino Management
- Customer Service Issues
- Leisure & Business Travel
- Travel Agency Management
- Service Training
- Health and Wellness Tourism

IGI Global is currently accepting manuscripts for publication within this series. To submit a proposal for a volume in this series, please contact our Acquisition Editors at Acquisitions@igi-global.com or visit: http://www.igi-global.com/publish/.

The Advances in Hospitality, Tourism, and the Services Industry (AHTSI) Book Series (ISSN 2475-6547) is published by IGI Global, 701 E. Chocolate Avenue, Hershey, PA 17033-1240, USA, www.igi-global.com. This series is composed of titles available for purchase individually; each title is edited to be contextually exclusive from any other title within the series. For pricing and ordering information please visit http://www.igi-global.com/book-series/advances-hospitality-tourism-services-industry/121014. Postmaster: Send all address changes to above address.

Titles in this Series

For a list of additional titles in this series, please visit:
www.igi-global.com/book-series/advances-hospitality-tourism-services-industry/121014

Employability and Skills Development in the Sports, Events, and Hospitality Industry
Vipin Nadda (University of Sunderland in London, UK) Ian Arnott (Westminster University, UK) Wendy Sealy (University of Chichester, UK) and Emma Delaney (University of Surrey, UK)
Business Science Reference • © 2022 • 315pp • H/C (ISBN: 9781799877813) • US $215.00

Handbook of Research on Sustainable Tourism and Hotel Operations in Global Hypercompetition
Hakan Sezerel (Anadolu University, Turkey) and Bryan Christiansen (Global Research Society, LLC, USA)
Business Science Reference • © 2022 • 430pp • H/C (ISBN: 9781668446454) • US $315.00

Entrepreneurship Education in Tourism and Hospitality Management
Satish Chandra Bagri (Hemwati Nandan Bahuguna Garhwal Central University, India) R.K Dhodi (Hemwati Nandan Bahuguna Garhwal Central University, India) and KC Junaid (Hemwati Nandan Bahuguna Garhwal Central University, India)
Business Science Reference • © 2022 • 330pp • H/C (ISBN: 9781799895107) • US $230.00

Global Perspectives on Strategic Storytelling in Destination Marketing
Ana Cláudia Campos (CinTurs, Universidade do Algarve, Portugal) and Sofia Almeida (Faculty of Tourism and Hospitality, Universidade Europeia, Portugal)
Business Science Reference • © 2022 • 300pp • H/C (ISBN: 9781668434369) • US $240.00

Challenges and Opportunities for Transportation Services in the Post-COVID-19 Era
Giuseppe Catenazzo (ICN Business School, France)
Business Science Reference • © 2022 • 268pp • H/C (ISBN: 9781799888406) • US $250.00

Handbook of Research on Cultural Tourism and Sustainability
Claudia Ribeiro de Almeida (University of the Algarve, Portugal) Joao Carlos Martins (University of the Algarve, Portugal) Alexandra R. Gonçalves (University of the Algarve, Portugal) Silvia Quinteiro (University of the Algarve, Portugal) and Maria Laura Gasparini (University of Bologna, Italy)
Business Science Reference • © 2022 • 482pp • H/C (ISBN: 9781799892175) • US $315.00

701 East Chocolate Avenue, Hershey, PA 17033, USA
Tel: 717-533-8845 x100 • Fax: 717-533-8661
E-Mail: cust@igi-global.com • www.igi-global.com

Table of Contents

Detailed Table of Contents

staff. It concludes with the need for a contribution of fiscal and financial support measures as well as the need for the adoption of biosafety protocols and promotion and marketing strategies with a view to recovery and resumption of tourist activity at the destination. Such measures will enable greater social inclusion for micro and small entrepreneurs affected by the pandemic.

The main purpose of this chapter is to investigate the effect of gender discrimination perceptions of hotel employees on their job satisfaction levels and turnover intentions. A second aim is to compare employees' perceptions of gender discrimination by their sex. A final aim is to investigate the moderator role of gender in the relationship between perceived gender discrimination and job satisfaction. For this purpose, a study was conducted, and 267 employees working in 4- and 5-star hotels operating in the city of Konya in Turkey were reached. The data were collected by questionnaire technique. As a result of the study, it was determined that perceived gender discrimination affects job satisfaction negatively and affects turnover intention positively. In addition, female employees feel more gender discrimination in the workplace than men. Gender moderates the relationship between perceived gender discrimination and job satisfaction. More clearly, the negative effect of perceived gender discrimination on job satisfaction is stronger for women than for men.

Tourism can promote different possibilities for gender equality such as empowering women, generating employment and income, and promoting equitable experiences in tourist destinations and attractions. This chapter aims to discuss the incorporation of gender equality through the inclusion of Sustainable Development Goal (SDG) 5 in tourism. For this, a theoretical essay is developed based on articles present in the

The objective of this chapter is to review the literature to identify the different marketing strategies used by different countries in promoting food tourism with special reference to the viewpoints of female tourists. The viewpoints of female tourists have been selected as female travelling category has seen rapid expansion in today's worldwide outbound tourism industry. This study contributes by becoming the first systematic literature review on different marketing strategies used by different countries in promoting food tourism with special reference to the viewpoints of female tourists during the period 2015 to 2021.

This research analyses the impact of the COVID-19 crisis on Brazilian expectation tourism. A questionnaire survey was used to assess the tourist expectation regarding safety in future travel. A total of 796 questionnaires were collected between 6 April and 6 May 2020. The data were analyzed with factorial analyzes and t-tests and revealed that the gender of respondents turns out to be an important variable in determining different expectations in future travels. The results show that there are new concerns from Brazilian tourists about safety at the destination, increasing interest in information about the health system and the endemic diseases of the region to which they intend to travel.

This work aims to discuss the barriers of access and permanence of Black woman crewmembers in the Brazilian airline industry as well as resistance strategies faced by them. Using intersectionality in a theoretical-methodological way, this research, of qualitative nature, carried out interviews with six Black women of the aforementioned sector. The work revealed how the airline industry is an elitist environment that excludes Black bodies, making use of the domination of structural, cultural, disciplinary, and interpersonal powers in order to give white subjects the advantage. However, it was also possible to perceive strategies of affronting, which involve the union of the Black airline industry workers into a collective—the Quilombo Aéreo—helmed by women who sought to open opportunities for the insertion of more Black people into the airline industry, taking care of the mental health of the ones who already work there, and also be a beacon for support.

Since the mid-1980s, studies on cultural heritage, whether material or immaterial, have been gaining prominence in tourism. However, there have been few debates and approaches dedicated to the understanding of socio-historical and ethnic-racial cultural peculiarities that promote the establishment of an agenda of tourist services that involve cultural heritage that recall Afro-Brazilian traditions. It is in this perspective that the authors propose a reflection elaborated from the intersection between the debate of ethnic-racial relations and tourism in Afro-religious communities, analyzing the challenges and contradictions of the promotion of tourist activities in Terreiros of Candomblé and Umbanda, in addition to gathering information that show the invisibility and prejudices in relation to these religions at the national level and valuing their tourist potential.

Perceiving that the fields of tourism and communication are linked with a certain degree of dependence of the former on the latter, this chapter reinforces the importance of media discourse as an element to sustain the orientation of tourism production. For this reason, discursive elements that permeate this type of production, especially, in institutional and official spaces on the internet are the main goal. This text is based in studies about racism from a theoretical-methodological perspective of the critical discourse analysis based on ethics and aims to recognize the abuse of power in language in order to empower those under such oppression. From this perspective, two discursive events will be analyzed in spaces of official and institutional touristic publicity in Rio Grande do Norte on the internet.

The chapter aims at studying the inclusion of these groups in a consumer market, especially in the tourism industry, and it is a continuation of a master study carried out by one of the authors of the text in the Graduate Program in Tourism at the University of São Paulo. To this end, the authors focus their attention on the NGO Eternamente SOU, a reference in welcoming LGBT+ elderly people in Brazil, and on the life stories of its participants, recently published in the book Os Brilhos das Velhices LGBT+ and as a supporting text, the book Introduction to Elderly LGBTI+.

This chapter tackles the need to incorporate strategies of linguistic and cultural accessibility that guarantee respect for diversity and equality in processes of dissemination and access to tourism information in the web environment. The proposal focuses on transcreation as a fundamental tool from the perspective, furthermore, of inclusive language. These reflections will contribute to establishing recommendations aimed at facilitating the creation of contents adapted to the characteristics of the new media. These guidelines may be of great use both for professionals in the tourism sector and for those in the field of communication or translation, amongst others. In addition, the contribution aims to favour the development of teaching resources linked to aspects of the specific language of communication and marketing, encouraging more holistic training for students of tourism and related areas. This rejuvenated professional profile will also require knowledge in post-digital communication to undertake this task in a global manner.

Foreword

One of the main reasons that people travel and venture into tourist activities is to have an immersion in different cultures, societies, and traditions, increasing their perspectives on the world and having different experiences from the ordinary. However, the tourism sector still does not present a coherent panorama with contemporary social panoramas, since the sector continues to reproduce historical and structural prejudices, especially with regard to women, people of color, and LGBTQIA+ people. In some cases, discrimination does not appear in quantitative data, but in looking at the career prospects and advancement of these groups in the area. Thus, despite advances, as long as decision-makers remain with the same profile: white and heterosexual men, the demands of socially marginalized groups will not be a priority and disparity will remain in the sector.

From that, it is essential to discuss tourist experiences related to issues with discrimination and equality such as racism, inherent prejudice, gender equality, indigenous rights, and experiences of the LGBTQIA+ community to ensure the tourism industry is inclusive and safe. One of the main ways to produce these debates is through the science and data exposed in leading industry reports. Thus, this book proposes to gather theoretical frameworks and the latest findings from empirical research, presenting the challenges, advances, and possibilities for improving tourism in the context of the well-being of marginalized social groups and, thus, promoting social and cultural equity. From that, promoting diversity in tourism has benefits that go beyond the limits of the industry, affecting society as a whole through the diffusion of ideas such as social justice and cultural equity through tourist activities.

This reference work makes a fundamental contribution to the promotion of equality in the tourism sector, as it brings together current data on issues related to the inclusion of women, LGBTQIA+, and people of color, as well as points out the relevance of creating strategies to promote the well-being of these groups in the sector and their possibilities for advancement, adapting the area to greater diversity. Another important point worth highlighting in this book is the focus on the global south present in some of its chapters, daring to think of a tourism sector that observes destinations beyond Europe and North America and having a decolonial perspective that is sometimes absent in the area studies. Thus, this reference work is crucial, not only in the academic field, but also for hotel managers, activists, travel agencies, tour organizations, industry professionals, government officials, policymakers, researchers, scholars, practitioners, instructors, and students.

The promotion of social and cultural equity is a challenge that is not limited to the area of tourism, since, as a reflection of its environment, the sector reproduces what inhabits the mentality of the population. Thus, public policies are necessary to instigate improvements in the tourism sphere, influencing the private sector and people who are inserted in the area, from employees to customers and managers. In recent decades, terms such as "diversity management" and "ethical commitment" have emerged as possibilities for greater diversity in tourism, yet there is a lack of data and the development of realistic adaptations so that not only the number of women, people of color and LGBTQIA+ people are in the sector, but can also advance in their careers, occupying leadership positions (Noguer-Junca, 2021).

Related to gender disparities, the World Tourism Organization stated that "tourism can empower women in multiple ways, particularly through the provision of jobs through income-generation opportunities in small and large-scale tourism enterprises" (UNWTO, 2015). Nevertheless, even though women are the majority of the tourism global workforce, there are considerable difficulties with their full inclusion in the sector, such as the salary gap of 14.7% between men and women and there are fewer leadership opportunities for women (UNWTO, 2019).

Although the financial emancipation of women has been increasing in recent decades, it does not occur in an egalitarian way geographically: in certain locations, whether for religious or political reasons, female autonomy remains low and women who seek their autonomy are discriminated against. From this perspective, the full empowerment of women across the globe can contribute to their insertion into the sector but it is a challenge that overcomes touristic activities (Zhang and Zhang, 2020).

Concerning race and ethnical equality, Kilomba (2021) points out that while white bodies are understood as belonging to all places, continents, and spaces, black bodies are socially considered inappropriate, and out of place. In the Brazilian context, for example, the black population is the quantitative majority, yet it is not the majority in leadership positions in the tourism sector or the majority of guests. The existence of spaces that are not racially inclusive is a legacy of the country's history of slavery that drives the present structural racism. Regarding the indigenous issue, the exclusion as a target public is even more intense. In addition, tourism in indigenous lands is rarely focused on the autonomy and self-determination of these groups, viewing them as objects, not subjects in the tourist activity (de Oliveira, 2021; dos Santos and Bomfim, 2021).

Within the scope of LGBTQIA+ populations, several challenges emerge with regard to representation. For example, the use of non-LGBTQIA+ actors in advertisements on the subject in the tourism sphere, offering caricatured representations that do not match the profile of the group, as well as the lack of hiring people in the field and the very few cases of LGBTQIA+ in positions management. In addition, the existence of homophobic legislation across the globe contributes to the little encouragement of people from the group in the sector, since their functions can be limited by cases of state homophobia (Moreira and Campos, 2019).

According to the organization Out Now (2012), LGBTQIA+ tourism is a relevant segment for the market, given that this category represents 6% of the global tourism market, being historically associated with marches, pride parades, and festivals, also contemporaneously with well-known places. for the safety of the group and non-discrimination. Thus, it is necessary to observe this group as a relevant target audience, a fact that sometimes does not happen due to the homophobia of the actors involved, negatively impacting social equity and the economic growth of the niche (Ram et al., 2019).

As exposed in the previous section, there are several challenges to the rise of social and cultural equity in the tourism sector. In this way, the solutions developed must be interdisciplinary, observing micro and macro scenarios, as well as combating structural and historical oppressions that go beyond the barriers of the sector and connect with society as a whole. Sexism, homophobia, racism, and other prejudices that remain in force in tourism are part of a mentality socially constructed and present in part of the collective unconscious. From socialization, privileges are treated as natural, making the historical origins of inequalities invisible to part of the population and making it difficult to take collective responsibility for their eradication.

Since the gender gap is not related to women's participation in the tourism sector but is associated with decent work and leadership opportunities, several strategies can be adopted in micro and macro spheres, such as the inclusion of tourism in gender-sensitive legal and macroeconomic policy to guarantee gender equality and women's empowerment, mainstream gender equality debates in regional and national tourism plans, including committing financial resources to ensure that these are implemented and the encouragement of research related to gender and tourism, once it enables the creation of reports with updated data and the development of new solutions (World Tourism Organization, 2019).

Besides that, leadership jobs exclusive to women must be designed, adapting the tourism sector to female needs. In this sense, all spaces where there is tourist activity should make adjustments in their selection processes, seeking not only the inclusion of women but possibilities for career growth by the occupation of leadership positions. In addition, the support of grassroots women's organizations is essential to female empowerment in the sector (Kuniyal et al., 2021).

In the racial sphere, one of the main factors that stimulate tourism is the feeling of belonging and this can only be achieved in environments without discrimination, where people of color feel welcome. However, building a sphere that enables the feeling of belonging goes far beyond that. World tourism continues to be Eurocentric, making explicit historical narratives that make black-centered perspectives invisible, especially with regard to slavery and Afro-descendant religiosities. In this sense, contemplating indigenous and black history is also essential to promote the permanence of these groups as customers, employees, and decision-makers in the sector (Hudson et al., 2018; Chio et al., 2020).

Therefore, initiatives such as the Black Travel Movement, an American tourist organization focused on the storytelling of black people, are fundamental to promoting racial diversity and denouncing cases of racism, provoking the public sector to create measures to combat racial discrimination in the field and encouraging practical changes in the private sphere (Benjamin and Dillette, 2021).

The good reception of LGBTQIA+ tourists is also an interdisciplinary issue, as it involves decision-makers, workers, and managers. In this scenario, dialogues between the actors involved are essential to combat homophobia in all spheres and contribute to ensuring that representation is not based on pink money, but on a structural change that allows the welcome of these populations in different destinations (Usai et al., 2020).

Besides that, hospitality is a relevant factor for promoting tourism for LGBTQIA+ people, since homophobia may not be institutionalized and still manifest itself in a structural way. Thus, an integration between the community and the sector is necessary to guarantee the well-being of this population, with state assistance to guarantee the preservation of the rights, autonomy, and dignity of LGBTQIA+ people. From this perspective, education for equity is essential for long-term inclusion (Silva and Vareiro, 2020)

Among all the initiatives mentioned and developed for each specific group, one characteristic is common to all three: the recognition of individuals as subjects, not objects. This perception is essential to understand their demands as a target audience or members of the sector's labor body. Historically, tourism was developed as a male, white, Eurocentric area. In this sense, the promotion of social and cultural equity will only be possible by deconstructing this narrative that is still seen by many managers as the only option (Chambers, 2021).

This book is organized into thirteen chapters. A brief description of each of the chapters follows:

Chapter 1 identifies that tourism activities were strongly impacted by the loss of revenue, reduction in revenue, and staff. In this sense, it highlights the need for a contribution of fiscal and financial support measures, for the companies in the sector, mostly micro and small companies, as well as the adoption of biosafety protocols and promotion and marketing strategies with a view to recovery and resumption of tourist activity at the destination.

Chapter 2 analyzes discursive manifestations of racism in institutional spaces of touristic publicity. In addition, it brings a reflection on communication and tourism. From this perspective, two discursive events will be analyzed in spaces of official and institutional touristic publicity in Rio Grande do Norte on the Internet.

Chapter 3 investigates women's tourism collective agency and its relationship with other forms of agency in a tourism-dependent rural community in Uganda. Findings show positive collective gains for women, in terms of economic independence, livelihood diversification, reduced drudgery, and acquisition of skills that have enhanced their agency and well-being. In turn, this is creating positive outcomes at the household and community levels.

Chapter 4 discusses the barriers to access and permanence of black woman crewmembers in the Brazilian airline industry, as well as resistance strategies faced by them using intersectionality in a theoretical-methodological way. It revealed how the airline industry is an elitist environment that excludes black bodies, making use of the domination of structural, cultural, disciplinary, and interpersonal powers to give white subjects the advantage.

Chapter 5 debates the incorporation of gender equality through the inclusion of Sustainable Development Goal (SDG) number 5 in tourism. The results demonstrate that gender equality must be substantially discussed by everyone involved in the tourism sector. In particular with regard to equal salary and opportunities and salary for women as a way to reduce gender stereotypes in companies in the sector.

Chapter 6 exposes the relevance of including LGBT+ elderly communities in a consumer market, especially in the tourism industry. To this end, it focuses on the NGO Eternamente SOU, a reference in welcoming LGBT+ elderly people in Brazil, and on the life stories of its participants, recently published in the book "Os Brilhos das Velhices LGBT+", and as a supporting text, the book "Introduction to Elderly LGBTI+", also organized by its members, through content analysis.

Chapter 7 discusses how what happens in tourist destinations is an insufficient and inadequate base of information on the natural and cultural heritage capable of arousing curiosity and interest in the differential values of places and communities in order to establish communication and assimilation of visitors for expanding your knowledge and enjoyment of the place and its hospitality.

Chapter 8 proposes a reflection elaborated from the intersection between the debate of ethnic-racial relations and tourism in Afro-religious communities, analyzing the challenges and contradictions of the promotion of tourist activities in terreiros of Candomblé and Umbanda, in addition to gathering information that shows the invisibility and prejudices concerning these religions at the national level, valuing their tourist potential.

Chapter 9 main purpose is to investigate the effect of gender discrimination perceptions of hotel employees on their job satisfaction levels and turnover intentions.

A second aim is to compare employees' perceptions of gender discrimination by their sex. A final aim is to investigate the moderator role of gender in the relationship between perceived gender discrimination and job satisfaction.

Chapter 10 aims to precipitate and reflect on the nature of tourism employability and examine the gender space and women's employability for inclusive tourism development. It also indicates how women-centric employee engagement is attained in a globalized world. The gender-centric perspective and women's empowerment in the hospitality business is assessed.

Chapter 11 tackles the need to incorporate strategies of linguistic and cultural accessibility that guarantee respect for diversity and equality in processes of dissemination and access to tourism information in the web environment. In addition, its contribution aims to favor the development of teaching resources linked to aspects of the specific language of communication and marketing, encouraging more holistic training for students of tourism and related areas.

Chapter 12 reviews the literature to identify the different marketing strategies used by different countries in promoting food tourism with special reference to the viewpoints of female tourists. It also contributes to becoming the first systematic literature review on different marketing strategies used by different countries in promoting food tourism with special reference to the viewpoints of female tourists during the period 2015 to 2021.

Chapter 13 analyzes the impact of the Covid-19 Crisis on Brazilians' expectations of tourism. The data were analyzed with factorial analyzes and t-tests and revealed that the gender of respondents turns out to be an important variable in determining different expectations in future travels. The results show that there are new concerns from Brazilian tourists about safety at the destination, increasing interest in information about the health system and the endemic diseases of the region to which they intend to travel.

Manoela de Oliveira Veras
University of Southern Santa Catarina (UNISUL), Brazil

REFERENCES

Benjamin, S., & Dillette, A. K. (2021). Black travel movement: Systemic racism informing tourism. *Annals of Tourism Research*, *88*, 103169. doi:10.1016/j.annals.2021.103169

Chambers, D. (2021). Are we all in this together? Gender intersectionality and sustainable tourism. *Journal of Sustainable Tourism*, 1–16.

Chio, J., Gill, T., Gonzalez, V. V., Harp, S. L., McDonald, K., Rosenbaum, A. T., Rugh, S. S., & Thomas, L. L. (2020). Discussion: Tourism and race. *Journal of Tourism History, 12*(2), 173–197. doi:10.1080/1755182X.2020.1756465

de Oliveira, N. A. (2021). Precisamos falar sobre racismo no turismo. *RITUR: Revista Iberoamericana de Turismo, 11*(2), 267–280.

Dos Santos, S., & Bomfim, C. (2021). *Mechanisms of trust in indigenous tourism: a study of the Pataxó Jaqueira community in Porto Seguro, Brazil* (Doctoral dissertation). Oxford Brookes University.

Figueroa-Domecq, C., Palomo, J., Flecha-Barrio, M., & Segovia-Perez, M. (2020). Technology double gender gap in tourism business leadership. *Information Technology & Tourism, 22*(1), 75–106. doi:10.100740558-020-00168-0

Hudson, S., Kevin, K. F. S., Meng, F., Cárdenas, D., & Li, J. (2018). Racial discrimination in tourism: The case of African-American travellers in South Carolina. *Current Issues in Tourism*. Advance online publication. doi:10.1080/13683500.2018.1516743

Kilomba, G. (2021). *Plantation memories: episodes of everyday racism*. Between the Lines.

Kourtesopoulou, A., & Chatzigianni, E. E. (2021). *Gender Equality and Women's Entrepreneurial Leadership in Tourism: A Systematic Review*. Gender and Tourism.

Kuniyal, J. C., Maiti, P., Kumar, S., Kumar, A., Bisht, N., Sekar, K. C., Arya, S. C., Rai, S., & Nand, M. (2021). Dayara bugyal restoration model in the alpine and subalpine region of the Central Himalaya: A step toward minimizing the impacts. *Scientific Reports, 11*(1), 16547. doi:10.103841598-021-95472-y PMID:34400660

Moreira, M. G., & Campos, L. J. D. (2019). The ritual of ideological interpellation in LGBT Tourism and the impossibility of the desire that moves. *Revista Brasileira de Pesquisa em Turismo, 13*(2), 54–68. doi:10.7784/rbtur.v13i2.1542

Noguer-Juncà, E., & Crespi-Vallbona, M. (2021). Gender Perspective in University Education: The Case of Bachelor's Degrees in Tourism in Catalonia. *International and Multidisciplinary Journal of Social Sciences, 10*(2), 81–111. doi:10.17583/rimcis.8156

Out Now. (2012). *Better LGBT* Retrieved from: http://www.outnowbusinessclass.com/learn/

Ram, Y., Kama, A., Mizrachi, I., & Hall, C. M. (2019). The benefits of an LGBT-inclusive tourist destination. *Journal of Destination Marketing & Management, 14*, 100374. doi:10.1016/j.jdmm.2019.100374

Silva, S., & Vareiro, L. (2020, October). Residents' Perceived Impacts of LGBT Tourism: A Cluster Analysis. In *International Conference on Tourism, Technology and Systems* (pp. 207-222). Springer.

UNWTO - World Tourism Organization. (2015). *Tourism in the 2030 Agenda*. Available at: https://www.unwto.org/tourism-in-2030-agenda

UNWTO - World Tourism Organization. (2019). *Global Report on Women in Tourism* (2nd ed.). UNWTO. doi:10.18111/9789284420384

Usai, R., Cai, W., & Wassler, P. (2022). A queer perspective on heteronormativity for LGBT travelers. *Journal of Travel Research, 61*(1), 3–15. doi:10.1177/0047287520967763

Zhang, J., & Zhang, Y. (2020). Tourism and gender equality: An Asian perspective. *Annals of Tourism Research, 85*, 103067. doi:10.1016/j.annals.2020.103067

Preface

Society is organized based on a variety of ideas, characteristics, situations, and environments. In this context, driven by curiosity and the desire to get to know places and cultures different from the ones they are used to, people venture into tourist activities to expand their worldviews and experiences. And it is common for them to face realities totally different from those they are used to. Therefore, it is essential to discuss tourist experiences related to diversity. Such as: racism, inherent prejudice, gender equality, indigenous rights, rights, and experiences of the LGBTQIA+ community, etc. It is hoped that this work will contribute to broaden the discussion about the nuances inherent to tourism activities and experiences at tourist destinations and different cultures.

This book provides relevant theoretical frameworks and the latest findings from empirical research on diversity and equity applied to tourism activity. It be written for professionals who wish to improve their understanding of the social, cultural, and legal issues regarding diversity applied to tourism experiences and land development. The relevance of the topic revolves around tourism experiences (tourists and residents) and solutions to problems to contribute to the improvement of society, diversity, equity, and inclusion. This book comes to fill a gap in the current demand, by jointly presenting texts that help in the debate on equity, inclusion, diversity, and equality in Tourism and in related areas.

Diversity is a sensitive topic to be explored by the market, society, and academic studies. This permeates the culture of peoples, their signs and meanings, laws, norms and even the territory in which they operate. In tourism, as in any other phenomenon, it is evidenced by how people are received in different countries, by the levels of tolerance and respect. And they can also be seen in advertising and in the preparation of the job market to meet the tourist demand.

Over the decades, the need to welcome diversity and recognize it for its cultural richness is perceived to embrace multiple life experiences in different countries. This can be evidenced by the increase in the number of women in the labor market, their professional valorization and a decrease in sexism and gender impositions.

In addition, it is important to emphasize the importance of adapting the hotel sector and tourist destinations to welcome the elderly population that grows every day and takes advantage of the possibilities of traveling after a lifetime of work. It can also be perceived by the investment in accessibility to welcome people with special needs and provide them with inclusive experiences.

Also noteworthy is the encouragement of LGBTQIA+ tourism, a public that, unfortunately, depends on laws and good management practices capable of guaranteeing safety and respect for basic rights to have a good experience in tourist destinations. The care with diversity must consider that, in low season, it is the minorities that heat the tourism economy. And for that there must be infrastructure, security and teams prepared to receive this audience. Likewise, there must be marketing actions aimed at attracting them to destinations.

The book is opportunity to discuss diversity in the tourism sector and research topics in this area. The book is suitable both for students of tourism, management, hospitality, gastronomy, anthropology, sociology, geography and many others who have Tourism as their focus and object of study (masters and doctoral students), as well as tourism professionals in the sector. Several of the chapters are current and practical examples that can be used in various university disciplines in tourism and related fields to broaden the discussion of the cultural nuances surrounding the experience in tourism destinations. It also proves useful information for research work. In addition, because diversity is an interdisciplinary and trans-disciplinary topic, the reader will be able to get more information about the tourism industry and the latest trends in a summarized and reliable way.

The book has 13 chapters. The first two, "Tourism, Health, and Quality of Life for All" and "The Social Impact of COVID-19 on the Tourism Economy: The Case of Joinville (Brazil)," provide a more general perspective. Following, the articles "The Relationship Among Perceived Gender Discrimination, Job Satisfaction, and Turnover Intention and the Moderator Role of Gender," "Tourism and Gender Equality From SDG 5's Perspective," "Gender Perspectives: Women and Employability in Tourism," "Interrogating Rural Women's Collective Tourism Entrepreneurship and Social Change in South Western Uganda," "The Perspectives of Female Tourists on Food Tourism in Different Countries: A Review on Different Marketing Strategies Used by Different Countries in Promoting Food Tourism," and "Gender Differences Among Brazilians' Perceptions About Safety When Selecting a Destination" address gender studies and the specific issues experienced by women in the tourism sector.

Still within the theme, the article "Intersectionality Between Racism and Sexism in the Brazilian Airline Industry: Perceptions and Strategies of Black Women Crewmembers" addresses the issue of black women and allows the adoption of the intersectional lens to understand the problems faced by them. There are the articles "Tourism, Contradiction, and Afro-Religious (In)Visibility" and "Tourism Promotion and Racism Against Indigenous People in Rio Grande do Norte (Brazil)." These address racism against Afro religions and against indigenous peoples. The last two articles, "Essay on the Appropriation of Tourism in LGBT+ Elderly Communities: A Look at the Book *The Shining of LGBT+ Old Ages*" and "Transcreation in Digital Tourism Information: An Inclusive Language Approach" deal with questions about LGBTQIA+ elderly people and language. inclusive, respectively.

In the chapter "Tourism, Health, and Quality of Life for All," the travel experience is addressed through its internal and external movements. External because the tourist moves in physical space and time. Internal because his intellectual and emotional prepare for unique experiences. This dichotomy is in line with the media stimuli received and incorporated into the individual and collective behavior of guests-consumers-tourists. In this sense, it is essential to harmonize what the destination has to offer tourists and what they expect to experience. The article also addresses the need for cities and their identities to represent and change with the needs and demands of local policies and social movements, linked to universals. This approach aims to generate identity and meaning for the tourist, whether materially or emotionally.

"The Social Impact of COVID-19 on the Tourism Economy: The Case of Joinville (Brazil)," the second chapter of the work, addresses the impact of COVID-19 on the events segment and its impact on the tourism economy in the city of Joinville (Santa Catarina). According to this, tourist activities were impacted by the loss of revenue, reduction of revenue and personnel, and they need fiscal and financial support measures for companies, the adoption of biosafety protocols and promotion and marketing strategies with a view to recovery and resumption of tourist activity to promote social inclusion for micro and small entrepreneurs affected by the pandemic.

The chapter "The Relationship Among Perceived Gender Discrimination, Job Satisfaction, and Turnover Intention and the Moderator Role of Gender" investigates hotel employees' perception of gender discrimination and turnover intentions with a focus on gender discrimination by sex and job satisfaction. According to the study, perceived gender discrimination negatively affects job satisfaction and positively affects turnover intention in female employees of 4 and 5-star hotels in Turkey.

In "Tourism and Gender Equality from SDG 5's Perspective," the fourth chapter, possibilities for women's empowerment, employment and income generation and equitable experiences for women are discussed as possibilities to generate gender equality in tourism. The findings address the need for equal pay and opportunities and pay for women as a way of reducing gender stereotypes in companies in the sector, as well as developing good practices in the graduation of higher education in tourism to promote equality.

The fifth chapter, "Gender Perspectives: Women and Employability in Tourism," reflects on the nature of tourism employability and examines the gender space and the employability of women for the development of inclusive tourism. The study reflects on the tourism industry, economic resilience and its role in the face of gender parity to promote the empowerment of women in the hospitality business.

"Interrogating Rural Women's Collective Tourism Entrepreneurship and Social Change in Southwestern Uganda," the sixth chapter, analyzes women's collective tourism agency and its relationship with other forms of agency in a rural community dependent on tourism in Uganda. For the study, women have positive gains related to financial independence and purchasing power when participating in the female tourism collective. This, at the same time contributes to the empowerment of women in the tourism economy, encourages policies aimed at this public and promotes the equitable development of the sector.

The seventh chapter, "The Perspectives of Female Tourists on Food Tourism in Different Countries: A Review on Different Marketing Strategies Used by Different Countries in Promoting Food Tourism," is a systematic review of the marketing strategies in food tourism perceived by women tourists. The study highlights the point of view of women and the importance of a less sexist lens in marketing actions.

The study "Gender Differences Among Brazilians' Perceptions About Safety When Selecting a Destination" is the eighth chapter of the work. It addresses the impact of the Covid-19 crisis on Brazilian tourist expectations and finds that women have less optimistic expectations regarding future trips. Well, the concern with security at the destination is greater among them. In addition, it shows that women seek more information about the health system and endemic diseases in the region to which they intend to travel.

The ninth chapter, "Intersectionality Between Racism and Sexism in the Brazilian Airline Industry: Perceptions and Strategies of Black Women Crewmembers," discusses the barriers to access and permanence of black crew members in the Brazilian airline sector and their strategies to face the problems they experience. The study highlights the elitist environment that excludes black bodies through structural, cultural, disciplinary and interpersonal domination to give advantage to white subjects. In addition, it also highlights the "Quilombo Aereo" group as a strategy of a women's collective to expand opportunities for insertion in the sector's job market.

"Tourism, Contradiction, and Afro-Religious (In)Visibility" is the tenth chapter. It discusses the socio-historical and ethnic-racial cultural peculiarities in the promotion of tourist services involving Afro-Brazilian traditions. In particular, regarding the challenges and contradictions of promoting tourism in Candomblé and Umbanda "terreiros". The article aims to denounce the invisibility and prejudices in relation to religion, as well as value its tourist potential.

The eleventh chapter, "Tourism Promotion and Racism Against Indigenous People in Rio Grande do Norte (Brazil)," addresses the media discourse and the connection between tourism and communication. According to this, the discursive manifestations of racism against the indigenous population in institutional spaces of tourist advertising highlights the importance of the abuse of power in language to empower those who suffer such oppression.

"Essay on the Appropriation of Tourism in LGBT+ Elderly Communities: A Look at the Book *The Shining of LGBT+ Old Ages,*" the twelfth chapter of the work, highlights the insertion of LGBT+ elderly people in the tourist consumption market. The study arises from the performance of a Non-Governmental Organization and addresses the importance of welcoming this audience and valuing their life story to understand their travel habits.

Finally, the last chapter, "Transcreation in Digital Tourism Information: An Inclusive Language Approach," highlights linguistic and cultural accessibility strategies to ensure respect for diversity and equality in the processes of dissemination and access to tourist information on the internet. The study defends the importance of these strategies for professionals in the tourism sector and for the community. It also highlights the need to develop didactic resources for communication and marketing and for the training of tourism students as the main resource for the inclusion of all those interested in the sector.

We editors of this book hope that you will enjoy our work as much as we enjoy the texts and contributions of many researchers around the world.

Priscila Cembranel
Universidade Sociedade Educacional de Santa Catarina, Brazil

Jakson Renner Rodrigues Soares
Universidad da Coruna, Spain

Andre Riani Costa Perinotto
Parnaiba Delta Federal University, Brazil

Chapter 1
Tourism, Health, and Quality of Life for All

André Riani Costa Perinotto
https://orcid.org/0000-0001-7094-3758
Parnaiba Delta Federal University, Brazil

Cintia Martins
Parnaiba Delta Federal University, Brazil

ABSTRACT

Some hospitals improving their service structure, a greater number of people having access to a quality medical service, and above all, greater demand from a public with special needs make many entrepreneurs combine medical treatment with a quality service, such as that provided by the hotel chain. Many definitions of quality are used in different sectors in different sciences. This chapter explores tourism, health, and quality of life.

INTRODUCTION

In 1963, the World Tourism Organization (WTO) defined tourism as "the sum of relationships and services resulting from a temporary and voluntary exchange of residence for non-business or professional reasons." (Beni, 1998, p. 46).

Trigo (1993) points out that one cannot analyze the tourist phenomenon outside the context comprising culture, art, leisure and quality of life concerns, inserted in the post-industrial dynamics and complexity. The author defines post-industrial societies as those that, from the 1950s, achieved a high level of technology, particularly in

DOI: 10.4018/978-1-6684-4194-7.ch001

developed countries, and have an economy marked by the growth of the third sector and a computerized industrial complex.

For Luchiari (1997, p.41), "tourists are concerned with the region itself, its accelerated and disordered growth; yet they do not think specifically about the well-being of local communities but rather the conservation of that one, which is to be used as a leisure resource." According to Krippendorf (1989, p. 191), "the local population must participate in the tourism development in their space, so as not to position themselves as invaded," thus damaging their quality of life.

Krippendorf (1989) points out that the habits of people facing mobile leisure (tourism) are no different from one country to another and the most widespread travel motivation nowadays is the desire to escape from everyday realities; that is, breaking out of routines, particularly those experienced in urban spaces since tourists seek space, images, and icons that are different from those found in their everyday lives.

In addition, Acerenza (2002) points to tourism as one of the factors of development, as tourism comes to collaborate so that certain goals are achieved not only in the economic sphere but also in the social, cultural, and even political ones. These goals are:

- In the economic sphere: to improve the budgetary balance (capturing foreign exchange resulting from the development of international tourism. However, tourism can also contribute to this achievement by reducing the outflow of foreign exchange by stimulating domestic tourism); increasing the domestic product (originated from tourist spending); redistributing income (through national tourism reaching different population strata); boosting less-developed zones and regions (due to the wide possibilities it offers in this sense, by the transport of relative economic resources in a given place).
- In the social sphere: to generate productive jobs (this goal can be considered economic and social, for it strengthens the production units of the "sector;" that is, the development of tourist companies in their entire scope and various modalities, thus creating direct and indirect jobs); to achieve the rest and relaxation of the population (that is, regarding leisure as a right of society);
- In the cultural sphere: to protect the historical-cultural heritage (to be an attractive and potential resource, in addition to being able to revitalize cultural traditions and protect them); to improve the educational level of the local population (everyone wants to be welcomed on their travels and be able to provide job opportunities in welcoming, hosting and providing information to visitors).
- In the political sphere: to achieve national integration (that is, the interchange of cultures and internal displacement of income, thus becoming able to achieve a national identity and integrate the population around shared development

goals); to project and improve the country's image abroad; to safeguard national sovereignty and security (this helps reaffirmation, particularly in border areas or sparsely populated regions of a country).

Development must be perceived as a complex process of changes and transformations of an economic, political, and, above all, human and social order. Development is nothing more than growth (defined as positive increments in product and income) transformed to satisfy the most diverse needs of human beings, such as health, education, housing, transportation, food, leisure, among others (Oliveira, 2003, p .40).

Travelling exerts a lot of influence on tourists since it will subjectively release the content of one's dreams, desires, projective imagination, and increase their existential experiences. And by engaging in such an experience, they will become pioneers of themselves.

According to Walker (2002), traveling is opening new horizons, getting to know new cultures, places, and landscapes. A trip can help one break out of their routine, reveal new scenarios, and typically surprises tourists in their expectations.

A trip is an external and internal movement for tourists. External because as one travels, they move in space and time. And internal because their imagination expands, instigating their emotions and intellect and preparing them to live the extraordinary through unique experiences that reveal what is unknown and unusual.

The tourist and hospitality space/scenarios often result from a person's ability to capture, absorb, and experience their imaginary and collectivity as they search for the content of dreams, desires, and impulses stimulated by the media, which generates and feeds this fanciful process.

Therefore, the contributions of the field of psychosociology, which investigates the perception and imagery expressed in the individual and collective behavior of guests-consumers-tourists are of paramount importance.

However, what is happening in tourist destinations nowadays constitutes an insufficient and inadequate base of information on the natural and cultural heritage capable of arousing curiosity and interest in the differential of places and communities to establish communication and assimilation of visitors for expanding their knowledge and enjoyment of the place and its hospitality.

Harmonization should always be sought between what the destination has to offer tourists and what they hope to experience. It is from this association between supply and consumption that the fruition of hospitality and the cultural dimension emerges, a component that is still poorly valued in travel planning.

The scientific analysis must significantly expand knowledge about leisure and the imaginary, everyday life, interpersonal relationships between diverse cultures, and the reaction of tourists to the interpreted heritage.

The urban phenomenon is linked to modern history. Cities are faithful representations of macro-social movements. They are a part of the world where, regardless of their dimensions or regional relevance, they vibrate and change according to the needs and demands of local social policies and movements, linked to universal elements. Urban changes invade and cause invasions, and this is not always beneficial to the interests of tourism policies.

Identity is associated with differences, that is, an object's singularities. It is recognized as a separable entity and, therefore, urban identity must have some meaning for the observer, whether material or emotional.

Brazil Attracting Visitors for Health

"To be glowing with health!" This popular idiom summarizes how Brazil stood out in various health segments, such as cardiology, oncology, dentistry, plastic surgery, among others.

Brazilian hospitals have reached a certain degree of international excellence, housing doctors and nurses of recognized and outstanding standards.

In addition to the country's attractions, those who are forced to travel due to medical treatments soon discover Brazil's exceptional cost/benefit.

Importance of Health for Tourism

To provide better infrastructure for urban cleaning services to the tourist municipalities that are part of the National Tourism Municipalization Program (PNMT), which is managed by EMBRATUR, through the implementation of systems for the collection, treatment, and/or disposal of solid waste.

To conduct studies on demand and capacity aiming at planning a location to host the client/visitor. The case of Barretos and Analândia, SP. The number of hospital beds, sewage training, basic infrastructure, water, electricity, transport.

Tourism has the ambiguous effect of promoting health conditions in host destinations while acting as a vehicle to disseminate certain diseases.

Endemic tropical diseases can affect tourists who, due to lack of information, natural resistance, adequate vaccines, or immediate medical care, may undergo serious complications in their travels. Ex: Bird flu, cholera, malaria, among others.

Health Tourism can be defined as the set of tourist activities that people carry out as they search for means to maintain or acquire good functioning and health of their body and mind. Indeed, this concept is directly linked to the Tourism of Aesthetics.

When travelers move around to undergo medical treatment in the country, this involves a wide range of complementary services, which fosters a part of tourism that has not been studied much, namely Health Tourism. In this case, someone who leaves their town looking for treatment in a big city will have to consume a series of services, namely transportation (whether by plane, bus or even car, thus paying the toll charges); food and catering services, either on the way or at the destination, to be used at all times); accommodation, as they need to stay in hotels or another form of lodging. Naturally, these services are not offered simply to those people who travel looking for health care, but their revenues are increased due to this modality of tourism.

Health Tourism: Countless foreigners visit Brazil not only for leisure but in search of health care services. Private doctors and dentists' offices have a busy schedule with clients who come from abroad. The difference in the exchange rate pays off for foreigners coming to Brazil. Brazil has medical specialties regarded as cutting-edge. For visitors, travel is more affordable, as they can pay for the trip, go on vacations, and still have the opportunity to undergo an operation, for example, at a more affordable rate.

Another niche that deserves to be highlighted is that of spas. In the 1970s there were only three of them in Brazil; in the 1980s, they added to 15, and now there are approximately 150 spas and clinics in the country subdividing themselves, prepared to serve an increasingly demanding public. In addition to the clinics, there are various other spa modalities, including holistic, aesthetic, medical, sports, and adventure, nutrition and fitness, thermal, wellness, and day spas.

Hospital events include national and international conferences, medical and other professionals' journeys, courses, lectures, telemedicine (surgeries broadcast live to conferences and auditoriums in other places over the internet), among others. However, although they are typically successful, they cost more and are less organized than if they were to be conducted by tourism and hospitality professionals.

The *Hospital do Coração*, for example, has a glass mural in the main lobby showing the various events that are held. Examples include international health symposiums held in Brazil, with the participation of authorities from Brazil, the USA, and the Netherlands, or the Abdominoplasty Course, with surgeons from all over the country, among others.

Aesthetics and Tourism: This practice emerged from human's tireless quest for the perfect body and the feeling of well-being that it provides. It is truly a break for one's body. There is no time to spend hours in gyms, taking long walks in the city, or starting unnecessary diets that can end up harming one's health.

Urban Spas and Aesthetics and Physiotherapy Clinics: These places help to break out of the routine without having to go far. They can help people to lose or control their weight, relieve stress, undergo sunless tanning, stretch marks and cellulite treatments, post-operative treatments, or take part in countless other conventional and alternative treatments that such places offer.

Hydrothermal resorts: resorts aimed at healing and pleasure. Baths and spas have always been associated with practices that navigate ambiguously between body control and pleasure. They were pointed out by Narciso (1944), a medical hydrologist, as the first tourist movement involving the journey of healing and pleasure.

Brazil has mineral waters of several types coming from various sources, so there is no need to beg for aerated, ferruginous, sulfurous waters abroad. They include sparkling water from Vila de Campanha, ferruginous water from Andaraí, Matacavalos, and sulphureous water from Vila de Caldas in Minas Gerais. The country also features thermal water spots including Caldas do Cubatão, Caxambu and Poços de Caldas, Vila de Itapicuru in Bahia, as well as the thermal springs of Santa Catarina and Goiás.

Medical Hotels: Luxury hospitals have entered a business previously reserved for hotels by absorbing specialized labor from the hotel and tourism. This opened a new range of work choices in hospitals, with the consequent benefit for patients and a greater transit of people to other locations, consuming products, and services hitherto uncommon, and fostering a part of a scarcely known tourism economy.

Some hospitals have improved their service structure, a greater number of people have achieved access to quality medical service and, above all, the demand from a public with special needs has expanded, so many entrepreneurs have combined medical treatment with quality services similar to those provided by hotel chains.

Many definitions of quality are adopted in various sectors in different sciences. "There is no single concept of quality. Various sciences (philosophy, economics, marketing, production) have developed concepts of Quality, each of them emphasizing aspects that are their own" (Castelli, 1998).

Campos (1992) defines quality as "the product or service that meets customer needs perfectly, reliably, affordably, securely and at the right time."

For Gianesi and Correa (1996), quality services are defined as "the degree to which customer expectations are met/exceeded by their perception of the service provided."

Although there is a macro view regarding the concepts of quality, the quality function was defined by Juran (1994) as "the set of activities through which the adequacy of the product or service is achieved for use, no matter in which part of the organization these activities are carried out."

In turn, according to Paladini (1995), quality "is a definition that compromises and requires effort from those who intend to adopt it: the commitment to always serve the consumer in the best conceivable way and the effort to optimize all the process actions that contribute to this end."

The answer seems to have various undertones: to develop a prospective vision and to create a set of skills within an organization aimed at understanding the options of the future; to confront them with the capacities available at present; and finally, to identify the paths that lead the destination to a future that finds them prepared to compete when it finally comes.

According to Trigo (1993, p. 27), today's organized tourism implies the presence of service structure in the tourist's place of origin, consisting of agencies or operators, guides or software that prepare the trip; carriers that can make the trip and the journey itself feasible, and; the hosting equipment at the destination, the services provided to the tourist and the entire network of relations between visitors and residents of the visited place, an aspect that has been regarded as the one that deserves the most attention in the scope of the tourist phenomenon.

REFERENCES

Acerenza, M. Á. (2002). Tourism administration: Conceptualization and organization [Administração do turismo: Conceituação e organização]. *Tradução de G. R. Hendges, 1*.

Beni, M. C. (1998). Structural analysis of tourism [Análise estrutural do turismo] (2nd ed.). SENAC.

Campos, V. F. (1992). TQC - Total quality control [TQC – Controle de qualidade total] (2nd ed.). São Paulo: Bloch Editores.

Castelli, G. (2001). *Hotel Administration* [Administração Hoteleira] (8th ed.). EDUSC.

Gianesi, I. G. N., & Corrêa, H. L. (1996). *Strategic service management* [Administração estratégica de serviços]. Atlas.

Juran, J. M. (1994). The Next Century of Quality [O Próximo Século da Qualidade]. Congresso Anual de Qualidade da ASQC.

Krippendorf, J. (1989). *Sociology of Tourism: For a new understanding of leisure and travel* [Sociologia do Turismo: para uma nova compreensão do lazer e das viagens]. Civilização Brasileira.

Luchiari, M. T. (1997). Tourism and culture fell on the north coast of São Paulo [Turismo e cultura caiçara no litoral norte paulista]. In Turismo Modernidade e Globalização. HUCITEC.

Oliveira, L. O. (2003). Endogenous elements of regional development: considerations about the role of local society in the development process [Elementos endógenos do desenvolvimento regional: considerações sobre o papel da sociedade local no processo de desenvolvimento]. *Revista FAE*, *6*(2).

Paladini, E. P. (1995). *Quality Management in the Process; quality in the production of goods and services* [Gestão da Qualidade no Processo; a qualidade na produção de bens e serviços]. Atlas.

Trigo, L. G. G. (1993). Tourism and Quality; Contemporary Trends [Turismo e Qualidade; Tendências Contemporâneas] (5th ed.). Academic Press.

Walker, J. R. (2002). *Introduction to hospitality* [Introdução à hospitalidade]. Manole.

Chapter 2
The Social Impact of COVID-19 on the Tourism Economy:
The Case of Joinville (Brazil)

Yoná da Silva da Silva Dalonso
University of the Region of Joinville, Brazil

Elaine Scalabrini
University of the Region of Joinville, Brazil

Jani Floriano
University of the Region of Joinville, Brazil

Fernanda Dalonso
https://orcid.org/0000-0002-4720-0371
University of the Region of Joinville, Brazil

Marcelo Leandro De Borba
University of the Region of Joinville, Brazil

ABSTRACT

Since March 2020, the world has been impacted by SARS-CoV-2, COVID-19. The effects of this pandemic closed business and segments including special tourism activities. This chapter aims to present the impact of the COVID-19 pandemic on the tourism economy in the city of Joinville (Santa Catarina), especially in the destination events segment, based on an empirical research. The results evidence that tourism activities were strongly impacted by loss of revenue and reduction in revenue and staff. It concludes with the need for a contribution of fiscal and financial support measures as well as the need for the adoption of biosafety protocols and promotion and marketing strategies with a view to recovery and resumption of tourist activity at the destination. Such measures will enable greater social inclusion for micro and small entrepreneurs affected by the pandemic.

DOI: 10.4018/978-1-6684-4194-7.ch002

INTRODUCTION

Tourism is a constantly growing, driven by globalization and by the desire for tourist consumption, enabling the development of the activity, mainly in the economic aspect. Social and cultural aspects are also influenced by the tourism, mentioning, as an example, the valorization of the artistic and cultural manifestations, as well as of the material and immaterial patrimony. This economic activity is of vital importance to society, not only for strengthening the business and trade balance of countries, but also for being one of the main leisure activities of today's society, favoring the promotion and cultural and environmental valorization.However, tourist activity is susceptible to crises, whether economic, social or health. This is the reality of 2020 when the world suffers the impacts of the COVID-19 pandemic reality.

In this sense, despite the prospects for tourism at the beginning of 2020, the pandemic caused practically total stoppage of tourism operations in mid-March, changing completely the future of this important economic sector worldwide.

Since the beginning of the pandemic, the travel market has been one of the sectors most affected by the crisis, as the policy of isolation resulting from contention measures to contagion by COVID-19 directly affects the economic dynamics of the sector, leaving almost no possibility of revenue. Worldwide, approximately 75 million people who work directly with tourism are at risk of losing their jobs. In addition, it is estimated a loss of US$ 2.1 trillion in GDP is related to tourism (Wordl Travel and Tourism Council, 2020). As it is an activity that generates jobs in all income groups in Brazil, mainly, and on a large scale, in areas of a lesser degree of specialization, its downsizing has significant consequences for the country.

As of March 2020, trips with different objectives have been reduced, which impacted the different sectors of tourism: transport (airlines, road transport, taxis, transport applications), accommodation (hotels, Airbnb, hostels), restaurants, events, and the entire production chain related to this activity.

Joinville, the largest city in the state of Santa Catarina (Brazil), also felt the impacts related to the crisis from COVID-19. The main tourism segment is business and events. Before the crisis, small, large, and medium-sized cultural and business events were held annually, attracting a large audience (Scalabrini & Dalonso, 2018). In addition, other segments are also relevant to Joinville like rural tourism and leisure tourism.

In this sense, this study aimed to identify the impacts of the COVID-19 on the tourism and it was developed by the University of the Region of Joinville - Univille, and the Joinville and Region Convention & Visitors Bureau, It was possible to identify a more precise scenario concerning the economic and social impacts of the pandemic on the city's tourism activity in all its segments, be they business, events, leisure, among others. It's important to consider that the events sector conglomerates a significant number of small family businesses, which, in many cases, are characterized as the only income of the family.

This paper is organized as follows. After the introduction, section 2 presents concepts that allow understanding the pandemic context. Research methods are presented in section 3, followed by the presentation of the data and a discussion of the results. Finally, considerations are presented.

COVID-19 and Tourism: Evolution and Impacts

The Coronavirus SARS-Cov-2 (COVID-19) disease, appeared in Wuhan, China and the first case was detected in December 2019 During the Carnival 2020, Italy decreed a curfew in the Lombardy region, hitherto the most affected, strongly impacting the region's tourism in the period. In March, with the cases already spread in different parts of the world, and with an increasing increase, a pandemic situation was declared and the disease was already characterized as a worldwide public health crisis (Ruiz Estrada & Lee, 2020).

Countries in Europe have closed their borders and, destinations previously discussed overtourism, have gone to zero tourism with restaurants and hotels closed and airlines prevented from operating (Gössling et al., 2021; Richards, 2020). Until the advent of COVID-19, the Tourism Industry could be understood as one of the largest markets in the world (Uğur & Akbıyık, 2020).

Epidemics and pandemics are constant in world history and one of the important epidemics in recent history was caused by the Severe Acute Respiratory Syndrome, SARS, in 2002, in the province of Guandong, China. Studies have shown that the impacts caused by SARS were negative, substantial, and significant (Škare & Porada-Rochoń, 2021).

Studies on SARS in Taiwan have identified two important factors, namely: the level of hysteresis, and institutional efficiency in coping with critical events. They also found that crises caused by epidemics affect the tourism sector differently (Škare & Porada-Rochoń, 2021).

Theses studies also revealed that the SARS has significantly impacted tourism demand in China, Hong Kong, Singapore, and Taiwan, while the Avian Influenza, another pandemic episode, has not had a significant negative impact on the Asian tourism sector, despite the high mortality rate (Škare & Porada-Rochoń, 2021).

In previous epidemics, travel industry tended to recovered quickly, which is not to be expected in the SARS-CoV- scenario since the current pandemic appears to require stricter measures than those taken in the other epidemics and pandemics moments. (Škare & Porada-Rochoń, 2021).

Previous pandemics have operated mainly through idiosyncratic shock channels so that the domestic tourism sector has suffered negative impacts. However, as soon as such shocks ceased to exist, that is, as soon as the contagion cases no longer appeared, the sector managed to recover. However, concerning COVID-19, the shock effects, globally, multiply very quickly and increase the crisis. A country at low risk, that is, without a state of alertness to the disease and, consequently, without idiosyncratic shock, will not be able to have such an immediate return as other countries are still alert to the disease (Škare & Porada-Rochoń, 2021).

According World Travel and Tourism Council, 2020, about 75 million workers are at risk of losing their jobs as a direct impact of the crisis caused by COVID-19. The same research also points out that Tourism GDP suffered the loss of up to US$ 2.1 trillion, and that around 1 million travel tourism workers are losing jobs daily (Škare & Porada-Rochoń, 2021).

Škare et al. (2021), affirms that the impact of COVID-19 on the travel tourism industry cannot be compared with those already exercised in previous pandemics. According to them, the best scenario, predicted from April 2020, points to a loss that starts from 2.93 to 7.82 percentage points in the contribution to GDP by the world tourism industry, and that the tourist expenses that are lost several from 25.0 to 35.0 percentage points. Total capital investments fall from 25.0 to 31.0 percentage points (Škare & Porada-Rochoń, 2021).

The pandemic caused by COVID-2019 will have an unparalleled negative impact on the global tourism industry, not only in the short term but also in the long term in a way that will require years until the sector's recovery. Studies show that the contribution of the tourism economy to GDP will fall from 4.1 US$ trillion to 12.8 US% trillion and that the total contribution of the tourism sector to employment will fall by 514.080 million to 164.506 million jobs. Not to mention the loss of tourist expenses that will fall from US$ 9.9 trillion to US$ 604.8 billion, which leads to a decrease in capital investments from US$ 1.1 trillion to US$ 362.9 billion (Škare & Porada-Rochoń, 2021; Uğur & Akbıyık, 2020).

Currently, the World Tourism Organization points out that before the global outbreak of COVID-19, the tourism growth expected for 2020 was 3-4%, which implies a mobilization of almost two million more international tourists compared to the last year. However, we are currently facing a health phenomenon, the COVID-19 pandemic, which has generated enormous global consequences, especially in terms of health and social-economic and, within it, the tourism sector.

The effects resulted in severe economic stagnation in several countries, due, among other things, to interruption or decrease in product supply chains, decrease in production in major economies, deterioration in raw material prices; all of the above was the result in the first instance by the confinement measures and travel restrictions established by the governments as a way of flattening the contagion curves of this virus (World and Tourism Council, 2020).

In the universe of research generated from the impact of the pandemic on the global economy, especially in tourism, there is a consensus among the authors that the pandemic will reflect negative results in the medium and long term that will undergo a significant recovery process for the resumption the economic heating of destinations (Baum & Hai, 2020; Beni, 2020; Couto et al., 2020; Gössling & Hall, 2021; Gullo, 2020; Mecca & Amaral, 2020; Qiu et al., 2020; To, 2020; Uğur & Akbıyık, 2020; Yeh, 2020).

The stoppage of tourist activity as a consequence of this situation has caused, in less than two months, going from a situation of growth to a very different one of collapse. This same collapse situation is not only present in the tourist segment. Its transversality makes the fall of the sector have a domino effect that not only affects the tourism system, but all those elements directly or indirectly dependent, including territories and local and national economies, therefore, it is knocking on the doors of tourism enterprises.

Study Site

Joinville, located in the northern region of the State of Santa Catarina, has a population of 597,658 inhabitants, characterized as the most populous city in the State of Santa Catarina (IBGE, 2020). Regarding the economic development the service sector has increased the advantage over the industry in Joinville in the labor market. Today, there are 86 thousand workers in the segment, while industrial companies employ 72 thousand people. The sector already accounts for a 54% share of GDP. Concerning the Ranking of the Municipalities with the highest Gross Domestic Product in Brazil, Joinville ranks among the 100 largest economies in the country, occupying the 28th position in the country and the 3rd. Position in the South region, being surpassed only by the cities of Curitiba and Porto Alegre (IBGE, 2017). In this scenario, the growing development of tourist activity in the city has contributed to the growth of the service sector in Joinville.

Present in a strategic region with a diversity of accessibility and counting on the preservation of cultural values, Joinville is an important tourist destination in the South of Brazil, especially in the segment of business tourism and events. For a greater perception and development of targeted market strategies, the study and application of research in destinations that receive events become fundamental tools for the real dimensioning of the socioeconomic impacts of tourist activity in local communities.

The development of this segment in the city allows the creation of more spaces for their execution, in addition to quality offers regarding infrastructure and superstructure, as well as, implies the displacement of tourists for their participation, presenting competitive advantages for the locality, such as the generation of jobs and income.

As in other world destinations, the pandemic resulting from COVID-19 had a marked impact on this tourist segment at Joinville, which is why the need to perform research to measure these impacts and propose strategies for the sustainable resumption of tourism in Joinville.

METHODOLOGY

The research, of an empirical nature and with a quantitative focus, was applied to 136 service providers and suppliers in the tourism and events sector in the municipality of Joinville - SC, members of the class entities: Joinville and Região Convention & Visitors Bureau, Gastronomy and Entertainment Sector of CDL Joinville and Tourism Center of the Joinvilense Association of Small, Micro and Medium Enterprises - AJORPEME. The survey was carried out over September 1 to September 28, 2020. It was conducted on the Google Forms Platform, A total of 104 completed and valid questionnaires were returned, which represented a sample with a margin of error of 3.5% and a 95% reliability level.

The questionnaire consisted of 23 closed questions (Chart 1), divided into two sections oriented to business characteristics and the impacts of COVID-19 (e.g. cancellations, prices, billing and employees). It is noteworthy that the companies in the events segment also answered specific questions about the events planned and cancelled in 2020.

Data were entered in Excel, where possible outliers were analyzed. After this, the data were analyzed using the statistical program IBM SPSS® v. 26, applying descriptive statistical techniques.

Data Analysis

Regarding the companies characteristics, the majority of respondents (47.2%) are connected to businesses that directly involve the provision of services or the supply of products for the sector of events. Next, 22.1% of respondents correspond to companies in the catering area (food and beverages), 13% of companies in the lodging area (hotels, hostels, inns), 7.7% travel agencies, 2.9% of companies in the field of culture and leisure, 1.9% tourist guides, 1% of transport companies and 3.7% of other branches related to tourism.

Regarding the size of the business, the majority of respondents (82.69%) fall into the category of micro-entrepreneur, small business, and micro-enterprises. This result follows the parameters as the reality of the State of Santa Catarina (Brazil), where 90% of active tourist companies are individual microentrepreneurs and microenterprises (JUCESC, 2020).

Table 1. Questionnaire framework

Section	Question
Section 1: Business Features	Q1: The business sector
	Q2: Business related to the events area
	Q3: Business size
	Q4: Time of existence of the business
Section 2: COVID-19 Impact on business	Q5: Performance concerning prices
	Q5.1: Percentage of price reduction
	Q5.2: Percentage of price increase
	Q6: 2020 billing forecast
	Q6.1: Estimated 2020 revenue loss
	Q7: Employee situation
	Q7.1: Number of layoffs
	Q7.2: Number of hires
	Q8: Percentage of employees who are in the home office
	Q9: Billing return forecast for the pre-Covid period 19
	Q10: Knowledge of government sector support measures
	Q11: Credit needs
	Q12: Required credit amounts
	Q13: Possible subsistence time with existing working capital
Specific section for event companies	Q2.1: Events were contracted or scheduled to be held in 2020
	Q2.2: Events contracted for 2020, which were held before State Decree 515 of March 17, 2020 (which prohibited the holding of events)
	Q2.3: Events canceled in 2020
	Q2.4: Events that have been rescheduled for 2021
	Q2.5: Expectation of the public that stopped circulating in 2020.

Source: own elaboration, based on the questionnaire applied to companies in Joinville, 2021.

In an analysis of how long the companies have been active in the tourism market, the survey shows that 70% of the companies have had business for 7 years. Considering that the Brazilian average survival rate for companies is 4 years and that the survival rate for companies with up to two years of activity is 76.6%, it can be said that the participating companies are consolidated in the market (Sebrae, 2016).

Specifically, about the impacts of COVID-19 on business, the first question was concerning prices. The establishments interviewed did not make any decision regarding the variation in prices (Table 2). As this moment of the pandemic created expectations of return, which were not confirmed, it is possible to understand the reasons why 48% of the companies participating in this research affirm the maintenance

Table 2. Economic impacts: prices and billing

Business performance concerning prices		Revenue forecast for 2020	
Variable	**%**	**Variable**	**%**
Prices have remained the same	48.1	Reduction of more than 75%	58.7
Prices have been reduced	29.8	Reduction between 51% and 74.99%	13.5
Prices have been increased	10.6	Reduction between 26% and 50.99%	15.4
No decision was made	11.5	Reduction of up to 25,99%	6.7
		Will remain stable	1.9
		Increase between 51% and 74.99%	1.0
		Increase between 26% and 50.99%	1.0
		Increase by up to 25.99%	1.9

Source: own elaboration, based on the results of the questionnaire, 2021.

of prices as a strategy. Still, analyzing the behavior related to prices, when compared to the time of existence of the business, it is evident that the companies that have 1 to 3 years in the market had a different behavior from the companies already consolidated (more than 3 years in the market). While the former had a higher percentage of price reductions (42.9%), companies already consolidated have chosen to maintain prices (56.5%). The fact that most of the responding companies are consolidated, leads to the understanding that knowledge of the market allows them to adopt more appropriate strategies, aiming to guarantee their audience.

In the billing aspect (Table 2), the expressive majority (87.6%) registered a significant drop in billing, mainly justified by the impossibility of holding events since March/2020. The non-holding of events, and the restriction of movement of people, impacted both the network of suppliers for the event and the support network for tourists and visitors.

In addition, the majority of the companies among those with 1 to 3 years of existence, affirm that they will have a 75% reduction in sales (71.4%). Regarding the type of company, it is autonomous companies (90.9%) and microentrepreneurs (65.5%) who will most feel the impacts of the crisis, concerning revenue, that is, a reduction of more than 75% in the year 2020.

Regarding the initial forecast of recovery in the face of the crisis caused by the pandemic, 43.3% of companies surveyed believe that only in 2021 will their business recover. However, 36.5% believe that it will occur only after 2021.

The survey was also dedicated to understanding the situation of company employees. The result shows that, among the measures taken with the staff, 52.9% affirm that they dismissed or will dismiss, which reflects the absence of business being generated in this period. At the same time, 45.2% assume that they used MP

Table 3. Employment situation during the pandemic

Employment situation		*Home office* **Employees**	
Variable	**%**	**Variable**	**%**
There were or will be hires	1.9	There is no way to work at home office	21.2
There have been or will be layoffs	5.9	No home office employees	44.2
There were no layoffs/hires	45.2	From 75% to 99% in home office	3.8
		From 51% to 75% in home office	1.9
		From 31% to 50% in home office	1.9
		From 11% to 30% in home office	2.9
		Up to 10% in home office	5.8
		All home office employees	1.9
		I do not know how to answer	5.8

Source: own elaboration, based on the results of the questionnaire, 2021.

936/2020 (Provisional Measure that suspends or reduces employment contracts in the State of Santa Catarina) or other measures to preserve employment (Table 3).

As it is about the provision of services, 65.4% responded that they do not have or have no means of working from home office (Table 3). This result reflects the routine work profile of professionals in the tourism sector, to which the provision is directly related to the need to use the equipment, and the interface with the consumer.

About knowledge of governmental measures to support the sector that were adopted since the pandemic, it is observed that 50% stated that they know all measures, and then 38.5% stated that they had little knowledge. The majority of respondents try to keep themselves informed about the actions that the government has been adopting for the sector.

Respondents were also asked about the need for credit during the pandemic period. In this scenario, the survey showed that 21% of the companies surveyed saw the need for access to credit, but did not apply. The same number, 21.2% of the interviewed companies stated that they do not need credit and, 19.2% stated that they need credit, which they applied for and are waiting for the result (Table 4).

Of the interviewed companies that stated the need for credit, 15.4% declare the need for a credit line between R$ 101 thousand to R$ 300 thousand, and 12.5% between R$ 11 thousand to R$ 35 thousand.

Analyzing the direct impact on the events sector, one of the questions sought to raise the number of events that were contracted to be held throughout that year. Within the chain of service providers for the survey respondents, it was informed that 2,770 different services were contracted to be carried out during the events scheduled for 2020 in Joinville.

Table 4. On the need for credit during the pandemic period

Need for credit		Required credit amounts	
Variable	**%**	**Variable**	**%**
I don't know how to evaluate yet	20.2	I do not know how to answer	16.3
I need it, but I couldn't	18.3	Up to R$ 10 thousand	6.7
I have the need, I am waiting	19.2	From R$ 11 thousand to R$ 35 thousand	12.5
I have a need, I didn't ask	21.2	From R$ 36 thousand to R$ 50 thousand	9.6
		From R$ 51 thousand to R$ 100 thousand	9.6
		From R$ 101 thousand to R$ 300 thousand	15.4
I have no need	21.2	From R$ 301 thousand to R$ 1 million	4.8
		Above R$ 1 million	3.8
		Not applicable	21.2

Source: own elaboration, based on the results of the questionnaire, 2021.

Another question, states that between the 1st of January and the 17th of March 2020 (previously the publication of State Decree 515 of the 17th of March 2020, which prohibited the holding of events), 504 service provision contracts were carried out services for the events scheduled during this period. Until the period of conducting the survey, it is possible to evidence a high impact on the economy of the event segment, with an average retraction of 81% in the segment's businesses.

According to data from the years 2018 and 2019, in the State of Santa Catarina each large event generates an average economic movement of R $ 15.3 million, and small events represent an average movement of R $ 200 thousand. In general, the tourism sector represents 12% of the State's GDP, which resulted in 2019, an ICMS tax collection linked to tourist activities was R $ 630 million (NSC TV, 2020).

Considering the uncertainties caused by COVID-19, for events in 2020, the interviewees affirmed that about 1040 contracted services were rescheduled to happen in 2021. It is estimated that the events impact 52 economic sectors, which, in this scenario, were affected measures adopted for social isolation and public restriction.

Purportedly, it could have a loss of R $ 11.5 million in the companies' revenues in 2020. This represents not only a loss of revenue but also a collection of taxes to the municipality and a reduction in GDP. Another relevant impact is concerning the profile of the companies, with the majority (82.69%) falling into the category of microentrepreneur, small business, and microenterprises, this drop in revenue directly impacts the family income of the owners. In addition to the precariousness of family income, the municipality's economy indirectly loses with the fall in the consumption of goods and services.

Finally, 94.2% of the companies interviewed, the absolute majority (94.2%) declared that applied research is relevant to measure the impact of the pandemic on the tourism economy.

Like Joinville, many other studies have demonstrated the effectiveness of the pandemic on Brazilian destinations, affecting not only tourism but the impact on the present and the near future in all dimensions of human life, from social, political, educational, emotional, and economic (Biz, 2020; Corbari & Grimm, 2020; Gil et al., 2020; Guimarães et al., 2020; Paixão et al., 2021; Siston et al., 2020). The pandemic context triggered several social impacts in the tourism sector. There are several issues that will be suitable for the development of sustainable tourism in social aspects, especially in relation to the adoption by governments of public policies that will subsidize micro and small businesses to resume their economic activities.

In the Getúlio Vargas Foundation study, based on the Characteristic Activities of Tourism (CAT), the estimated economic losses of the sector will be R $ 165.5 billion, which represents 38.9% concerning 2019. The total loss of the Brazilian tourism sector will be R $ 116.7 billion in the 2020-2021 biennium. To recover from this loss, it will be necessary to grow 16.95% per year in 2022 and 2023 in activities to recover the economic loss caused by the Covid-19 pandemic crisis (Barbosa et al, 2020).

Although the health control measures implemented by governments, aimed at controlling contagion, result in positive impacts on health, such measures affect economic activity, since social distance generally implies a slowdown in production or even its total interruption and activities such as tourism and events are directly affected by these measures, as seen in the results of the survey conducted in Joinville.

CONCLUSION

It is a fact that the COVID-19 pandemic has had unprecedented impacts in recent history and this also refers to tourism. Worldwide destinations were impacted by the fact that tourism has practically stopped and the main reflexes are focused on economic aspects, one of the most noticeable being the dismissal of thousands of employees in the tourism area and the closing of many companies in the sector, being the hotel industry, catering, and agency the most affected businesses.

Given this fact, tourism will need to be reinvented and there are already some perspectives for its resumption. Overtourism, a reality until the beginning of 2020, is no longer a concern for destinations. On the contrary, there is a trend towards domestic tourism, short distance and shorter trips, and also destinations of nature and outdoor activities. This was already a reality during the last European summer, where domestic destinations were the preference of tourists (Remoaldo, 2020).

Another concern that has been highlighted is the search for safe destinations, that is, those that demonstrate efficacy in health security measures and also security in cancellation policies. Examples to be cited are the Clean & Safe Seal adopted by the Portuguese Tourism Office, where companies, which meet health safety requirements, receive a seal that demonstrates to consumers their concern with biosafety and Responsible Tourism, launched by the Ministry of Tourism of Brazil, with characteristics similar to the previously mentioned.

These short trips have better quality and interaction with the local culture and responsibility for sustainability, authenticity, and the local community, this can be an social incentive to tourism. With a focus on these perspectives, Joinville essentially a business and event destination, needs to plan and be attentive to new trends towards the resumption of tourism, minimizing the impacts caused by the pandemic period.

Although the moment is critical, and the balance between economic impacts and health concerns is extremely challenging for governments, this can represent an opportunity for tourism, in its different instances (national, state, and municipal) to reinvent itself. It is a time when new segments of tourism can be strengthened, such as creative tourism and cultural tourism.

These short trips have better quality and interaction with the local culture and responsibility for sustainability, authenticity, and the local community. With a focus on these perspectives, Joinville essentially a business and event destination, needs to plan and be attentive to new trends towards the resumption of tourism, minimizing the impacts caused by the pandemic period.

Although the moment is critical, and the balance between economic impacts and health concerns is extremely challenging for governments, this can represent an opportunity for tourism, in its different instances (national, state, and municipal) to reinvent itself. It is a time when new segments of tourism can be strengthened, such as creative tourism and cultural tourism.

In sum, a survey carried out in the Joinville - SC enterprises, points to a relevant economic and, consequently social impact, caused by the pandemic COVID-19. It is important to bear in mind the need to implement public and private measures that guarantee, in a safe way, the resumption of tourist activity. It is extremely important to take into account the biosafety protocols, demonstrating to visitors and consumers the commitment to the well-being of all.

Likewise, it is considered relevant, based on the research result, the need to identify local, regional and federal policies that promote the resumption of the tourist activity in Joinville, especially in the event and food segments, as well as the continuous monitoring of the performance of the activity at the destination.

REFERENCES

Barbosa, L. G., Coelho, A. M., & Motta, F. do A., & Guimarães, I. L. (2020). Economic Impact of Covid-19 Proposals for Brazilian Tourism [Impacto Econômico do Covid-19 Propostas para o Turismo Brasileiro]. *Fundação Getúlio Vargas*, *1*, 1–24.

Baum, T., & Hai, N. T. T. (2020). Hospitality, tourism, human rights, and the impact of COVID-19. *International Journal of Contemporary Hospitality Management*, *32*(7), 2397–2407. doi:10.1108/IJCHM-03-2020-0242

Beni, M. C. (2020). Tourism and COVID-19: some reflections. *Revista Rosa Dos Ventos - Turismo e Hospitalidade*, *12*, 1–23. . doi:10.18226/21789061.v12i3a02

Biz, A. A. (2020). Initial Perspectives of Covid-19 Impacts on Tourism in the State of Santa Catarina – Brazil [Perspectivas Iniciais Dos Impactos Da Covid-19 No Turismo Do Estado De Santa Catarina –Brasil]. *Revista Turismo & Cidades*, *2*, 139–152.

Corbari, S. D., & Grimm, I. J. (2020). The COVID-19 pandemic and the impacts on the tourism sector in Curitiba (PR): A preliminary analysis [A pandemia de COVID-19 e os impactos no setor do turismo em Curitiba (PR): uma análise preliminar]. *Ateliê Do Turismo*, *4*(2), 1–26.

Couto, G., Castanho, R. A., Pimentel, P., Carvalho, C., Sousa, Á., & Santos, C. (2020). The Impacts of COVID-19 Crisis over the Tourism Expectations of the Azores Archipelago Residents. *Sustainability*, *12*(18), 7612. doi:10.3390u12187612

Gil, G. D. E. S., Noel, M., & Hirschfeld, C. (2020). Border in disenchantment notes on the state, tourism and Covid-19 in Foz do Iguaçu-BR. [Fronteira em desencanto notas sobre o estado, turismo e Covid-19 em Foz do Iguaçu-BR]. *Revista SURES*, *15*, 22–42.

Gössling, S., Scott, D., & Hall, C. M. (2021). Pandemics, tourism and global change: A rapid assessment of COVID-19. *Journal of Sustainable Tourism*, *29*(1), 1–20. do i:10.1080/09669582.2020.1758708

Guimarães, V. L., Catramby, T., Moraes, C. C. de A., & Soares, C. A. L. (2020). Covid-19 pandemic and higher education in tourism in the state of Rio De Janeiro (Brazil): Preliminary research notes. *Revista Rosa Dos Ventos - Turismo e Hospitalidade*, *12*, 1–18. . doi:10.18226/21789061.v12i3a09

Gullo, M. C. R. (2020). The Economy in the Covid-19 Pandemic: Some Considerations [A Economia na Pandemia Covid-19: Algumas Considerações]. *Rosa Dos Ventos*, *12*(3), 1–8. doi:10.18226/21789061.v12i3a05

IBGE, Instituto Brasileiro de Geografia e Estatística. (2017). *Gross Domestic Product of Municipalities* [Produto Interno Bruto dos Municípios]. Avalaible online: https://cidades.ibge.gov.br/brasil/sc/joinville/pesquisa/38/47001?tipo=ranking

IBGE, Instituto Brasileiro de Geografia e Estatística. (2020). *Cities and States* [Cidades e Estados]. Avalaible online: https://www.ibge.gov.br/cidades-e-estados/sc/joinville.html

JUCESC. Junta Comercial do Estado de Santa Catarina. (2020). *Statistics 2020* [Estatísticas 2020]. Avalaible online: http://www.jucesc.sc.gov.br/index.php/informacoes/estatisticas/503-estatisticas-2020

Mecca, M. S., Gorete, M., & Amaral, D. O. (2020). Covid-19: Reflexos no Turismo. *Rosa Dos Ventos*, *12*(3), 1–5. doi:10.18226/21789061.v12i3a06

NSC TV. (2020). *SC tourism sector adds losses with cancelled events and fears impact in high season* [Setor turístico de SC soma prejuízos com eventos cancelados e teme impacto na alta temporada]. Avalaible online: https://www.nsctotal.com.br/noticias/os-impactos-da-pandemia-no-setor-turistico-de-sc

Paixão, W., Cordeiro, I., & Körössy, N. (2021). Effects of the COVID-19 pandemic on tourism in Fernando de Noronha during the first half of 2020 [Efeitos da pandemia do COVID-19 sobre o turismo em Fernando de Noronha ao longo do primeiro semestre de 2020]. *Revista Brasileira de Pesquisa em Turismo*, *15*(1), 2128. doi:10.7784/rbtur.v15i1.2128

Qiu, R. T. R., Park, J., Li, S., & Song, H. (2020). Social costs of tourism during the COVID-19 pandemic. *Annals of Tourism Research*, *84*, 102994. doi:10.1016/j.annals.2020.102994 PMID:32834228

Remoaldo, P. (2020). Creativity in tourism in pandemic period COVID-19 - the ambition and role of the local in the global [Criatividade em turismo em período de pandemia COVID-19 - a ambição e o papel do local no global]. doi:10.21814/uminho.ed.25.13

Richards, G. (2020). Tourism and Resilience: From “overtourism” to no tourism. *Conference: Summer School on the Management of Creativity Organized by HEC Montreal and the University of Barcelona*.

Ruiz Estrada, M. A., Park, D., & Lee, M. (2020). The Evaluation of the Final Impact of Wuhan COVID-19 on Trade, Tourism, Transport, and Electricity Consumption of China. SSRN *Electronic Journal*. doi:10.2139/ssrn.3551093

Scalabrini, E. C.B., & Dalonso, Y. (2018). Impacts Of Events On Tourist Destinations: a case study in the city of Joinville, SC, Brazil [Impactos Dos Eventos Em Destinos Turísticos: um estudo de caso na cidade de Joinville, SC, Brasil]. *Revista Turismo Em Análise, 29*(2), 332–348.

Sebrae. (2016). Study on Business Survival in Brazil 2016 [Estudo Sobre Sobrevivencia das Empresas no Brasil 2016]. *Sebrae.* http://www.sebrae.com.br/Sebrae/Portal Sebrae/Anexos/sobrevivencia-das-empresas-no-brasil-102016.pdf

Siston, T. G., Camara, J., Federal, U., Grande, R., Com, I. R., & Federal, G. (2020). Impacts of Covid-19 on tocantins tourism [Impactos da Covid-19 no turismo do Tocantins]. *Revista Espaço e Tempo Midiáticos, 3*(2), 1–12.

Škare, M., Soriano, D. R., & Porada-Rochoń, M. (2021). Impact of COVID-19 on the travel and tourism industry. *Technological Forecasting and Social Change, 163*, 120469. doi:10.1016/j.techfore.2020.120469 PMID:35721368

To, W. M. (2020). *How Big is the Impact of COVID-19 (and Social Unrest) on the Number of Passengers of the Hong Kong International Airport? Sustainability analysis View project Soundscape View project How Big is the Impact of COVID-19 (and Social Unrest) on the Number of P.* Working Paper. doi:10.13140/RG.2.2.12999.04002

Uğur, N. G., & Akbıyık, A. (2020). Impacts of COVID-19 on global tourism industry: A cross-regional comparison. *Tourism Management Perspectives, 36*, 100744. doi:10.1016/j.tmp.2020.100744 PMID:32923356

World Travel and Tourism Council. (2020). *Crisis readiness: Are you prepared and resilient to safeguard your people & destinations?* Global Rescue Report.

Yeh, S.-S. (2020). Tourism recovery strategy against COVID-19 pandemic. *Tourism Recreation Research*, 1–7. doi:10.1080/02508281.2020.1805933

Chapter 3
The Relationship Among Perceived Gender Discrimination, Job Satisfaction, and Turnover Intention and the Moderator Role of Gender

Gamze Temizel
https://orcid.org/0000-0001-6576-1634
Selçuk University, Turkey

ABSTRACT

The main purpose of this chapter is to investigate the effect of gender discrimination perceptions of hotel employees on their job satisfaction levels and turnover intentions. A second aim is to compare employees' perceptions of gender discrimination by their sex. A final aim is to investigate the moderator role of gender in the relationship between perceived gender discrimination and job satisfaction. For this purpose, a study was conducted, and 267 employees working in 4- and 5-star hotels operating in the city of Konya in Turkey were reached. The data were collected by questionnaire technique. As a result of the study, it was determined that perceived gender discrimination affects job satisfaction negatively and affects turnover intention positively. In addition, female employees feel more gender discrimination in the workplace than men. Gender moderates the relationship between perceived gender discrimination and job satisfaction. More clearly, the negative effect of perceived gender discrimination on job satisfaction is stronger for women than for men.

DOI: 10.4018/978-1-6684-4194-7.ch003

"Human community consists of two kinds of people, called men and women. Is it possible to advance a part of this mass and neglect the other so that the whole of the mass can advance? Is it thinkable that while half of an object is tied to the ground with chains, the other part can rise to the sky?"

Mustafa Kemal ATATÜRK

Founder of the Turkish Republic

INTRODUCTION

Perceived gender discrimination (will be stated as PGD from now on) is a concept related to employees' beliefs that they are limited or excluded in organizations because of their gender. Studies on the perception of gender discrimination focus on the employee's personal perception of discrimination rather than whether he or she is actually exposed to this situation (Foley et al., 2015, p. 652). The concept of discrimination is one of the interesting topics in the business literature. PGD has various negative consequences in terms of employees' work-related attitudes and behaviors (Foley et al., 2005). Policies and practices that discriminate against gender cause many negative consequences for both employees and organizations.

In studies examining the behavioral responses of employees to practices in the workplace that discriminate against gender, it has been stated that PGD causes conflicts with management, neglect of work, low motivation, less excitement towards work and work conflict. It has also been revealed that while PGD is negatively related to job satisfaction, organizational commitment and self-esteem, it is positively related to turnover intention (Jaffe, 2017; Channar et al., 2011; Kara & Yıldıran, 2011; Foley et al., 2005, pp. 421-423; Onay, 2009; Gutek et al., 1996; Kim & Park, 2018). Besides, women experience a higher level of perception of gender discrimination compared to men (Northcraft & Gutek, 1993; Gutek et al., 1996; Shaffer et al., 2000; Ngo et al., 2002; Foster et al., 2004; Foley et al.; Foley et al., 2006; Peng et al., 2009; Channar et al., 2011; Foley et al., 2015). If women perceive a higher level of gender discrimination than men, they will encounter more problems in the workplace compared to men and they will react more negatively to the work and the organization (Foley et al., 2005, pp. 421-423).

Tourism, which takes part in the service sector, is an industry that provides high employment opportunity due to its structure open for improvement, labor-intensive character and interaction with other sectors. In the tourism industry, hotels that need a high number of employees due to their manpower-based production structure are also enterprises with a high labor turnover rate (Lam et al., 2002, p. 218; Aydın, 2005, p. 265). Women in the workforce of tourism have equal capacity with their male counterparts, besides they have better skills to be more effective in the industry. They communicate better, they are careing and nurturing, and they adopt supporting behaviors that make them advantageous in the service industry (Marinakou, 2014). However women in the working life face gender discrimination because of the preference of men in recruitment, wage inequality, the recognition of career opportunities to male employees, harassment, the fact that women with young children are not preferred in recruitment, and women who work part-time are chosen in case someone is fired. In the study of Marinakou (2015) it is stated that in hospitality industry only few women are found in high managerial positions and they are mainly found in positions that are stereotypically ascribed to their gender, such as housekeeping, sales and marketing. Campos-Soria et al. (2009) stated that women in hospitality industry take part in jobs that are less paid and earn less than men. Similarly Thrane (2008) stated that male employees receive about 20% more wages annually than their female colleagues in the tourism industry.

As in other organizational structures, a negative perception that will be developed by the employees towards gender discrimination in the hotel enterprises will decrease job satisfaction and increase the turnover intention. This situation will cause various problems in the organizations. The high rate of labor turnover leads to problems such as decreased organizational effectiveness, and a series of costs to be incurred in hiring new employees. From this point of view, the negative effects of PGD on employees is a situation that should be emphasized both at the individual level and organizational context.

In this chapter, it is aimed to determine whether the gender discrimination perceived by the employees of the hotel establishments has an impact on their job satisfaction and turnover intention. Another aim is to test the moderator role of gender in the relationship between PGD and job satisfaction. In this way, it is aimed to provide a theoretical framework for the consequences of PGD in the workplace, regarding the employees and the organizations. The results of the study are expected to contribute to the existing literature base and support the understanding of the reactions of the employees to unfair treatments in the workplace. In addition, it is aimed to reveal results that can be used for human resources management. The data to be revealed about the employees is expected to contribute to reduce pecuniary loss and intangible damages that the hotel businesses will incur as a result of the dissatisfaction of employees with their job, their intention to leave and finally their actions to quit their job.

In studies examining the behavioral responses of employees to PGD, the relation of PGD with various variables such as job satisfaction (Channar et al., 2011; Foley at al., 2005; Shaffer et al., 2000), turnover intention (Foley at al., 2005; Kara & Yıldıran, 2011; Onay, 2009; Shaffer et al., 2000) and organizational commitment (Channar et al., 2011; Jaffe, 2017; Kara & Yıldıran, 2011; Onay, 2009) have been examined in different sectors. There are also studies that examine PGD and compare employees' perceptions of gender discrimination by their sex (Foley at al., 2005; Ngo et al., 2002; Channar et al., 2011). As a result of the literature review and to the best of author's knowledge, no study was encountered that examines the impact of gender discrimination perceptions of hotel employees on their job satisfaction levels and their turnover intentions. Besides, any studies that compare hotel employees' perceptions of gender discrimination by their sex, and that investigate the moderator role of gender in the relationship between PGD and job satisfaction of hotel employees was not encountered. Therefore, it is expected that the results of the research will contribute to the existing literature at this point.

BACKGROUND

Perceived Gender Discrimination (PGD)

Gender discrimination is defined as unfair treatment caused by gender-related prejudices (Piethyläinen et al., 2020, p. 311). Unjust behavior towards a part of the society due to characteristics such as gender, language, religion, race and age is called discrimination. Making these unfair behaviors on the basis of gender is expressed as gender discrimination. Gender discrimination occurs when decisions about employees are made according to their gender, regardless of their qualifications or work-related performance (Gutek et al., 1996, p. 792). Employees feel gender discrimination when they see members of their own gender at a disadvantage compared to other gender in the workplace. Gender discrimination against women is a more common attitude compared to men. Women are less represented in business life, they do not have equal rights with men and they are exposed to negative discrimination (Kartal, 2014, p. 33). Besides, they experience a higher perception of gender discrimination compared to men, considering that they are disadvantaged in business life because of their gender (Foley at al., 2005).

PGD is related to an individual's belief that she/he is personally limited or removed at work because of her/his gender. This situation focuses on the perception that the person has developed regarding discrimination, rather than actually experiencing gender discrimination (Foley et al., 2015, p. 652). Employees experience lower job satisfaction when they perceive that their gender is the cause of discrimination in the workplace (Foley at al., 2005, pp. 428-429). PGD is associated with poor job attitudes such as low job satisfaction, physical health, psychological health and work-related outcomes (Triana, et al. 2019, p. 2443; Raver & Nishii, 2010). Discrimination has many consequences for employees and their happiness. Adverse working conditions, such as gender discrimination, can deter employees from continuing their careers (Piethyläinen et al., 2020, p. 311). However, it is stated that there are few studies examining how employees respond to discrimination, which is an important issue for the management of human capital by affecting the workforce turnover rate (Ngo et al., 2002: 1206).

Job Satisfaction

Job satisfaction is defined as the positive thinking that occurs when employees consider their job, the job environment and the results of the work done. The concept expresses the combination of psychological, physiological and environmental conditions that cause the employee to be satisfied with his job (Hoppock, 1935, p. 47). The concept aims to evaluate the attitudes, behaviors, beliefs and feelings of employees towards their jobs. Employees' attitudes towards work began to be examined in the 1920s, and the importance of the subject has increased with the studies carried out in the 1930s and 1940s (Sevimli & İşcan, 2005, p. 55).

Job satisfaction, which is one of the most widely studied concepts in the field of organizational behavior, emphasizes the positive mood of the employee towards the work environment and the attitudes formed through interactions in this environment. The concept arises from the interaction of thoughts and emotions and is examined in two dimensions, cognitive and emotional (Froese & Peltokorpi, 2011, p. 50).

It is seen that the relationship between PGD and job satisfaction is the subject of many studies in the literature. Studies on the negative effects of PGD in the workplace have concluded that PGD negatively affects job satisfaction (Channar et al., 2011; Foley at al., 2005).

Turnover Intention

Turnover intention is one of the concepts that is frequently discussed in the field of organizational behavior, just like job satisfaction. High employee turnover rate as a result of high turnover intention in employees and its transformation into turnover behavior will emerge as a loss of productivity and profitability for businesses. Turnover intention is one of the concepts that should be carefully examined in order to retain talented employees and to prevent the costs caused by the leaves of employees and recruitments.

Turnover intention is briefly expressed as the possibility of an employee to resign from his/her current job (Fong & Mahfar, 2013, p. 35). Employees' intention to leave their current job voluntarily and consciously exhibiting attitudes and behaviors that cause them to realize this purpose are expressed as turnover intention (Mobley, 1977). In another definition, turnover intention is defined as the desire of employees to voluntarily terminate their job and leave the organization permanently, which arises for personal reasons or organizational reasons such as the organization's inability to meet the expectations of employees (Griffeth et al., 2000; Özdemir & Özdemir, 2015, p. 337).

It is not possible to measure quitting behavior before it happens. Planned behavior theory (Ajzen, 1991) shows that behavioral intention is a good predictor of actual behavior. In this regard, turnover intention is accepted as a precursor of quitting behavior. Although every thought on this subject does not result in quitting behavior, this may be the beginning of the quitting process for employees who express their intention to quit their job. For this reason, examining the factors that will cause employees to leave their job will increase profitability by preventing the costs caused by employee turnover.

LITERATURE REVIEW

When the literature on the negative effects of PGD on employees is examined, national and international studies in this field are encountered. Details of these studies are given below:

In the study of Triana et al. (2019) examining perceived workplace gender discrimination and employee outcomes, the gender discrimination perceptions of employees and the consequences of this situation in the workplace are examined using the meta-analysis method and two complementary empirical studies. Research results show that PGD is negatively related to job attitudes, physical health, psychological health, and work-related outcomes (work-based and relational).

A study was conducted by Kim and Park (2018) in which they investigated the relationship between gender discrimination, belief in a just world, self-esteem and depression perceived by Korean working women. As a result of the study, it was concluded that PGD was negatively related to self-esteem at high levels of belief in a just world.

In the study of Foley et al. (2015) to examine the effects of gender and gender identification power on the perception of gender discrimination, a questionnaire was applied to the employees of 3 large enterprises serving in China. The results reveal that gender and gender identification power are associated with PGD. The study aims to help managers understand why and how their subordinates create their perceptions of gender discrimination. According to research findings, in order to influence such perceptions in organizations; the importance of gender identity, gender comparison and gender bias in organizational practices should be considered.

In the study of Arlı (2013) which aims to determine the perceptions of university students' gender discrimination and gender bias who are having marine tourism education, a questionnaire was applied to male and female students. As a result of the research, it was determined that there was a statistically significant difference between female and male students' perceptions of gender discrimination and prejudices against women. It was also determined that female students were aware of the gender discrimination applied to women in the workplace.

Kara and Yıldıran (2011) conducted a study to determine; how female trainers and administrators working in private sports facilities perceive gender identity, gender prejudices and discrimination against women and the relations of these perceptions with organizational belonging and turnover intention. As a result of the research, it was determined that PGD negatively affected the organizational commitment of female trainers and managers and positively affected their turnover intention.

Channar et al. (2011) in their study investigating gender discrimination in the workforce and its effects on employees, they conducted a survey on the employees of health and education enterprises serving in two different regions of India and Pakistan. As a result of the study, it was concluded that while gender discrimination perceived in the workplace decreases job satisfaction, motivation, organizational commitment and enthusiasm for work, it increases the stress level of employees.

In Onay (2009)'s study to explain the consequences of PGD, a survey was conducted on blue-collar and white-collar employees in two different enterprises. As a result of the research, it was concluded that there was gender discrimination in both companies and that female employees perceived this discrimination more than men. Apart from this, it has been stated that gender discrimination among employees affects their organizational commitment negatively and their turnover intention positively.

In the study of Foley et al. (2005) they examined the relationship between PGD, organizational justice and work-related attitudes (job satisfaction, organizational commitment, and turnover intention). They also investigated the moderator role of gender in these relationships. As a result of the study conducted on the example of Protestant clergy in Hong Kong, it has been determined that there is a significant correlation between perceptions of justice, perceptions of discrimination and job attitudes such as job satisfaction, organizational commitment and turnover intention. However, the moderator role of gender in the relationship between PGD and job satisfaction could not be proven.

Shaffer et al. (2000) researched the work-related consequences of gender discrimination and collected data through questionnaires they conducted with 583 business women working in the United States, China and Hong Kong. According to the results of the research, while the perception of gender discrimination is negatively related to job satisfaction and emotional commitment; It was found to be positively related to turnover intention and life stress.

There are various studies in the literature in which gender discrimination is evaluated in terms of tourism industry employees. Among these studies, some of the subjects mentioned are; gender discrimination in job applications in hotels (Temizkan et al., 2020), gender pay gap in the tourism industry (Guimarães & Silva, 2016), attitudes of managers towards gender discrimination in accommodation enterprises (Dalkıranoğlu & Çetinel, 2008), gender perception in the tourism sector (Tekin, 2017), career challenges of female managers in the hospitality industry (Kattara, 2005), and the glass ceiling perception of female managers in tourism (Remington & Kitterlin-Lynch, 2018; Aydın et al., 2007; Anafarta et al., 2008). In addition to these studies, the following studies were examined in terms of the relationship between tourism industry employees and gender discrimination:

In the study of Nalçacı İkiz (2020), it is aimed to determine the attitudes of managers from tourism enterprises towards gender discrimination and female employees. As a result of the research, it is stated that managers have positive perceptions and attitudes towards female employees, but they lack knowledge about gender discrimination and they normalize some gender inequality in the working environment. Other results obtained from the research are; the current representation of women in the management level is low in the sector, the departments and jobs in the sector are separated by gender, the most important factor pushing women to work is to gain economic independence and the main reason for women leaving the job is work-family conflict.

In the study of Ersoy and Ehtiyar (2021) it is aimed to investigate the effects of gender thoughts and perceptions of female managers working in various managerial positions in accommodation enterprises on their career processes. It is also aimed to reveal their experiences and difficulties in these processes on the basis of gender. As a result of the study, it has been determined that the gender role is effective in the career processes of female managers. Despite this, it has been concluded that women have the skills to carry out multiple roles, they prefer to advance in their careers by not giving up despite all these obstacles and they struggle in this sense.

Carvalho et al. (2019) investigated the gendering processes of female managers in their careers in tourism enterprises. It was concluded that the effect of hidden gender discrimination on female employees is more common than open discrimination.

In the study of Russen et al. (2021) hotel managers' perspectives on the promotion process of hotel employees were examined based on the gender of the promoted employee, their perceived organizational justice and PGD against women. In the study, the sample of 87 hotel managers working in the USA was studied. The study emphasizes gender inequality in promotion opportunities among hotel employees.

According to the results of the research, when female employees are promoted the level of organizational justice perceived by the employees in the organization increases.

The study of Qu et al. (2020) examines the relationships between PGD, organizational justice and deviant behavior among hotel workers in China. In addition, organizational attachment is considered as a mediator on these relationships. The results show that PGD is negatively related to organizational commitment; distributive and procedural justice is positively related to affective commitment and organizational identification; turnover intention causes organizational deviance behavior. In addition organizational identification and turnover intention mediate the effect of PGD on organizational deviation.

In the study of Çiçen, et al. (2020) it was aimed to measure whether women employed in accommodation enterprises are exposed to gender discrimination and the level of difference in gender discrimination perceptions according to demographic characteristics. A questionnaire was applied by interviewing a total of 157 women working in 58 accommodation enterprises in Edirne. As a result of the research, it was determined that the participants were not exposed to gender discrimination in issues such as hiring, wages and promotion.

In studies examining the behavioral responses of employees to PGD, job satisfaction and turnover intention have been expressed as critical components of employee attitudes that are likely to be affected by PGD. In the above-mentioned studies about the negative effects of PGD in the workplace on employees, it has been stated that the PGD negatively affects job satisfaction (Channar et al., 2011; Foley at al., 2005; Shaffer, 2000) and positively affects the turnover intention (Foley at al., 2005; Kara & Yıldıran, 2011; Onay, 2009; Shaffer, 2000).

Studies have shown that both women and men perceive discrimination based on gender (Cameron, 2001; Gutek et al., 1996). Although it is stated that men also experience discrimination based on gender, gender discrimination against women is a more common phenomenon globally (Shaffer et al., 2000, p. 396). Parallel to this, studies have reported that women experience a higher level of perception of gender discrimination compared to men (Northcraft & Gutek, 1993; Gutek et al., 1996; Shaffer et al., 2000; Ngo et al., 2002; Foster et al., 2004; Foley at al., 2005; Foley et al., 2006; Peng et al., 2009; Channar et al., 2011; Foley et al., 2015). The collective relative deprivation theory expresses the distress a person feels about an issue on behalf of the group to which he/she belongs. The person may react to this situation such as resentment and dissatisfaction (Crosby, 1982). In line with the theory of relative deprivation women believe that their fellows are disadvantageous compared to men, when they perceive gender discrimination against their sex in the workplace. Working women in this direction may perceive that women are generally disadvantaged in business life. According to the research results of Gutek et al. (1996), when women think that they are exposed to gender discrimination, they are faced with situations such as a lower sense of power and prestige in their jobs, more job conflicts, and a decrease in the desire to make the same career choice again (Gutek et al., 1996). According to Foley et al. (2006), the reason why women perceive higher levels of gender discrimination compared to men is that while gender-based discrimination in the workplace is a disadvantage for women, it is seen as a privilege and an advantage for men (Foley et al., 2006, p. 200). In addition, if women perceive more gender-based discrimination than men and, if they expect to be a victim of this situation more than men; the relationship between PGD and negative reactions (such as low job satisfaction) that the employee may develop against his/her job and the organization will be stronger in female employees (Foley at al., 2005, p. 430). When evaluated in this context, hypotheses of the research have been developed in parallel with the literature as follows:

- **Hypothesis One:** PGD has an effect on job satisfaction
- **Hypothesis Two:** PGD has an effect on turnover intention
- **Hypothesis Three:** The perceived level of gender discrimination differs according to gender. Women feel gender discrimination more than men
- **Hypothesis Four:** Gender will moderate the relationship between PGD and job satisfaction. The negative impact of perceived gender discrimination on job satisfaction will be stronger for women than for men.

The model developed to measure the effect of gender discrimination perceived by employees in hotel enterprises on their job satisfaction and turnover intention and to measure the moderator role of gender in the relationship between PGD and job satisfaction is as shown in Figure 1 below.

RESEARCH METHODOLOGY

The aim of the research is to measure the effect of the level of gender discrimination perceived by the employees of hotel enterprises on the level of their job satisfaction and turnover intention. Quantitative research method was used in the study. Questionnaire technique was used to collect the data. The details of the questionnaire created with the literature review are shared under the title of "Factor and Reliability Analysis Results".

Universe and Sample of the Research

The universe of the research consists of the employees of 4 and 5 star hotels operating in Konya. The sample of the study consists of hotel employees selected by the

Figure 1. Model of the research

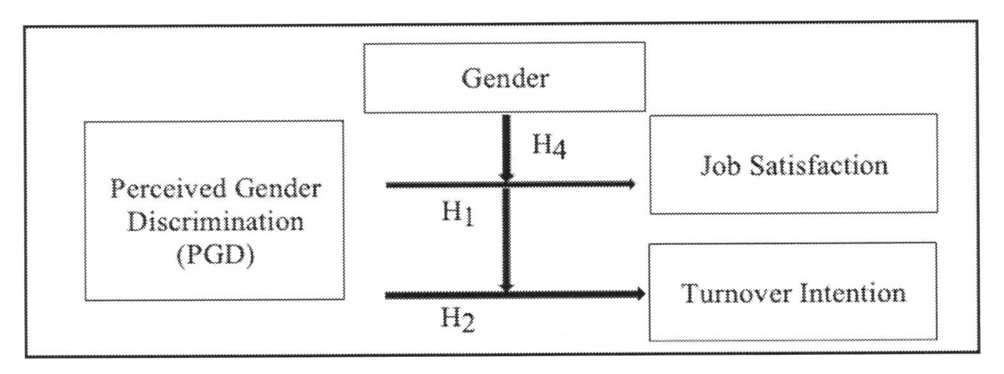

purposeful (intentional) sampling method, which is one of the non-random sampling methods. The research was carried out during the spring of 2021. The questionnaires were applied to hotel employees by contacting the hotel general managers, on a voluntary basis in all 4 and 5 star hotels, except for one 4 star hotel, which were serving in Konya on the above-mentioned dates. With the help of human resources personnel, a self-administered questionnaire was distributed to the employees and their anonymity was preserved by reassuring them about the confidentiality of the questionnaires. A total of six 4-star and eight 5-star hotels were included in the research. During the survey implementation process, 350 questionnaires were distributed and feedback was received from 295 employees. Within the 295 questionnaires obtained, 28 could not be evaluated for various reasons and a total of 267 questionnaires were included in the research.

Data Collection Tools

In the research, in order to measure the perceptions of gender discrimination in the workplace, Perceived Gender Discrimination Scale was used. The original 10-item scale used in Sanchez and Brock (1996) was created to measure ethnic discrimination in the workplace. The scale of Sanchez and Brock was adapted to gender discrimination by Foley et al. (2005) with 4 questions and one-dimension. A 5-point Likert type rating was used in the questionnaire. In the study, the Perceived Gender Discrimination Scale of Foley et al. (2005) was used as adapted into Turkish in the study of Barış (2009). While the Cronbach Alpha reliability coefficient of the scale was 0.868 in the study of Foley et al. (2005), the Alpha value was 0.90 in the study of Barış (2009).

In order to measure the turnover intention, the Turnover Intention Scale developed by Mobley, Horner and Hollingsworth (1978) and adapted into Turkish by Örücü and Özafşarlıoğlu (2013) was used. The scale is 3-item, one-dimensional and uses 5-point Likert type rating.

The Job Satisfaction Sub-Scale developed by Hackman and Oldman (1975) used in the studies of Çatalsakal (2016), Canberk (2019) and Erol Korkmaz (2021) was used to measure job satisfaction of the participants. The scale is 3-item, one-dimensional and uses 5-point Likert type rating.

Data Analysis Method

The data obtained in the research were analyzed using SPSS 25.0 for Windows (Statistical Package for Social Sciences), SPSS Process and G-Power programs. The construct validity of the PGD, Job Satisfaction and turnover Intention Questionnaires were determined by Exploratory Factor Analysis. The consistency of the answers given to the questionnaires was measured with the Reliability Analysis. In the study, Cronbach's Alpha reliability values were higher than 0.90 in all scales indicating that the questionnaire had excellent high reliability (Baker, 1991, p. 8; Cronbach, 1951, p. 16).

The relationship between continuous variables with a normal distribution was analyzed with the Pearson correlation coefficient. The Pearson correlation coefficient is a measure of the linear dependence between two continuous random variables. Pearson correlation coefficient provides information on the strength of the linear relationship between random continuous variables. The sign of the correlation coefficient is positive if the variables are straight related and negative if they are inversely related. The hypotheses of the study were estimated by linear regression and the moderation effect by the process analysis developed by Hayes. The statistical power of the study was determined as $1\text{-}\beta=0.82$ with $\alpha=0.05$ significance level and $d=0.5$ effect size. In the research, the statistical power criterion which was aimed to be found above 80% in the studies was reached (Cohen, 1977; Hinton, 2007). While interpreting the analysis results, the error was kept at $\alpha=0.05$ and $\alpha=0.01$ significance levels, so the decisions were made at 0.95 and 0.99 confidence levels.

RESULTS

Factor and Reliability Analysis Results

Within the scope of the research, 4 different types of questionnaires were used. In the first part of the questionnaire, there are questions about the demographic characteristics of the participants. The second part includes the Job Satisfaction Scale, the third part includes the Turnover Intention Scale and the last part includes

Table 1. Reliability analysis findings

Scales	*Items*	*Cronbach's Alpha*	*Between Items*	*Tests for non-additivity*
Job Satisfaction	3	0.911	F=13.451 p<0.00	F=0.040, p=0.841>0.05
Turnover Intention	3	0.924	F=37.471 p<0.00	F=1.530, p=0.216>0.05
Perceived Gender Descrimination	4	0.968	F=45.668 p<0.00	F=0.010, p=0.921>0.05

the Perceived Gender Discrimination Scale. Except for the questionnaire form in which demographic information was investigated, all scale expressions were graded as a 5-point Likert scale. Factor Analysis and Reliability Analysis findings are summarized with Table 1 and Table 2 below.

In the light of the data in Table 1 and Table 2, the Factor and Reliability Analysis results of the scales used in the study are as follows:

Exploratory factor analysis was applied to test the construct validity of the Job Satisfaction Scale. First of all, compliance with factor analysis was tested with the values of Kaiser Mayer Olkin (KMO) and Barlett tests. The KMO test result value was 0.758 for the job satisfaction scale and the Barlett test significance test value was observed as $p<0.00$. Thus, it has been proven that the sample size is sufficient, and the data set is suitable for principal component analysis. The Job Satisfaction Scale was measured in its one-dimensional form, as in the referenced publication. The factor loads of the statements of the scale ranged from 0.917 to 0.926 and were found to be quite high. Cronbach's Alpha value for the Job Satisfaction Scale was determined as 0.911. It was found that the items forming the job satisfaction questionnaire were homogeneous and related to each other ($F=13.451$, $p<0.00<0.05$). In addition, it was determined that the test was non-additivity ($F=0.040$, $p=0.841>0.05$). Hotelling's T-Squared Test was performed to determine whether the test design of the Job Satisfaction Scale was appropriate or not, and according to the test results, the model was found to be in an appropriate structure ($F=13.205$, $p<0.00<0.05$).

The construct validity of the Turnover Intention Scale was checked with Kaiser Mayer Olkin (KMO) and Barlett tests. After the analyses, the KMO test result value for the Turnover Intention Scale was determined as 0.747 and the Barlett test significance test value as $p<0.000$. It has been proven that; the relations of the factors in line with the values are explained at a high level by their values, the sample number is sufficient, and the data set is suitable for principal components analysis. The scale was applied unidimensionally and the factor loads of the expressions were found to be between 0.912 and 0.951. Cronbach's Alpha value for the Turnover

Table 2. Factor Analysis Findings

	Load	*Eigen value*	*Eigenvalues % of Variance*	$\overline{X}$	*KMO*	*Bartlett*
Job Satisfaction				4.219		
My job satisfies me.	0.926	2.550	85.004	4.191	0.758	p<0.00
The works I do in my job satisfies me.	0.923			4.172		
I love my job.	0.917			4.341		
Turnover Intention				1.797		
I frequently think of leaving my job.	0.912	2.621	87.352	1.992	0.747	p<0.00
I am actively looking for a job in other institutions and companies.	0.940			1.685		
I will probably leave my job soon.	0.951			1.715		
Perceived Gender Discrimination				2.048		
I think that my gender can sometimes be an obstacle in working life.	0.942	3.650	91.244	1.982	0.836	p<0.00
I think my gender may have a negative impact on my career progression.	0.972			2.452		
I think that many people in working life have prejudices about gender and they will treat me in line with these prejudices.	0.948			1.975		
I think that I may be excluded from some activities in working life because of my gender.	0.959			1.780		

Intention Scale was determined as 0.924. It was determined that the items of the scale were homogeneous and related to each other and the test was non-additivity (F=37.471, p<0.00<0.05; F=1.530, p=0.216>0.05). It was also determined that the test design was appropriate in terms of reliability analysis applications of the Turnover Intention Scale (F=26.959, p<0.00<0.05).

The construct validity of the PGD Scale was checked with Kaiser Mayer Olkin (KMO) and Barlett tests. After the analysis, the KMO test result value for PGD was determined as 0.836 and the Barlett test significance testing value was determined as p<0.00. It has been proven that the sample size of the scale is sufficient, and the data set is suitable for principal component analysis. The scale was applied unidimensionally and the factor loads of the expressions were found to be between 0.972 and 0.942. Cronbach's Alpha value for PGD was found to be 0.968. It was determined that the scale items were homogeneous and related to each other. Besides, the test was non-additivity (F=45.668 p<0.00<0.05; F=0.010, p=0.921>0.05). The appropriate structure of the test design of the scale was also determined with the help of Hotelling's T-Squared Test ($F=9.377$, $p<0.00<0.05$).

In consideration of the above-mentioned values, it has been seen that the scales fulfill the reliability conditions accepted in the literature and their internal consistencies are at acceptable levels independently.

Demographic Characteristics of Participants

Demographic characteristics and some descriptive features of the participants are as mentioned in Table 3 below.

According to Table 3 it has been observed that 60.3% of the participants in the study were women and 39.7% were men. A significant majority (33.3%) of the people participating in the research were between the ages of 19-25. It was observed that 50.9% of the participants were married and 49.1% were single. Besides, considerable majority (33.0%) of the participants are high school graduates. In addition, 66.7% of the individuals in the research work in 4-star hotels and 33.3% in 5-star hotels. A significant majority of people (37.1%) were working in the front office department. 74.2% of the employees were not in a managerial position in their department and considerable majority (31.5%) of the people in the study have been serving in the tourism sector for 1-4 years.

Hypotheses Testing

The Relationship between Perceived Gender Discrimination and Turnover Intention

The correlation and regression analysis findings, which were conducted to examine the relationship between PGD and Turnover Intention, are given below. First of all, the existence and degree of the relationship between the two scales was examined by correlation analysis. The mean values, standard deviation and correlation coefficients of the scales are as shown in Table 4 below.

In the table, information about the correlation relationships for the Gender Discrimination and Turnover Intention scales of the people participating in the research and the mean ± standard deviation values of the scales are reported. The correlation relationship and the summarized average values were carried out on the Gender Discrimination and Turnover Intention scores. The said scores were created on the basis of the data obtained from the applied questionnaires. It represents the findings obtained at the 99% confidence level.

According to the Table 4, the mean score of the PGD Scale was obtained as 2.048 ± 1.299. On an average, the participants responded to the statements directed

Table 3. Demographic characteristics and descriptive features

Demographic Characteristics	Sample Size (n=267)	
	n	%
Gender		
Woman	161	60.3
Man	106	39.7
Age		
Between 19-25	89	33.3
Between 26-35	84	31.5
Between 36-45	79	29.6
Between 45-55	15	5.6
Marital Status		
Married	136	50.9
Single	131	49.1
Educational Background		
Primary Education	44	16.5
High School	88	33.0
Associate Degree	49	18.4
Bachelor and Above	86	32.2
How Many Stars is the Hotel Worked for?		
4 Stars	178	66.7
5 Stars	89	33.3
Departmant Worked in		
Front Office	99	37.1
Housekeeping	54	20.2
Kitchen	41	15.4
Food&Beverage	32	12.0
Sales&Marketing	24	9.0
Accounting&Finance	17	6.4
Current Position		
Executive	69	25,8
Not Executive	198	74,2
How Many Years Have You Worked in Tourism Industry		
Less than 1 year	27	10,1
1-4 years	84	31,5
5-9 years	76	28,5
10-14 years	33	12,4
15-19 years	24	9,0
More than 20 years	23	8,6

Table 4. Mean, standard deviation and correlation coefficients of variables

		Perceived Gender Discrimination	Turnover Intention
Perceived Gender Discrimination	Mean ± Standard Deviation	2.048 ± 1.299	1.797 ± 0.949
	Correlation Coefficient (r)	1	0.502
	p-value		<0.000
	Sample Size (n)	267	267

to them with the PGD Scale, as they felt discrimination from time to time. The Turnover Intention Scale score was determined as 1.797±0.949. In line with the average answers given to this scale, it was also determined that the participants generally did not have an intention to quit their jobs. In addition, there is a positive correlation with a coefficient of 0.502 between PGD and Turnover Intention scales. A one-unit increase in the PGD Scale score creates a 0.502-unit increase in the Turnover Intention score. In the light of the information obtained, it has been determined that there is a strong relationship between gender discrimination and turnover intention and this relationship is statistically significant ($r=0.502$, $p<0.00<0.01$).

Within the scope of the study, after the relationship between PGD and Turnover Intention scales was statistically significant, the causality relationship between the mentioned parameters were investigated. The findings were analyzed by regression analysis, aiming to investigate the effect of gender discrimination perceptions of the employees on their turnover intention. The results are shown in Table 5 below. In line with the findings obtained, A model of "Turnover Intention = 2.059 + 0.459 PGD + Ɛ" was created.

In line with the data expressed in Table 5, a one-unit increase in employees' PGD score increases their turnover intention by 45.9%. The effect of the mentioned parameter on the turnover intention is also statistically significant ($p<0.05$). With this current model, 41.2% of the total variation could be explained. The unexplained part of the variation is due to other factors apart from the investigated parameters

Table 5. Regression analysis results of turnover intention

Turnover Intention	ß (95% CI)	t-value	Coefficents p-value	Adj. R^2	p-value
Constant	2.059 (1.880 – 2.639)	12.632	<0.000	**0.412**	**<0.00***
Perceived Gender Discrimination	0.459 (0.386 – 0.532)	9.699	<0.000		

Turnover Intention Scale is summarized with predictors, confidence intervals and statistical significance values. $p<0.05$

Table 6. Mean, standard deviation and correlation coefficients of variables

		Perceived Gender Discrimination	Job Satisfaction
Perceived Gender Discrimination	Mean ± Standard Deviation	2.048 ± 1.299	4.219 ± 0.820
	Correlation Coefficient (r)	1	-0.475
	p-value		<0.00
	Sample Size (n)	267	267

that affect turnover intention. The established model is statistically significant ($p<0.00<0.05$). As a result of the findings, it was determined that the PGD has a significant effect on the turnover intention and the alternative Hypothesis 1, expressed as "PGD has an effect on the turnover intention" could not be rejected.

The Relationship between Perceived Gender Discrimination and Job Satisfaction

The relationship between PGD Scale and Job Satisfaction Scale was analyzed by correlation and regression analysis. The findings of the obtained results such as the mean values, standard deviation and correlation coefficients of the scales are as shown in Table 6 below.

In the table, information about the correlation relations for the PGD and Job Satisfaction scales of the participants and the mean ± standard deviation values of the scales are reported. The correlation relationship investigated and the summarized average values were carried out on PGD and Job Satisfaction Scores, and these scores were created based on the data obtained from the applied questionnaires. Represents the findings obtained at 99% confidence level.

According to the Table 6, the mean score of the PGD Scale was obtained as 2.048 ± 1.299. The participants' Job Satisfaction Scale score was determined as 4.219 ± 0.820 and it was determined that the participants were satisfied with their jobs. It's also determined, in line with the average answers given to the statements that the participants felt the perception of gender discrimination from time to time. There is a negative correlation with a coefficient of 0.475 between the PGD scores of the people in the study and their Job Satisfaction scores. It was determined that the relationship between the two scales was statistically significant ($r=0.475$, $p<0.00<0.01$).

Since the relationship between PGD and Job Satisfaction scales was statistically significant during the research process, the causal relationships between the mentioned parameters were investigated. The findings were analyzed by regression

Table 7. Regression analysis results of job satisfaction

Job Satisfaction	ß (95% CI)	t-value	Coefficents p-value	Adj. R^2	p-value
Constant	4.811 (4.652–4.970)	49.687	<0.00	**0.375**	**0.0001***
Perceived Gender Discrimination	-0.388 (-0.352–-0.223)	-8.779	<0.00		

Job Satisfaction Scale is summarized with predictors, confidence intervals and statistical significance values. p<0.05

analysis, aiming to investigate the effect of gender discrimination perceptions of the employees on their job satisfaction. The results are shown in Table 7 below. In line with the findings obtained, the "Job Satisfaction = 4.811 - 0.388 PGD +Ɛ" model was created.

In line with the data expressed in Table 7, a one-unit increase in employees' PGD scores decreases their job satisfaction scores by 38.8%. The effect of the mentioned parameter on job satisfaction is also statistically significant ($p<0.05$). With this current model, 37.5% of the total variation could be explained. The established model is statistically significant ($p<0.00<0.05$). The unexplained part of the variation is due to other factors apart from the investigated parameters, that affect job satisfaction. As a result of the findings, it was determined that PGD has a significant effect on job satisfaction. Thus, the alternative Hypothesis 2, expressed as "PGD has an effect on the job satisfaction" could not be rejected.

The Relationship between Perceived Gender Discrimination and Gender

How the PGD differs by gender is explained in Table 8 below by mean values, standard deviation values and statistical results. In line with the results obtained, the PGD score of women in the study was 2.178 ± 1.425 while the PGD score of men was 1.851 ± 1.056. PGD score of women was statistically and significantly higher than men ($p=0.032<0.05$). As a result of the findings, the alternative Hypothesis 3, expressed as "Women feel gender discrimination more than men" could not be rejected.

The Moderator Role of Gender in the Relationship Between Perceived Gender Discrimination and Job Satisfaction

The moderator effect of the gender factor on the relationship between PGD and job satisfaction was examined by Hayes Model 1 moderator variable regression

Table 8. Perceived gender discrimination by gender test

Gender	*Sample Size (n)*	*Mean*	*Standard Deviation*	*t-value*	*p-value*
Woman	161	2.178	1.425	2.150	**0.032**
Man	106	1.851	1.056		

p<0,05

analysis. The results are described in Table 9 and Figure 1 below. According to the findings, "Job Satisfaction = 5.642 - 0.638 PGD + 0.595 Women - PGD * Gender + Ɛ" model was created. Experiencing gender discrimination reduces job satisfaction by 63.8%. Women's job satisfaction is 59.5% higher than men's. In the model, the effect of gender discrimination and gender interaction on job satisfaction is also significant ($\beta = -0.228$, $p<0.05$). Accordingly, it was determined that the gender factor played a moderator role between PGD and job satisfaction. In addition, when women feel gender discrimination, their job satisfaction decreases by 47.1%, while the same rate is determined as 14.2% for men. Both effect values are statistically significant ($p<0.05$).

In line with the results, the alternative Hypothesis 4, expressed as "Gender has a moderator role in the relationship between PGD and job satisfaction" could not be rejected. As can be seen in Figure 2, the job satisfaction values of women who felt more gender discrimination were found to be much lower than those who felt less. The range values for job satisfaction in women are wider than in men. Therefore, women are more exposed to the negative impact of PGD on job satisfaction.

CONCLUSION

This chapter aimed to examine the effect of gender discrimination perceptions of hotel employees on their job satisfaction levels and their turnover intentions. According to the results of the study, both female and male employees experience gender discrimination perception towards their own gender in the workplace. Besides, gender discrimination perceived by these employees reduces their job satisfaction and increases their intention to leave their job. On the other hand, level of PGD among employees differs according to gender, and women feel gender discrimination more than men. In addition, it is possible to talk about the moderator role of gender in the relationship between PGD and job satisfaction. Accordingly, it's possible to say that the negative effect of PGD on job satisfaction is stronger in women than in men. This situation highlights that women are more dissatisfied with their jobs than men because they think that they are exposed to gender discrimination in the

Table 9. Regression analysis results of the Moderator Role of Gender in the Relationship Between Perceived Gender Discrimination and Job Satisfaction

Job Satisfaction	ß (95% CI)	t-value	F-value	Adj. R^2	p-value
Constant	5.642* (5.156–6.129)	22.831	31.337	**0.413**	**<0.00**
Perceived Gender Discrimination	-0.638* (-0.80–-0.397)	-5.861			
Gender (women)	0.595* (0.255–0.977)	3.451			
Perceived Gender Discrimination *Gender	-0.228* (-0.378–-0.078)	2.997			
Women	-0,471* (-0.547–-0.293)	-9.432	8.983		**0.003**
Men	-0,142* (-0.271–-0.013)	-2.167			

Job Satisfaction Scale is summarized with predictors, confidence intervals and statistical significance values. $p<0.05$

workplace. Women's job satisfaction is particularly affected by their perceptions of gender discrimination.

The chapter contributes to the existing database by expanding our understanding of the impact of PGD on job attitudes. Within the scope of the study, the perceptions of both male and female employees regarding gender discrimination were examined.

Figure 2. Moderator role of gender in the relationship between perceived gender discrimination and job satisfaction

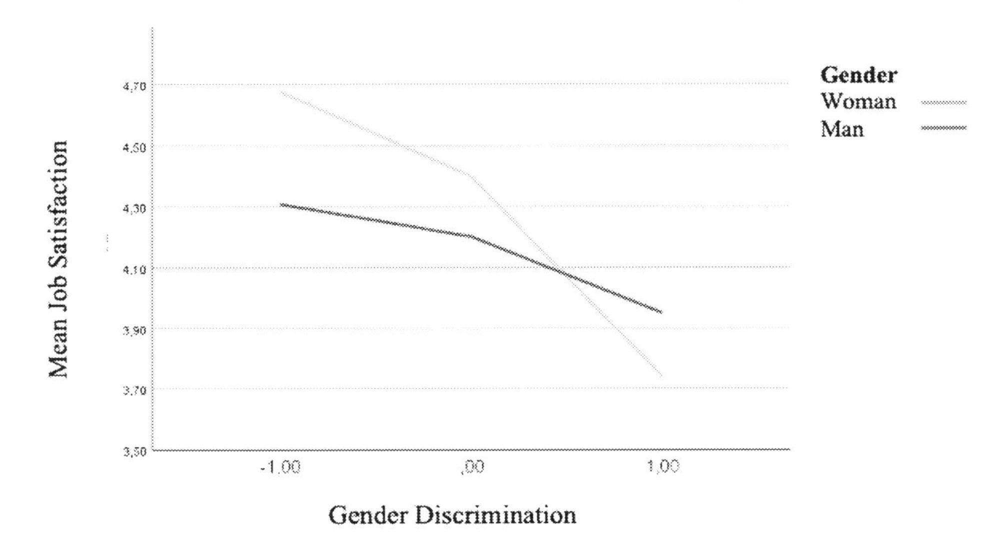

In the study, the perception of discrimination was examined in line with the information declared by employees who may have been exposed to discrimination and from the perspective of these persons. In this way, the results of the research give an idea about the reactions of employees who think that they experience discrimination because of their gender, through their work-related attitudes. To the best of author's knowledge, there is no other study that (1) examines the effect of gender discrimination perceptions of hotel employees on their job satisfaction levels and their turnover intentions; (2) compares hotel employees' perceptions of gender discrimination by sex and (3) investigates the moderator role of gender in the relationship between PGD and job satisfaction of hotel employees. Therefore, the results of the study are expected to contribute to the tourism industry literature.

With the first hypothesis tested within the scope of the research, the effect of PGD on job satisfaction was examined. In line with the findings, it was concluded that job satisfaction decreases in employees with a high perception of gender discrimination. Similarly, in studies investigating the negative effects of PGD on employees, a negative relationship was found between these two variables (Channar et al., 2011; Foley et al., 2005). In this direction, the results of the tested hypothesis have parallels with the results of the studies in the literature.

The second hypothesis tested in the research was to examine the effect of PGD on turnover intention. In line with the findings, it was concluded that the intention to leave the job increases in the employees with a high perception of gender discrimination. Similarly, in studies investigating the negative effects of PGD on employees, a linear relationship was found between these two variables (Foley et al., 2005; Kara & Yıldıran, 2011; Onay, 2009). At this point, the results of the hypothesis tested are similar to other studies available in the literature.

As a third hypothesis of the research, it was tested whether the PGD level differs according to gender. According to the results obtained, the perception of gender discrimination differs according to gender, and female hotel employees experience a higher level of gender-based discrimination perception than male employees. In the studies of Gutek et al. (1996), data were collected from independent psychologists and managers to examine the relationship between perceived discrimination, and the individual's reactions to work and organization. As a result of the research, women perceived gender discrimination against themselves more than men. The study results of Gutek et al. (1996) are in line with the results of the H_3 tested in this study. In the study of Foley et al. (2006), data were collected with questionnaires administered to lawyers in Hong Kong. According to the results of the study, women perceived more gender discrimination and gender bias against women than men. The results of this study show parallelism with the results of $H_{3.}$ Similarly, in different studies conducted in the literature, it has been stated that women experience a higher level of perception of gender discrimination compared to men (Northcraft & Gutek, 1993;

Shaffer et al., 2000; Ngo et al., 2002; Foster et al., 2004; Foley et al., 2005; Peng et al., 2009; Channar et al., 2011; Foley et al., 2015). Therefore, the results of the hypothesis tested are similar to other studies available in the literature.

As the fourth hypothesis, the moderator role of gender in the relationship between PGD and job satisfaction was investigated. In line with the findings, it has been confirmed that gender has a moderator role in the relationship between PGD and job satisfaction. Foley et al. (2005) conducted a study in which they examined the effects of PGD and organizational justice on job satisfaction, organizational commitment and turnover intention in the case of Protestant clergy in Hong Kong. The moderator role of gender in the relationship between PGD and job satisfaction, and the moderator role of gender in the relationship between PGD and organizational commitment were also investigated in the study. While the moderator role of gender in the relationship between PGD and organizational commitment was confirmed in the study, the moderator role of gender in the relationship between PGD and job satisfaction could not be confirmed. In this respect, the results of H_4 confirm that, unlike the study in the current literature, the negative effect of PGD on job satisfaction among female hotel employees is stronger than that of male employees.

This study has several limitations. Within the scope of the study, data were collected only from hospitality industry employees. Besides, the data were collected from hotel employees working in a single city in a country (Konya/Turkey). The fact that the data were collected from enterprises operating in a single industry and in a single city is limiting, in terms of the generalizability of the results. The data were also obtained in line with the answers declared by the participants themselves, and are limited to the subjective point of view of the participants.

Another limitation of the study is that the data were collected only by quantitative research method. Conducting a qualitative study focused on obtaining data through one-on-one interviews on a subjective phenomenon such as the perception of gender discrimination may provide an advantage in order to investigate the subject thoroughly. In future studies, it can be suggested to carry out a mixed method research by supporting the quantitative data with a qualitative method.

In the study, job-related attitudes such as job satisfaction and turnover intention were chosen as the possible results of the gender discrimination perceptions of the employees. In future studies, focusing on the behavioral responses (stress level, excitement, etc.) to PGD may be useful to more comprehensively measure the impact of the concept on employee well-being. Besides, the moderator role of gender in the relationship between PGD and job satisfaction was investigated within the research. In future studies, examining the mediation relationship between PGD, job satisfaction and turnover intention may also be meaningful in determining the effects of PGD on employees.

Within the scope of the research, the data were collected from accommodation enterprises, which is a sub-sector of the tourism industry. In future studies, collecting data from other components of the industry, such as food & beverage and recreation enterprises, may be beneficial due to the different nature of gender stereotypes in each of these sectors. In this way generalizability of the results to the tourism industry may be provided. In future studies, in order to reach comparative results from the accommodation industry; the differentiation between national and international hotels, city hotels and resort hotels, four-star and five-star hotels can also be investigated.

The data were obtained from the employees of a single country. In future studies, collecting data from different countries, and conducting an intercultural comparative study may provide an opportunity to broaden the perspective on the subject by revealing similarities and differences.

SOLUTIONS AND RECOMMENDATIONS

According to the World Tourism Organization data, women constitute 54% of employment in the tourism industry worldwide (World Tourism Organization, 2019). Despite that women in the tourism industry may experience disadvantages such as; customers' negative attitudes towards female employees due to sexualized marketing activities and working environments, high social contact that is susceptible to misperception by customers, inappropriate customer behaviors due to alcohol use, employers that encourage female employees to use their sexual identities to achieve higher income and customer satisfaction (Morgan & Pritchard, 2018), and earning less than men doing the same job (World Tourism Organization, 2019). In addition to these problems, female employees think that they are professionally disadvantaged because of their gender, and they feel the perception of gender discrimination more intensely than men.

In line with the results of the study, female employees who perceive gender discrimination in the workplace are more likely to think about leaving the organization by experiencing dissatisfaction with their jobs. It is possible to mention a few potential results, and suggestions about what this will mean for businesses and human resources managers. In organizations where discrimination based on gender is common, increased turnover due to the decrease in job satisfaction of successful female employees may reduce organizational effectiveness. It is also possible for these employees to be recruited by competitors. Managers should take into account the negative reactions of female employees to discrimination based on gender, and exhibit egalitarian approaches between men and women in practices such as recruitment, wages, salaries, rewards etc.

Managers' focus on reducing employees' perceptions of gender discrimination will help to reduce employee turnover intention by increasing job satisfaction. In this way, it will be ensured that organizational efficiency losses, and costs that can be caused by high labor turnover will be prevented. The Bureau of Labor Statistics estimated that the average employee replacement costs are $13,996 per employee (O'Connell and Kung, 2007) and replacing an entry-level employee costs 50% to 100% of the employee's salary (Porter, 2011). So managers' efforts to reduce employees' gender discrimination perceptions will benefit the organizations because of the high costs of employee turnover. In addition, the existing employees confidence and positive attitudes towards the organization will increase if they do not perceive any discrimination within the organization, which will in return increase the satisfaction and effectiveness. Managers should behave in administrative processes, and communicate with employees in a way, to prevent the perception of discriminative treatment based on gender. Methods such as opinion surveys, one-on-one meetings with each employee and focus group interviews to be applied to employees can be used to determine the employee's perception of gender discrimination. Managers should also consider complaints from employees. They can increase the welfare of employees, and avoid financial problems caused by the perception of gender discrimination, by correctly analyzing the gender discrimination situations that are reported and not reported by the employees.

REFERENCES

Ajzen, I. (1991). The theory of planned behavior. *Organizational Behavior and Human Decision Processes*, *50*(2), 179–211. doi:10.1016/0749-5978(91)90020-T

Anafarta, N., Sarvan, F., & Yapıcı, N. (2008). The perception of glass ceilings by women managers in hospitality enterprises: A study in Antalya [Konaklama işletmelerinde kadın yöneticilerin cam tavan algısı: Antalya ilinde bir araştırma]. *Akdeniz İİBF Dergisi*, *08*(15), 111–137.

Arlı, E. (2013). Gender discrimination and gender prejudice perceived in the marine tourism sector: A study on Karamürsel Vocational School students [Deniz turizm sektöründe algılanan cinsiyet ayrımcılığı ve cinsiyet önyargısı: Karamürsel Meslek Yüksekokulu öğrencileri üzerine bir araştırma]. *Çalışma ve Toplum*, *2013*(3), 283-302.

Aydın, Ş. (2005). *Human resource management in hospitality businesses: principles and practices* [Konaklama işletmelerinde insan kaynakları yönetimi: ilkeler ve uygulamalar]. Nobel Yayın Dağıtım.

Aydın, Ş., Özkul, E., Tandoğan, K.G., & Şahin, N. (2007). A study on the effect of glass ceilings on the promotion of women to the top and top management in hotel enterprises [Otel işletmelerinde kadınların üst ve tepe yönetime yükseltilmesinde cam tavan etkisi üzerine bir araştırma]. *Ulusal Yönetim ve Organizasyon Kongresi,* 312-319.

Baker, R. (1991). The reliability and criterion validity of a measure of patients' satisfaction with their general practice. *Family Practice, 8*(2), 171–177. doi:10.1093/fampra/8.2.171 PMID:1874365

Cameron, J. E. (2001). Social identity, modern sexism, and perceptions of personal and group discrimination by women and men. *Sex Roles, 45*(11/12), 743–766. doi:10.1023/A:1015636318953

Campos-Soria, J. A., Ortega-Aguaza, B., & Ropero-GarcÃa, M. A. (2009). Gender segregation and wage difference in the hospitality industry. *Tourism Economics, 15*(4), 847–866. doi:10.5367/000000009789955152

Canberk, G. (2019). *The mediating effect of organizational commitment and job satisfaction in the relationship between workplace incivility and turnover intention* (Unpublished master's thesis). Middle East Technical University, Turkey.

Carvalho, I., Costa, C., Lykke, N., & Torres, A. (2019). Beyond the glass ceiling: gendering tourism management, *Annals of Tourism Research, 75,* 79-91. doi:10.1016/j.annals.2018.12.022

Çatalsakal, S. (2016). *How trait mindfulness is related to job performance and job satisfaction: self-regulation as a potential mediator* (Unpublished master's thesis). Middle East Technical University, Turkey.

Channar, Z. A., Abbassi, Z., & Ujan, I. A. (2011). Gender discrimination in workforce and its impact on the employees. *Pakistan Journal of Commerce and Social Sciences, 5*(1), 177-191.

Çiçen, C., Boyacıoğlu, E. Z., & Oğuzhan, A. (2020). Examination of female labor force performance in the tourism sector: The case of accommodation enterprises in Edirne [Turizm sektöründe kadın işgücü performansının incelenmesi: Edirne ili konaklama işletmeleri örneği]. *Güncel Turizm Araştırmaları Dergisi, 4*(1), 123–150. doi:10.32572/guntad.666727

Cohen, J. (1977). *Statistical power analysis for the behavioral sciences.* Academic Press.

Cronbach, L. (1951). Coefficient alpha and the internal structure of tests. *Psychomerika*, 297-334. . doi:10.1007/BF02310555

Crosby, F. J. (1982). *Relative deprivation and working women*. Oxford University Press.

Dalkıranoğlu, T., & Çetinel, F. G. (2008). Comparison of the attitudes of male and female managers towards gender discrimination in hospitality enterprises [Konaklama işletmelerinde kadın ve erkek yöneticilerin cinsiyet ayrımcılığına karşı tutumlarının karşılaştırılması]. *Dumlupınar Üniversitesi Sosyal Bilimler Dergisi*, *20*, 277–298.

Erol Korkmaz, H. T. (2021). The relationship between emotional labor in the health sector with personality and psychological well-being [Sağlık sektöründe duygusal emeğin kişilik ve psikolojik esenlikle ilişkileri]. *Mersin Üniversitesi Sosyal Bilimler Enstitüsü Dergisi*, *5*(1), 59–83. doi:10.55044/meusbd.993646

Ersoy, A., & Ehtiyar, V. R. (2021). Social burden and career: Analysis of gender factors affecting the career development of women managers in the hospitality sector [Toplumsal yük ve kariyer: konaklama sektöründeki kadın yöneticilerin kariyer gelişimlerini etkileyen toplumsal cinsiyet faktörlerinin analizi]. *Journal of Economy Culture and Society*, *63*, 237–255. doi:10.26650/JECS2020-0072

Foley, S., Ngo, H. Y., & Loi, R. (2006). Antecedents and consequences of perceived gender discrimination: A social identity perspective. *Sex Roles*, *55*(3/4), 197–208. doi:10.100711199-006-9073-4

Foley, S., Ngo, H. Y., Loi, R., & Zheng, X. (2015). Gender, gender identification and perceived gender discrimination: An examination of mediating processes in China. *Equality, Diversity and Inclusion*, *34*(8), 650–665. doi:10.1108/EDI-05-2015-0038

Foley, S., Ngo, H. Y., & Wong, A. (2005). Perceptions of discrimination and justice: Are there gender differences in outcomes? *Group & Organization Management*, *30*(4), 421–450. doi:10.1177/1059601104265054

Fong, Y. L., & Mahfar, M. (2013). Relationship between occupational stress and turnover intention among employees in a furniture manufacturing company in Selangor. *Jurnal Teknologi*, *64*(1), 33–39.

Foster, M. D., Arnt, S., & Honkola, J. (2004). When the advantaged become disadvantaged: Men's and women's actions against gender discrimination. *Sex Roles*, *50*(1/2), 27–36. doi:10.1023/B:SERS.0000011070.24600.92

Froese, F. J., & Peltokorpi, V. (2011). Cultural distance and expatriate job satisfaction. *International Journal of Intercultural Relations, 35*(1), 49–60. doi:10.1016/j.ijintrel.2010.10.002

Griffeth, R. W., Hom, P. W., & Gaertner, S. (2000). A meta-analysis of antecedents and correlates of employee turnover: Update, moderator tests, and research implications for the next millennium. *Journal of Management, 26*(3), 463–488. doi:10.1177/014920630002600305

Guimarães, C. R. F. F., & Silva, J. R. (2016). Pay gap by gender in the tourism industry of Brazil. *Tourism Management, 52,* 440-450. doi:10.1016/j.tourman.2015.07.003

Gutek, B. A., Cohen, A. G., & Tsui, A. (1996). Reactions to perceived sex discrimination. *Human Relations, 49*(6), 791–813. doi:10.1177/001872679604900604

Hackman, J. R., & Oldham, G. R. (1975). Development of the job diagnostic survey. *The Journal of Applied Psychology, 60*(2), 159–170. doi:10.1037/h0076546

Hayes, A. F. (2013). *Introduction to mediation, moderation, and conditional process analysis a regression-based approach* (3rd ed.). The Guilford Press.

Hinton, P. R. (2007). *Statistics explained* (2nd ed.). Taylor & Francis.

Hoppock, R. (1935). *Job satisfaction*. Harper and Brothers.

Jaffe, R. (2017). *The relationship between perceived gender discrimination and counterproductive work behaviors* (Unpublished Honors Undergraduate Thesis). University of Central Florida. https://stars.library.ucf.edu/honorstheses/198

Kara, F. M., & Yıldıran, İ. (2011). The perception of the other: The prejudices and discrimination perceived by women in the sports sector [Öteki'nin algısı: spor sektöründe kadınlarca algılanan cinsiyet önyargıları ve ayrımcılığı]. *Gazi Beden Eğitimi ve Spor Bilimleri Dergisi, 16*(1), 3–13.

Kartal, M. (2014). *Gender discrimination against women employees in the labor market: The example of Kahramanmaraş textile sector* [Emek piyasasında kadın çalışanlara yönelik cinsiyet ayrımcılığı: Kahramanmaraş tekstil sektörü örneği] (Unpublished master's thesis). Selçuk University, Turkey.

Kattara, H. (2005). Career challenges for female managers in Egyptian hotels. *International Journal of Contemporary Hospitality Management, 17*(3), 238–251. doi:10.1108/09596110510591927

Kim, E., & Park, H. (2018). Perceived gender discrimination, belief in a just world, self-esteem, and depression in Korean working women: A moderated mediation model. *Women's Studies International Forum, 69,* 143-150. doi:10.1016/j.wsif.2018.06.006

Lam, T., Lo, A., & Chan, J. (2002). New employees' turnover intentions and organizational commitment in the Hong Kong hotel industry. *Journal of Hospitality & Tourism Research (Washington, D.C.), 26*(3), 217–234. doi:10.1177/1096348002026003002

Marinakou, E. (2014). Women in hotel management and leadership: Diamond or glass? *Journal of Tourism and Hospitality Management, 2*(1), 18–25.

Mobley, W. H. (1977). Intermediate linkages in the relationship between job satisfaction and employee turnover. *The Journal of Applied Psychology, 62*(2), 237–240. doi:10.1037/0021-9010.62.2.237

Mobley, W. H., Horner, S. O., & Hollingsworth, A. T. (1978). An evaluation of precursors of hospital employee turnover. *The Journal of Applied Psychology, 63*(4), 408–414. doi:10.1037/0021-9010.63.4.408 PMID:701211

Morgan, N., & Pritchard, A. (2018). Gender matters in hospitality. *International Journal of Hospitality Management, 76,* 38–44. Advance online publication. doi:10.1016/j.ijhm.2018.06.008

Nalçacı İkiz, A. (2020). Gender discrimination and women employees in tourism enterprises: Attitudes and practices of managers on the subject [Turizm işletmelerinde cinsiyet ayrımcılığı ve kadın çalışanlar: yöneticilerinin konuya ilişkin tutum ve uygulamaları]. *Yüzüncü Yıl Üniversitesi Sosyal Bilimler Enstitüsü Dergisi, 0*(50), 373–396.

Ngo, H. Y., Tang, S. C., & Au, W. W. T. (2002). Behavioural responses to employment discrimination: A study of Hong Kong workers. *International Journal of Human Resource Management, 13*(8), 1206–1223. doi:10.1080/09585190210149484

Northcraft, G., & Gutek, B. A. (1993). Discrimination against women in management: Going, going, gone? or going, but never gone? In E. Fagenson (Ed.), *Women in management: trends, issues, and challenges in managerial diversity* (pp. 219–245). Sage.

O'Connell, M., & Kung, M. C. (2007). The cost of employee turnover. *Industrial Management (Des Plaines), 49,* 14–19.

Onay, M. (2009). The consequences of perceived gender discrimination and an empirical study on the topic [Algılanan cinsiyet ayrımcılığının sonuçları ve konuyla ilgili ampirik bir araştırma]. *Ege Akademik Bakış / Ege Academic Review, 9*(4), 1101-1125.

Örücü, E., & Özafşarlıoğlu, S. (2013). The effect of organisational justice on employees' intention to leave the job: A practice in the Republic of South Africa [Örgütsel adaletin çalışanların işten ayrılma niyetine etkisi: Güney Afrika Cumhuriyetinde bir uygulama]. *Mustafa Kemal University Journal of Social Scienes Institute, 10*(23), 335–358.

Özdemir, S., & Özdemir, Y. (2015). Examination of academic studies related to the intention to leave the job and the intention to leave the job [İşten ayrılma niyeti ve işten ayrılma niyeti ile ilgili akademik çalışmaların incelenmesi]. In R. Ö. Kutanis (Ed.), *Türkiye'de örgütsel davranış çalışmaları I* (pp. 335–356). Gazi Kitabevi.

Peng, K. Z., Ngo, H. Y., Shi, J. Q., & Wong, C. S. (2009). Gender differences in the work commitment of Chinese workers: An investigation of two alternative explanations. *Journal of World Business, 44*(3), 323–335. doi:10.1016/j.jwb.2008.08.003

Pietiläinen, M., Nätti, J., & Ojala, S. (2020). Perceived gender discrimination at work and subsequent long-term sickness absence among Finnish employed women. *European Journal of Public Health, 30*(2), 311–316. doi:10.1093/eurpub/ckz156 PMID:31697306

Porter, J. (2011). Attract and retain top talent. *Strategic Finance., 92*(12), 56–60.

Qu, Y., Jo, W., & Chris, C. H. (2020). Gender discrimination, injustice, and deviant behavior among hotel employees: Role of organizational attachment. *Journal of Quality Assurance in Hospitality & Tourism, 21*(1), 78–104. doi:10.1080/152800 8X.2019.1619498

Raver, J. L., & Nishii, L. H. (2010). Once, twice, or three times as harmful? Ethnic harassment, gender harassment, and generalized workplace harassment. *The Journal of Applied Psychology, 95*(2), 236–254. doi:10.1037/a0018377 PMID:20230066

Remington, J., & Kitterlin-Lynch, M. (2018). Still pounding on the glass ceiling: A study of female leaders in hospitality, travel, and tourism management. *Journal of Human Resources in Hospitality & Tourism, 17*(1), 22–37. doi:10.1080/15332 845.2017.1328259

Russen, M., Dawson, M., & Madera, J. M. (2021). Gender discrimination and perceived fairness in the promotion process of hotel employees. *International Journal of Contemporary Hospitality Management*, *33*(1), 327–345. doi:10.1108/IJCHM-07-2020-0647

Sanchez, J. I., & Brock, P. (1996). Outcomes of perceived discrimination among Hispanic employees: Is diversity management a luxury or a necessity? *Academy of Management Journal*, *39*(3), 704–719. doi:10.5465/256660

Seçer B. (2009). The impact of women's attitudes towards trade unions and perceptions of gender discrimination on the desire to become a union member [Kadınların sendikalara yönelik tutumları ile cinsiyet ayrımcılığı algılarının sendika üyesi olma isteğine etkisi]. *Çalışma ve Toplum, 4,* 27-60.

Sevimli, F., & İşcan, Ö. F. (2005). Job satisfaction in terms of individual and business environment factors [Bireysel ve iş ortamına ait etkenler açısından iş doyumu]. *Ege Akademik Bakış Dergisi*, *5*(1), 55–64.

Shaffer, M. A., Joplin, J. R., Bell, M. P., Lau, T., & Oguz, C. (2000). Gender discrimination and job-related outcomes: A cross-cultural comparison of working women in the United States and China. *Journal of Vocational Behavior*, *57*(3), 395–427. doi:10.1006/jvbe.1999.1748

Tekin, Ö. A. (2017). Gender perception in the tourism industry: a study on five-star hotel employees [Turizm sektöründe toplumsal cinsiyet algısı: beş yıldızlı otel çalışanları üzerine bir araştırma]. *Eurasian Journal of Researches in Social and Economics, 4*(12), 669-684.

Temizkan, R., Oğuz, Y. E., & Timur, B. (2020). Gender discrimination at job application process: An experimental study at hotels. *Journal of Business Research-Turk.*, *12*(2), 1121–1129. doi:10.20491/isarder.2020.900

Thrane, C. (2008). Earnings differentiation in the tourism industry: Gender, human capital and socio-demographic effects. *Tourism Management*, *29*(3), 514–524. doi:10.1016/j.tourman.2007.05.017

Triana, M. C., Jayasinghe, M., Pieper, J. R., Delgado, D. M., & Li, M. (2019). Perceived workplace gender discrimination and employee consequences: A meta-analysis and complementary studies considering country. *Journal of Management*, *45*(6), 2419–2447. doi:10.1177/0149206318776772

World Tourism Organization. (2019). *Global report on women in tourism* (2nd ed.). UNWTO. doi:10.18111/9789284420384

KEY TERMS AND DEFINITIONS

Discrimination: The unjust or prejudicial treatment to one person or to a group due to certain characteristics such as race, age, sex, etc.

Gender Discrimination: Discrimination based on gender such as sexual harassment, pregnancy discrimination, and unequal pay for women doing the same jobs as men.

Job Satisfaction: An employee's contentedness from his/her job or positive feelings about his/her work environment.

Perceived Gender Discrimination: An individual's belief that she/he is discriminated against because of her/his gender.

Turnover Intention: An employee's intention to leave his/her current job consciously and voluntarily.

Chapter 4
Tourism and Gender Equality From SDG 5's Perspective

Priscila Cembranel
https://orcid.org/0000-0002-9560-686X
Santa Catarina Educational Society University, Brazil

Raissa Mariana Rita
Santa Catarina Educational Society University, Brazil

Manoela de Oliveira Veras
University of Southern Santa Catarina, Brazil

Ana Paula Xavier Fonseca
Santa Catarina Educational Society University, Brazil

Giselle Domingos
Santa Catarina Educational Society University, Brazil

ABSTRACT

Tourism can promote different possibilities for gender equality such as empowering women, generating employment and income, and promoting equitable experiences in tourist destinations and attractions. This chapter aims to discuss the incorporation of gender equality through the inclusion of Sustainable Development Goal (SDG) 5 in tourism. For this, a theoretical essay is developed based on articles present in the Web of Science (WoS) database. The results demonstrate that gender equality must be substantially discussed by everyone involved in the tourism sector. In particular with regard to equal salary and opportunities and salary for women as a way to reduce gender stereotypes in companies in the sector. In addition, it is understood that one of the ways to improve gender equality is in the development of practices in undergraduate higher education in tourism, as there are studies that indicate better academic results on the part of women.

DOI: 10.4018/978-1-6684-4194-7.ch004

1 INTRODUCTION

Sustainability becomes every day a criterion of consumer preference. And, it causes, even today, changes in social paradigms in sectors that have always favored economic and practical logics. This is no different in the tourism sector (Hall, 2019). This contributes significantly to the GDP of countries, besides being directly linked to the various goals of the Sustainable Development Goals established by the UN through the 2030 Agenda. This presents 17 goals with specific targets for each of them. Its fulfillment is the responsibility of the government, civil society, and also the private sector (Peña-SumaNchez; Ruiz-Chico; JiméNez- Garceuuma & López-SimaNchez, 2020).

Tourism accounts for 1 in 10 jobs worldwide and is one of the most prominent sectors in many countries. For this reason, the SDGs are discussed in the sector to improve people's awareness and their relationship with their environment. Among them is SDG 5, focus of this study which aims to achieve gender equality and women's empowerment through reforms in laws and regulations that enable this purpose to be achieved. (Peña-SumaNchez; Ruiz-Chico; JiméNez- Garceuuma & López-SimaNchez, 2020).

Although the presence of women has been growing in the industry in the last century, women's work suffers a number of variations when compared to men's work. This occurs because women are seen as fragile figures and susceptible to stereotyped opinions based on gender, such as of care activities (Ferreras-Garcia, 2021). In this sense, despite being an SDG, gender equality is still little discussed in tourism. Similarly, female empowerment is idealized, but in reality, there are few opportunities for women in the sector due to the social inferiorization of women and the lack of public policies related to gender equality (Alarcón, 2019).

The lack of knowledge about gender equality is a problem since higher education for tourism. For, although there is discussion of generic concepts such as "diversity management" and "ethical commitment", no teaching plan mentions the gender perspective and equality management as a current challenge for organizations. The study also reveals that just over 20% of respondents are aware of SDG 5, which may compromise the future management leadership of public and private organizations in the tourism sector (Noguer-Junca, 2021).

The media and stereotypical representation of genders further exacerbates this problem. While men are presented as a form of strength and superiority, women are represented as the "weaker sex" in a trivialized or eroticized way. This portrayal imposes on the public gender roles and types of behaviors are deemed more appropriate and valuable in the eyes of society (Smith, 2021). Therefore, women are coerced into remaining in the private sphere, maintaining care activities.

Considering that women equally occupy university benches and that there are difficulties related to gender equality since the graduation in tourism, this article aims to answer the following problem: "How can the adoption of SDG number 5 contribute to promote gender equality in the tourism sector?". In this way, we intend to discuss the incorporation of the gender equality theme through the inclusion of SDG number 5 in tourism.

This article is divided into: introduction, theoretical framework, methodological aspects, results and discussions, and final considerations.

2 THEORETICAL REFERENCES

Without gender equality there is no sustainability. Thus, gender studies in tourism usually confront stakeholders with the sector's difficulties regarding the lack of policies, projects, and decent working conditions for women (Alarcón & Mullor, 2018).

Sustainable tourism development makes it necessary for women to participate fully and equally in decision-making and processes that affect their lives. In addition, it brings uncomfortable discussions about unpaid care work and the invisibilization of women and girls in front of the market, the lack of representatives in parliaments, unions, cooperatives and community associations, and the urgency to create laws, policies and practices capable of increasing gender equality (UN Women, 2018).

Thus, SDG 5 presents goals aimed at reducing discrimination against women and girls, eliminating violence, trafficking and sexual exploitation, early and forced marriages, genital mutilation, recognizing care and domestic work and encouraging shared responsibility in homes and families, providing women with the opportunity to occupy leadership positions and access to sexual and reproductive health and reproductive rights. It also includes aspects related to economic resources, access to property, financing, and inheritance, and access to basic technologies to promote women's empowerment. And, it seeks to strengthen policies and legislation to promote gender equality at all levels (ONU Brazil, 2015).

For this reason, discussing gender equality presupposes recognizing the violence committed against women and girls throughout their journey in society. And to admit that, despite being in greater numbers in the tourism sector, they still assume less prestigious roles due to the difficulties imposed by society's invisible norms, domestic overload, and low access to certain services (Esquivel & Sweetman, 2016). While men are educated to occupy roles in the public sphere as leaders, female socialization focuses on activities related to care, whether at home or for children. For this reason, women who enter the market face two major obstacles: the triple shift, two of them usually unpaid, and the lack of public policies aimed at their inclusion in the market from the reduction of the sexist view that privileges hiring men due to the historical perception of the male protagonism (Sultana, 2012).

From that, unpaid work is pointed out as a major ally in the lack of women in leadership roles. According to data from the United Nations (2020), less than 50% of working-age women are in the labor market, a gap that has remained relatively constant in the past 25 years. One of the central causes of that is the disparity of dedicated hours to unpaid domestic and care work: on an average day, men spend 1.7 hours while women address 4.2 hours to those activities. Hence, this lopsided distribution restricts female participation in the labor market.

Thus, the incorporation of women as workers requires not only changes in public policies, but an adjustment in a socially constructed mentality that reduces women to home activities and assigns the market to men. This adjustment is required in all sectors, including tourism. Gender and tourism are directly related. The majority of its workforce globally is female. However, women earn 14.7% less than men. Women also continue to be poorly represented in leadership roles and they are concentrated in low-level jobs (World Tourism Organization, 2019)

Tourism is one of the most prominent sectors for the fulfillment of the 2030 Agenda. Among the goals set by this agenda, there is SDG 5 focused on gender equality and women's empowerment. This is understood as an indispensable criterion for the success of the tourism sector, and despite presenting gradual advances, it still lacks substantial advances to make the situation adequate and fair (Boluk, Cavaliere & Higgins-Desbiolles, 2019). This is because, the social and media view of women's role in society continues to hamper them in their achievements. Thus, lack of opportunities in the labor market is at the top of an extensive list of daily difficulties faced by women around the world (Noguer-Juncà & Crespi-Vallbona, 2021).

In tourism, as in other economic sectors, the disparity between men and women is clear. For, despite having greater knowledge and training than men, there are few women who manage to reach leadership positions or higher salary range. And when they do, they must deal with discrimination in their daily lives (Alarcón, 2019).

Thus, the gender roles assigned to certain activities affect women's demand for positions at higher hierarchical levels. This happens because of discrimination and causes them to focus on jobs with lower pay, but able to reconcile their performance in the corporate environment and family environment (Smith, 2021).

3 METHODOLOGICAL ASPECTS

The data included in this study comes from a review of academic articles published between 2016 and 2021, and peer-reviewed to ensure credibility. The search allowed to identify 18 articles based on keywords "SGD 5" and "tourism" and inclusion criteria.

In the Web of Science database, the inclusion criteria were: Articles presenting the inclusion indicators: Published in an academic journal (with a peer review committee), and published in English between 2016 and 2021.

Articles considered irrelevant were eliminated, either after a careful reading of the article title, abstract, or full text. With this process, it was possible to identify a total of 06 articles that provided data for the literature review. They are: Peña-SumaNchez, Ruiz-Chico, JiméNez-Garceuuma & López-SimaNchez (2020), Ferreras-Garcia, Sales-Zaguirre & Serradell-Lópes (2021), Kuniyal et al. (2021), Noguer-Juncà & Crespi-Vallbona (2021), Smith; Kimbu; Jong & Cohen (2021) and Alarcón (2019).

4 RESULTS AND DISCUSSION

4.1 Gender Issues in the Tourism Sector

The training of tourism professionals with a gender perspective is essential to eliminate norms that privilege men and transform traditional gender relations. However, it is something that occurs in a deficit way, because the students' knowledge on the subject is small. This highlights the maintenance of inequalities in educational institutions. These, in turn, will generate professionals who reproduce the problems that already exist in society. The problem is also perceived within universities, where women do not assume management positions, for example. (Noguer-Juncà & Crespi-Vallbona, 2021).

In hotels, the most important administrative jobs are commonly entrusted to men, while customer service and reception are functions occupied by women. Even in these places, when the supervisors are women, it is common for female students to feel more comfortable (Ferreras-Garcia, Sales-Zaguirre & Serradell-Lópes, 2021).

Still, regardless of the gender of the supervisor, female tourism graduates usually perform better in the learning required by companies. These include: communication and practical application of knowledge, foreign language skills, entrepreneurship, decision making, problem solving, and recognition of operating procedures. However, when women self-assess themselves, they tend to think they are worse than they really are (Ferreras-Garcia, Sales-Zaguirre & Serradell-Lópes, 2021).

When analyzing specific contexts, it can be seen that support for gender empowerment and equality does not yet occur through laws and regulations in all countries of the European Union. This is in addition to the fact that there is no data collection on women's wages in the tourism sector. However, it is possible to state that it is lower than men's wages. Another problem is access to leadership positions

Table 1. List of included and excluded articles.

Reference	Theme	Brief study summary	Justification for inclusion/ exclusion of the study in the analysis
Koide & Akenji (2017)	Sustainable production and consumption policies and SDG 12	Evaluates the national policies of EU, Asian, Latin American and African governments on the sustainable production and consumption targets of SDG 12	Excluded, as it does not address tourism or SDG 5
Lützendorf & Balouktsi (2019)	Climate change and greenhouse gas emissions and SDG	Discusses climate protection in cities, projects zero greenhouse gas emission targets presented through global agendas, Agenda 2030 and the Paris Agreement, and the SDG.	Excluded, as it does not address tourism.
Adshead (2019)	SDG performance in the EU	Assesses performance on infrastructure-driven SDGs in EU countries and the UK	Excluded, as it does not address tourism
Yeh, Chiou, Wu, Lee & Wu (2019)	Communication Industry and the SDGs	The study explores the similarities and differences of the SDGs between the academic community and the media.	Excluded, as it is not focused on the tourism sector.
Alarcón (2019)	Tourism from a Gender Perspective and the SDG	Highlights gender inequality in tourism and the lack of indicators and jobs for women in the sector.	Included
Peña-SumaNchez, Ruiz-Chico; JiméNez- Garceuuma & López-SimaNchez (2020)	Tourism and the SDGs	Analyzes tourism activity in the EU (2009-2018) from an employment perspective and adaptations to SDGs 5 and 8	Included
Jia, Wu, Niu, Tang & Mu (2020)	UN sustainability monitoring (SDG 9) in Africa	The study monitors a region in northern Algeria where expressways were built by China, linking it to SDG 9.	Excluded, as it only addresses SDG 9.
Chen, Cheng, Edwards & Xu (2020)	Vulnerability of the sharing economy in the COVID-19 pandemic	Reports the difficulty of the sharing economy model (Airbnb) exposed by the COVID-19 pandemic in Sydney, Australia	Excluded, since although it is about the sharing economy, it does not address SDG 5
Cherrington (2020)	Monitoring Forest and Coastal Ecosystems in Belize	The article presents an analysis of the monitoring of Belize's coastal forest and marine ecosystems through the Earth Observation System (NASA) with the goal of achieving SDGs 14 and 15	Excluded, as it does not address tourism and SDG 5
Passer, Lützendorf, Habert, Kromp-Kolb, Monsberger, Eder & Truger (2020)	Climate change and greenhouse gas emissions and SDG	Reports on the emergency climate and Greenhouse Gas emission situation in the European Union in line with the SDG	Excluded, as it does not address tourism.
Ferreras-Garcia, Sales-Zaguirre & Serradell-López (2021)	The Impact of Gender on Innovation Competencies	Analyzes gender competencies and skills in the field of management and innovation	Excluded, as it does not address tourism and SDG 5
Ferreras-Garcia, Sales-Zaguirre & Serradell-López, (2021)	The Impact of Gender on Skills in the Tourism Sector	Analyzes the relevance of the gender gap in the competencies of higher education students, trainees in the tourism sector in Spain	Included.
Kuniyal, Maiti, Kumar, Bisht, Sekar, Arya, Rai & Nand (2021)	Ecological restoration in the Dayara grasslands (India)	The study evaluates an eco-restoration model for the Indian Himalayan region correlating to the SDG (1, 2, 3, 4, 5, 6, 13 and 17)	Included, as it addresses SDG 5 in specific tourist region
Noguer-Juncà & Crespi-Vallbona, (2021)	Gender Perspective of University Education	Studies learning of university students of Tourism, Hotel and Tourism Management in Catalonia with respect to the implementation of gender equality policies and initiatives	Included.
Smith, Kimbu, Jong & Cohen (2021)	Gender Representations on Instagram in the aviation industry	Reports representation of gender issues at work in the aviation industry. Maps the organizational representation of flight attendants and pilots on Instagram.	Included.
Balsalobre-Lorente, Sinha, Driha & Mubarik (2021)	Impacts of aging and natural resource extraction	Analyzes the impact of natural resource extraction, globalization, economic growth, energy consumption and an aging population on carbon emissions in the European Union (EU-5), addresses SDG 7, 8 and 13.	Excluded, as it does not address tourism.

Source: the authors (2021).

and the division of labor. For, the positions assigned to women are marked by the sexual division of labor and precariousness (Peña-SumaNchez, Ruiz-Chico, JiméNez-Garceuuma & López-SimaNchez, 2020).

In addition to the lack of standards and laws, there are no specific resources to address gender issues in tourism. And, this has not been adequately addressed by the World Tourism Organization (WTO), because the issue is not simply to include women, it is necessary that they stay in the activities and grow professionally (Alarcón, 2019).

It is also observed that Eastern European countries have more women employed in the tourism sector. However, the pay gap between women and men is still large, as they also have lower overall pay levels among the EU-28 member countries. Another point is that women have more chances of employment in recently acceded countries such as: Lithuania, Estonia, Finland, Poland, Latvia, Austria, Bulgaria, Slovenia, and Slovakia (Peña-SumaNchez, Ruiz-Chico, JiméNez-Garceuuma & López-SimaNchez, 2020).

The Indian Himalayan region has had its tourism potential highlighted in terms of employability, quality of life, and environmental impacts. In the search for improvements in this territory, women started to be included in the process of discussion and development of the territory. Thus, one way to keep people involved and also to value local women was to develop activities using locally available materials as a way to preserve the local culture, empower families, and generate income (Kuniyal et al., 2021).

As well as some territories, the way to reach them is also part of the tourism industry. Air transport, the most traditional way to travel long distances, allows the development of tourist destinations and markets around the world. However, although airlines try to sell an image of diversity, cabin space is hyper-feminine and objectified. Furthermore, organizational images portray employees based on their gender: pilots are white, experienced men and flight attendants are predominantly white, young, thin women. This makes the male audience the main target for travel (Smith; Kimbu; Jong & Cohen, 2021).

4.2 Ways to Achieve Gender Equality

One of the possibilities for improving things in the EU is for the tourism sector to work in partnership with national and international institutions on strengthening gender equality in the tourism sector and in different socio-cultural contexts. For, the sector generates more female jobs, stable and decent jobs for women than other sectors, especially in the countries that last entered the EU (Peña-SumaNchez, Ruiz-Chico, JiméNez-Garceuuma & López-SimaNchez, 2020).

In this sense, it is noteworthy that about 55.78% (2009-2014) and 55.16% 2015-2018) of people hired are women. Similarly, countries with better economic development have smaller disparities in hiring by gender when compared to countries with lower levels of development. (Peña-SumaNchez, Ruiz-Chico, JiméNez-Garceuuma & López-SimaNchez, 2020).

In the hospitality industry, it is common for men to assume management positions. And, although women have the ability to perform them, this can represent a barrier to career growth because it is not seen in a positive way in general. Thus, it is important that companies and universities strengthen the training of women employed in the tourism and hospitality industry to empower them in this sector. (Ferreras-Garcia, Sales-Zaguirre & Serradell-Lópes, 2021).

In this sense, Spain can be taken as an example. There, universities follow a plan with gender equality policies. This is focused on the promotion of egalitarian values and models, promotion of gender equality, eradication of chauvinistic violence, political participation, personal and community empowerment of women, visibility of women and non-sexist communication, and transversal adoption of the gender perspective in public policies (Noguer-Juncà & Crespi-Vallbona, 2021).

Another interesting case is the development of the Indian Himalayan region that becomes possible by involving, in particular, the surrounding villages. For this, women and men have been trained to act as tour guides. It is also suggested that a committee be created with 50% women members so that the activities can generate income for more women. (Kuniyal et al., 2021).

Airlines, as part of the tourism industry, try to include SDG 5 among their commitments by articulating, among their content in traditional and virtual media, messages of equality, diversity, and inclusion. However, the images conveyed with these messages are not in sync. Gender stereotypes are still present in advertising and in aviation where, less than 6% of pilots are women and more than 80% of the cabin, responsible for less prestigious services, is composed of women (Smith; Kimbu; Jong & Cohen, 2021).

One of the main points that the tourism sector can contribute is the creation of jobs for women. However, it is not enough just to create these jobs, it is essential that there are growth prospects for them to reach more prestigious occupations. There is also the need to change the social dynamics of gender, otherwise the problems will continue to occur in interpersonal and interprofessional relationships. This will mean that, despite being active in the sector, they will not be able to contribute with their full potential to the growth of the sector (Alarcón, 2019).

4.3 Improvements/Initiatives Implemented After Incorporating the SDGs into the Lives of Women in the Tourism Sector

Although changes are considered minimal in the EU, the gender pay gap has narrowed in some countries between 2010-2014. These are: Lithuania, Slovenia, Latvia, Bulgaria, Croatia, Finland, Denmark, Portugal, Sweden, and Romania. In addition, there was more stable job creation in the tourism sector. Thus, SDG 5 can be connected with SDG 8, sustainable economic growth and decent employment (SumaNchez, Ruiz-Chico, JiméNez-Garceuuma & López-SimaNchez, 2020).

Women's ratings in the hospitality industry are usually higher when compared to those of men. However, being stereotyped based on gender creates barriers for women to assume leadership positions. For this reason, women supervising other women can positively influence the assignment of tasks and functions. Nevertheless, the process of evaluating learning outcomes is not influenced by the gender of the supervisor versus the student (Ferreras-Garcia, Sales-Zaguirre & Serradell-Lópes, 2021).

The work developed and suggested for women in the Indian Himalayas receives support from the government and community groups, because among the results are the improvement of the territory's ecological index, increased education and income for village women (Kuniyal et al., 2021).

The adoption of gender equality-oriented policies in universities in Spain promotes a critical perspective on sexist prejudices, behaviors, beliefs, and practices. Moreover, it promotes non-sexist knowledge, ethical and moral principles. There are also university programs aimed at gender equality for professors and university management. These programs generate research, hold conferences, and debate this issue with the faculty and student community. There are also programs that award undergraduate, master's, and doctoral studies focused on the gender perspective (Noguer-Juncà & Crespi-Vallbona, 2021).

Over time, the aviation industry has started to adopt the diversity banner, increasing the hiring of women and LGBTQIA+. However, most of them work in less prestigious jobs, this does not bring about proper gender integration in all aviation roles. Thus, for this to be properly represented it is important that the organizational images of airlines are modified (Smith; Kimbu; Jong & Cohen, 2021).

Initiatives to implement gender equality in tourism should involve political aspects, resource mobilization and society. Another point to be highlighted is that while SDG 5 is not properly implemented in tourism, all other SDGs will not be fully achieved. An example of this is the fact that tourism brings water and sanitation to remote communities (SDG 6), but induces mismanagement of these resources that substantially affects women in these places. Similarly, when generating jobs (SDG 8), they often do not support gender equality (SDG 5). Thus, it is understood

Figure 1. Goals of SGD 5 contemplated
Source: authors

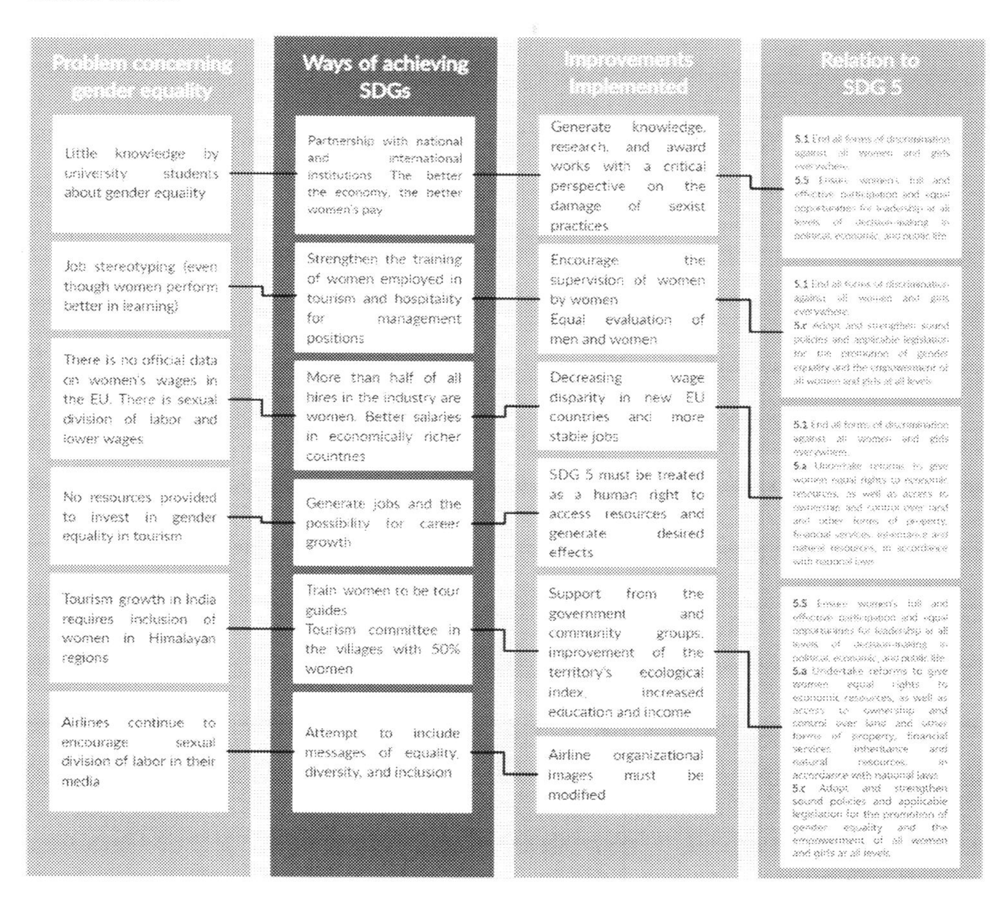

that SDG 5 must be treated as a human right in order for it to benefit from laws and resources in an adequate manner (Alarcón, 2019).

In order to systematize the ways to achieve the SDGs, Figure 1 was built. It presents the goals related to SDG **5:** that are contemplated by the cases analyzed in this theoretical review. According to the studies, the tourism sector contributes little, but works to achieve the following goals: **5.1**: end all forms of discrimination against all women and girls everywhere, **5.5:** Ensure women's full and effective participation and equal opportunities for leadership at all levels of decision-making in political, economic, and public life, **5a**: Carry out reforms to give women equal rights to economic resources, as well as access to ownership and control over land and other forms of property, financial services, inheritance and natural resources, in accordance with national laws and **5.c** Adopt and strengthen sound policies and applicable legislation for the promotion of gender equality and the empowerment of all women and girls at all levels.

5 CONCLUSION

Tourism achieves one of the sustainability criteria by including gender equality and empowerment of women and girls (SDG 5). This action, according to the articles analyzed, generates knowledge, research and awards, and allows partnerships between national and international institutions. In addition, it contributes to the empowerment of women to assume management positions. Other aspects highlighted were: the decrease in the salary disparity, job generation, and possibilities for career growth.

This study contributes by pointing out practical ways to achieve gender equality and the empowerment of women in tourism. It also shows how far the tourism sector is from achieving SDG 5. There are movements in the university education of tourism professionals and, still, the results are incipient. There are also attempts to generate employment, income, and career opportunities that include women, but they run into cultural practices, domestic work overload, and the sexual division of labor. And, no matter how many measures are taken to ensure gender equality, there is still society and its predominantly patriarchal culture that influence work structures and lifestyles. In this regard, it is fundamental to increase the female representation in leadership roles and guarantee the salary disparity.

These findings are in line with the study by Alarcón (2019), who argues for the need to treat SDG 5 and its goals as a fundamental human right so that it receives incentives, resources, and the creation of laws in all countries to effectively ensure gender equality and the empowerment of girls and women.

The limits of this research are related to the number of databases consulted and to the time frame set by the researchers. For this reason, it is suggested as a possibility of future research to analyze other databases and include other key words to perform the search. It is also suggested the development of a theoretical framework on the subject and how the competence in gender perspective can be properly implemented by the tourism sector to promote SDG 5.

REFERENCES

Adshead, D., Thacker, S., Fuldauer, L. I., & Hall, J. W. (2019). Delivering on the Sustainable Development Goals through long-term infrastructure planning. *Global Environmental Change*, *59*, 101975. doi:10.1016/j.gloenvcha.2019.101975

Alarcón & Cañada. (2018). *Gender dimensions in tourism.* Alba Sud Publishing Informes en Contraste Series, no. 4. Retrieved from: http://www.albasud.org/publ/docs/81.en.pdf

Alarcón, D. M., & Cole, S. (2019). No sustainability for tourism without gender equality. *Journal of Sustainable Tourism, 27*(7), 903–919. doi:10.1080/09669582.2019.1588283

Balsalobre, D., Sinha, A., Driha, O. M., & Mubarik, S. (2021). Assessing the Impacts of Ageing and Natural Resource Extraction on Carbon Emissions: A proposed Policy Framework for European Economies. *Journal of Cleaner Production, 296*, 126470. doi:10.1016/j.jclepro.2021.126470

Boluk, K. A., Cavaliere, T., & Higgins-Desbiolles, F. (2017). A critical framework for interrogating the United Nations Sustainable Development Goals 2030 Agenda in tourism. *Journal of Sustainable Tourism, 27*(7), 847–864. doi:10.1080/09669582.2019.1619748

Brasil, O. N. U. (2015). *SGD 5: Gender equality: Achieving gender equality and empowering all women and girls* [SGD 5: Igualdade de gênero: Alcançar a igualdade de gênero e empoderar todas as mulheres e meninas]. Retrieved from: https://brasil.un.org/pt-br/sdgs/5

Chen, G., Cheng, M., Edwards, D., & Xu, L. (2021). COVID-19 pandemic exposes the vulnerability of the sharing economy: A novel accounting framework. *Journal of Sustainable Tourism.* Advance online publication. doi:10.1080/09669582.2020.1868484

Cherrington, E. A., Griffin, R. E., Anderson, E. R., Hernandez Sandoval, B. E., Flores-Anderson, A. I., Muench, R. E., Markert, K. N., Adams, E. C., Limaye, A. S., & Irwin, D. E. (2020). Use of public Earth observation data for tracking progress in sustainable management of coastal forest ecosystems in Belize, Central America. *Remote Sensing of Environment, 245*, 111798. doi:10.1016/j.rse.2020.111798

Esquivel, V., & Sweetman, C. (2016). *Gender and the Sustainable Development.* Academic Press.

Ferreras-Garcia, R., Sales-Zaguirre, J., & Serradell-López, E. (2021). Competency assessment and learning results in tourism internships: is gender a relevant factor? Higher Education, Skills and Work-Based Learning. doi:10.1108/HESWBL-05-2021-0096

Ferreras-Garcia, R., Sales-Zaguirre, J., & Serradell-López, E. (2021). Sustainable Innovation in Higher Education: The Impact of Gender on Innovation Competences. *Sustainability*, *13*(9), 5004. doi:10.3390u13095004

Hall, C. M. (2019). Constructing sustainable tourism development: The 2030 agenda and the managerial ecology of sustainable tourism. *Journal of Sustainable Tourism*, *27*(7), 1044–1060. doi:10.1080/09669582.2018.1560456

Jia, Z., Wu, M., Niu, Z., Tang, B., & Mu, Y. (2020). Monitoring of UN sustainable development goal SDG-9.1.1: Study of Algerian "Belt and Road" expressways constructed by China. *PeerJ*, *8*, e8953. doi:10.7717/peerj.8953 PMID:32547851

Koide, R., & Akenji, L. (2017). Assessment of Policy Integration of Sustainable Consumption and Production into National Policies. *Resources*, *6*(4), 48. doi:10.3390/resources6040048

Kuniyal, J. C., Maiti, P., Kumar, S., Kumar, A., Bisht, N., Sekar, K. C., Arya, S. C., Rai, S., & Nand, M. (2021). Dayara bugyal restoration model in the alpine and subalpine region of the Central Himalaya: A step toward minimizing the impacts. *Scientific Reports*, *11*(1), 16547. doi:10.103841598-021-95472-y PMID:34400660

Lützkendorf, T., & Balouktsi, M. (2019). On net zero GHG emission targets for climate protection in cities: More questions than answers? *IOP Conference Series: Earth and Environmental Science*, 323. 10.1088/1755-1315/323/1/012073

Nassani, A. A., Aldakhil, A. M., Abro, M. M. Q., Islam, T., & Zaman, K. (2019). The impact of tourism and finance on women empowerment. *Journal of Policy Modeling*, *41*(2), 234–254. doi:10.1016/j.jpolmod.2018.12.001

Noguer-Juncà, E., & Crespi-Vallbona, M. (2021). Gender Perspective in University Education: The Case of Bachelor's Degrees in Tourism in Catalonia. *International and Multidisciplinary Journal of Social Sciences*, *10*(2), 81–111. doi:10.17583/rimcis.8156

Passer, A., Lützkendorf, T., Habert, G., Kromp-Kolb, H., Monsberger, M., Eder, M., & Truger, B. (2020). Sustainable built environment: Transition towards a net zero carbon built environment. *The International Journal of Life Cycle Assessment*, *25*(6), 1160–1167. doi:10.100711367-020-01754-4

Peña-Sánchez, A. R., Ruiz-Chico, J., Jiménez-García, M., & López-Sánchez, J. A. (2020). Tourism and the SDGs: An Analysis of Economic Growth, Decent Employment, and Gender Equality in the European Union (2009–2018). *Sustainability*, *12*(13), 5480. doi:10.3390u12135480

Smith, W. E., Kimbu, A. N., de Jong, A., & Cohen, S. (2021). Gendered Instagram representations in the aviation industry. *Journal of Sustainable Tourism*. Advance online publication. doi:10.1080/09669582.2021.1932933

Sultana, A. (2012). Patriarchy and Women's Subordination: A Theoretical Analysis. *Arts Faculty Journal*, *4*, 1–18. doi:10.3329/afj.v4i0.12929

United Nations. (2020). *World's Women 2020: Trends and Statistics*. Retrieved from: https://worlds-women-2020-data-undesa.hub.arcgis.com/

ONU Women. (2018). *Turning promises into action: Gender equality in the 2030*. Author.

World Tourism Organization. (2019). *Global Report on Women in Tourism* (2nd ed.). UNWTO. doi:10.18111/9789284420384

Yeh, S. C., Chiou, H. J., Wu, A. W., Lee, H. C., & Wu, H. C. (2019). Diverged Preferences towards Sustainable Development Goals? A Comparison between Academia and the Communication Industry. *International Journal of Environmental Research and Public Health*, *16*(22), 4577. doi:10.3390/ijerph16224577 PMID:31752324

Chapter 5
Gender Perspectives:
Women and Employability in Tourism

Bindi Varghese
Christ University, India

Emilda K. Joseph
Christ University, MG University, India

Tomy K. Kallarakal
Christ University, India

ABSTRACT

The travel business is an extensively engaging sector, and it is quite a paradox to see how tourism businesses play a leadership role within the industry and in the business community. This chapter aims to precipitate and reflect on the nature of tourism employability and examine the gender space and women employability for inclusive tourism development. This chapter examines varied aspects affecting the tourism industry and addresses economic resilience building. The significance of the gender parity revolves around the dynamic capacities related to the women in the private business space in the hospitality sector. This chapter indicates how women-centric employee engagement is attained in a globalized world. The gender-centric perspective and the women empowerment in the hospitality business are assessed.

INTRODUCTION

One of the most significant advantages of the tourism industry is the creation of jobs for residents in tourist locations. While this is commonly acknowledged, there is a lack of understanding of a gender bias in the kind of jobs offered to men and

DOI: 10.4018/978-1-6684-4194-7.ch005

women (Boonabaana, 2014). Gender discrepancies in tourism employment have been documented in research, with more women than males being impacted negatively and it has been linked in large part to conventional gender perceptions and relationships in diverse locations. (Xu, 2018).

According to Kinnaird and Hall (1996) tourism is founded on the grounds of gendered societies, and gender relations infect all aspects of tourist-related development and activity as a result. Societal factors impact and are influenced by gender relations in several ways like economic, political, social, cultural, and environmental factors. Tourism does not exist in isolation; it has an impact on all of them. Tourism has become such an important component of growth, the social, economic, and political linkages that have resulted are part of wider power and control systems that can be defined by race, class, or gender. However, female members are often marginalized in government policies and development programs compared to their male counterparts. Therefore, understanding women's and men's power and agency, as well as the cross-cultural creative techniques used regarding their political, economic, social, and cultural roles, is fundamental. (Ridgeway & Correll, 2004)

Ferguson et al. (2021) say 54% of people employed in tourism are women, which shows that the tourism industry appears to be a particularly significant sector for women. On a global scale, women's engagement in the tourist business has increased significantly and this rise in female participation might be attributed to the tourist industry's expansion. (Kladeen, 2020). They have attained higher levels of education than ever before. Despite this, their representation in managerial roles remains unacceptably low, with only a small percentage breaking past the "glass ceiling." (Nguyen, 2022). In comparison to males, women are more likely to work as chambermaids, cleaners, receptionists, phone controllers, housekeepers, handicraft merchants, and restaurant waiters in the tourist industry (Xu, 2018). Several interconnected elements contribute to the tourist labor market's gender segregation.

Gender Stereotyping

Gender stereotypes exist in most cultures and are more culturally generic than culturally particular. Gender stereotypes have an impact on how we view each other and ourselves. (Wojtowicz, 2021). Gender stereotypes and gender roles are not unique to the tourist industry; rather, it appears that the tourism industry is another example of conventional preconceptions and roles at work. (Skalpe, 2007). Women are seen to be particularly well-suited to filling specific tourist professions; they regard themselves as "well-suited" and are interested in conventional occupations. As a result, women are more appropriate to some vocations, such as caring and household-related tasks, as well as service positions. On the one hand, this contributes to the perpetuation of gender stereotypes and women's positioning as a result.

This is unfavorable in general, especially because the majority of gender-stereotyped jobs are low-paying and do not feature crucial management roles (Sabina & Nicolae, 2013). Women, on the other hand, can enter the tourist profession based on their traditional roles and their confidence in their ability to fulfill them. Gender stereotypes and gender roles are not unique to the tourist industry; rather, it appears that the tourism industry is another example of conventional preconceptions and roles at work. (Skalpe, 2007).

Conventional Gender Norms

Furthermore, conventional gender norms place the primary responsibility for raising children, caring for the elderly, and conducting domestic chores on women (Koc, 2019). As a result, women are frequently forced to pick between informal, part-time, and seasonal work. Although this allows people to balance their many obligations as well as their job outside the house, it comes with several disadvantages, including lower compensation per working hour, fewer promotion chances, less formal training, and less unemployment protection (Kladeen, 2020).

Gender Identity

Recognizing gender identity in labor markets is a widespread issue that implies when considering tourism because of its size, quick expansion, and incredibly diversified and dynamic character (Alshareef & AlGassim, 2021). The tourism business appears to be an especially suitable "candidate" for participating in initiatives to advance and this will allow the sector to launch important programs for women's growth women (Alshareef & AlGassim, 2021). In many nations, the large number of women in the tourist industry offers a vital foundation for women's growth. There are, however, countless examples of women and women's groups starting their income-generating operations. These activities assist local women in gaining financial independence while also challenging them to learn the essential skills and further their education. Financial freedom and strong education, contribute to higher women's self-esteem and more fair family and community interactions (Mitra, 2019). Women may find community-based tourism efforts, particularly those run by local women's groups and cooperatives, to be an accessible and viable entry point into paid labor. They appear to inspire greater long-term motivation than outside initiatives (McCall & Mearns, 2021).

CULTURAL PERCEPTIONS AND GENDER PERSPECTIVE

Gender has been a significant topic in tourism research during the last few decades (Ridgeway & Correll, 2004). It is an institutionalized system of social practices for classifying people into two distinct groups, men and women, and organizing inequitable social connections based on that distinction (Indra Munshi, 2006). Gender is also a cultural construct, and men's and women's perspectives vary from culture to culture, and even within the same culture or society, at various times (Ridgeway & Correll, 2004). There are a variety of reasons to believe that the gender system is influenced by both cultural and social relationship circumstances. If the gender system is a system for defining difference and organizing inequity based on that difference, then widely held cultural ideas that describe men's and women's differentiating qualities and how they are expected to behave are a major component of the gender system (Indra Munshi, 2006).

According to Garcia-Ramon et al. (1995), gender stereotypes are universal portrayals of women and men with a limited range of characteristics. If cultural gender ideas are the rules for enacting the gender system, social-relational settings are the venues in which these rules are applied to individual behavior and appraisal.

There are two elements to the process of connecting gender ideas and the social-relational environment (Garcia-Ramon et al., 1995):

1. **Categorization:** We can assume that the behavior expectations for men and women included within gender beliefs will be implicitly invoked for individuals in social-relational situations since cultural views about gender are implicated in the initial processes of categorization.
2. **Background Identity:** Human perception studies reveal that people almost always categorize themselves and others in different ways based on culturally significant and situationally appropriate identities and responsibilities. Specifics for self and others, such as boss and employee, are present in the most socially connected circumstances, and they carry with them assigned behavior requirements that are important to the scenario.

This shift of what gender is as a social phenomenon is one of the most significant advances in gender knowledge in the last decade. As cultural beliefs are an integral part of the gender system, social relativity situations are where these ideas or regulations are put to the test (Indra Munshi, 2006). The key initiative towards a progressive economy and a developed world is to provide an equal opportunity to the women to sustain their livelihood through tourism. An imperative study of this nature, examines the role of women employee engagement and career path choices especially in the leisure business. The financial aspects in leisure business embrace gender parity and inclusive practices towards female employment, and women empowerment.

According to Kinnaird and Hall (1996) tourism is founded on the grounds of gendered societies, and gender relations infect all aspects of tourist-related development and activity as a result. Societal factors impact and are influenced by gender relations in several ways like economic, political, social, cultural, and environmental factors. Tourism does not exist in isolation; it has an impact on all of them. Tourism has become such an important component of growth, the social, economic, and political linkages that have resulted are part of wider power and control systems that can be defined by race, class, or gender. However, female members are often marginalized in government policies and development programs compared to their male counterparts. Therefore, understanding women's and men's power and agency, as well as the cross-cultural creative techniques used regarding their political, economic, social, and cultural roles, is fundamental. (Ridgeway & Correll, 2004)

It is observed that there is a male bias in the tourism industry, which subsumes distinct female experiences and behaviors in the tourism and tourism-related activity in the domain of male experience. There are significant differences between men and women in terms of the nature and sorts of tourism-related jobs accessible. This, of course, has far-reaching societal consequences. (Ridgeway & Correll, 2004) The ongoing pay disparity between men and women in the tourist industry has also been discussed. Even though they work in the same roles, males frequently earn more than women. Due to the reciprocal interaction between religion and society, religious systems are engaged in a circle of mutual influence with societal norms and patterns of social organisation as a result it prohibits women's mobility in public locations and prevent them from working in professional tourist jobs in some places (Wilson & Ypeij, 2012). On the other hand, have been able to gain financial independence and can support themselves and their families by working in tourism. Women's tourist labor and income have provided them self-confidence, increased social respect, reduced workloads, and gainful social services. Women's engagement in tourism has repositioned women's identities by stretching their local geographical and moral boundaries (Wilson & Ypeij, 2012).

Community Engagement and Inclusive Practices

Commitment to promote tourism and community wellbeing, has not only improved the quality of life of but has also become a differential element when its destination development is sought after. This, in a crux, is what an inclusive approach in tourism with gender perspective entails. It is required to develop a wholesome experience for destinations with capabilities to improve governance, management facilitates, and product innovation. Gender perspectives with inclusive business practices in tourism will enhance the role of women and thereby enhance the competitiveness of the service sector. Considering tourism as an important and integral sector in national economies, an empowered woman in the tourism system will enable value network and provide a favourable direction for development. Way forward, the service sector demands complete integrated and a synergistic business-space to be competitive globally.

Women have an important role in tourism throughout, whether as visitors, hosts, or professionals in the tourist industry. It discovered that women in tourism firms require more assistance and empowerment to demonstrate their managerial qualities and thrive in leadership and top management (Hasanat et al., 2021).

Gender segregation arises for both developed and developing economies (Hutchings et al., 2020). Gender-based research must include analytic considerations for social factors that may explain differences in behavior and tourism opportunities (Figueroa-Domecq & Segovia-Perez, 2020). Especially in global crises, doing housework and caring for relatives hinders their chances of advancement and improvement (Araújo-Vila et al., 2021). Not only do they have to bear the poor conditions of the sector, but also the failure of public administration. Other causes of the persistence of gender inequalities in employment are gender stereotypes that adapt men and women to specific gender roles, and practices that are rooted in corporate culture and hinder women's career advancement (Koc, 2019).

Women may be better able to act efficiently and successfully in the service industry. However, the education, personality traits, talents, and other skills of an individual employee can influence the decision on their level of job performance (Koc, 2019). The government and the corporate sector should endeavour to break down existing structural obstacles by promoting gender equality in the tourist field to recognize the harmful impact of career limits. Targeted initiatives by public, private, and civil society actors, such as advocating equal pay, combatting sexual harassment, and hiring women into senior positions, help to promote decent employment for women in tourism. (Costa et al., 2011). Therefore, investing in women's talents, social skills, and knowledge of various training options, improves gender equality outcomes throughout the industry (Ferguson et al., 2021).

Similarly, gender-sensitive macroeconomic and legal measures at the national level, if implemented effectively, strengthen the economic empowerment of women in the tourism sector. (Costa et al., 2011). Understanding rural women as economic actors and appreciating their knowledge and skills will maintain their efforts in the face of several obstacles. That emphasizes how the variety of factors outside the control of rural women entrepreneurs inhibit the growth of rural tourism businesses (Makandwa et al., 2021). It is in light of the increasing social responsibility in tourism development and the emergence of sustainability as an important issue at global level that CBT (Community Based Tourism) gains prominence as part of the governmental strategies for development while safeguarding social justice. Rationales behind the CBT development have typically portrayed a few key aspects which include poverty alleviation, economic diversification and greater local participation. CBT is advocated for the economic gains generated from tourism which can be widely distributed thereby supporting the poverty alleviation objective. This effort is further enhanced through diversifying the local livelihood so that the local people do not solely rely on agriculture as they come to have tourism activity as an additional source of income. In practice, the structure, objectives and themes of a CBT project are greatly shaped by the host community's needs. In order to encourage local participation, the search for leadership within the community is crucial (Murphy, 1988; Kiss, 2004; Manyara & Jones, 2007; Hamzah & Khalifah, 2009; López-Guzmán et al., 2011).

In many CBT projects, there was always a local leader who anticipated the potential of tourism and kick-started the project, while others adopted 'wait and see' attitude until they saw the success of similar projects elsewhere. Due to remote location, many CBT project face the challenge of lack of access to tourist market and infrastructure (Sarkar & Sinha, 2015). In this regard, the importance of linking up with other stakeholders in tourism development such as the tourism industry which could assist in the marketing and promotion of products. This aspect is a dynamic evolution involving a good connection with other industry players to create a stronger economic chain in tourism business. Community-based tourism has been promoted as a means of development whereby the social, environmental and economic needs of local communities. Community based tourism (CBT) could be one way of creating a more sustainable tourism industry and community readiness for participation in development include existing activities, leadership as a resource of capital (Murphy, 1988; Kiss, 2004; Manyara & Jones, 2007; Hamzah & Khalifah, 2009; López-Guzmán et al., 2011). Community-based tourism development is receiving increased attention from a variety of sectors: for those in government and non-governmental organizations who have long been working with communities on wildlife and natural resource management, tourism enterprises are seen as one form of sustainable utilization with potential to bring economic, as well as social, benefits to communities.

CASE STUDY: INCLUSIVE MECHANISM AND COMMUNITY ENGAGEMENT SCENARIO – KERALA, INDIA

Tourism largely has a wide scope of economic empowerment opportunities which leads to dynamic effects. It is exponentially seen that tourism affects the livelihood strategies of the local households, especially women in the informal sector. The economic independence has also enhanced women's position in the community and help overcome the gender disparities or barriers.

Kerala is the first state in India to declare tourism as an industry. The State is highly proactive in strategizing innovative policies and it's pro-tourism approaches; navigate right interventions for effective tourism policy frameworks. Apparently the state welcomes an integrated business model engaging all stakeholders whilst working collaboratively. The collaborative mechanism devised by the State facilitates a strong alliance where government led initiatives embrace all segments of the society for an integrated tourism growth. As per official statistics, tourism account for 10 per cent of the states GDP and contributes 23.5 per cent towards the employment in the state (Nair & Dhanuraj, 2018). Role of women and women centralism creates great scope for gender parity and engages a localized approach in financial independence.

Kerala is very progressive and is remarkably successful in establishing a brand for itself by positioning a favourable tourism image globally with the title of God's Own Country (Vasudevan, 2008). The dynamic cumulative effects of all State driven initiatives, positively engages the tourism stakeholders in Kerala with social, political and economic integration.

Role of Women and Inclusive Mechanism

The state-initiated strategies and articulated effective measure to build Kerala tourism industry by empowering women to participate fully in the social and economic life across all sectors and at all levels to build strong economies. The local governments, as the torch bearers and real promoters of women empowerment; work primarily at the grass root level. With the interventions of local governments; the State has been very successful in helping women to empower socially and economically through selected schemes implemented by the Grama Panchayats of Kerala. These initiatives drastically improve the social and economic status of women in the community space and position them well. A pro-tourism system aids joint and integrated effort in framing policies and schemes to practice an inclusive business mechanism. The public sector leads collaborative efforts and works jointly with community and private sectors to enable growth and development.

Role of Kudumbasree and Community Engagement

One of the promising schemes led by the local governing body- A scheme initiated for the grass root level development and planning are channelized by the panchayats and other local bodies. The term A Malayalam coinage - 'Kudumbasree' indicates- prosperity of the family. Kudumbasree programmes are charted out by the local body since 1998 and works as a sub system of the government wing; which connects women to the forefront and embrace economic independence and social recognition. This scheme embraces and support the local economic growth and development, foster social development and enable women empowerment through its network of neighbourhood groups. The financial inclusion projects under this scheme facilitate a strong mechanism to promote gender equity by ensuring economic independence and apt interventions for alleviation of poverty and capacity building function.

Gender Disparities in Employability in the Hospitality Business

Gender disparity can be a paradox in the hospitality sector, but in the tourism trade; it is quite pronounced -an type casted roles for employment opportunities for women. Over the years, hospitality businesses may indicate certain challenges pertaining to gender parity. The service sector to a larger extent demands a sustainable outlook towards development; as gender equality and empowerment of women. The Sustainable Development Goals (SDGs) on the 2030 Agenda, also emphasizes on promoting sustained, inclusive, and fair-trade practices for all. Tourism has an important role in achieving the commitments of the 2030 Agenda, since the service sector is widely accepted for engaging a larger ratio of women on employment (United Nations, 2021). In the wake of the Covid-19 pandemic, large number of gender equality issues cropped up and therefore, it is of great interest to know how the gender parity concerns are to be addressed (Power, 2020). The Inclusive Tourism business practices determine competence development among the counterparts using a value chain approach to identify linkages with tourism stakeholders. Inclusive mechanisms can be best examined by integrated efforts by the stakeholders of the hospitality business and allied segments in the tourism value chain. Adopting a local approach to economic development, it works directly with the poor or unempowered to integrate them into the tourism value chains. This process of 'mainstreaming' that indicate economies of scale has a greater capacity to enhance financial capacity and embrace community-based tourism development. The Inclusive Tourism pedagogy capacitate project stakeholders in the areas of hospitality services and linkages to the tourism industry. The potential involvement of women to expand the tourism supply chains, has recognized economic and social dimensions. An Inclusive approach engaging more strata of society can aid physical and socio-economic growth and development of not just women, but also other unempowered segments of a pro tourism community.

Figure 1. Gender space in tourism sector and economies of growth (source: developed by the authors, 2022)

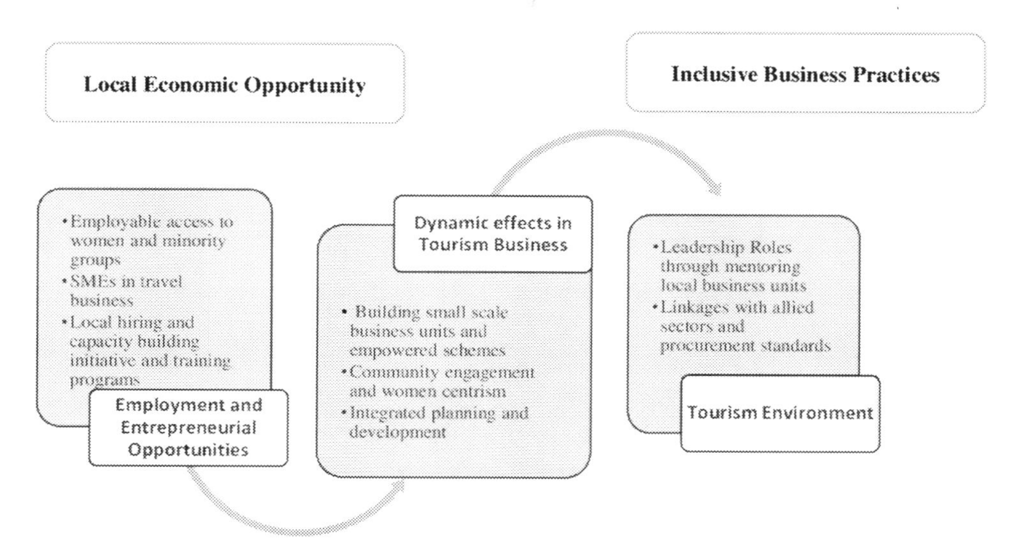

LITERATURE ROADMAP

Inequality between men and women exists in every business, but it is especially prevalent in the tourism industry. Women may be politically and socially empowered through tourism when they are involved in activities through tourism organizations and the local community. Women's involvement and progress in the tourism industry are hampered by cultural hurdles. Gender discrimination, segregation in the labor market, segregation in the workplace, and socio-cultural discrimination are all issues that women encounter.

As presented in the Literature Roadmap (Figure 2) Women's employment and participation in tourism planning and management influence gender norms, women's employment, and sexual objectification. (Sabina & Nicolae, 2013). Even though women can demonstrate strong leadership abilities and general leadership traits, they still make up a tiny percentage of the tourism industry's workforce and leadership and, are under-represented in managerial positions. (Hutchings et al., 2020).

Similarly, the application of a gender perspective in tourist evaluation has found massive disparities between men and women on a range of issues like low pay, dangerous working conditions, sexual discrimination, sexual harassment, prostitution, slavery, and human trafficking. (Sabina & Nicolae, 2013).

Though, Gender inequality is common in all industries, it is even more pronounced in the tourism industry and, women are more affected by these conditions than men in an industry characterized by a broad range of job rotation, seasonality, precarious work, and part-time work. Therefore, it is important to required more assistance and empowerment at national. global and regional level. (Araújo-Vila et al., 2021). Likewise, Women's empowerment is a strong emphasis in tourism equality programs. It is critical, and institutional and financial assistance is required. When women are engaged in the community through community groups and civil society, they may be politically and socially empowered through tourism. When women receive gender-specific training and have access to suitable technology, tourism digitalization may unleash an exciting new avenue for creativity and empower women (Koc, 2019). It will help them grow economically, socially and culturally.

According to Hutchings et al. (2020) cultural barriers play a significant role in women's participation and advancement in tourism employment. Women face gender discrimination, labor market segregation, workplace segregation, socio-cultural discrimination, and Gender stereotypes. Therefore, investing in women's talents, social skills, and knowledge of various training options, improves gender equality outcomes throughout the industry (Ferguson et al., 2021). In addition, tourism Human Resource Development (HRD) should provide training programs and counselling sessions to help women entrepreneurs overcome their leadership weaknesses (Kourtesopoulou & Chatzigianni, 2021).

IMPLICATIONS

In tourism-led growth policy, there is an opportunity to mainstream gender equality in policy discourse and settings. That is, governments must consider gender concerns while developing tourism policy. Furthermore, governments may establish policies geared at women in tourism, such as training and education to increase their abilities, therefore empowering women in tourism jobs (Chambers & Airey, 2001). In this regard, language training and other capacity building program for female tourism employees, particularly for self-employed women in this profession, may be a valuable program, boosting their capacity to obtain advantages from tourist visits.

In addition, to balance tourist growth with gender equality, proper rules and regulations to empower women in tourism are required, such as tax exemptions for tourism enterprises with long-term contracts for female workers or businesses with female owners.

Figure 2. Literature roadmap (source: developed by the authors, 2022)

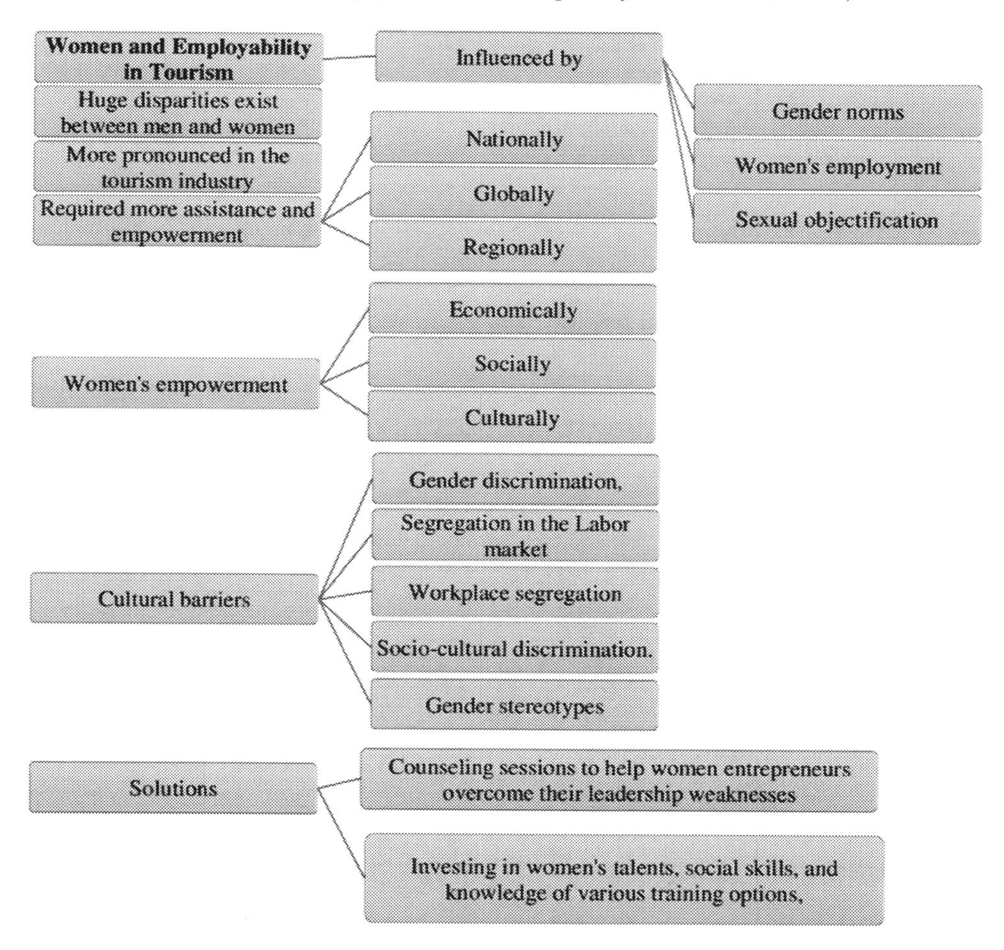

CONCLUSION

Despite significant growth in tourism research, it's really interesting to see how gender perspective research is evolving. The inclusion of gender management in the broader domain of diversity management will soon become a need in the tourist sector, due to the rising number of women in the labour market and shifting career paradigms. This is expected to reduce gender stereotypes and their influence on leaders' perspectives on how women-centric employee engagement is practiced and the impacts on the overall economic upliftment in a globalized world.

REFERENCES

Alshareef, F. M., & AlGassim, A. A. (2021). Women empowerment in tourism and hospitality sector in Saudi Arabia. *International Journal on Recent Trends in Business and Tourism*, *5*(4), 11–20. doi:10.31674/ijrtbt.2021.v05i04.003

Araújo-Vila, N., Otegui-Carles, A., & Fraiz-Brea, J. A. (2021). Seeking Gender Equality in the Tourism Sector: A Systematic Bibliometric Review. *Knowledge (Beverly Hills, Calif.)*, *1*(1), 12–24. doi:10.3390/knowledge1010003

Boonabaana, B. (2014). Negotiating gender and tourism work: Women's lived experiences in Uganda. *Tourism and Hospitality Research*, *14*(1–2), 27–36. doi:10.1177/1467358414529578

Chambers, D., & Airey, D. (2001). Tourism Policy in Jamaica: A Tale of Two Governments. *Current Issues in Tourism*, *4*(2–4), 94–120. doi:10.1080/13683500108667884

Costa, C., Carvalho, I., & Breda, Z. (2011). Gender inequalities in tourism employment: The portuguese case. *Revista Turismo & Desenvolvimento*, *15*, 37–52.

Ferguson, L., Boonabaana, B., Lattimore, C. K., & Alarcon, D. M. (2021, December). *Global Report on Women in Tourism* (No. 2). UNWTO.

Figueroa-Domecq, C., & Segovia-Perez, M. (2020). Application of a gender perspective in tourism research: A theoretical and practical approach. *Journal of Tourism Analysis: Revista de Análisis Turístico*, *27*(2), 251–270. doi:10.1108/JTA-02-2019-0009

Garcia-Ramon, M., Canoves, G., & Valdovinos, N. (1995). Farm tourism, gender, and the environment in Spain. *Annals of Tourism Research*, *22*(2), 267–282. doi:10.1016/0160-7383(94)00096-4

Hasanat, O., Alhelalat, J. A., & Valeri, M. (2021). Women Leadership in the Jordanian Hospitality Sector: Obstacles and Future Opportunities. In M. Valeri & V. Katsoni (Eds.), *Gender and Tourism: Challenges and Entrepreneurial Opportunities* (1st ed., pp. 149–158). Emerald Publishing. doi:10.1108/978-1-80117-322-320211009

Hutchings, K., Moyle, C. L., Chai, A., Garofano, N., & Moore, S. (2020). Segregation of women in tourism employment in the APEC region. *Tourism Management Perspectives*, *34*, 1–15. doi:10.1016/j.tmp.2020.100655

Indra Munshi. (2006, October). *Tourism Processes and Gender Relations: Issues for Exploration and Intervention* (No. 42). Economic and Political Weekly. https://www.jstor.org/stable/4418837

Kinnaird, V., & Hall, D. (1996). Understanding tourism processes: A gender-aware framework. *Tourism Management, 17*(2), 95–102. doi:10.1016/0261-5177(95)00112-3

Kladeen, M. (2020). Women and Tourism: Hindering Factors of Women Employment in the Hotel Sector in Sri Lanka. *International Journal of Psychosocial Rehabilitation, 24*(03), 2005–2013. doi:10.37200/IJPR/V24I3/PR200947

Koc, E. (2019). Do Women Make Better in Tourism and Hospitality? A Conceptual Review from A Customer Satisfaction and Service Quality Perspective. *Journal of Quality Assurance in Hospitality & Tourism, 21*(4), 402–429. doi:10.1080/15280 08X.2019.1672234

Kourtesopoulou, A., & Chatzigianni, E. (2021). Gender Equality and Women's Entrepreneurial Leadership in Tourism: A Systematic Review. In M. Valeri & V. Katsoni (Eds.), *Gender and Tourism: Challenges and Entrepreneurial Opportunities* (1st ed., pp. 11–36). Emerald Publishing. doi:10.1108/978-1-80117-322-320211002

Makandwa, G., de Klerk, S., & Saayman, A. (2021). Understanding the Experiences of Rural Women in Sustaining Tourism Enterprises. In M. Valeri & V. Katsoni (Eds.), *Gender and Tourism: Challenges and Entrepreneurial Opportunities* (1st ed., pp. 93–112). Emerald Publishing. doi:10.1108/978-1-80117-322-320211006

McCall, C. E., & Mearns, K. F. (2021). Empowering Women Through Community-Based Tourism in the Western Cape, South Africa. *Tourism Review International, 25*(2), 157–171. doi:10.3727/154427221X16098837279967

Mitra, S. (2019). What Works in Girls' Education: Evidence for the World's Best Investment? *Social Change, 49*(3), 556–558. doi:10.1177/0049085719863903

Murphy, C., & Halstead, L. (2003). *The person with the idea for the campsite is a hero: Institutional arrangements and livelihood change regarding community-owned tourism enterprises in Namibia*. Directorate of Environmental Affairs, Research Discussion Paper 61, Government of Namibia, Ministry of Environment and Tourism, Windhoek, Namibia.

Nair, L. R., & Dhanuraj, D. (2018). *Kerala Tourism - The Role of the Government and Economic Impacts*. Centre for Public Policy Research.

Nguyen, C. P. (2022). Tourism and gender (in)equality: Global evidence. *Tourism Management Perspectives, 41*, 100933. doi:10.1016/j.tmp.2021.100933

Power, K. (2020). The COVID-19 Pandemic Has Increased the Care Burden of Women and Families. *Sustain. Sci. Pract. Policy*, *2020*(16), 67–73. doi:10.1080/15487733.2020.1776561

Ridgeway, C. L., & Correll, S. J. (2004). Unpacking the Gender System: A Theoretical Perspective on Gender Beliefs and Social Relations. *Sage Publication*, *18*(4), 510–531. doi:10.1177/0891243204265269

Sabina, J. M., & Nicolae, J. C. (2013, October). Gender Trends in Tourism Destination. *Procedia: Social and Behavioral Sciences*, *92*, 437–444. doi:10.1016/j.sbspro.2013.08.698

Sarkar, R., & Sinha, A. (2015). The village as a social entrepreneur: Balancing conservation and livelihoods. *Tourism Management Perspectives*, *16*, 100–106. doi:10.1016/j.tmp.2015.07.006

Skalpe, O. (2007). The CEO gender pay gap in the tourism industry—Evidence from Norway. *Tourism Management*, *28*(3), 845–853. doi:10.1016/j.tourman.2006.06.005

United Nations. (2021). *Transforming Our World: The 2030 Agenda for Sustainable Development*. A/RES/70/1. 2015. Available online: https://sdgs.un.org/2030agenda

Vasudevan, S. (2008). The Role of Internal Stakeholders in Destination Branding: Observations from Kerala Tourism. *Place Branding and Public Diplomacy*, *4*(4), 331–335. doi:10.1057/pb.2008.24

Wilson, T. D., & Ypeij, A. (2012). *Introduction: Tourism, Gender, and Ethnicity*. Sage Publications, Inc. https://www.jstor.org/stable/41702290?seq=1&cid=pdf

Wojtowicz, E. (2021). Stereotypes in management-Does leadership have a gender? *Humanities and Social Sciences Quarterly*, *28*(1), 125–134. doi:10.7862/rz.2021.hss.10

Xu, H. (2018). Moving toward gender and tourism geographies studies. *Tourism Geographies*, *20*(4), 721–727. doi:10.1080/14616688.2018.1486878

Zhang, J., & Zhang, Y. A. (2021). Qualitative Comparative Analysis of Tourism and Gender Equality in Emerging Economies. *Journal of Hospitality and Tourism Management*, *46*, 284–292. doi:10.1016/j.jhtm.2021.01.009

Chapter 6
Interrogating Rural Women's Collective Tourism Entrepreneurship and Social Change in South Western Uganda

Brenda Boonabaana
https://orcid.org/0000-0003-2739-3142
Makerere University, Uganda

Amos Ochieng
Makerere University, Uganda

ABSTRACT

This chapter analyses women's tourism collective agency and its relationship with other forms of agency in a tourism-dependent rural community in Uganda. Findings show positive gains for women in terms of economic independence, livelihood diversification, reduced drudgery, and acquisition of skills that have further enhanced their capabilities and wellbeing. This has in turn enabled positive outcomes at the household and community levels. The authors argue that the outcomes of collective agency have contributed to other forms of agency (instrumental and intrinsic) while opening space for women's empowerment and social change. The chapter contributes to current debates on tourism, women's empowerment, and social change and informs policy and programming geared at enabling women's collective capacity and equitable tourism outcomes.

DOI: 10.4018/978-1-6684-4194-7.ch006

INTRODUCTION

The importance of women in development has been recognized as both a fundamental human right and a pathway for attaining equitable and sustainable outcomes. This is fully enshrined in the United Nation's 2015 Sustainable Development Goals (SDGs). The 17 interlinked SDGs adopted by the United Nations General Assembly in 2015 call for an end to poverty, protection of the planet, peace and prosperity by 2030 (UNDP, n.d.). Women's participation in tourism specifically contributes to SDG 5 (achieve gender equality and empower women and girls); SDG 1 (end poverty in all its forms everywhere); SDG 8 (promote sustained, inclusive and sustainable economic growth, full and productive employment and decent work for all); and SDG16 (promote peaceful and inclusive societies for sustainable development, provide access to justice for all and build effective, accountable and inclusive institutions at all levels (United Nations, n.d.).

The tourism sector promotes gender equity and women's agency mainly through the employment and entrepreneurship pathways. Although women tourism entrepreneurs often operate as individuals, in collaboration with their spouses, or collectively work with other women, they face a number of gender constraints that limit their meaningful engagement in tourism (Handaragama & Kusakabe, 2021; Boonabaana, 2014; Tucker and Boonabaana, 2012; World Tourism Organization, 2011). In Africa, patriarchal norms and practices often limit women's meaningful participation in the public tourism entrepreneurial space while compared to their male counterparts (World Tourism Organization, 2019). However, in many contexts, women continue to navigate their gender constraints to work as tourism entrepreneurs and employees (World Tourism Organization, 2019). Centrering the concept of collective agency/ 'power with' (Malapit et al., 2019), the authors interrogate the intricate experiences of rural women's tourism entrepreneurship by examining how women are exercising their collective power to achieve their common goals and social change, and the relationship with other forms of agency - instrumental agency/ 'power to' and intrinsic agency/'power within' (Malapit et al., 2019). Next, the chapter presents a review of relevant literature followed by the conceptual framework, methodology, study context, findings, discussions and conclusions.

LITERATURE REVIEW

Tourism Development in Uganda

Uganda has identified tourism as a priority sector for enabling social economic development and poverty alleviation (National Planning Authority, 2020). Before the COVID-19 pandemic, Uganda registered over 1.5 million tourist arrivals that contributed about US$ 1.6 billion in foreign exchange and 7.7 percent of the country's gross domestic product (GDP) (Ministry of Tourism, Wildlife and Antiquities [MoTWA], 2020). Although Uganda's tourism is diverse-including culture and heritage, religion, food, entertainment, MICE, the country's tourism is largely nature-based. The top most tourist attractions in Uganda are the primates, including the mountain gorilla in the Bwindi Impenetrable National Park and Mgahinga Gorilla National Park in Southwestern Uganda, and Chimpanzees in Kibale National Park and other conservation areas in the country (Ochieng, Ahebwa & Twinomuhangi., forthcoming). Gorilla ecotourism is the most sought-after tourist activity (Tumusiime and Vedeld, 2015), contributing the highest amount of tourism revenue for the country (MoTWA, 2020).

Uganda has a conducive policy environment that encourages community entrepreneurship and women empowerment that has cascaded to the conservation and tourism spaces. Both the National Development Plan (National Planning Authority, 2020) and the National Tourism Development Masterplan (MoTWA,2014) encourage community participation in tourism activities to enable sustainable development. One of the 10-year development objectives for tourism in Uganda is to promote community involvement and enterprise development in the tourism economy (MoTWA,2014). The country's gender policy (2007) provides a framework for designing, implementing and monitoring gender equality and women's empowerment programmes across all development sectors (Republic of Uganda, 2007). Therefore, community members (men, women and youth) living close to the major conservation sites have embraced tourism as key livelihood (Ayorekire et al., 2021; Boonabaana, 2012).

Tourism Entrepreneurship and Gender

Globally, women make up a large proportion of tourism workers (54%) than any other sector (World Tourism Organization, 2019). Within the accommodation and food services sector, they represent 57% in the Americas, 69% in Africa, 53% in Asia and the pacific, 53% in Europe and 9% in the Middle East (World Tourism Organization, 2019). Available evidence reveals how women tourism entrepreneurship is gaining ground in several developing contexts (see Vukovic, Petrovic, Maiti, & Vujko, 2021; Nomnga, 2017; Handaragama & Kusakabe,2021; World Tourism Organization, 2019; Kimbu and Ngoasong, 2016; Boonabaana, 2012), with opportunities to addresses both commercial and social transformation goals (Kimbu and Ngoasong, 2016).

In Africa, women constitute about 31% of tourism entrepreneurs (World Tourism Organization, 2011), although the majority still occupying low status and low paying jobs as artisans, retail vendors, running family businesses (World Bank, 2013; Baum, 2013). Women also earn 10-15% less than their male counterparts (World

Tourism Organization, 2011, 2019). By far, the nature of women's participation and remuneration within the sector reflects the deep-rooted gender inequalities (Handaragama & Kusakabe, 2021; World Bank, 2013; Baum, 2013; Tucker & Boonabaana, 2012; World Tourism Organization, 2011).

Despite women's entrepreneurship potential, they are constrained by limited financial resources, care roles, skills, mobility and social stereotypes that perceive men as risk takers than women (World Tourism Organization, 2019; United Nations Conference on Trade and development [UNCTAD], 2017; Nomnga, 2017; Tshabalala & Ezeuduji, 2016; World Bank, 2013). As revealed by Guloba et al. (2017), although Ugandan women are more entrepreneurial than men, they have limited access to finance.

Further, ethnicity, race and nationality may intersect with gender to further restrain women's entrepreneurial opportunities (World Tourism Organization, 2019; World Bank, 2013). In South Africa, black African women are least likely to be employed in male-dominated occupations across all sectors (Parashar, 2014). The double tragedy of racial and gender discrimination in South Africa has affected women's meaningful participation in, and benefits from tourism (Tshabalala & Ezeuduji, 2016). In Kenya, majority of tour companies are male dominated and run as family businesses, with the most successful owned and managed by white and Asian Kenyans (World Tourism Organization, 2019; World Bank, 2013; UNCTAD; 2017). Yet, in many developing countries, there is growing policy emphasis on the need to catalyse rural women's entrepreneurship to enable poverty alleviation and development (Guloba, et al., 2017).

Nevertheless, several case studies in Asia, Africa, Latin America and the Caribbean demonstrate women's potential to push their gender boundaries to tap into tourism's social-economic opportunities (World Tourism Organization, 2019). In several localities, rural women are active entrepreneurs and workers in community tourism enterprises associated with handcraft production, cultural performances, guiding and accommodation (Buzinde et al., 2017; Kimbu & Ngoasong, 2016; Boonabaana, 2014; Tucker & Boonabaana, 2012; Scheyvens, 2000; 2002; Al-Dajani & Marlow, 2013). Scheyvens (2000, 2002) has explained some ecotourism projects that have enabled women's economic, psychological, social and political empowerment in Africa. Women's Siyabonga craft co-operative in Kwazulu Natal, South Africa and the pastoral Masaai women in Tanzania were economically empowered through bead work, campsites and walking safaris. Women tourism entrepreneurs have been found to prioritise and pursue social transformation goals rather than the commercial gains (Kimbu & Ngoasong, 2016). In Uganda, Kibale Association for Rural and Environmental Development (KAFRED) in Bigodi, Kibale National Park has adopted a community tourism model that is enabling local men and women to engage in and gain from Chimpanzee tourism (Biodigitourism, 2021).

While the growing literature on gender and tourism entrepreneurship sheds light on how women are navigating gender barriers to create opportunities for themselves as tourism entrepreneurs, little attention has been paid to the role of collective agency and its interaction with other forms of agency to enhance women empowerment and social change in developing tourism contexts. This chapter endeavors to show this relationship. The chapter contributes to the ongoing debates around tourism, women's empowerment and social change as well as tourism policy and programming.

The Concept of Agency

Women's agency influences their capacity to engage in the tourism development arena. According to Kabeer (1999), agency is the capacity to define one's own goals and making strategic choices in pursuit of the identified goals, especially, in a context where this ability was previously denied. It also includes processes of decision-making, negotiation, and manipulation (Kabeer, 2001). Malapit et al. (2019) describe agency in three forms (i) instrumental agency or 'power to' (ii) intrinsic agency or 'power within' and; (iii) collective agency or 'power with.' Instrumental agency relates to a person's ability to access and own financial resources (credit, income); ownership of productive resources (such as land and other assets); work-life balance; and mobility (visiting important locations). Intrinsic agency is about a woman's sense of self-worth/efficacy, autonomy of income, knowledge, confidence, and respect from others, especially, family members. Collective agency is measured by a woman's capacity to collaboratively function in influential groups towards a common goal, and gaining respect from other household members (Malapit et al., 2019).

van Eerdewijk et al. (2017) have argued that when women exercise their agency, they begin to confront power relations, make strategic choices, have a voice while empowering themselves and enabling social change. Agency can be enhanced through access to resources - material, human, and social (Kabeer, 2001), as well as a conducive social and policy environment (van Eerdewijk et al., 2017). In this chapter, we draw on the concept of agency to provide empirical experiences of two rural women associations that have embraced tourism as an alternative livelihood to substance farming, including implications to their wellbeing, empowerment and social change. The evidence adds value to theoretical debates and praxis in the area of women's tourism entrepreneurship, empowerment and social change in a developing tourism context.

METHODOLOGY

This study was conducted in August and September 2018, in a rural tourism destination of Buhoma community in Southwestern Uganda, that largely depends on gorilla ecotourism in Bwindi Impenetrable National Park. The chapter also benefits from the longitudinal ethnographic research conducted by the first author over the last 12 years (2009-2021). The study utilized ethnographic semi-structured in-depth interviews with women group members (22), informal interviews with community members, key informant interviews with national park officials and community leaders (6), focus group discussions (2) and participant observations. A total of 30 interviews and discussions were held. Participants were identified using purposive and snowball sampling techniques that enabled the identification of the relevant participants. Field observations and informal interviews were conducted during community visits to women group businesses, conservation authorities and local leaders. Raw data were transcribed verbatim, coded and categorized following inductive thematic analysis that generated key themes that guided writing of the results section.

STUDY CONTEXT

Gorilla Ecotourism in Bwindi Impenetrable National Park

Following its gazettement as Bwindi Impenetrable National Park (BINP) in 1991, the area was declared a UNESCO Natural Heritage site in 1994 (Ampumuza, 2021). The park is most popular as a gorilla tourism destination in Uganda (Uganda Wildlife Authority, 2018). The neighbouring communities, majority Bakiga and indigenous minority Batwa/Pygmy, traditionally depended on forest resources for survival but were later displaced due to conservation restrictions. To enable them have alternative livelihoods, government authorities and conservation partners encouraged and supported them to engage in community-based tourism initiatives. Batwa also survive on casual farm labour, illegal hunting, and donations from development organizations (Boonabaana, 2012; Ampumuza, 2021)

The community enterprises are implemented through community owned organizations such as the Buhoma-Mukono Community Development Organization (BMCDA) and the Batwa Development Organization (BDO). The organization brings together seven thousand (7000) community members living in Mukono Parish to tap into the tourism opportunities. While the BDO focuses on Batwa/pygmy targeted initiatives, the BMCDA targets both the Bakiga and Batwa ethnic people. Through these organizations, a number of initiatives have been developed to sustain the local people. These include a community walk (has six cultural sites), the Batwa/

pygmy cultural experience, vegetable project (demonstrates local vegetable types and cooking), community lodges, schools and hospitals (Boonabaana, 2012; Tucker & Boonabaana, 2012). There are also tourism revenue sharing programmes that enable the community to receive a share of tourism revenue from Uganda Wildlife Authority. These initiatives have been supported by the government of Uganda through its tourism policy that encourages local community participation in tourism, input from non-governmental organizations (NGOs), enthusiastic tourists that support local initiatives and community members willing to engage with tourism. As noted by Yanes, Zielinski, Cano and Kim (2019), partnership arrangement by the community and other stakeholders is key in enabling successful community tourism entrepreneurship.

To better tap into ecotourism opportunities, women have formed groups and organizations through which they collectively operate. The two women's groups selected for the study are described in the following.

WOMEN'S TOURISM COLLECTIVES: TWO CASE STUDIES FROM BUHOMA COMMUNITY

Case 1: Ride 4 a Woman

Ride 4 a woman is a women focused organization located in Buhoma, the closest village to BINP in Uganda. It was founded in 2009 as a Non-Governmental Organization (NGO) and aims at empowering women with skills and income opportunities. It has a membership of three hundred (300) women that are mainly poor, illiterate, widowed, HIV positive and drop out school girls. Most of the group members also experience a high care burden of up to eight children and grandchildren. To join, members pay membership fees of about UGX 2000 (less than half a dollar) per year. The organization operates multiple enterprises ranging from accommodation facilities/guest house, craft businesses, bicycle rentals to tourists, microfinance, bakery, safe water provision, and agriculture livelihood support. The guest house doubles as a temporary shelter for women experiencing domestic violence and accommodation facility for tourists. The organization is mainly funded by former tourists especially for its physical infrastructure and microfinance seed grants. It is also supported by government entities such as the Uganda Wildlife Authority in areas of marketing, advisory and capacity development. Fifty (50) of the 300 women are directly employed by the organization in sewing, cultural dancing, basket weaving including demonstration through a programme dubbed "a day with a woman", and homestay/accommodation. The women work in shifts of 25 women a day, and are paid between UGX5000-UGX9000 (approx. US$ 1.75-2.75) each day they work.

Case 2: Buhoma-Mukono Women's Group

Buhoma - Mukono women's group is also located in Buhoma. The group started in 1995 and is involved in handcraft businesses, cultural dances, and microfinance. It is affiliated to the bigger community development organization – BMCDA. The women's group brings together 8 women subgroups with a membership of about 200 members, aimed at achieving social, cultural and economic benefits through tourism. To be a member, each woman contributes one basket as capital for group's craft shop, a one-off fee of UGX 50000 (US$13) and a monthly subscription of UGX2000 (less than half a dollar) to qualify for the group's microfinance membership. The group charges members an interest rate of 10% per annum.

FINDINGS

Women's Collective Agency and Outcomes

This section presents findings on the outcomes of women's collective agency, and how it relates to other forms of agency– instrumental and intrinsic agency.

Gains in Instrumental Agency: 'The power to'

This section explains women's achievements within the domain of instrumental agency (power to) due to their collective tourism work. These are assessed in relation to women's ability to access and own financial resources (credit, income), own productive resources (such as land and other assets), exercise work-life balance and visit important locations (mobility), as suggested by Malapit et al. (2019). The section further interrogates elements of instrumental agency that have not been influenced by women's collective agency.

Enhanced Economic Capabilities for Women

As a result of women's collective tourism activities, they have been able to access income and to diversify their agricultural livelihoods. With their incomes, women have been able to acquire personal assets such livestock (goats, sheep, chicken), land, sewing machines. This has in turn enabled the group members to pay school fees for their children, cater for family health demands, and purchase of household items such as mattresses, chairs, blankets, sewing machines and kitchen utensils. Aligned to this, a female group member of Ride 4 a woman explained that: "*Yes, we have benefitted by investing in small projects of our own and paying school fees...*"

A member of Buhoma-Mukono women's group expressed how the members had acquired the ability to purchase household basic items noting that:

We are paying for family requirements like buying sugar, clothes but I have also bought land and built a house from craft business and my other small income sources like selling food and saving groups.

Another group member explained that:

I have bought mattresses, plates, cups and I am happy as a woman because I have my own money that I can spend on what I need without waiting upon my husband to provide. When there is money and I buy such things, my husband feels very happy (Member, Buhoma-Mukono women's group).

The community leaders also noted that women were increasingly developing their capacity to educate their children, as men continue to spend their resources on alcohol.

Ownership of Productive Resources

While some women have invested their incomes as individuals, other women have invested collectively in land and commercial houses especially, for Buhoma-Mukomo women's group. Women have also been able to self-organise and manage affordable credit and loan schemes that support members with economic emergencies and business capital. The Ride 4 a woman organization's credit and loan scheme had reached a total of about $14000 (by 2018), with an interest rate of 3% per annum. Buhoma-Mukono women group's interest was found to be three times higher (at 10%) than that of Ride 4 a woman. Women in both groups were finding the interest rate affordable and helpful. The funding portfolio for ride 4 a woman has increased overtime from $5000 in 2015; $5000 in 2016 and $4000 in 2018, which was attributed to good management practices. There is a nine-member team that oversees the loan management programme and investment portfolios. The women's economic capabilities have stimulated women's capacity to access and control financial resources and own productive resources as key ingredients for instrumental agency.

Livelihoods Alternatives

Due to group-based tourism opportunities, women have been able to diversify their survival options, including having a livelihood fall back that has reduced their agricultural related drudgery. Women expressed their experiences associated with farming drudgery and 'tiredness', and as such, tourism work was seen to be a great opportunity for them to "rest" from farming while earning an income. This links to the developing opportunity of women's autonomy of income translating into better work-life balance, as key elements of intrinsic and instrumental agency. Some of the women's voices below illustrate their changing perspectives, lives and experiences:

We were saved from the hoe. We were tired of digging. Our gardens are very far and it is usually tiresome since reaching there takes about 3 hours and there is also time for digging. It is tiresome (FGD member, Ride 4 a woman).

We were tired of digging up the hills, you walk from 8am up to 11am and reach there and dig till late evening. We got tired and we wanted to rest when we got this opportunity (FGD member, Ride 4 a woman)

I used to dig but I no longer dig, I got a sowing machine and now I make items am called an officer and supply to people, I bought trees – which I got when I sold goats (In-depth interview participant, Ride 4 a woman)

Better Hygiene and Wellbeing

Women participants further mentioned that during group meetings, women intentionally focus on issues of hygiene and wellbeing. With this, women have developed important networks that are not only facilitating their economic capacity, but also, their health and general wellbeing. One of the group leaders shared about the emerging improvements in women's personal hygiene and outlook by noting that: *"If you do not bathe or brush, women will tell you. Their homes have changed by being vanished, painted"*. This key outcome connects to the acquisition of life skills pertinent to instrumental agency.

International Connections, Networks and Children's Education

Women members have also been able to form important international networks with tourists that eventually support their children with education requirements (school fees and other personal needs). Women shared how almost all members had their children sponsored by former tourists up to university level. This has reduced women's burden to provide school fees and enabled them to save and spend on better family nutrition, health insurance and hiring gardening help. About this, a woman member of the group noted that: *"My daughter got a sponsor....in primary six. A former tourist from Switzerland is sponsoring her...I also get a salary that I use to buy my personal and family requirements"*. Women expressed being previously burdened by school fees demands, which limited them to live decent lives and to fend for their families as depicted below:

I got friends. The pioneer is called [name withheld) who pays for my daughter in senior two. Even for my elder son [she] bought for him an ipad and a computer. I have 4 children and they have all managed to study. One finished Makerere university, the other is in Kabale University, another in senior 4 and the last born is in primary 4 and is a girl. Now the one who finished university sends me money to pay for gardenig labour (In-depth interview participant, Ride 4 a woman).

A similar view was raised as follows;

I used to put on one dress and couldn't buy food for my mother, but now things are better. I get a salary and save money, I have bought a sewing machine, that I use to make dresses in the evenings and sell them to Ride 4 a Woman. I have also bought land with a banana plantation that I paid in instalments which is fully mine now. I took a small loan from the group and bought another small plot of land (In-depth interview participant, Ride 4 a woman).

These outcomes depict the growing trend by women tourism group members to access and control their own income and spending it on things that matter to their lives, including purchasing and owning property, investment resources, better food and wellbeing, which is in turn, enhancing their instrumental agency (the power to). Findings depict substantial positive outcomes across all elements of instrumental agency due to women's collective work, except input in productive decisions and visiting important locations.

Gains in Intrinsic Agency: 'The power within'

This section explains women's achievements within the domain of intrinsic agency (power within) as a result of women's collective tourism work. Intrinsic agency is assessed in terms of women's sense of self-worth/efficacy, autonomy of income, knowledge, confidence, and respect from others, especially, family members as suggested by Malapit et al. (2019). The section further interrogates elements of intrinsic agency that have not been influenced by women's collective agency.

Community Appreciation and Increased Member Confidence

Because of the positive benefits being realised by women group members, they are being appreciated and respected by both men and women community members.

Participants unanimously mentioned how women that are not part of any groups admire them and perceive them as 'officers' because they consider them to be living better lives. They too wished to join the footsteps of women tourism group members. A member of Buhoma-Mukono women's group noted that; "*when they see me getting money, they feel they should also join. They envy me because they see that I am helping myself and my family*". Because of the positive gains, women's self-confidence has been boosted. This is being manifested through their ability to speak in public with confidence as was expressed by their leader (*Ride 4 a Woman)*; "*the women were shy to speak but now can stand and speak in a congregation of 50 people*" This demonstrates women's self-worth, confidence and respect from others, as key indicators of intrinsic agency that women experiencing due to their group activities.

Addressing Domestic Violence

Through their collective work, women have received several trainings, including a focus on domestic violence. Women have been trained about the different forms of violence and prevention measures, and provided with opportunities to share experiences and to work out solutions together. Below is an example of the lessons acquired by women from the training:

They have now learnt different forms of domestic violence for example when a man takes away your money, its domestic violence. Physical violence, a man forcing for sex, lack of decision-making power are all forms of domestic violence (Leader, Ride 4 a woman).

The Ride 4 a woman group has gone ahead to construct a domestic violence facility that provides free temporary shelter to both women group and non-group members experiencing domestic violence. The facility also doubles as a budget tourist accommodation whose 50% revenue is used to support domestically abused women while another 50% supports the operations of the facility. The excessive consumption of alcohol by men common in the area often fuels violence against women. However, due to the training and support interventions, participants were optimistic about their wellbeing. There were some observations about men beginning to be more cautious about battering their wives, as was stated by the women group leader; "*we have had three cases and now men fear to touch their wives because they know there is a shelter...*" This speaks to the development of women's intrinsic agency due to their ability to take charge of their lives by addressing domestic violence. Due to tourism, women have also refined their skills in craft making, sewing and leadership that have stimulated their self-efficacy/ worth, confidence and autonomy of income, while addressing common challenges such as severe poverty and domestic violence. Because of these achievements, they are gaining respect from their family and community members. This points to enhancement of women's intrinsic agency through their collective efforts.

Enhanced Leadership Capabilities

The various management and committees across the various group activities have provided space for women to take up leadership opportunities that have enabled them to acquire relevant leadership experience and skills. . Women leaders have played a key role in group formation, mobilizing, strategic direction, fundraising, networking and capacity building for group members. The leaders are also recognized, appreciated and supported at the local, national and international levels, with one of the leaders recently recognized with an award by the President of Uganda. She explained about the growing local, national and international recognition of their work as follows:

...I am honored, lucky and blessed for starting out something and it works. I talk to people and they believe in me... People are wondering how the organization has grown. I run it with honesty. I have learnt to manage large numbers of people. It has added on my list of friends and knowing new people. I am also recognised. People call us on every social function thinking we have a lot of money. I have attained some medals and Awards. I got an award from Uganda Women's Network (UWONET) for empowering women. I also got a medal from the President of Uganda...

As with the instrumental agency domain, findings depict some positive outcomes across all elements of intrinsic agency due to women's collective work.

Women's Collective Agency: Persistent Constraints

Despite positive gains in both instrumental and intrinsic agency, there are still persistent gaps in women's control of income, managing group dynamics, freedom of mobility and access to resources (for weaving baskets). Some participants spoke about their spouses' interest to manage their tourism income although they were resisting the unwelcome move. Some members of Buhoma women's group explained as follows:

Our husbands want us to give them the money we work for so that they spend it on alcohol, yet, they do not know even the price of salt (In-depth interview participant, Buhoma Mukono women's group)

I don't give him my money. I know he will spend it on alcohol. But he always wants me to give it to him, so I can't accept (In-depth interview participant, Buhoma Mukono women's group)

Women also shared how they apply negotiation skills to secure their money and employment. They donate some little monies to their husbands in attempt to 'silence them' against asking them not to work as expressed by a focus group participant: *"I give him part of the money I earn to keep peace in the home."* Other women echoed a similar view by noting that:

... we are struggling. Some of us came by force. Like me, my husband had refused but I insisted. I didn't want to miss the opportunity, yet, he doesn't give me whatever I want (FGD participant, Buhoma-Mukono Group)

Even me it was like that. He first refused but I insisted and came. He has now given up, given that he sees the benefits." (FGD participant, Buhoma-Mukono Group)

Such gender-based obstacles continue to limit women's freedom to actively participate in the tourism work space. A male community leader corroborated the above sentiments by citing the limitations of domestic roles and unfriendly working conditions for women as follows:

They leave house work unattended and when their husbands find it not done, they complain. Confidence of the public is negative. Giving women lead positions is sometimes perceived negative by the public. The perception is that they always as: Why does this person bring in women in key positions when there are men who can do the work. There are also internal conflicts among women themselves (Male, community leader).

Managing Group Dynamics

All group and community leaders cited the problem of managing group dynamics characterized by some *"fights and quarrels"* among women group members. The Buhoma-Mukono community group experienced group conflicts associated with leadership trust grounded in complaints about unequal sharing of income from dancing activities, disagreements, mismanagement and general leadership problems. The prolonged conflicts resulted into the group's suspension to offer cultural dances in some of the lodges, hence loss of income. Below are examples of participant excerpts about their group conflicts and the negative effects that followed;

We had leadership challenges because the groups that would dance would not bring back the money to the entire group. At times they would buy like a sowing machine but would never bring cash. When we brought in people to count books of accounts, we found that UGX 3 million was lost. Corruption was too much. There was also too much gossip among the women (Leader, Buhoma-Mukono Women's group).

We are no longer called to dance for tourists yet that's where we would sell our baskets and also get sponsors for our children. We used to get connections whenever we went to dance for the tourists. We are no longer invited but another group has started going (FGD participant, Buhoma-Mukono Women's group).

We got disagreements as women groups so we were stopped from dancing. We had 8 women groups and leadership was a problem. This led to a decision to come up with only one community group. We kept having leadership challenges and we gave up on dancing (In-depth interview participant, Buhoma-Mukono Women's group)

Limited Market

All participants from the two women groups complained about the limited market for their craft, guesthouse and cultural dance products mainly due to the fierce competition from other service providers. The Bwindi area has several groups (youth, orphaned children and Batwa/pygmies) and investors that offer some similar tourism products offered by the two women groups. Besides, women have limited access to weaving materials due to strong national park regulations to access the forest. This has forced women to look for materials very far from home, including acquiring them expensively from the Democratic Republic of Congo (DRC). This has led to reduced income, increased working time and cost to produce crafts and low morale. The above constraints curtail women's ability to meaningfully exercise their instrumental and intrinsic agency and their associated opportunities.

DISCUSSION AND CONCLUSIONS

Findings of the two case studies demonstrate how women's collective agency has translated into outcomes that build their instrumental and intrinsic agency, through their community tourism initiatives. Particularly, women's instrumental agency has been enabled in the areas of access to and control over financial resources, ownership of productive resources and assets, and work-life balance. Collective agency thus plays a key role in enhancing instrumental and intrinsic agency demonstrated by enhanced women's financial inclusion, independence, esteem and challenged negative norms around domestic violence. Our analysis further reveals that the three forms of agency are manifesting through women's ability to achieve their common goals of addressing household and community poverty while achieving their immediate and strategic needs. The case studies further demonstrate how collective agency is a key input to instrumental/'power to' and intrinsic/'power within,' and an enabler of other dimensions of empowerment – resources and achievements (Kabeer, 1999). While women's agency may be enhanced in certain perspectives, it may remain invisible in others, which calls for continued interrogation of the interactions occurring between tourism developments, women's collective agency and outcomes.

Findings further demonstrate the enhanced women's ability to meet immediate family needs and address their common challenges of severe poverty and gender-based violence. Their growing economic independence has meant affording better education opportunities for their children and attainment of key development resources. Their ability to invest portions of their income in their families and the wider community is well aligned to other case study findings associated with the community-based tourism model in Africa (Kimbu and Ngoasong, 2016; Boonabaana, 2012; Tucker and Boonabaana, 2012; Scheyvens, 2000; 2002). Community tourism that has been widely adopted in Africa has gained prominence in Zimbabwe, Namibia, Kenya, Uganda, South Africa, Tanzania, while enabling rural women to join the paid work space for the first time (Boonabaana, 2012).

While gender norms continue to play a critical role in affecting women's agency and outcomes, findings allude to women's resilience to counter their social constraints to deliver positive social-economic outcomes for themselves, their families and community members. Positive outcomes in women's lives have occurred as precursors for social transformation – including economic independence and subtle confrontation of domestic violence.

Women are working out ways to resist male pressure to control their income, to move out of the domestic space for paid tourism work and to reduce their economic dependence on men. However, as women tap into tourism opportunities, there is an emerging pattern of power relations where local men are instead becoming economically dependent on the women while maintaining their patriarchal control on women. Nevertheless, as Laverack and Wallerstein (2001) have explained, when individuals, groups and communities begin to organize and mobilise themselves, they can indeed achieve the social and political changes necessary to redress their powerlessness.

However, as they push their gender boundaries, Buhoma women still face constraints that limit their full potential to exercise their agency. These need to be addressed if rural women living in tourism destinations are to join the tourism space, consolidate their gains, and further their operations.

RECOMMENDATIONS

The authors recommend that women groups should be encouraged and supported to tap into tourism opportunities in their localities. Women collectives have a lot to offer in terms of personal, family and social transformation. There is need for the relevant stakeholders to innovate diverse opportunities that can synergize, boost and sustain women's rural tourism entrepreneurship. The innovations should be informed by an in-depth understanding of the various gender-based opportunities and constraints experienced in the various tourism destinations. Another recommendation relates to the need to engage men as spouses, parents and brothers, towards creating a conducive household and community environment for women to better operate. The authors recommend similar studies on how women's collective work in various tourism destinations is translating into different forms of women's agency and social outcomes.

Given that this study was conducted before the COVID19 pandemic, in future, it would be good to examine the impacts of the COVID19 shocks on women's gains, their resilience to the shocks and outcomes.

REFERENCES

Al-Dajani, H., & Marlow, S. (2013). Empowerment and entrepreneurship: A theoretical framework. *International Journal of Entrepreneurial Behaviour & Research*, *19*(5), 503–524. doi:10.1108/IJEBR-10-2011-0138

Ampumuza, C. (2021). *Batwa, gorillas and the Ruhija road: a relational perspective on controversies at Bwindi Impenetrable National Park, Uganda* [Doctoral Dissertation]. Wageningen University and Research.

Ayorekire, J., Mugizi, F., Obua, J., & Ampaire, G. (2021). Community-Based Tourism and Local People's Perceptions Towards Conservation: The Case of Queen Elizabeth Conservation Area, Uganda. In *Prospects and Challenges of Community-based Tourism and Changing Demographics* (pp. 56–82). IGI Global Publishers.

Baum, T. (2013). *International perspectives on women and work in hotels, catering and tourism. Bureau for Gender Equality*. Working Paper No. 1/2013, Sectoral Activities. Department Working Paper No. 289. International Labour Organization: Geneva

Bigoditourism. (2021, December 7). *Bigodi tourism*. Bigodi Tourism. Retrieved from https://bigoditourism.com/

Boonabaana, B. (2012). *Community-based Tourism and Gender Relations in Uganda* [Doctoral Dissertation]. University of Otago, Dunedin, New Zealand.

Boonabaana, B. (2014). Negotiating Gender and Tourism Work: Women's Lived Experiences in Uganda. *Journal of Tourism and Hospitality Research, 14*(1-2), 27–36. doi:10.1177/1467358414529578

Buzinde, C., Shockley, G., Andereck, K., Dee, E., & Frank, P. (2017). Theorizing Social Entrepreneurship within Tourism Studies. In P. J. Sheldon & R. Daniele (Eds.), *Social Entrepreneurship and Tourism, Philosophy and Practice* (pp. 21–34). Springer International Publishing. doi:10.1007/978-3-319-46518-0_2

Guloba, M., Ssewanyana, S., & Birabwa, E. (2017). Rural Women Entrepreneurship in Uganda: A Synthesis Report on Policies, Evidence, and Stakeholder. Research Series No. 134, Economic Policy Research Centre (EPRC).

Handaragama, S., & Kusakabe, K. (2021). Participation of women in business associations: A case of small-scale tourism enterprises in Sri Lanka. *Heliyon, 7*(11), e08303. doi:10.1016/j.heliyon.2021.e08303 PMID:34778588

Kabeer, N. (1999). Resources, agency, achievements: Reflections on the measurement of women's empowerment. *Development and Change, 30*(3), 435–464. doi:10.1111/1467-7660.00125

Kimbu, A. N., & Ngoasong, M. Z. (2016). Women as vectors of social entrepreneurship. *Annals of Tourism Research, 60*, 63–79. doi:10.1016/j.annals.2016.06.002

Laverack G, & Wallerstein, N. (2001). Measuring community empowerment: A fresh look at organizational domains. *Health Promotion International, 16*(2).

Malapit, H. J., Quisumbing, A. R., Meinzen-Dick, R. S., Seymour, G., Martinez, E. M., Heckert, J., Rubin, D., Vaz, A., & Yount, K. M. (2019). *Development of the project-level Women's empowerment in agriculture index (pro-WEAI).* https://ebrary.ifpri.org/utils/getfile/collection/p15738coll2/id/133061/filename/133271.pdf

Ministry of Tourism, Wildlife, and Antiquities [MOTWA]. (2014). *Uganda Tourism Development Master Plan (2014-2024).* Author.

Ministry of Tourism, Wildlife, and Antiquities [MoTWA]. (2020). *The impact of COVID-19 on the tourism sector in Uganda*. Government of Uganda.

National Planning Authority [NPA]. (2020). *Third National Development Plan (NDPIII), 2020/2021-2024-2025.* The Republic of Uganda.

Nomnga, V. J. (2017). Unlocking the Potential of Women Entrepreneurs in the Tourism and Hospitality Industry in the Eastern Cape Province, South Africa. *Journal of Economics and Behavioral Studies*, *9*(4), 6–13. doi:10.22610/jebs.v9i4.1817

Nomnga, V. J. (2021). Empowering Rural Women in the Hospitality Industry through Small, Medium and Micro Enterprises. *International Journal of Innovation, Creativity and Change, 15*(8).

Ochieng, A., Ahebwa, W. M., & Twinomuhangi, R. (forthcoming). *Nexus between biodiversity, climate change and tourism: implications for sustainable tourism in Uganda*. Academic Press.

Parashar, S. (2014). Marginalized by race and place: A multilevel analysis of occupational sex segregation in post-apartheid South Africa. *The International Journal of Sociology and Social Policy*, *34*(11/12), 747–770. doi:10.1108/IJSSP-01-2014-0003

Republic of Uganda. (2007). *The Uganda Gender Policy*. Ministry of Gender, Labour and Social Development.

Scheyvens, R. (2000). Promoting women's empowerment through involvement in ecotourism: Experiences from the third world. *Journal of Sustainable Tourism*, *8*(3), 232–249. doi:10.1080/09669580008667360

Scheyvens, R. (2002). *Tourism for development: Empowering communities*. Pearson Education Limited.

Tshabalala, S. P., & Ezeuduji, I. O. (2016). Women Tourism Entrepreneurs in KwaZulu-Natal, South Africa: Any Way Forward? Acta Universitatis Danubius, 12(5).

Tucker, H., & Boonabaana, B. (2012). A critical analysis of tourism, gender and poverty reduction. *Journal of Sustainable Tourism*, *20*(3), 437–455. doi:10.1080/09669582.2011.622769

Tumusiime, D. M., & Vedeld, P. (2015). Can Biodiversity Conservation Benefit Local People? Costs and Benefits at a Strict Protected Area in Uganda. *Journal of Sustainable Forestry*, *34*(8), 761–786. doi:10.1080/10549811.2015.1038395

Uganda Wildlife Authority. (2018). *Bwindi Impenetrable National Park*. https://ugandawildlife.org/wp-content/uploads/2022/01/Bwindi-cc-2018-2.pdf

UNDP. (n.d.). *Sustainable development goals: United Nations Development Programme*. Retrieved from https://www.undp.org/sustainable-development-goals

United Nations. (n.d.). *The 17 goals | sustainable development*. United Nations. Retrieved from https://sdgs.un.org/goals

United Nations Conference on Trade and development [UNCTAD]. (2017). *Economic development in Africa Report, Tourism for Transformative and Inclusive Growth*. The United Nations.

van Eerdewijk, A., Wong, F., Vaast, C., Newton, J., Tyszler, M., & Pennington, A. (2017). *White paper: A conceptual model of women and girls' empowerment*. https://www.kit.nl/wp-content/uploads/2018/10/BMGF_KIT_WhitePaper_web-1.pdf

Vukovic, D.B., Petrovic, M., Maiti, M. & Vujko, A. (2021). Tourism development, entrepreneurship and women's empowerment – Focus on Serbian countryside. *Journal of Tourism Futures*. doi:10.1108/JTF-10-2020-0167

World Bank. (2013). *Case Studies of the Horticulture, Tourism, and Call Center Industries*. The World Bank Group.

World Tourism Organization. (2011). *Global Report on Women in Tourism*. United Nations World Tourism Organization.

World Tourism Organization. (2019). *Global Report on Women in Tourism* (2nd ed.). UNWTO. doi:10.18111/9789284420384

Yanes, A., Zielinski, S., Diaz Cano, M., & Kim, S. I. (2019). Community-based tourism in developing countries: A framework for policy evaluation. *Sustainability*, *11*(9), 2506. doi:10.3390u11092506

Chapter 7
The Perspectives of Female Tourists on Food Tourism in Different Countries:
A Review of Different Marketing Strategies Used by Different Countries in Promoting Food Tourism

Nirma Sadamali Jayawardena
Griffith University, Australia

Sanjeewa Kumara Karunarathne
Cardiff Metropolitan University, UK

ABSTRACT

The objective of this chapter is to review the literature to identify the different marketing strategies used by different countries in promoting food tourism with special reference to the viewpoints of female tourists. The viewpoints of female tourists have been selected as female travelling category has seen rapid expansion in today's worldwide outbound tourism industry. This study contributes by becoming the first systematic literature review on different marketing strategies used by different countries in promoting food tourism with special reference to the viewpoints of female tourists during the period 2015 to 2021.

DOI: 10.4018/978-1-6684-4194-7.ch007

1. INTRODUCTION

Many nations consider tourism to be a significant commercial sector (Smith, Suthitakon, Gulthawatvichai, & Karnjanakit, 2019). The main scope of this paper is to review the papers to identify the different marketing strategies used in promoting tourism destinations through tea and coffee products with special reference to the viewpoints of female tourists. The viewpoints of female tourists been selected as female travelling category has seen rapid expansion in today's worldwide outbound tourism industry (Kim & Choi, 2012; Zhang & Hitchcock, 2017). When considering 'Destination Tourism', some academic publications have highlighted the importance of adding food and tourism in managing destinations from both demand and supply sides (Rachão, Breda, Fernandes, & Joukes, 2019). Several authors discussed that food experiences can add value to tourism (Hall, Sharples, Mitchell, Macionis, & Cambourne, 2004; Rachão et al., 2019; Rachão, Breda, Fernandes, & Joukes, 2020). In the tourism industry, food and beverage experiences are a growing and important segment (Ignatov & Smith, 2006). Using the definition from the World Tourism Organization in 2012, tourism is defined as the actions of humans traveling to and staying in places beyond their usual environment for a period of not more than one year for pleasure, business, or other purposes. Tourism for food and beverage experiences is a growing and important part of the industry (Ignatov & Smith, 2006).

Tourism networks are becoming a more essential instrument for economic growth (Gibson, Lynch, & Morrison, 2005; Scott, Cooper, & Baggio, 2008). Such networks have the potential to make a substantial contribution to sustainable tourism that incorporates both community and business interests at the local destination level (Gibson et al., 2005; Scott et al., 2008). The destination related motivation is a vital element in tourism. However, what has been missing from the current literature is that, up to date none of the studies reviewed the literature to identify the different marketing strategies used by different countries in promoting food tourism destinations with special reference to the viewpoints of female tourists (Li et al., 2011). Female travellers now account for half of the world's leisure travellers (Li et al., 2011) and they have become the major target market for many tourism enterprises. Women have an important part in tourism all around the world, as guests, hosts, and employees (Tan & Bakar, 2016). Women are travel influencers, and their prominence in travel consumption is growing (Tan & Bakar, 2016). Female travellers have higher purchasing power and are more likely than their male counterparts to spend more money at tourist spots (Chan, 2007; Larsen et al., 2009). This study can be considered as the **first** cross country analysis study which categorised the coffee and tea-based tourism promotion by considering the viewpoints of female tourists.

Globally, coffee and tea are two of the most widely traded commodities. According to Menke (2018), coffee has an estimated net worth of more than US$100 billion, with 500 billion cups consumed annually. According to Bedford (2020), tea is worth approximately US$52 billion, and is expected to reach almost US$81.6 billion by 2026. The commodities in question are also represented on global stock exchange indices by companies such as Starbucks Coffee and Tata Tea, which reflect the importance of these agricultural products. Also, coffee and tea are enshrined in tradition and custom. Coffee and tea are consumed throughout the world for a range of reasons, including health and well-being, ceremonies, and gift-giving (Hedrick et al., 2010; Kaplan, 2017; Lin, 2017). Typically, markets for women's tourism products are small and not sufficiently diversified. Numerous case studies in this report demonstrate that the market for women's handicrafts and cultural tourism products is compact and crowded (Brain, 2018; Wipulasena, 2020). To encourage innovation, it is necessary to improve product development and market outlets Brain, 2018; Wipulasena, 2020). Female travellers account 34% globally as travellers as of November 2021 (Statista, 2021). In a survey conducted in November 2021, the percentage of adults who subscribed to travel-related paid subscription services in several countries were examined (Statista, 2021). Most of the subscribers in the countries surveyed were males. Men constituted 66 percent of all adults who subscribed to a paid subscription program for travel in the United States (Statista, 2021). Japan had the highest proportion of female subscribers among the countries studied after the impact from COVID-19 (Statista, 2021). Therefore, the main objective of this study is to identify the different marketing strategies used by different countries in promoting food tourism with special reference to the viewpoints of female tourists.

Research objective: To identify the different marketing strategies used by different countries in promoting tea and coffee products with special reference to the viewpoints of female tourists

1.1 Importance of Tea and Coffee Product-based Tourism for Female Tourists

The World Food Travel Association (2020) estimates that more than one quarter of tourists' travel budgets are spent on food. Tourism satisfaction at destinations is significantly influenced by food (Yousaf & Xiucheng, 2018). The main beverages of coffee and tea are consumed globally for a variety of reasons, such as a daily beverage, health and well-being, ceremonies, and gift-giving (Hedrick et al., 2021). Both commodities are also versatile and can be used in a wide range of products and services, such as cooking condiments, baking flavours, and making desserts (Hedrick et al., 2021). Nevertheless, the intersection of coffee and tea remains understudied in terms of tourism (Besky, 2014). However, the intersection of coffee and tea remains understudied from the perspective of tourism (Besky, 2014). This is due to coffee and tea being reduced to objects of consumption within the broader tourism sector (Petit, 2007). Recent years have seen an increase in coffee and tea tourism in destinations such as Uganda and Sri Lanka due to their respective expertise in crop production (Brain, 2018; Wipulasena, 2020).

The markets for women's tourism products are typically small and not sufficiently diverse. In this report, numerous case studies demonstrate that the market for women's handicrafts and cultural tourism products is compact and crowded (Brain, 2018; Wipulasena, 2020). In order to encourage innovation, it is necessary to improve product development and distribution channels (Brain, 2018; Wipulasena, 2020). Despite this, the enablers and returns on investment to attract potential market segments are largely under researched and needs a call for a systematic literature review to determine the current scope of coffee and tea tourism for female tourists. A growing body of academic research has focused on coffee and tea tourism as different destinations attempt to position their agricultural landscapes in service-oriented industries such as tourism (Mahendra et al., 2020; Wang et al., 2019). Such a phenomenon is caused by two main factors. The yields of agricultural crops such as coffee and tea are highly sensitive to market forces as well as adverse weather conditions (Woyesa and Kumar, 2020).

1.2 The Lack of Sustained Theory

While the case studies offered rich insights into a relatively under-explored area of coffee and tea tourism, there is a lack of sustained theory that could be used to guide future research and practice (Candelo et al., 2019; Jayasooriya, 2019; Su et al., 2020; Ummiroh and Hardiyani, 2013; Woyesa and Kumar, 2020). There appears to be a wide variety of authors who have published on coffee and tea tourism (Candelo et al., 2019; Jayasooriya, 2019; Su et al., 2019; Su et al., 2020; Ummiroh and Hardiyani, 2013; Woyesa and Kumar, 2020). Among other things, the authors should be commended for advancing the case studies to build theory from a range of paradigms. For instance, consumer behaviour and marketing perspectives constitute the premises on coffee and tea conceptual frameworks focusing the female tourists (Anbalagan and Lovelock, 2014; Fernando et al., 2016; Koththagoda and Thushara, 2016; Sultana and Khan, 2018; Wang et al., 2019, 2020). Some authors have conceptualized coffee and tea tourism through the perspective of agricultural livelihoods and coffee/tea heritage (Candelo et al., 2019; Jayasooriya, 2019; Su et al., 2020).

Although there are similarities and subtle differences between these studies, there are few citations and theoretical developments that can be used to formulate a refined coffee or tea tourism model (Candelo et al., 2019; Jayasooriya, 2019). It could be interpreted in two ways: one, that there is a large body of literature on coffee and tea tourism focusing the female tourists, which has been compiled within this review, thus justifying a systematic literature review (Ummiroh and Hardiyani, 2013; Woyesa and Kumar, 2020). Two, replication or validation of the constructs and propositions in the existing coffee and tea tourism models is very much in its infancy and the reason for this could be the heterogeneous operating landscapes of governance, local cultures, and a lack of a coherent strategy to guide such segments into the future (Smith et al., 2019). Therefore, the destination marketing strategies would be advantageous to approach coffee and tea tourism in a cross-cultural manner (Smith et al., 2019). Although the use of case studies can be useful in gaining an understanding of coffee or tea tourism in specific places or contexts, it is also valuable to compare between different cultures to reveal similarities and differences in the global landscape (Candelo et al., 2019; Jayasooriya, 2019).

1.3 Importance of Food Tourism in Destination Marketing Strategies

Food tourism may be viewed as a form of niche or alternative tourism and due to escalating competition and a change in what travellers want in terms of destination experiences, is now more often being included as a new or additional factor in the travel and tourism industry (Poon, 1993; Ritchie & Crouch, 2000). As a result, food tourism can serve as a valuable source of marketable images and experiences for tourists, enhancing the competitiveness and sustainability of the destination (Quan & Wang, 2003). This interaction benefits both food and tourism industries, as local and regional food products provide a means for promoting the identity and culture of a destination, and allow food producers to create tourism experiences around the raw materials (Quan & Wang, 2003). Food is considered to be a reflection of a country's culture and its people. Therefore, it is an ideal product to offer as an attraction in a destination, and it can be effectively used as a marketing tool. Many authors have discussed food and wine as expressions of place and their use as marketing tools (Cohen & Avieli, 2004; Hall & Sharples, 2003). **However, the focus on coffee and tea which are daily consumed beverages in some countries lacks focus with reference to female tourists** (Candelo et al., 2019; Jayasooriya, 2019; Su et al., 2019; Su et al., 2020; Ummiroh and Hardiyani, 2013; Woyesa and Kumar, 2020).

It would be beneficial for future studies to consider coffee and tea tourism from a cross-cultural perspective (Candelo et al., 2019; Jayasooriya, 2019). In addition to the usefulness of case studies when learning about coffee or tea tourism in various places and contexts, comparative studies do offer valuable insight into similarities and differences among different cultures. In addition, these studies can also be examined through the lived experiences of visitors living in the local cultures for an extended period of time, where methods as diverse as ethnography, journal entries,

Table 1. Inclusion and exclusion criteria

Inclusion criteria	Exclusion criteria
English only articles	Articles published in different languages
Journal papers, conference papers and book reviews	Websites, blogs, and new paper reviews
Scope and contribution: Female tourists Promoting Tourism Usage of coffee and tea products Published between 2015 to 2021	Scope and contribution: Male tourists Not applicable for Tourism Not focused on coffee and tea products Not Published between 2015 to 2021

or blogs could provide insights into the unique characteristics and experiences of coffee and tea tourists Cohen & Avieli, 2004; Hall & Sharples, 2003).

2. SYSTEMATIC LITERATURE REVIEW APPROACH

The systematic literature reviews (SLR) can be defined as the reviews which follows a systematic structure with an objective (Weed, 2005). The main purpose of this systematic literature review is to categorise the various promotion strategies used by different countries to promote tourism through food products. A review of the current literature was conducted using the 'Publish or Perish' software across Google Scholar. As one of the most widely used web-based academic search engines, Google Scholar has between 2 and 100 million records in both academic and grey literature (Haddaway, Collins, Coughlin, & Kirk, 2015). Authors included the articles published during the period of 2015 to 2021, a period of six years been selected to avoid using outdated content in the reviewing process (Behl et al., 2022; Jayawardena, 2021; Jayawardena et al.,2021). This can be further justified based on the precedents of reviews that focussed on only a five- to six-year review period with findings indicating the most recent research gaps (Jarquin et al., 2011; Park et al., 2015; Setati et al., 2009; Jayawardena, 2020; Jayawardena, Ross, & Grace, 2020).

The main keyword used is promoting tourism through food products, food tourism and female tourists and food tourism and gender roles. Since the main aim of this review paper is to categorise the various promotion strategies used by different countries to promote tourism through food, this paper used several inclusion and exclusion criteria as follows.

2.1 The Article Selection Process

A total of 998 studies were appeared from the Google Scholar. Nevertheless, all the articles were not qualified for the review due to out-of-scope issues. For instance, some studies focused on promoting culture, about different marketing strategies, advertising, human resource management and trade agreements and not about promoting tourism through tea and coffee products. Moreover, after removing the duplicated records and through reviewing the scope and contribution, a total of 428 studies had to remove from the reviewing process and the remaining 570 articles were identified as initially qualified articles for further investigation. After careful reading of the abstracts and results sections, another set 323 of articles were removed due to unavailability of the promotion strategies to promote tourism through tea and coffee products. Further, to maintain the quality of the review, the articles published in high impact factor journals were selected. For example, based on the journal quality rankings mentioned through ABDC ranking system, the A* and A ranking journals are considered as higher quality journals. Similarly, in SC imago ranking the Q3 and Q4 ranking journals. Other than these rankings, several studies been considered due to the contribution of the paper. Therefore, due to quality maintenance, a total of 212 articles has been removed. Finally, a total of 35 studies were found as qualified to be added for the review. Figure 1 further illustrates the filtering criteria used in this review.

3. SUMMARY OF THE SELECTED STUDIES

The final studies (n=45) include thirty-one (41) journal papers, three (3) conference papers and the one (1) book review and these were summarised using the Table 2 as follows.

Based on the Table 1, authors identified several promotion strategies used by different countries to promote food tourism and perspectives of female tourists regarding the food tourism. The next section discusses these findings as follows.

4. DISCUSSION OF THE FINIDNGS BASED ON THE FOOD PROMOTION STRATEGIES OF THE COUNTRIES

Most coffee tourism papers focused Indonesia, by investigating the links between coffee and tourism in a major coffee-producing country. Thailand, Korea, Taiwan, Brazil, Costa Rica, Switzerland, Rwanda and Pakistan are the next highest recorded context for coffee tourism studies. Comparatively, tea tourism was almost exclusively

Figure 1. Flow chart of the literature search process

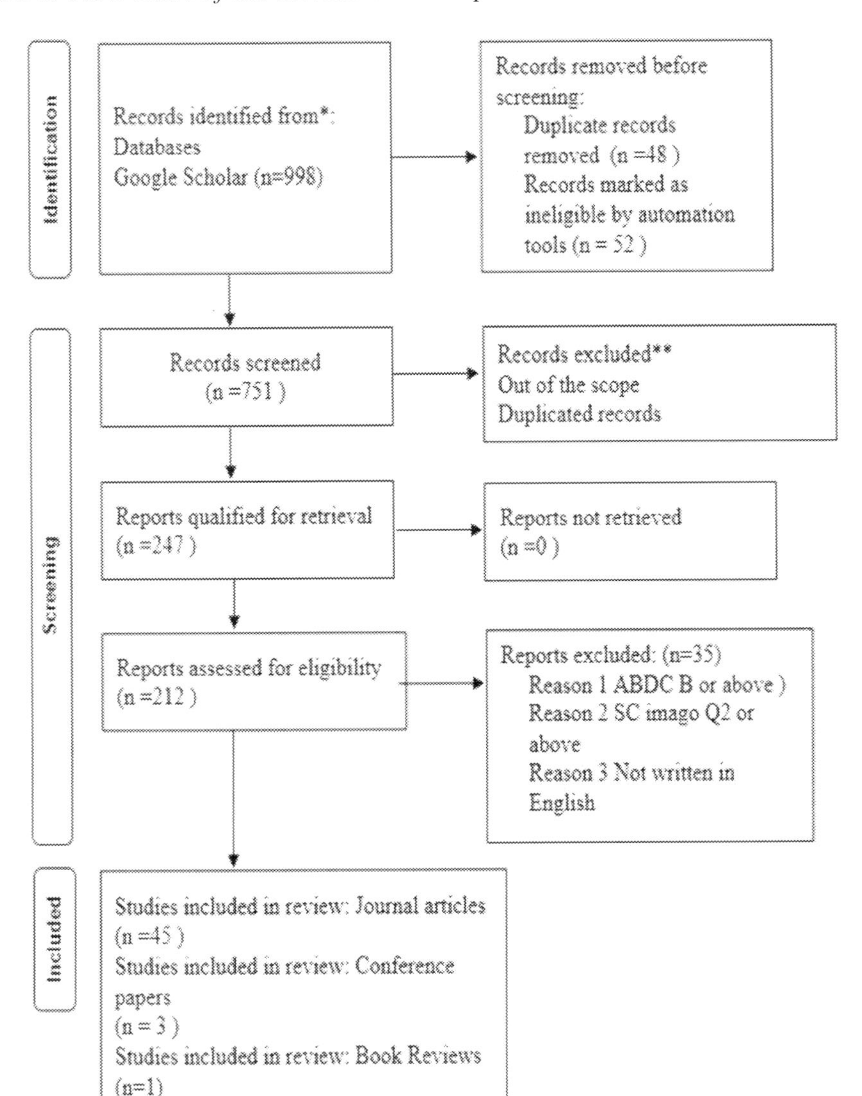

analysed within three countries, namely China, India, and Sri Lanka. According to this interesting distinction between coffee and tea tourism, tea production may be more widely dispersed than coffee production, which has been largely concentrated in a few selected regions throughout the world. As a result of the above presented systematic literature review on cross country analysis, the key themes emerged were categorized under country and continent sections as follows.

Table 2. Summary of the key studies reviewed in this paper

Source	Journal	Context	Key Concepts	Focus	Findings based on the tea and coffee-based food tourism promotion strategies in different countries
Findings based on the tea and coffee-based food tourism strategies in different countries					
Smith et al. (2019)	Local Economy	Thailand /Asia	To provide directions on coffee tourism administration and to establish a coffee tourism network among the communities of Thailand	Coffee tourism administration	-The findings consist of the results of three projects: the community-based tourism by coffee farmers in Chiang Mai, the pilot study of a coffee tour program in Huay Hom Village, Mae Hong Son, and the project "Good Coffee in Lampang" -Thailand lacks coffee tourism and it is essential to explore whether Northern Thailand can flourish as a coffee tourism attraction
Candelo, Casalegno, Civera, and Büchi (2019)	Tourism Analysis	Costa Rica/North America	Investigated the coffee tourism based on multiple stakeholder perspectives	Coffee tourism based on multiple stakeholder perspectives	-Empowerment and cooperation, business diversification, sustainability, and creation of a destination image are the four main benefits for the local communities of farmers to attract tourists
Anbalagan and Lovelock (2014)	Tourism and Hospitality Research	Rwanda/ Africa	Explored the opportunity for synergistic, cross-sectoral development of coffee tourism in Rwanda	Cross-sectoral development of coffee tourism	-Coffee tourism also offers a supplementary attraction for Rwanda's uni-dimensional (gorilla tourism) product which could increase length of stay and visitor spend
Wang, Chen, Su, and Morrison (2019)	Tourism Management Perspectives	Taiwan/ Asia	Analysed the tourism experiences offered by coffee estates in Taiwan	Tourism experiences	- Tourist satisfaction (among females) is high when they interact with local citizens - More qualitative research with coffee estate guests and coffee lovers are still required to determine whether the coffee estate brands established by the Taiwan owners are recognized and fit consumer needs and expectations
Kim and Lee (2017)	Journal of Services Marketing	South Korea/ Asia	Investigated how service brand loyalty can be enhanced through customer involvement, based on involvement theory and symbolic interaction theory	Brand loyalty	- Results identified customer–brand identification and service value influenced both service brand involvement and service brand-decision involvement.
Lee, Wall, and Kovacs (2015)	Journal of Rural Studies	Canada /North America	Analysed the place branding processes of two not-for-profit organizations that are engaged in promoting rural development based on the formation of food clusters through creative economic perspectives	Brand loyalty	- The nature of agricultural production, the availability of other supporting cultural and tourism products, and proximity to markets vary from place to place
Farsani, Ghotbabadi, and Altafi (2019)	Asia Pacific Journal of Tourism Research	Iran / Asia	-Explored the tendencies of tourists towards organizing Agri-tours - Investigated the tendencies of tourists towards intangible and tangible agricultural heritage	Agricultural heritage	-Tourists are interested in Agri tours and both tangible and intangible agricultural heritage
Aslam and Jolliffe (2015)	Journal of Heritage Tourism	Sri Lanka/ Asia	Identifies the heritage accommodations related to the legacy of the tea industry and discusses their role in heritage tourism, interpreting the region's tea heritage and industry to contemporary visitors.	Agricultural heritage	-The various forms of historic lodging and recreation facilities for the plantation industries of planters' bungalows, rest houses, and planters' clubs being repurposed as contemporary lodging -The reuse of many tea heritage properties for tourism today contributes to tourism development and to improved livelihoods of workers on tea plantations through employment related to tourism accommodations
Okumus and Cetin (2018)	Journal of Destination Marketing & Management	Turkey / Asia	Investigated whether and how Istanbul, Turkey is marketed and promoted as a culinary destination	Agricultural heritage	. Utilizing local foods and other culinary resources in tourism development and destination marketing in a developing country can prevent local foods from becoming standardized or internationalized
Zhou, Hsieh, and Canziani (2016)	Conference paper	USA, China, and Taiwan / North America, and Asia	Surveyed a total of 246 university faculty members in United States, China, and Taiwan regarding their perceptions of tea tourism, including their levels of interest in various tea tourism activities and importance of tour components	Tea tourism	-Demographic factors, cultural backgrounds, and self-reported expertise regarding tea culture were significantly associated with respondents' expectations towards tea tourism
Xu and Ye (2016)	Journal of China Tourism Research	China / Asia	Explored tourist experiences through an empirical study on the Old Town of Lijiang, a leisure and romantic destination	Tourist experiences	-This paper is the first empirical study on the phenomenon of Yanyu at tourist destinations. It explores gender relationships between tourists in the unique environment of the capital of Yanyu, and enriches the related tourism literature, which is mostly concerned with host–tourist relationships
Smith (2015)	Tourism Recreation Research	Canada / North America	Explored the importance of place in the context of tourism product development and marketing, particularly the linkage between place and culture as a tourism experience	Tourist experiences	-Cultural tourism and place-based activity in the context of marketing and product development could be done using event-based or attractions-based marketing, word-of-mouth promotion and through video and photography of the destinations
Mahaliyanaarachchi (2016)	Journal of Agricultural Sciences	Sri Lanka / Asia	Reviewed literature on potential of Agri tourism as a risk management strategy in rural agriculture sector with special reference to developing countries	Agricultural heritage and Agri-tourism	-Risk management in agriculture is vital both for individual farmers and for agriculture as a sector because higher risks threaten sustainability of agriculture sector, and it results in the collapse of both micro and macro economies in a country

continued on following page

Table 2. Continued

Source	Journal	Context	Key Concepts	Focus	Findings based on the tea and coffee-based food tourism promotion strategies in different countries
Islam, Ahmed, Ali, and Ahmer (2019)	British Food Journal	Pakistan / Asia	Investigated the impact of authenticity, interpersonal justice and prior experience on customer's revisit intention, taking involvement as a mediator	Agricultural heritage and Agri-tourism	-The findings reveal that revisit intention of coffee users is based on various factors, including their involvement, authenticity, interpersonal justice and prior experience with the cafe. These findings, thus, use a valuable message for cafe managers as they are required to ensure that customers should repeat their visits
Wijaya (2019)	Journal of Ethnic Foods	Indonesia / Asia	This study aimed to portray how Indonesian food culture has been shaped, developed, and held as the value embedded in the society	Food culture	-This study is anticipated to function as a starter contribution to increase the market awareness of Indonesian cuisine and its richness particularly through the exploration of socio-cultural aspect
Jordan (2018)	History of Retailing Consumption	Switzerland / Europe	This article probes the consumption of tea and coffee in seventeenth- and eighteenth-century Bern	Food culture	-First, it first looks at their public consumption – in coffeehouses, taverns, and inns. Second, using a serial run of bankruptcy inventories, it investigates their private consumption in Bern, and whether there were marked differences in the chronology and levels of consumption of a global good like tea and coffee between polities with and without trading companies, port cites, and colonies
Wang, Chen, et al. (2019)	Tourism Management	China/ Asia	This paper reports the application of the concept of deconstruction to urban heritage sites. Such locations are divided into the tourism zones of cultural, leisure and landscape spaces	Tourism and cross-cultural links	This paper reports the application of the concept of deconstruction to urban heritage sites.
Soltani, Pieters, Young, and Sun (2018)	Asia Pacific Journal of Tourism Research	Japan / Asia	Argued that five main factors contributed to the success of *Kumamon*: government support, power of emotional attachment and anthropomorphism, efficient public transport and tourism services, the mascot branding, and social media	Tourism and cross-cultural links	Argued that five main factors contributed to the success of Kumamon: government support, power of emotional attachment and anthropomorphism, efficient public transport and tourism services, the mascot branding, and social media
Ramsey, Thimm, and Hehn (2019)	European Journal of Tourism, Hospitality Recreation	Germany and Switzerland / Europe	This paper presented a unique example of a border region with two-way traffic for cross-border shopping tourism: the border between Germany and Switzerland	Tourism and cross-cultural links	The results indicated high levels of traffic for various products and services. And while residents are generally satisfied with cross-border shopping in their communities, there are emerging issues related to volume and too many in Konstanz and not enough in Kreuzlingen
Su, Wall, and Wang (2019)	Journal of Sustainable Tourism	China / Asia	This study has identified and synthesized potential links between multiple components of the tea industry and those of the tourism sector, and the benefits would flow to agriculture, tourism, culture and arts and crafts as reflected in community livelihoods	Tourism and cross-cultural links	Identified several tea and tourism integration techniques such as; appreciating tea landscapes, visiting tea shops and tea museums, demonstration of tea processing, tea ceremony and cultural events, tea tasting, tea featured cuisine and tea featured accommodations
Su and Zhang (2020)	Tourism Geographies	China / Asia	-First, this study explored why and how guesthouse owners in Lijiang organize tea activities to socialize with tourists -Secondly, this study examined why some tourists favour tea drinking for relaxation and comfort	Tourist experiences	Findings indicated that building closeness to nature, sparked by absorption into the place that tourists visit; temporally, slowing down to taste tea and thus enjoy a different rhythm of life; and socially, building connection with hosts and other tourists through tea conversations as effective strategies
Lin and Wen (2018)	Journal of China Tourism Research	China / Asia	This research indicates that the intermarriage radius of local people is greater than ever before, as local people have more and wider encounters.	Tourist experiences	Tea tourism provides a platform for individual development within the social evolution. This article reflects the swift changes in remote Yunnan, where gender roles, the tea industry and social changes are interwoven
Fernando, Rajapaksha, and Kumari (2017)	Kelaniya Journal of Management	Sri Lanka / Asia	Identified the potentials to promote Sri Lanka as a tea tourism destination	Tourism destination	When considering tourists' experience profile, more than half of the respondents have never visited the tea tourism regions in the world. More than half of tea tourists desired to have day tour in tea tourism area and lack of activities in tea tourism outlets highlighted. The Attitudes on spending for accommodation, food and beverages, transportation, tea tourism activities and other pleasure activities, majority of tea tourists expected to spend less than US$ 200. Tourists had good awareness about Ceylon tea tourism activities moderately. When considering about attractions, tea tourism destinations have peaceful atmosphere and more manmade attractions but less events and leisure activities.
Liu (2019)	World Scientific Research Journal	China / Asia	This article first introduces the present status of Xinyang tea culture tourism resources, and then conducted a SWOT analysis	Tourism destination	Government should intervene more on the development of the tea culture tourism

continued on following page

Table 2. Continued

Source	Journal	Context	Key Concepts	Focus	Findings based on the tea and coffee-based food tourism promotion strategies in different countries
Torabi Farsani, Zeinali, and Moaiednia (2018)	Journal of Heritage Tourism	Iran / Asia	This research has two major purposes: to investigate innovation and strategies for promoting herbal-medicine based tourism and to demonstrate strategies for integrating tourism and medicinal plants for the purpose of education and knowledge transfer	Tourist experiences	Herbal medicine tourism as an integrated type of tourism that involves outdoor activities, including festivals, workshops in herbal medicine tourist parks/ farms, and the natural habitats of plants to popularize the therapeutic properties of medicinal plants and to preserve traditional medicine as f intangible cultural heritage
Qi, Li, Lu, and Pu (2019)	Conference paper	China / Asia	This paper envisages the present situation, existing problems, and future development direction of tea mountain tourism	Tourist experiences	Some of the identified strategies in promoting tea culture are leisure tour with professional tea merchants, senior tea friends travel as the main tea mountain free travel, team travel by enterprise customers and employees and self-driving tour with family
Mu, Chen, and Liang (2019)	Conference paper	China / Asia	This paper introduces the history of tea culture development, analyses the possibility of combining tea culture experience with urban leisure tourism development	Tourism development	-The combination of tea culture experience and urban leisure tourism can promote the further development of tourism industry, can realize the transformation of local tourism industry, and has important significance in the inheritance and development of culture --Future development of leisure tourism in this city must rely on its integration with tea culture; by integrating from the economic model and the development model of the tourism industry; the cultural advantages of tea culture will be fully revealed, so as to further promote the high-speed development of urban leisure tourism
Lee (2017)	Book Name: A Multi-Industrial Linkages Approach to Cluster Building in East Asia	Korea / Asia	Presented the characteristics and current conditions of governmental cluster programs in regional agriculture in the Republic of Korea	Tourism development	The existence of central resources, continuous local government support, and the actors' interorganizational learning and mutual complementarity have been confirmed as important factors in the formation and growth of a cluster
Ageeva and Foroudi (2019)	Journal of Business Research	Russia / Eastern Europe and Northern Asia	Identified how branding of places influences both supply and demand sides' perspectives and leads to changes in travellers' behaviour towards Russia	Brand loyalty	A conceptual model was designed which illustrates that the tangible and intangible factors of place identity influence the archetypical nation trait and regional place brand, which further results in a positive place image, authentic lifestyle, and entrepreneurship
Agyeiwaah, Otoo, Suntikul, and Huang (2019)	Journal of Travel Tourism Marketing	Thailand / Asia	Examined the relationships between antecedents and outcomes of culinary tourist participation in cooking classes.	Tourist experiences	Culinary tourists' motivation positively influences both the culinary experience and satisfaction; and that the culinary tourist experience is positively associated with both culinary tourist satisfaction and loyalty, suggesting that the more tourists are motivated to participate in cooking classes, the more experiential value and satisfaction are perceived
Shin, Hwang, Lee, and Cho (2015)	The Journal of Business Economics Environmental Studies	Korea / Asia	Examined how franchise coffee shop service quality and store atmosphere influence customer satisfaction and loyalty.	Brand loyalty	First, taste is revealed to be the most influential factor among components that have an impact on service quality. Second, taste also turned out to have the most impact on service quality among components influencing customer loyalty. Last, customer satisfaction affected customer loyalty
Ting, De Run, Cheah, and Chuah (2016)	British Food Journal	Malaysia / Asia	Investigated the determinants of ethnic food consumption intention in the context of developing markets	Tourist experiences	Attitude, subjective norm and perceived behavioural control all have positive effect on consumption intention of non-Dayak Malaysians towards Dayak food. However, food neophobia is only found to have a moderation effect on the relationship between subjective norm and consumption intention.
Ting, Fam, Hwa, Richard, and Xing (2019)	Tourism Management	Malaysia / Asia	Used the theory of planned behaviour to investigate tourists' intention to consume Dayak food when they visit Malaysia	Brand loyalty	While these tourists appear to share a lot in common in their consumption intention, they are different in terms of how they intend to consume Dayak food in Sarawak
Kwanya (2015)	Conference Paper	Kenya / Africa	Investigated the potential and the actual use of indigenous knowledge in leveraging the other efforts being made to develop and cushion tourism in Kenya.	Tourist experiences	There are several challenges such as lack of relevant business development skills; lack of adequate capital to develop and promote indigenous tourism products, services and facilities; remoteness of indigenous tourism sites; insecurity; poor infrastructure; modernisation; environmental degradation and consequences of climate change; stiff competition; and intra or inter-ethnic resource-based conflicts
Samoggia and Riedel (2018)	Appetite	None	A systematic literature review of consumer research towards coffee with the objective to identify and categorize motives, preferences and attributes of coffee consumption and purchasing behaviour	Tourism destination	Results provide a model of key determinants for coffee consumption that can be grouped into the categories, (1) personal preferences, (2) economic attributes, (3) product attributes, (4) context of consumption, and (5) socio-demographics
Findings based on the perspectives of female tourists					

continued on following page

Table 2. Continued

Source	Journal	Context	Key Concepts	Focus	Findings based on the tea and coffee-based food tourism promotion strategies in different countries
Sengel et al. (2015)	Procedia-Social Behavioral Sciences	Turkey/ Middle East	This study seeks to uncover which visitors are interested in local cuisine as an attraction by analysing the elements influencing local food demand in tourism.	Tourism destination	Restaurants that cater to visitors may be able to maximise the influence of positive word of mouth by focusing on married men and single women, since these groups are more likely to share their local cuisine experiences with their friends and family. Food has become a travel motivator for males, whereas females are more interested with gathering knowledge before to their excursions, so management may aim their advertisements to female tourists.
Robinson and Getz (2014)	British Food Journal	Australia/ Asia Pacific	The purpose of this paper is to convey the findings of a research of self-proclaimed "foodies." This report, in particular, presents a demographic and socioeconomic description of the sample, as well as their behavioural and travel choices.	Behavioural and travel choices	The key findings indicate that food tourists are typically females with well-education and money. They desire diverse, regional, and authentic experiences that are tactile rather than passive, and they are prepared to travel for food (and drink) that is matched by cultural and tourist activities.
Chen and Huang (2018)	British Food Journal	China/ Asia	The goal of this article is to examine the food-related motivation, engagement, satisfaction, and behavioural intentions of Chinese domestic visitors in order to assess the potential of local cuisine to operate as a destination attraction and contribute to the development of local areas in China.	Tourism destination	The findings indicate three categories of food-related behaviour. While gender appears to be important, other demographic criteria, such as age and educational level, do not appear to impact Chinese domestic visitors' degree of interest and participation in local food.
Gupta, Khanna, and Gupta (2019)	International Journal of Tourism Cities	India/ Asia	The goal of this article is to examine and analyse international visitors' street food preferences in Delhi. It will also investigate the reasons underlying the tourists' preference for certain dishes.	Tourist experiences	Street food preference is higher among male tourists than female tourists It was shown that there is a substantial association between the age of the visitors and their taste for street cuisine.
Chavarria and Phakdee-auksorn (2017)	Tourism Management Perspectives	Thailand/ Asia	The purpose of this study was to describe the overall attitude of foreign visitors towards street cuisine in Phuket and to determine which variables are most essential in predicting their behavioural intentions.	Tourist experiences	Both men and women have a good attitude towards street food. Furthermore, both groups appeared to rank each of the food features fairly similarly, they are concerned about hygiene, and they perceive food quality to be good in the same areas. It was believed that there would be a difference in attitudes between Western and Asian tourists, because food in Phuket may be more familiar to Asian travellers. However, in this study, both groups indicated comparable attitudes, which might be attributed to globalisation, access to information, and the growing presence of ethnic Thai restaurants in both Western and Asian nations.
Knollenberg, Duffy, Kline, and Kim (2021)	Tourism Planning Development	USA/ America	This study investigates how food tourism locations in North Carolina (NC), United States of America, can best advertise food and beverage experiences to various sorts of food tourists.	Tourism destination	Foodies are often women with higher salaries who desire active travel experiences. Foodies are complicated and multidimensional, and various sorts of foodies have different location choices.
Ying, Wen, Law, Wang, and Norman (2018)	Asia Pacific Journal of Tourism Research	USA/ America	The purpose of this study is to experimentally validate the efficacy of a single-item self-classification technique.	Tourist experiences	All respondents stated that they were interested in experiencing a place through the consumption of local food. The robustness of this study self-classification measure is investigated by comparing it to a data-driven multidimensional psychographic method in terms of its capacity to predict tourist behaviours towards food-related destination consumption.
Wang, Lehto, and Cai (2019)	Journal of Hospitality Tourism Research	USA/ America	This study compares tourist food consumption trends and food choice reasons while on vacation to their eating behaviour in regular life.	Behavioural and travel choices	The findings show that consumers' food selection intentions and behaviours when travelling are discordant with their diet routines at home. In the everyday environment, both male and female respondents consumed considerably more whole grains, vegetables, and fruits than in the trip scenario. The difference in intake frequency of fats and sweets between the two settings, however, was significant only for male respondents.
Sirigunna (2015)	Procedia-Social Behavioral Sciences	Thailand/ Asia	The study was designed largely to elicit European Union tourists' concerns about various food safety management practises experienced during their vacation to Thailand.	Tourism destination	Food safety was not a severe concern for international visitors in Thailand because just one instance, or.25 percent of respondents, had become ill several times as a result of food and beverage intake in Thailand. However, the vast majority of responders, up to 87.5 percent, had not been unwell at all throughout their trip to Thailand.

continued on following page

Table 2. Continued

Source	Journal	Context	Key Concepts	Focus	Findings based on the tea and coffee-based food tourism promotion strategies in different countries
Wang, Filimonau, and Li (2021)	Journal of Cleaner Production	China/ Asia	With an exploratory survey in Lhasa, a popular tourist destination in China, this study aimed to establish the size of food waste by tourists and explain the role of various socio-demographic and food consumption-related factors in its occurrence through statistical analysis and multiple linear regression analysis, respectively.	Behavioural and travel choices	Findings indicated that female tourists waste significantly more food. Concurrently, data suggests that females are more inclined to try unfamiliar foods implying that females are more likely to order food that they do not like and hence waste.

Source: Developed by authors

Thailand

According to the Ministry of Tourism and Sports in 2017, it was reported that "Tourism as a significant business sector to the Thai economy, producing 16% of the country's GDP". Further, Smith et al. (2019) mentioned that, Thailand lacks coffee tourism and it is important to explore whether Northern Thailand can flourish as a coffee tourism attraction. As a main tourism promotion strategy, the perceived awareness of local communities in several areas of Thailand is essential as the role in tourism had influenced their perceived knowledge of tourism principles. Similarly, most of the host communities should be aware of the importance of community participation in tourism development for example the facilities provided to tourists, tourist carrying capacity and e substantial tourism and environment administration etc. (Cole, 2006; Saufi, O'Brien, & Wilkins, 2014). Agyeiwaah et al. (2019) examined the relationships between antecedents and outcomes of culinary tourist participation in cooking classes using a structural equation modelling approach and found that more tourists are motivated to participate in cooking classes, the more experiential value and satisfaction are perceived.

Kenya

When considering Kenya, Tea is mainly grown in several districts which include Kericho, Bomet, Nandi, Kiambu, Thika, Maragua, Muranga, Sotik, Kisii, Nyamira, Nyambene, Meru, Nyeri, Kerinyaga, Embu, Kakamega, Nakuru and Trans-nzoia (Gesimba, Langat, Liu, & Wolukau, 2005). Kwanya (2015) investigated the potential and the actual use of indigenous knowledge in leveraging the other efforts being made to develop and cushion tourism in Kenya. Even though indigenous tourism holds a great socioeconomic possibility in Kenya, there are quite a few challenges such as lack of relevant business development skills; lack of adequate capital to develop and promote indigenous tourism products, services and facilities; remoteness of indigenous tourism sites; insecurity; poor infrastructure; modernisation;

environmental degradation and consequences of climate change; stiff competition; and intra or inter-ethnic resource-based conflicts (Kwanya, 2015).

Malaysia

Ting et al. (2019) used the theory of planned behaviour to investigate tourists' intention to consume Dayak food when they visit Sarawak, Malaysia. As the food tourism is slowly emerging as a new area in tourism, there is an opportunity for Sarawak to strengthen their region's identity and endure cultural heritage through the promotion of Dayak food categories among tourists (Ting et al., 2019). The several other food promotion strategies for the tourists includes maintenance of blogs or cuisine reviews, local tourism groups can provide free Dayak tastings and events that help cultivate proper consumer attitudes and narratives around the Dayak cuisine and culture (Ting et al., 2019). Further, Ting et al. (2016) attitude, subjective norm and perceived behavioural control all have positive effect on consumption intention towards Malaysian food, which means that due to the substantial increase of tourists visiting Malaysia, the understanding of ethnic food consumption intention from not only Malaysian but also tourist perspectives is of great need. An authentic way to engage with a destination is through glamping in tea gardens (Tayibnapis & Sundari, 2020).

Korea

Kim and Lee (2017) investigated how service brand loyalty can be enhanced through customer involvement, based on involvement theory and symbolic interaction theory. Findings indicated that coffee shop experience could be enhanced through proper brand names or a favourable reputations and coffee shops should create an environment where customers can positively express themselves and convey a positive self-image (Kim & Lee, 2017). Moreover, coffee shop managers need to create multidimensional values for customers, enhancing their consumption experiences (Kim & Lee, 2017). Therefore, mainly the research identified that layout and store design as essential in attracting consumers. Lee (2017) identified that the existence of central resources, continuous local government support, and the actors' interorganizational learning and mutual complementarity as significant factors in the formation and growth of a cluster. Shin et al. (2015) outlined the importance of focusing on the taste, as taste is revealed to be the most influential factor among components that have an impact on service quality and consumer satisfaction.

Russia

It is highlighted in the literature that, place image as a critical component for selecting a place to visit and is also a challenge for destination management organisations (Ageeva & Foroudi, 2019). Positive impression about the place is identified as essential in brand formation (Ageeva & Foroudi, 2019). Therefore, it is highly recommended for the decision makers to take into consideration multi-stakeholder perspectives when deciding about the place brand formation in Russia.

Taiwan

Wang, Chen, et al. (2019) analysed the tourism experiences offered by coffee estates in Taiwan and identified several strategies to promote tourism using coffee products. For example, it was found that rural tourism offers opportunities for visitors specially the tourists to have contact with nature, scenic landscapes, and culture in the countryside and also helps to enhance the sustainability of local communities (Wang, Chen, et al., 2019). Further, Zhou et al. (2016) found that demographic factors, cultural backgrounds, and self-reported expertise regarding tea culture is also identified as influential factors towards tea tourism for USA, China and Taiwan.

Costa Rica

Similar to Taiwan, Candelo et al. (2019) identified that for coffee tourism the empowerment and cooperation, business diversification, sustainability, and creation of a destination image are the four main benefits for the local communities of farmers to attract tourists.

Rwanda

The possible tourism development research in many African nations remains largely unexplored due to many destination management and image issues (Anbalagan & Lovelock, 2014). The rural Rwandan farmers can link various tourism activities associated with coffee farming as a long term survival method of tourism development (Anbalagan & Lovelock, 2014). Further, infrastructural issues are identified as a main barrier for tourism development in Rwanda at the destination level, and are perceived to pose concomitant obstacles for coffee tourism (Anbalagan & Lovelock, 2014).

Figure 2. Summary of the findings based on the food promotion strategies of the countries

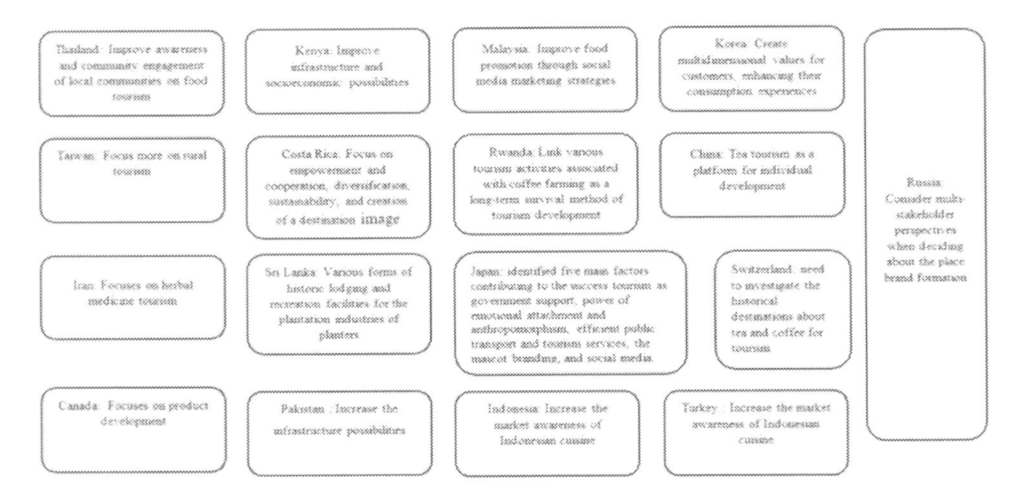

China

Mu et al. (2019) introduced the history of tea culture development, analysed the possibility of combining tea culture experience with urban leisure tourism development, and discusses how to achieve the path of combining the two industries, in order to provide a theoretical basis for further promoting tea culture tourism. Further findings indicated that combination of tea culture experience and urban leisure tourism can promote the further development of tourism industry. Moreover, Qi et al. (2019) indicated several strategies in promoting tea culture in China as leisure tour with professional tea merchants, senior tea friends travel as the main tea mountain free travel, team travel by enterprise customers and employees and self-driving tour with family. Liu (2019) identified government intervention as the most essential factor in developing the tea culture tourism. Further, Lin and Wen (2018) identified tea tourism as a platform for individual development. Tourist visits, nature and the tea taste plays a major role in tea tourism (Su & Zhang, 2020). Further some of the several tea and tourism integration techniques in China are; appreciating tea landscapes, visiting tea shops and tea museums, demonstration of tea processing, tea ceremony and cultural events, tea tasting, tea featured cuisine and tea featured accommodations (Su et al., 2019). Wang, Chen, et al. (2019) highlighted the importance of deconstruction to urban heritage sites as such locations are divided into the tourism zones of cultural, leisure and landscape spaces. Further gender plays a major role in developing the inter-tourist relationships (Xu & Ye, 2016).

Iran

Tourists are interested in Agri tours and both tangible and intangible agricultural heritage (Farsani et al., 2019). Torabi Farsani et al. (2018) indicated that herbal medicine tourism as an integrated type of tourism that involves outdoor activities, including festivals, workshops in herbal medicine tourist parks/ farms, and the natural habitats of plants to popularize the therapeutic properties of medicinal plants and to preserve traditional medicine as for intangible cultural heritage.

Sri Lanka

When considering tea tourism in Sri Lanka, lack of activities in tea tourism outlets and other pleasure activities dissatisfied the tourists (Fernando et al., 2017). Mahaliyanaarachchi (2016) identified that potential of Agri tourism as a risk management strategy in rural agriculture sector with special reference to developing countries. Aslam and Jolliffe (2015) found that various forms of historic lodging and recreation facilities for the plantation industries of planters' such as bungalows, rest houses, and planters' clubs contributes to tourism development.

Japan

Soltani et al. (2018) identified five main factors contributing to the success tourism as government support, power of emotional attachment and anthropomorphism, efficient public transport and tourism services, the mascot branding, and social media. It was during the late nineteenth and early twentieth centuries that Japanese department stores such as Mitsukoshi, Takashimaya, and Daimaru first emerged as "display palaces for Western imports, which the Japanese were eager to see and purchase (Loh,2020). By offering instruction in cooking, the use of cutlery, and table setting, and by hiring sales assistants to instruct customers in Western dress, they played a pivotal role in introducing Western food and dress to the Japanese (Loh,2020). In the 2000s, the Japanese manga and magazine industry reaffirms these sentiments and exploits them to its own advantage, manipulating both young Japanese women's perceptions of their cultural belatedness and their desire to purchase both British heritage commodities as well as the Japanese 'heritage texts' that promote these commodities (Loh,2020).

Switzerland

Jordan (2018) investigated the consumption of tea and coffee in 17th and 18th centuries Bern. During the 17th and 18th centuries, Europe imported consumer goods such as porcelain, spices, tea and coffee, textiles, silk, and cotton etc. It was identified that public coffee consumption was done in coffeehouses, taverns, and inns. which further illustrates the need to investigate the historical destinations about tea and coffee for tourism. Ramsey et al. (2019) presented an example of a border region with two-way traffic for cross-border shopping tourism specifically considering Germany and Switzerland and identified that shopping tourism in Konstanz persuades non-shopping tourism activity such as visitors frequenting restaurants or cultural institutions in the old town of Konstanz, stay overnight, or expand their demand for other goods and services such as wellness, medical care, car repair and real estate.

Canada

Smith (2015) demonstrated the importance of linking the culture with the tourism as cultural tourism and place-based activity in the context of marketing and product development could be done using event-based or attractions-based marketing, word-of-mouth promotion and through video and photography of the destinations. However, the nature of agricultural production, the availability of other supporting cultural and tourism products, and proximity to markets vary from place to place (Lee et al., 2015).

Pakistan

Islam et al. (2019) revealed that revisit intention of coffee users is based on various factors, including their involvement, authenticity, interpersonal justice, and prior experience with the cafe. These findings, thus, use a valuable message for cafe managers as they are required to ensure that customers should repeat their visits. Therefore, infrastructure development is identified as a necessary component in promoting tourism.

Indonesia

This study aimed to portray how Indonesian food culture has been shaped, developed, and held as the value embedded in the society and has been passed from one generation to the next (Wijaya, 2019). This study is anticipated to function as a starter contribution to increase the market awareness of Indonesian cuisine and its richness particularly through the exploration of socio-cultural aspect (Wijaya, 2019).

Turkey

For Turkey food was rarely presented in the marketing communications for Istanbul, and it was often called a supplementary product rather than a major destination attraction (Okumus & Cetin, 2018). Researchers have found that rural tourism experiences are diverse and heterogeneous, depending on the type of experience, activity, local food and beverage, accommodation, souvenirs, testify wildlife rehabilitation, transportation, and negative experiences. Tourism companies may be asked to design and manage their products and services for rural tourism experiences (Akay, 2020). As defined by the definition of rural tourism, it refers to the presence of people in natural environments, the ability to rest and the desire to be in close contact with people from different cultural backgrounds, to travel to rural settlements and stay in accommodation businesses specific to those areas, to enjoy the foods and beverages of that region, as well as to discover and discover and experience the abstract and concrete culture of that region (Akay, 2020).

Cetin, 2018). Similar to Indonesia, the awareness on traditional cuisine is identified as an important promotional strategy.

5. DISCUSSION OF THE FINDINS BASED ON THE PERSPECTIVES OF FEMALE TOURISTS

Food consumption is a key concept in hospitality literature. In spite of its importance in ensuring tourists have an enjoyable travel experience as well as its influence on tourists' perceptions of a destination, the impact of travellers' local food consumption on tourist behaviour remains unclear (Rousta & Jamshidi, 2020). A major topic for destination managers, researchers, and marketers is the topic of food (culinary) tourism, especially since food consumption is an integral part of the tourism business (Robinson & Getz, 2014; Rousta & Jamshidi, 2020). Food has become a major driving force for male tourists, whereas females are more interested in gathering knowledge before their excursions, so advertising may be targeted at female tourists (Sengel et al., 2015).

The study examined different methods of promoting food tourism in seventeen (17) different countries. The authors reviewed the latest literature published during the period 2015 to 2020 in top management, food, and nutrition journals based on Asia, Europe, Africa, and North America (Sengel et al., 2015). Restaurants that cater to visitors may be able to maximise the influence of positive word of mouth by focusing on married men and single women, since these groups are more likely to share their local cuisine experiences with their friends and family (Sengel et al., 2015). Food has become a travel motivator for males, whereas females are more interested with gathering knowledge before to their excursions, so management may aim their advertisements to female tourists (Sengel et al., 2015). Robinson and Getz (2014) **suggested that** food tourists are typically females with well-education and money. They desire diverse, regional, and authentic experiences that are tactile rather than passive, and they are prepared to travel for food (and drink) that is matched by cultural and tourist activities (Robinson and Getz, 2014). The findings indicate three categories of food-related behaviour (Chen and Huang, 2018). While gender appears to be important, other demographic criteria, such as age and educational level, do not appear to impact Chinese domestic visitors' degree of interest and participation in local food (Chen and Huang, 2018).

Researchers identified several promotional strategies based on tea, coffee, and food products. As an example, Thailand may be perceived as having a high level of awareness of the local community; Kenya may lack the necessary resources and infrastructure facilities to promote tourism. In addition, traditional food blogs and reviews are prevalent in Malaysia. In Korea, it was found that coffee shop managers must create multidimensional value for customers by enhancing their consumption experiences. Establishing a strong brand in Russia was identified as a vital strategy. Taiwan, Costa Rica, and Rwanda need to focus on long-term methods of tourism development. Gupta, Khanna, and Gupta (2019) found that street food preference is higher among male tourists than female tourists and it was shown that there is a substantial association between the age of the visitors and their taste for street cuisine. Chavarria and Phakdee-auksorn (2017) stated that the overall attitude of foreign visitors towards street cuisine in Phuket and to determine which variables are most essential in predicting their behavioural intentions. Chavarria and Phakdee-auksorn (2017) mentioned that both men and women have a good attitude towards street food.

Furthermore, both groups appeared to rank each of the food features fairly similarly, they are concerned about hygiene, and they perceive food quality to be good in the same areas. It was believed that there would be a difference in attitudes between Western and Asian tourists because food in Phuket may be more familiar to Asian travellers (Chavarria and Phakdee-auksorn, 2017). However, in this study, both groups indicated comparable attitudes, which might be attributed to globalisation, access to information, and the growing presence of ethnic Thai restaurants in both Western and Asian nations. Foodies are often women with higher salaries who desire active travel experiences. Foodies are complicated and multidimensional, and various sorts of foodies have different location choices (Knollenberg, Duffy, Kline, Kim, 2021).

Ying, Wen, Law, Wang, and Norman (2018) experimentally validated the efficacy of a single-item self-classification technique. Further, all respondents stated that they were interested in experiencing a place through the consumption of local food and the robustness of this study self-classification measure is investigated by comparing it to a data-driven multidimensional psychographic method in terms of its capacity to predict tourist behaviours towards food-related destination consumption (Ying, Wen, Law, Wang, and Norman, 2018). As a result, China was identified with several destination marketing strategies, such as leisure tours with professional tea merchants, appreciation of tea landscapes, visiting tea shops and tea museums, demonstrations of tea processing, traditional tea ceremonies and cultural events, tea tastings, tea themed cuisine, as well as tea themed accommodations. Herbal medicine tourism is popular in Iran.

There is evidence in Sri Lanka that Agritourism through various forms of historical lodging and recreation facilities for the plantation industries of planters such as bungalows, rest houses, and planters' clubs contributes to the development of tourism (Chen and Huang, 2018). The governments of Japan, Switzerland, and Canada are using social media marketing to promote tea tourism, as well as event-based, attraction-based, word-of-mouth, and location-based promotions (Ying, Wen, Law, Wang, and Norman, 2018). Pakistan, Indonesia, and Turkey were identified with several promotional strategies such as infrastructure development and market awareness on traditional cuisine (Ying, Wen, Law, Wang, and Norman, 2018). The findings of this study are of great value to companies engaged in food tourism (such as hotels, restaurants, clubs, and pubs) regarding how to promote tourism through unique cultural food products. The principal limitation of the study is that it focuses solely on promoting tourism through food products with a particular focus on female tourists and excludes other food types such as wine, traditional cuisine, and healthy products (Chen & Huang, 2018).

A study of Chinese female travellers revealed three types of food-related behaviour. Other demographic factors such as age and education level do not appear to influence the level of interest and engagement in local food among Chinese tourists (Chen & Huang, 2018). In the Indian setting, men visitors love street food more than female tourists. It was shown that there is a significant relationship between the age of the tourists and their preference for street food (Gupta et al., 2019). As both female and male visitors focus on food safety, both men and women have a positive view of street food in Thailand (Chavarria & Phakdee-auksorn, 2017; Sirigunna, 2015). According to Wang et al. (2021), female visitors waste much more food, meaning that females are more likely to order and waste meals that they do not enjoy.

Sengel et al. (2015) study found that visitors are interested in local cuisine as an attraction by analysing the elements influencing local food demand in tourism. Restaurants that cater to visitors may be able to maximise the influence of positive word of mouth by focusing on married men and single women, since these groups are more likely to share their local cuisine experiences with their friends and family (Sengel et al., 2015). Further when considering the perspectives of female tourists, food has become a travel motivator for males, whereas females are more interested with gathering knowledge before to their excursions, so management may aim their advertisements to female tourists (Sengel et al., 2015). Food tourists in Asia Pacific countries are generally females with a good education and a lot of money (Robinson & Getz, 2014). They are looking for different, regional, and authentic experiences that are tactile rather than passive, and they are willing to travel for food (and drink) that is accompanied by cultural and tourism activities (Robinson & Getz, 2014). Similarly, in the United States, food-based tourism is frequently undertaken by women with greater incomes who seek active vacation experiences. Foodies are complex and diverse, and different types of foodies have distinct location preferences (Knollenberg et al., 2021).

In Asia Pacific countries mostly food tourists are typically females with well-education and money (Robinson & Getz, 2014). They desire diverse, regional, and authentic experiences that are tactile rather than passive, and they are prepared to travel for food (and drink) that is matched by cultural and tourist activities (Robinson & Getz, 2014). Similarly, in USA food-based tourism was done often by women with higher salaries who desire active travel experiences. Foodies are complicated and multidimensional, and various sorts of foodies have different location choices (Knollenberg et al., 2021). Further, consumers' food selection intentions and behaviours when travelling are discordant with their diet routines at home. In the everyday environment, both male and female respondents consumed considerably more whole grains, vegetables, and fruits than in the trip scenario (Wang, Lehto, et al., 2019).

When considering the Chinese female tourists, findings indicated three categories of food-related behaviour. While gender appears to be important, other demographic criteria, such as age and educational level, do not appear to impact Chinese domestic visitors' degree of interest and participation in local food (Chen & Huang, 2018). In Indian context, street food preference is higher among male tourists than female tourists. It was shown that there is a substantial association between the age of the visitors and their taste for street cuisine (Gupta et al., 2019). Both men and women have a good attitude towards street food in Thailand (Chavarria & Phakdee-auksorn, 2017; Sirigunna, 2015) as both female and male tourists focuses on food hygiene. Wang et al. (2021) indicated that female tourists waste significantly more food implying that females are more likely to order food that they do not like and hence waste.

6. CONCLUSION

This study discussed different promoting strategies of food tourism in seventeen (17) different countries. To this end, the authors reviewed the latest literature published during the period 2015 to 2020 in top management, food and nutrition journals based on the regions of Asia, Europe, Africa, and North America. Authors identified several promotional strategies based on tea, coffee, and different food products. This study contributes to the current literature in two ways. Firstly, this study contributes by becoming the first systematic literature review on different marketing strategies used by different countries in promoting food tourism with special reference to the viewpoints of female tourists during the period 2015 to 2021. Secondly, when considering the theoretical contribution, this study used several PRISMA guidelines (Preferred Reporting Items for Systematic Reviews and Meta-Analyses) in selecting the articles. By using these guidelines, this paper was able to provide an impartial analysis through selecting most relevant papers to be added for the review based on the inclusion and exclusion criteria.

REFERENCES

Ageeva, E., & Foroudi, P. (2019). Tourists' destination image through regional tourism: From supply and demand sides perspectives. *Journal of Business Research, 101*, 334–348. doi:10.1016/j.jbusres.2019.04.034

Agyeiwaah, E., Otoo, F. E., Suntikul, W., & Huang, W.-J. (2019). Understanding culinary tourist motivation, experience, satisfaction, and loyalty using a structural approach. *Journal of Travel & Tourism Marketing, 36*(3), 295–313. doi:10.1080/10548408.2018.1541775

Akay, H., & Baduna Koçyiğit, M. (2020). Flash flood potential prioritization of sub-basins in an ungauged basin in Turkey using traditional multi-criteria decision-making methods. *Soft Computing, 24*(18), 14251–14263. doi:10.100700500-020-04792-0

Anbalagan, K., & Lovelock, B. (2014). The potential for coffee tourism development in Rwanda–Neither black nor white. *Tourism and Hospitality Research, 14*(1-2), 81–96. doi:10.1177/1467358414529579

Aslam & Jolliffe. (2015). Repurposing colonial tea heritage through historic lodging. *Journal of Heritage Tourism, 10*(2), 111-128.

Bedford, E. (2020). *Value of the global tea market from 2018 to 2026*. Retrieved on November 8th, 2021, available at: www.statista.com/ statistics/326384/global-tea-beverage-market-size

Behl, A., Jayawardena, N., Pereira, V., Islam, N., Del Giudice, M., & Choudrie, J. (2022). Gamification and e-learning for young learners: A systematic literature review, bibliometric analysis, and future research agenda. *Technological Forecasting and Social Change, 176*, 1–24. doi:10.1016/j.techfore.2021.121445

Besky, S. (2014). The labor of terroir and the terroir of labor: Geographical indication and darjeeling tea plantations. *Agriculture and Human Values, 31*(1), 83–96. doi:10.100710460-013-9452-8

Brain, L. (2018). *Uganda chooses coffee tourism to boost its revenues*. Retrieved on December 9th 2021, available at: www. tourism-review.com/coffee-tourism-in-uganda-to-boost-profits-news10856

Brain, L. (2018). *Uganda chooses coffee tourism to boost its revenues?* Retrieved on 3rd December 2021. www. tourism-review.com/coffee-tourism-in-uganda-to-boost-profits-news10856

Candelo, E., Casalegno, C., Civera, C., & Büchi, G. (2019). A ticket to coffee: Stakeholder view and theoretical framework of coffee tourism benefits. *Tourism Analysis, 24*(3), 329–340. doi:10.3727/108354219X15511864843830

Chan. (2007). Film-induced tourism in Asia: A case study of Korean television drama and female viewers' motivation to visit Korea. *Tourism Culture Communication, 7*(3), 207-224.

Chavarria, & Phakdee-auksorn. (2017). Understanding international tourists' attitudes towards street food in Phuket, Thailand. *Tourism Management Perspectives, 21*, 66-73.

Chen & Huang. (2018). Local food in China: A viable destination attraction. *British Food Journal, 120*(1), 146-157.

Cohen, E., & Avieli, N. (2004). Food in tourism. *Annals of Tourism Research, 31*(4), 755–778. doi:10.1016/j.annals.2004.02.003

Cole. (2006). Qualitative research: a challenging paradigm for infection control. *British Journal of Infection Control, 7*(6), 25-29.

Farsani, N. T., Ghotbabadi, S. S., & Altafi, M. (2019). Agricultural heritage as a creative tourism attraction. *Asia Pacific Journal of Tourism Research, 24*(6), 541–549. doi:10.1080/10941665.2019.1593205

Farsani, T. (2018). Food heritage and promoting herbal medicine-based niche tourism in Isfahan, Iran. *Journal of Heritage Tourism, 13*(1), 77–87. doi:10.1080/1743873X.2016.1263307

Fernando, Rajapaksha, & Kumari. (2017). Tea tourism as a marketing tool: a strategy to develop the image of Sri Lanka as an attractive tourism destination. *Kelaniya Journal of Management, 5*(2).

Gesimba, Langat, Liu, & Wolukau. (2005). The tea industry in Kenya; The challenges and positive developments. *Journal of Applied Sciences*, *5*(2), 334–336. doi:10.3923/jas.2005.334.336

Gibson, L., Lynch, P. A., & Morrison, A. (2005). The local destination tourism network: Development issues. *Tourism Hospitality Planning Development*, *2*(2), 87–99. doi:10.1080/14790530500171708

Gupta, K., Khanna, K., & Gupta, R. K. (2019). Preferential analysis of street food amongst the foreign tourists: A case of Delhi region. *International Journal of Tourism Cities*, *6*(3), 511–528. doi:10.1108/IJTC-07-2018-0054

Haddaway, N. R., Collins, A. M., Coughlin, D., & Kirk, S. (2015). The role of Google Scholar in evidence reviews and its applicability to grey literature searching. *PLoS One*, *10*(9), 138–237. doi:10.1371/journal.pone.0138237 PMID:26379270

Hall, C. M., & Sharples, L. (2003). The consumption of experiences or the experience of consumption? An introduction to the tourism of taste. In C. M. Hall, L. Sharples, R. Mitchell, N. Macionis, & B. Cambourne (Eds.), *Food Tourism around the World*. Butterworth Heinemann. doi:10.1016/B978-0-7506-5503-3.50004-X

Hall, M., Sharples, L., Mitchell, R., Macionis, N., & Cambourne, B. (2004). *Food tourism around the world*. Routledge. doi:10.4324/9780080477862

Hedrick, J., Yeiser, M., Harris, C. L., Wampler, J. L., London, H. E., Patterson, A. C., & Wu, S. S. (2021). Infant Formula with Added Bovine Milk Fat Globule Membrane and Modified Iron Supports Growth and Normal Iron Status at One Year of Age: A Randomized Controlled Trial. *Nutrients*, *13*(12), 4541. doi:10.3390/nu13124541 PMID:34960093

Hedrick, V. E., Comber, D. L., Estabrooks, P. A., Savla, J., & Davy, B. M. (2010). The beverage intake questionnaire: Determining initial validity and reliability. *Journal of the American Dietetic Association*, *110*(8), 1227–1232. doi:10.1016/j.jada.2010.05.005 PMID:20656099

Ignatov, E., & Smith, S. (2006). Segmenting Canadian culinary tourists. *Current Issues in Tourism*, *9*(3), 235–255. doi:10.2167/cit/229.0

Islam, T., Ahmed, I., Ali, G., & Ahmer, Z. (2019). Emerging trend of coffee cafe in Pakistan: Factors affecting revisit intention. *British Food Journal*, *121*(9), 2132–2147. doi:10.1108/BFJ-12-2018-0805

Jarquin, W., Wiggins, L. D., Schieve, L. A., & Van Naarden-Braun, K. (2011). Racial disparities in community identification of autism spectrum disorders over time; Metropolitan Atlanta, Georgia, 2000–2006. *Journal of Developmental and Behavioral Pediatrics, 32*(3), 179–187. doi:10.1097/DBP.0b013e31820b4260 PMID:21293294

Jayasooriya, S. S. W. (2019). Exploring the potentials, issues, and challenges for community-based tea tourism development (with reference to hanthana mountains). *International Journal of Advance Research, Ideas and Innovations in Technology, 5*(2), 475–480.

Jayawardena, N. S. (2020). The e-learning persuasion through gamification: An elaboration likelihood model perspective. *Young Consumers, 22*(3), 480–502. doi:10.1108/YC-08-2020-1201

Jayawardena, N. S. (2021). The role of culture in student discipline of secondary schools in cross-cultural context: A systematic literature review and future research agenda. *International Journal of Educational Management, 35*(6), 1099–1123. doi:10.1108/IJEM-06-2020-0325

Jayawardena, N. S., Ross, M., & Grace, D. (2020). Exploring the relationship between Australian university websites and international student enrolments. *International Journal of Educational Management, 34*(10), 1527–1557. doi:10.1108/IJEM-02-2019-0068

Jayawardena, N. S., Ross, M., Quach, S., Behl, A., Gupta, M., & Lang, D. (2021). Effective online engagement strategies through gamification: A systematic literature review and a future research agenda. *Journal of Global Information Management, 30*(5), 1–25. doi:10.4018/JGIM.290370

Jordan, J. (2018). Global goods away from global trading points? Tea and coffee in early modern Bern. *History of Retailing Consumption, 4*(3), 217–234. doi:10.1080/2373518X.2018.1549401

Kaplan, U. (2017). From the tea to the coffee ceremony: Modernizing buddhist material culture in contemporary korea. *Material Religion: the Journal of Objects, Art and Belief, 13*(1), 1–22. doi:10.1080/17432200.2016.1271969

Kim, E. H., & Choi, C. (2012). Men's talk: A Korean American view of South Korean constructions of women, gender, and masculinity. In *Dangerous Women* (pp. 75–126). Routledge. doi:10.4324/9780203379424-7

Kim & Lee. (2017). Promoting customers' involvement with service brands: evidence from coffee shop customers. *Journal of Services Marketing*.

Knollenberg, D., Duffy, L. N., Kline, C., & Kim, G. (2021). Creating competitive advantage for food tourism destinations through food and beverage experiences. *Tourism Planning & Development, 18*(4), 379–397. doi:10.1080/21568316.2020.1798687

Kwanya, T. (2015). *Indigenous knowledge and socioeconomic development: indigenous tourism in Kenya.* Paper presented at the International Conference on Knowledge Management in Organizations. 10.1007/978-3-319-21009-4_26

Larsen, B., Brun, W., & Øgaard, T. (2009). What tourists worry about–Construction of a scale measuring tourist worries. *Tourism Management, 30*(2), 260–265. doi:10.1016/j.tourman.2008.06.004

Lee, W., Wall, G., & Kovacs, J. F. (2015). Creative food clusters and rural development through place branding: Culinary tourism initiatives in Stratford and Muskoka, Ontario, Canada. *Journal of Rural Studies, 39*, 133–144. doi:10.1016/j.jrurstud.2015.05.001

Lee. (2017). The Agriculture-Food-Tourism Industry Cluster in the Republic of Korea: The Formation and Growth Factors of Clusters in Regional Agriculture. In *A Multi-Industrial Linkages Approach to Cluster Building in East Asia* (pp. 55-71). Springer.

Li, W., Wen, T., & Leung, A. (2011). An Exploratory Study of the Travel Motivation of Chinese Female Outbound Tourists. *Journal of China Tourism Research, 7*(4), 411–424. doi:10.1080/19388160.2011.627020

Lin, Q., & Wen, J. J. (2018). Tea tourism and its impacts on ethnic marriage and labor division. *Journal of China Tourism Research, 14*(4), 461–483. doi:10.1080/19388160.2018.1511490

Liu, Y. (2019). Study on the Development of Tea Culture Tourism in Xinyang City. *World Scientific Research Journal, 5*(7), 17–22.

Loh, W. (2020). Japanese tourists in Victorian Britain: Japanese women and the British heritage industry. *Textual Practice, 34*(1), 87–106. doi:10.1080/0950236X.2018.1539031

Mahaliyanaarachchi, R. (2016). Agri Tourism as a Risk Management Strategy in Rural Agriculture Sector: With Special Reference to Developing Countries. *Journal of Agricultural Sciences–Sri Lanka, 11*(1), 1. doi:10.4038/jas.v11i1.8075

Mahendra, I.W., Sumantra, I.K., Widnyana, I.K., & Vipriyanti, N.U. (2020). Identification of potentials and community perceptions in tourism village planning based on potential resources. *International Journal of Research-GRANTHAALAYAH, 8*(4), 13-22.

Menke, A. (2018). *The global coffee industry*. Retrieved on November 8th, 2021, available at: https://globaledge.msu.edu/blog/post/ 55607/the-global-coffee-industry

Mu, L., Chen, Q., & Liang, F. (2019). *Research on the Combination Path of Tea Culture Experience and Urban Leisure Tourism.* Paper presented at the 2019 International Conference on Management, Education Technology and Economics (ICMETE 2019). 10.2991/icmete-19.2019.141

Okumus, B., & Cetin, G. (2018). Marketing Istanbul as a culinary destination. *Journal of Destination Marketing & Management, 9*, 340–346. doi:10.1016/j.jdmm.2018.03.008

Park, Satoh, Miki, Urushihara, & Sawada. (2015). Medications associated with falls in older people: systematic review of publications from a recent 5-year period. *European Journal of Clinical Pharmacology, 71*(12), 1429-1440.

Petit, N. (2007). Ethiopia's coffee sector: A bitter or better future? *Journal of Agrarian Change, 7*(2), 225–263. doi:10.1111/j.1471-0366.2007.00145.x

Poon, A. (1993). *Tourism, Technology and Competitive Strategies*. CAB International.

Qi, J., Li, J., Lu, Y., & Pu, Y. (2019). *A Study on the Tourism Development of Tea Mountain in Yunnan Province—Take Baiying Mountain in Lincang City as an example*. Paper presented at the 2019 2nd International Conference on Education, Economics and Social Science (ICEESS 2019).

Quan, S., & Wang, N. (2003). Towards a structural model of the tourist experience: An illustration from food experiences in tourism. *Tourism Management, 25*(3), 297–305. doi:10.1016/S0261-5177(03)00130-4

Rachão, S., Breda, Z., Fernandes, C., & Joukes, V. (2019). Food tourism and regional development: A systematic literature review. *European Journal of Tourism Research, 21*, 33–49. doi:10.54055/ejtr.v21i.357

Rachão, S., Breda, Z., Fernandes, C., & Joukes, V. (2020). Cocreation of tourism experiences: Are food-related activities being explored? *British Food Journal, 122*(3), 910–928. doi:10.1108/BFJ-10-2019-0769

Ramsey, D., Thimm, T., & Hehn, L. (2019). Cross-border Shopping Tourism: A Switzerland-Germany Case Study. European Journal of Tourism. *Hospitality Recreation, 9*(1), 3–17. doi:10.2478/ejthr-2019-0002

Ritchie, J. R. B., & Crouch, G. I. (2000). The competitive destination: A sustainability perspective. *Tourism Management, 21*, 1–7.

Robinson & Getz. (2014). Profiling potential food tourists: An Australian study. *British Food Journal, 116*(4), 690-706.

Rousta & Jamshidi. (2020). Food tourism value: Investigating the factors that influence tourists to revisit. *Journal of Vacation Marketing, 26*(1), 73-95.

Samoggia, A., & Riedel, B. (2018). Coffee consumption and purchasing behavior review: Insights for further research. *Appetite, 129*, 70–81. doi:10.1016/j.appet.2018.07.002 PMID:29991442

Saufi, A., O'Brien, D., & Wilkins, H. (2014). Inhibitors to host community participation in sustainable tourism development in developing countries. *Journal of Sustainable Tourism, 22*(5), 801–820. doi:10.1080/09669582.2013.861468

Scott, C., Cooper, C., & Baggio, R. (2008). Destination networks: Four Australian cases. *Annals of Tourism Research, 35*(1), 169–188. doi:10.1016/j.annals.2007.07.004

Sengel, K., & Cetin, D. (2015). Tourists' approach to local food. *Procedia: Social and Behavioral Sciences, 195*, 429–437. doi:10.1016/j.sbspro.2015.06.485

Setati, Chitera, & Essien. (2009). Research on multilingualism in mathematics education in South Africa: 2000–2007. *African Journal of Research in Mathematics, Science Technology Education, 13*(1), 65-80.

Shin, C.-S., Hwang, G.-S., Lee, H.-W., & Cho, S.-R. (2015). The impact of Korean franchise coffee shop service quality and atmosphere on customer satisfaction and loyalty. *The Journal of Business Economics Environmental Studies, 5*(4), 47–57. doi:10.13106/eajbm.2015.vol5.no4.47.

Sirigunna. (2015). Food safety in Thailand: A comparison between inbound senior and non-senior tourists. *Procedia-Social Behavioral Sciences, 197*, 2115-2119.

Smith, N., Suthitakon, N., Gulthawatvichai, T., & Karnjanakit, S. (2019b). "Creating a coffee tourism network in the North of Thailand", Local Economy. *The Journal of the Local Economy Policy Unit, 34*(7), 718–729. doi:10.1177/0269094219893272

Smith, S., Suthitakon, N., Gulthawatvichai, T., & Karnjanakit, S. (2019). Creating a coffee tourism network in the north of Thailand. *Local Economy, 34*(7), 718–729. doi:10.1177/0269094219893272

Smith. (2015). A sense of place: Place, culture and tourism. *Tourism Recreation Research, 40*(2), 220-233.

Soltani, A., Pieters, J., Young, J., & Sun, Z. (2018). Exploring city branding strategies and their impacts on local tourism success, the case study of Kumamoto Prefecture, Japan. *Asia Pacific Journal of Tourism Research, 23*(2), 158–169. doi:10.1080/10941665.2017.1410195

Statista. (2021). Retrieved on 2nd December 2021. https://www.statista.com/statisticsshare-of-subscribers-to-travel-programs-worldwide-by-gender

Su, M. M., Sun, Y., Wall, G., & Min, Q. (2020). Agricultural heritage conservation, tourism and community livelihood in the process of urbanization – Xuanhua grape garden, Hebei province, China. *Asia Pacific Journal of Tourism Research, 25*(3), 205–222. doi:10.1080/10941665.2019.1688366

Su, W., Wall, G., & Wang, Y. (2019). Integrating tea and tourism: A sustainable livelihoods approach. *Journal of Sustainable Tourism, 27*(10), 1591–1608. doi:10.1080/09669582.2019.1648482

Su & Zhang. (2020). Tea drinking and the tastescapes of wellbeing in tourism. *Tourism Geographies*, 1-21.

Tan, E., & Bakar, B. A. (2016). The Asian Female Tourist Gaze: A Conceptual Framework. In Asian genders in tourism (pp. 65-87). Channel View Publications.

Tayibnapis, A. Z., & Sundari, M. S. (2020). Boosting indonesia's tourism sector to be competitive. *International Journal of Management & Business Studies, 10*(1), 9–14.

Ting, H., De Run, E. C., Cheah, J.-H., & Chuah, F. (2016). Food neophobia and ethnic food consumption intention. *British Food Journal, 118*(11), 2781–2797. doi:10.1108/BFJ-12-2015-0492

Ting, H., Fam, K.-S., Hwa, J. C. J., Richard, J. E., & Xing, N. (2019). Ethnic food consumption intention at the touring destination: The national and regional perspectives using multi-group analysis. *Tourism Management, 71*, 518–529. doi:10.1016/j.tourman.2018.11.001

Ummiroh, I. R., & Hardiyani, R. (2013). Agro-ecotourism management through cooperative based coffee plantation commodity to increase welfare of coffee farmer. *Journal of Economics, Business and Management, 1*(4), 347–349. doi:10.7763/JOEBM.2013.V1.75

Wang, C., Chen, L.-H., Su, P., & Morrison, A. M. (2019). The right brew? An analysis of the tourism experiences in rural Taiwan's coffee estates. *Tourism Management Perspectives, 30*, 147–158. doi:10.1016/j.tmp.2019.02.009

Wang, F., Filimonau, V., & Li, Y. (2021). Exploring the patterns of food waste generation by tourists in a popular destination. *Journal of Cleaner Production, 279*, 1–16. doi:10.1016/j.jclepro.2020.123890

Wang, L., Lehto, X., & Cai, L. (2019). Creature of habit or embracer of change? Contrasting consumer daily food behavior with the tourism scenario. *Journal of Hospitality & Tourism Research (Washington, D.C.), 43*(4), 595–616. doi:10.1177/1096348018817586

Weed. (2005). *"Meta interpretation": A method for the interpretive synthesis of qualitative research.* Paper presented at the Forum Qualitative Sozialforschung/ Forum: Qualitative Social Research, Forum Qualitative Sozialforschung.

Wijaya, S. (2019). Indonesian food culture mapping: A starter contribution to promote Indonesian culinary tourism. *Journal of Ethnic Foods, 6*(1), 9. doi:10.118642779-019-0009-3

Wipulasena, A. (2020). *Tea tourism: Beyond just a cup of tea.* Retrieved on 2nd December 2021.www.dailynews.lk/2020/08/ 25/features/226821/tea-tourism-beyond-just-cup-tea

World Food Travel Association. (2020). *What is food tourism?* Retrieved on 3rd November 2021. https://worldfoodtravel.org/what-is-food-tourism-definition-food-tourism

Woyesa, T., & Kumar, S. (2020). Potential of coffee tourism for rural development in Ethiopia: a sustainable livelihood approach. *Environment, Development and Sustainability*. doi: 2Fs10668-020-00610-7 doi:10.1007%

Woyesa, T., & Kumar, S. (2020). Potential of coffee tourism for rural development in Ethiopia: a sustainable livelihood approach. *Environment, Development and Sustainability*. doi: 2Fs10668-020-00610-7 doi:10.1007%

Xu & Ye. (2016). Tourist Experience in Lijiang—The Capital of Yanyu. *Journal of China Tourism Research, 12*(1), 108-125.

Ying, W., & Law, W. (2018). Examining the efficacy of self-classification approach in segmenting special-interest tourists: Food tourism case. *Asia Pacific Journal of Tourism Research, 23*(10), 961–974. doi:10.1080/10941665.2018.1513048

Yousaf, S., & Xiucheng, F. (2018). Halal culinary and tourism marketing strategies on government websites: A preliminary analysis. *Tourism Management, 68*(1), 423–443. doi:10.1016/j.tourman.2018.04.006

Zhang & Hitchcock. (2017). The Chinese female tourist gaze: A netnography of young women's blogs on Macao. *Current Issues in Tourism, 20*(3), 315-330.

Zhou, M., Hsieh, Y. J., & Canziani, B. (2016). *Tea Tourism: Examining University Faculty Members' Expectations*. Academic Press.

Chapter 8
Gender Differences Among Brazilians' Perceptions About Safety When Selecting a Destination

Jakson Renner Rodrigues Soares
https://orcid.org/0000-0002-9859-8009
University of A Coruña, Spain & Universidade Estadual do Ceará, Brazil

Larissa Paola Macedo Castro Gabriel
Tourism, Economy, and Sustainability Research Group, UECE, Italy

Raquel Santiago-Romo
University of Santiago de Compostela, Spain

André Riani Costa Perinotto
https://orcid.org/0000-0001-7094-3758
Parnaíba Delta Federal University, Brazil

ABSTRACT

This research analyses the impact of the COVID-19 crisis on Brazilian expectation tourism. A questionnaire survey was used to assess the tourist expectation regarding safety in future travel. A total of 796 questionnaires were collected between 6 April and 6 May 2020. The data were analyzed with factorial analyzes and t-tests and revealed that the gender of respondents turns out to be an important variable in determining different expectations in future travels. The results show that there are new concerns from Brazilian tourists about safety at the destination, increasing interest in information about the health system and the endemic diseases of the region to which they intend to travel.

DOI: 10.4018/978-1-6684-4194-7.ch008

1. INTRODUCTION

World tourism activity in the year 2020 was affected, just like all major industries, due to the restrictions on mobility as a result of a pandemic (Gössling, Scott & Hall, 2020). Concretely, world tourism is expected to shrink a number within the 60% to 80% in that year (Urraco, 2020). Additionally, according to the highest tourism-related body, the hard blow suffered could mean the disappearance of millions of jobs in one of the sectors of the economy that employs the most of the labor force. In Brazil, the sector accounts for a lost around $25 billion dollars and about 400 thousand layoffs, it is possible to reach 700 thousand jobs this year (CNC, 2020). Also, according to CNC, the sector is important not only for the direct expenditure made by tourists, but it is also important for all the subsectors where individual investment in travel can reach such as transportation, shopping for handicrafts, accommodation, restaurants and bars.

While analyzing the evolution of tourism in this country, it is found that in the latest (most recent) study by the Consumer Survey—Travel Intention, which portrays the expectation of Brazilian families to consume tourism-related services in the next six months. FGV (2017) identified that 82.8% of Brazilians intend to travel domestically in the next months and 16.3% prefer the international destinations. Likewise, in the year before the Covid-19 pandemic, Brazilians traveled mostly within the country (96.1%) and for leisure reasons (86.5%), staying overnight between 2 and 5 nights (Hosteltur, 2020). However, this data certainly do not match the results expected for 2020, due to the environment developed since the beginning of the year.

Tourism is a social economic activity, which suffer influences from many different factors. Thus, many stakeholders are responsible for the tourism development of a specific place: local community, businesspersons, public and academic authorities. In this sense, knowing that in the process of choosing the destination of their next trip, potential tourists consider several aspects that would define the image of the destination, it is essential to know these factors and to work together to seek the real development for the place. Likewise, tourism was one of the most affected activities by the COVID-19 pandemic crisis (Couto et al., 2020). In that study Couto et al (2020), the authors investigated the impacts of COVID-19 crisis over the tourism expectations of the Azores Archipelago residents. They considered the health and safety of tourism.

Besides the tourist infrastructures such as restaurants, bars, museums, hotels… (Echtner & Ritchie, 1991; Baloglu & Mccleary, 1999; Chen & Uysal, 2002), there are number of factors that are understood to have gained special attention due to the atypical and unimaginable situation like the one which occurred with the worldwide pandemic. We are specially talking about safety and hospitality. Several authors (Fakeye & Crompton, 1991; Beerli & Martín, 2004) understand that these two aspects are relevant for potential tourists in their decision-making process regarding the destination where to travel. Videlicet, to feel safe and hospitality (understood as the interpersonal relationships between the local community and the visitor) are essential issues that many tourists assess before making their decision (George, 2003). Both are factors that are analyzed by consumers in the election of the next trip (Soares, 2015). Not only that, there were few studies that analyzed the attitudes and intentions of travel of tourists (Abraham et al., 2020).

From there derives this study, understanding that to act and manage to influence future behavior after the pandemic, it is also necessary to know the travel expectations of potential tourists. The main objective of our paper is to evaluate the relationship between the perception of safety and the tourists' choice of the destination while residing in Brazil after the Covid-19 pandemic, taking into account the gender differences of respondents. Even so, there is a focus on aspects related to safety because it is understood that it will be one of the first factors that Brazilian tourists will evaluate before choosing the destination where they will travel. Hence, this paper is organized in 5 sections. In addition to this introduction, the paper presents in the second part a review of the bibliography related to tourism and safety. In addition, the variables analyzed in the following stage of the study were identified. The next section will address the methodological steps and it analyzes performed with the SPSS software. The next section there are results discussion and finally it presents the conclusions found in this piece.

2. THE STUDY OF SAFETY IN THE TOURSIM SECTOR

Since the beginning of the crisis generated by the SARS-cov-2 coronavirus early 2020, there have been, worldwide, debates raised to try to understand how this new situation would influence tourism activity. Both in the general press or specialist in the tourist area, as well as in the academic circles, regardless of the content of the discussion, it is important the understanding how this new tourism will become a frequent theme in the media. With regard to recent news and less academic studies or reports, we can highlight conclusions such as those of (Herrera, 2020), who affirms that many of the pre-pandemic habits will recover in the short and medium term, however, others news affirm that habits will change over the years. For this tourist specialist, one of the sectors, which will suffer greatly the effects, is foods and beverages during touristic visits. In this sense, it is relevant to say that it is believed the small bars and restaurants will be more affected. By attracting the eye from the customer's point of view, a family restaurant can pass on a perception of unsafety; this is something that the new tourist will take into account when choosing. According to Tomaello (2020), some conclusions from specialists of the tourist trade collected in the Infobae Dialogue indicate that the interactions and liaisons with the residents or the immersion in the core of the places will be impacted in the near future by new habits. In the same venue, Crosby (2020) also states that social distance will be a major factor in the future post-pandemic. In the *Informe Viajes National Geographic: Las claves del turismo post covid-19*, indicates that there will be a change in tourist behavior regarding the distance of their next trip (Adamuz, 2020). This report states that there will be more domestic than international trips (both for reasons of perceived safety and legal limitations). States that people will continue to have the same interest in traveling (Urraco, 2020), given that the situation is temporary and soon the pandemic will resume to forgetness. But it is also worth noting that there will be an increase in the hiring of travel assistance, that is, the new tourist will be more concerned with hiring travel insurance (Hosteltur, 2020). On the other hand, Rubio Gil (2020) indicates that the quality of accommodation is an aspect to be considered by the demand. Nonetheless, endemic diseases will be something that will be present in the daily life of the new tourist (Galo, 2020), because there will be a greater need for sanitary control and it will require international vaccination certificates. Finally, it is also worth highlighting that the concern for safety will redefine the priorities of tourists when choosing a beach destination for their next vacation (Botero, Mercadé, Cabrera & Bombana, 2020).

While reviewing studies in academic circles, safety has been discussed for several years from different perspectives (George, 2003; Lovelock, 2004; Maclaurin, 2004), indeed, people pay more and more attention to travel risks (Cui, Liu, Chang, Duan & Li, 2016). Tourist safety is a pertinent global issue affecting travellers and destinations (Zou & Meng, 2019). That risk in tourism is studied to improve management (Fuches & Pizam, 2011), as an example, the situations experienced nowadays (Covid-19 pandemic) do not consider territories and policies nor do they respect structural limits. This discussion is very well presented in the book "Safety and Security in Tourism: Relationships, Management, and Marketing". In the editors' words, this book examines tourism safety and security issues to give a better knowledge base from which to respond to future events (Hall et al., 2003). They relate image, security and safety perceptions, consumer behavior, crisis and other aspects, which are key to destination management. Another factor that also appears in the academic review is food safety. Maclaurin (2004) investigated the influence of the perceived risk of foodborne diseases on the choice of destination and as well as how the sources of information on food safety influence this choice. Likewise, in tourism the concern with the quality of food is evident (Almeida & Hostins, 2011). However, it confirms that the experience with the gastronomic heritage prevails in the visitor's experience (Bahls et al., 2020). On the other hand, George (2003) researched the perception of physical security and safety of tourists in Cape Town and found that a number of personal factors (nationality or previous experience with crime) were also found to affect respondent's perceptions of safety and security. In his studies on the perception of security of tourism agents (Lovelock, 2004) found that these workers tend to have a more critical view. In this sense, we understand that the potential tourist will feel safer if they hire the services from an intermediary, since these people are trained to offer more realistic information about the chosen destination for the next trip. Also highlights the importance of communication in a time of crisis such as this, as both information and disinformation are spreading faster in current times, which can help or hinder the tourist industry very quickly (Wall, 2006). Finally, we identified that gender is a recurrent feature in the literature review on safety travel (Zou & Meng, 2019; Karagöz, Işık, Dogru & Zhang, 2020]. This is because perceptions are different and have a distinct impact on consumer intention and behavior. This study has a number of practical implications travel safety aiming to improve expectations among male and female tourists.

3. METHODOLOGY

To design the questionnaire, it was performed a literature review regarding the perception of safety. It was identified that tourists evaluate security at different levels: integrity (related to physical security) (George, 2003; Lovelock, 2004; Tarlow, 2014), food security (Maclaurin, 2004; Almeida & Hostins, 2011; Bahls, Beleze, Pires & Krause, 2020) and health-related security (Hall et al., 2003; Cui, Liu, Chang, Duan & Li, 2016). To justify the variables that would be analyzed, 13 tourism researchers were consulted on this topic. Finally, the scholars identified the items in the questionnaire that measure the reasons which influence the election of the next destination after the pandemic of Covid-19 (Figure 1). The Snowball sampling method was used in a non-probabilistic sample to reach the highest number of responses. There were 796 completed questionnaires, they were collected throughout Brazil based on the initial question "Do you have or did you have any trips planned for the next months?". Considering the Brazilian population, this allowed us a 5% margin of error and a 95% confidence interval. They were applied from April 6 to May 6, 2020, during the period when the country was immersed in the Covid-19 pandemic. For data analysis, the SPSS software (version 24) was used and the following statistical procedures were applied: 1. The First Stage, univariate statistical data were calculated for all items in the questionnaire. From this point on, we also performed the scale reliability test with the Cronbach alpha test. 2. The Second Stage, it was performed the t-tests in order to identify the subjects' perception by grouping them by gender.

Figure 1. Methodological approach.

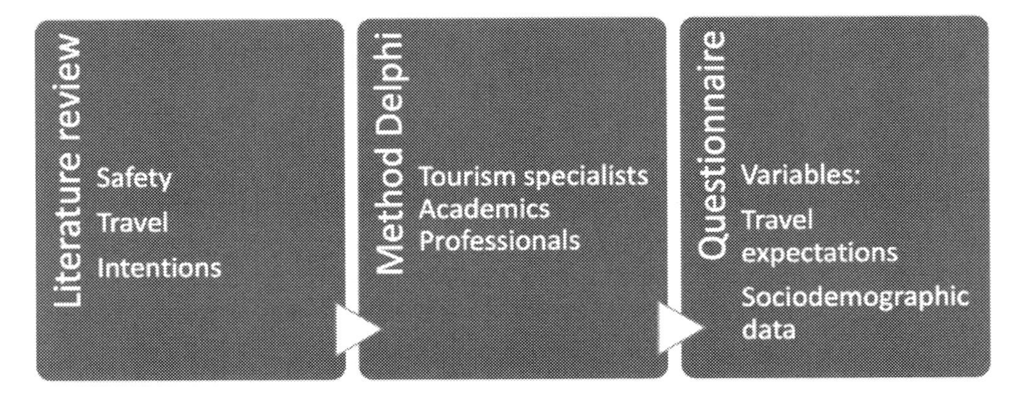

3.1 Questionnaire Design

A questionnaire was developed with the intention to evaluate and understand the expectations of Brazilian tourists and their future behavior in a post-pandemic world. Therefore, in addition to reviewing the literature and considering the impact of an unexpected situation on tourist behavior, it was decided to rely also on the vision of specialists in the tourism sector, by using the Delphi method, to identify a scale to be tested that could influence in choosing the destination after this moment of international stress. A group of 13 tourism specialists (academics and professionals) were consulted and asked how it will affect safety in this so-called new tourism. All highlighted aspects related to safety; hence this aspect has so far been little questioned by tourists when choosing a destination for their holidays. Each expert indicated their level of agreement with the previous expert's response until closing the indicators used in the questionnaire. In this approach to the tourism specialists, there was a need to seek information about the destination (not only sanitary, but also about the quality of the specifications). In carrying out Delphi, it was also identified that the tourist will have a perception of a greater need to feel secure in their decisions making process (knowledge about the destination's health situation, to hire services from brokers to complete the travel experience with a travel health insurance purchase) or during the stay at the destination (reduction on the interaction with locals or changes on eating habits while in the trip). As a result, the questionnaire was composed of two parts. The first part contained 13 variables adapted to the specifications of this study on travel expectations. The second part includes sociodemographic characteristics in respect of age, sex, education level and employment status. The items were measured with a Likert scale that ranged from 1 "strongly disagree" to 5 "strongly agree". Finally, the questionnaire has conformed to eighteen variables and an open question for the respondent to identify the country of the next trip.

4 RESULTS

The results listed below are given by direct analysis by the performed questionnaires. The sample researched is consisted of 34.3% men and 65.5% women. In general, there is a large presence of people with university and post-university studies (25.8% and 69% respectively). Regarding the employment situation, only 3.5% of respondents say they are unemployed; however, it highlights that the vast majority of probable responses that are active: the government employs 34.8%, 22.6% work with a formal contract and 20.7% have their own business. Finally, 8.2% of the responses are from students and 10.2% are from retired people. The main motivation for the planned trips was for leisure reasons such as visiting relatives and friends, studying abroad their usual place of residence, doing business or participating in congresses, tradeshows or meetings.

Table 1 below illustrates the profile of the sample by gender. As it is shown, there are no major representations in the age distribution by gender, except for those under 25, where females represent up to 10 times more than the percentage of males. Regarding the level of education, even if there is no great difference among the levels of one and the other, the group of females is composed largely from university-educated individuals on contrary with the male respondents. While verifying the employment situation, it is where differences are most noticeable when respondents are studying (the number of males in this situation is 3 times greater than females). Another aspect to be noticed is that there are more females in public jobs in than males, just as in the case of retired people, they are more retired females than males. Finally, note that the main reasons for travel coincide for both genders.

Thereafter, tow closed-ended questions regarding future travel were formulated (Table 2). The investigation inquired about the intentions of future trips (Table 2). Regardless of gender, Brazilian tourists have no interest in changing their intention to travel. The averages are quite high for the two statements related to not changing traveling behavior. Likewise, more than half of the sample agrees that they will continue to travel at the same frequency as before and that they do not intend to change the destination of the next trip. Therefore, in this new tourism, as soon as it is possible to travel again, Brazilians will continue to travel with the same frequency as before the situation resulting from the Covid-19 pandemic. An important fact to take into account is that there is no intention to change the destination they had planned.

Therefore, we try to identify the destinations, where in which the respondents indicate no intention to change their trip itinerary in case of their next trip after

Table 1. Sociodemographic aspects of the participants.

		Males 34.3%	**Females 65.5%**
Age	15 > 25	0.8%	7%
	26 > 25	21.5%	23.4%
	36 > 45	31.6%	29.5%
	46 > 55	23.3%	21.5%
	56 > 65	12.7%	15.2%
	>65	2.9%	3.2%
Education	(upper) secondary education	3.7%	2.9%
	Technical	2.9%	1.7%
	University	26.5%	25.5%
	Post-university	66.9%	69.9%
Employment Status	Student	11.6%	4.6%
	Unemployed	2.9%	3.8%
	Self-employed	22.5%	19.8%
	Formal jobs holder	23.6%	21.7%
	Public sector	32.4%	36.2%
	Retired	6.9%	12%
Motives for traveling	Leisure	4.09	4.23
	Friends and family	2.53	2.76
	Business	2.58	2.20
	Education	2.51	2.43
	Tradeshow Congress	2.36	2.26
	Concerts/Cultural events	1.72	1.72
	Shopping	1.84	1.82
	Religious	1.18	1.41
	Pilgrimage	1.16	1.26
	Sports	1.23	1.11

Source: Own elaboration with research data.

the isolation restrictions period is over. We identified that among the international destinations Portugal, Italy, France and Spain were the countries that most retained the tourists' interests. Although Europe was the first western continent to be hit by the health crisis, the preference for these destinations is due to several factors. The factors range from historical and cultural heritage interest, curiosity for a taste of local European gastronomy, European tourism products diversification, no visas

Table 2. Future travel intentions

Study Variables	Total			Males		Females		
	Agree	Average	Standard Deviation	Agree	Average	Agree	Average	*p*-Value
When this coronavirus situation is over, I will travel again with the same frequency.	66.2%	3.87	1.20	70.5%	3.93	64.0%	3.85	0.362
I will not change the destination of my next trip	56.2%	3.66	1.34	56.7%	3.66	56.2%	3.66	0.992

Source: Own elaboration with research data.

requirements, variety of different affordable direct air routes for the Brazilian middle class, easy travelling logistics within European countries, the knowledge of languages (Portuguese and Spanish) and as well as the interest in learning a new language (Spanish and French) (Tarlow, 2014).

Subsequently, eleven closed-ended questions regarding the perception of safety on the next trips (Table 3). As it can be observed in the averages for the statements, it was found that this new tourist would seek for a lot regarding the destination prior traveling. This is notorious because the averages of the statement I will seek more information about the destination before deciding where to travel (4.47) and I will find out if the destination is safe, (4.57) are the highest. In addition to being also, the statements where there is a higher level of agreement (87.5% and 92.3% respectively). On the other hand, the lowest average (2.20) indicates that this sample has no interest in changing their eating habits during the trip. That is, this new tourist does not believe that eating on familiar food chains generates more security on both trips.

To identify whether all variables explain expectations for future trips, we performed a factor analysis with principal component analysis extraction method with Varimax rotation method. To assess the degree of consistency between the variables, we followed the criterion of analyzing the reliability of the sample by controlling Cronbach's alpha and the total item correlation. The eleven items result in two factors (Table 4). All items must be considered because the factor loading is greater than 0.400 (Hair Jr, Anderson, Tatham & Black, 2005). Even so, in the analysis of the Showcase Adequacy Measure, the result for KMO was higher than the 0.80 of admirable performance. And Bartlett's Test of Sphericity indicates that the result is significant, since $p < 0.05$ (Hair Jr, Anderson, Tatham & Black, 2005). Thus, all items were respected; this measure is within the acceptable limit for the scale's reliability (Hair Jr., Gabriel & Patel, 2014).

The next step taken was to identify significant differences among the perceptions of the items that make up the measurement scale (Table 5). An examination of the

Table 3. Results for the statements regarding the perception of safety on the next trips

Study Variables	Total		
	Agree	Average	Standard Deviation
I will probably seek less possibilities to relate to the local population on my next trips	31.2%	2.70	1.35
I will definitely hire health insurance on my next trips	75.6%	4.17	1.16
The health system of my next destination will be an important factor in future trips	79.2%	4.13	1.02
I will taste the local food and gastronomy of the place because it is not dangerous	73.6%	4.07	1.14
I will eat at international food franchises because they are safer	18.2%	2.20	1.23
I will seek to travel closer	26.8%	2.45	1.37
I will seek better quality accommodation	74.6%	4.09	1.1
I will seek more information about the destination before deciding where to travel	87.5%	4.47	0.86
In order to decide where I am going, I will first consult the diseases characteristic of the place	74.6%	4.07	1.10
I'll find out if the destination is safe	92.3%	4.57	0.70
I will definitely book my trip at a travel agency	33.2%	2.74	1.47

Source: Own elaboration with research data.

available data reveals that there are some differences between the perceptions of males and females regarding how safety will influence their future tourist behavior.

Table 5 presents the results for the statements regarding the safety perception in travel decisions. Similarly, it is possible to affirm that males and females will expect the same way with respect to some aspects. In this fashion, this new tourist will not decrease contact with the local population, that is, the relational exchanges provided by tourism will continue to form part of the tourist experiences of Brazilian tourists. Unlike the assumptions, at the beginning of this investigation, tourists have no intention of traveling closer, which means that distance does not create a feeling of unsafety. Another aspect to note is that Brazilian tourists do not intend to hire intermediary services for their next trips. Finally, the new tourist considers that the quality of accommodation will be decisive in his choices.

The focus of this paper was the relevance of the Brazilian tourist's expectations according to their perceptions about travel safety from a gender perspective, thus, according to performed analyzes, it was identified that the intention of both will be subject to issues of safety. The lowest averages are in the items "decrease contact with the local population", "trust more in international catering chains" and "seek

Table 4. Factors that conform the expectations of Brazilian tourists in postpandemic

Study Variables	Factor 1	Factor 2
I will definitely hire health insurance on my next trips	0.515	
The health system of my next destination will be an important factor in future trips	0.664	
I will seek better quality accommodation	0.599	
I will seek more information about the destination before deciding where to travel	0.736	
In order to decide where I am going, I will first consult the diseases characteristic of the place	0.694	
I'll find out if the destination is safe	0.780	
I will probably seek less possibilities to relate to the local population on my next trips		0.676
I will taste the local food and gastronomy of the place because it is not dangerous		0.786
I will eat at international food franchises because they are safer		0.749
I will seek to travel closer		0.649
I will definitely book my trip at a travel agency		0.404
Cronbach's alpha	**0.772**	**0.703**
Bartlett's Test of Sphericity Qui-cadrado	**2035,802 sig. 0,000**	
KMO Measure	**0.838**	

Source: Own elaboration with research data.

to travel closer". That is, Brazilian tourists indicate with their responses that they do not realize that contact with people at the destination (hospitality), that gastronomy and that distance are aspects that offer a feeling of insecurity. In other words, for Brazilian tourists, these aspects will not cause changes in the way they travel.

Nonetheless, there are some significant differences in relation to gender, understanding that females are a little more concerned with some of the items questioned in this study. In addition, they agree that these are also the highest averages, that is, these are the items of greatest concern.

5. MAIN RESULTS AND CONTRIBUTIONS

Significant differences are perceived in 6 of the 11 items that make up this measurement scale. Thus, in order to characterize the future behavior of Brazilian tourists, it possible to say that females will be more concerned with safety than males. This is because they are more intent on "Hiring health insurance", "Consult the health system", "Search for varied information before traveling", "Consult endemic diseases" and "Check if the destination is safe". Corroborating this result

Table 5. Results for the statements regarding the perception of safety on the next trips

Study Variables	Males		Females		
	Agree	Average	Agree	Average	*p*-Value
I will probably seek less possibilities to relate to the local population on my next trips	29.5%	2.67	32.2%	2.71	0.680
The health system of my next destination will be an important factor in future trips	73.8%	3.93	82.1%	4.23	0.000
I will taste the local food and gastronomy of the place because it is not dangerous	77.8%	4.22	71.4%	4.00	0.008
I will eat at international food franchises because they are safer	15.3%	2.13	19.8%	2.24	0.210
I will seek to travel closer	24.7%	2.39	28.0%	2.48	0.384
I will seek better quality accommodation	70.9%	3.99	76.6%	4.14	0.057
I will seek more information about the destination before deciding where to travel	81.8%	4.31	90.7%	4.56	0.000
In order to decide where I am going, I will first consult the diseases characteristic of the place	69.5%	3.87	77.1%	4.18	0.000
I'll find out if the destination is safe	89.5%	4.45	93.7%	4.64	0.000
When this coronavirus situation is over, I will travel again with the same frequency	70.5%	3.93	64.0%	3.85	0.362
I will not change the destination of my next trip	56.7%	3.66	56.2%	3.66	0.992
Cronbach's alpha: 0.791					

Source: Own elaboration with research data.

(Araújo, Martins & Perinotto, 2020), the safety aspect is one of the most important for women, being a concern in choosing a destination. Women feel vulnerable and exposed to dangerous situations when they are unaccompanied. Violence against women means a neat form of the sexist patterns introduced by society, generating in them insecurities with everything and everyone, directly interfering in their choices.

The average for the item related to continue tasting local cuisine is high for both genders. It will continue to arouse interest for both males and females. However, the results indicate that there is a significant difference between gender expectations. That is, males will be more willing to taste the gastronomy than females are. Thus, our results match with those of Maclaurin (2004), who found that women consider food safety more important than males.

It is noteworthy that the people surveyed have no intention, in general terms, to renounce tourism as part of their leisure agenda. This first result is an important contribution to the management of tourist destinations, since tourism planning policies must continue to act in such a way as to continue to position the destination in the mind of the potential tourist. While it is certain that the time is not to sell trips, a correct point is that from the moment they can travel, Brazilian tourists intend to continue traveling with the same intensity as they traveled before the pandemic. Therefore, it is up to the destinations to become competitive in order to attract this tourist. Thus, it is worth highlighting the resilient character of the sector, which despite being affected by the balance of payments due to a lower inflow of foreign currency in the destination, it is easy to recover in the short and medium term (Sánchez, 2020).

The COVID-19 has substantially changed the paradigm of residents' attitudes in choosing the form of vacation (Couto et al., 2020). Regardless of, a relevant aspect that deserves to be highlighted is that, unlike what was identified in recent studies on the increase of domestic tourism as a solution for the tourism sector (Herrera, 2020; Rubio Gil, 2020; TRLV, 2020), according to the analyzes carried out, the Brazilian tourist has no intention of changing his trips and starting to travel closer. That is, this expectative is not identified in the data analysis. Which shows that Brazilian tourists are loyal to the destinations they would travel to and trust the brand of the destination (Tarlow, 2014). Concretely, according to the data, the tourist understands that the pandemic is a passing thing and that the destination to which they had planned their trip has a negative impact due to the health crisis. In addition, new concerns are noted among tourists residing in Brazil about safety at the destination, increasing the search for information about the health system and diseases endemic to the region to which they will travel.

6. CONCLUSION

Based on the results of the study, we conclude that tourist destinations must communicate quickly to generate more security for potential Brazilian tourists. Our results highlight the need for Brazilian tourists to obtain more information to organize their trip. Therefore, it is up to marketers to work to meet this need. It can be concluded that the concern of females for getting informed about the destination increases before choosing the next trip. These results coincide with (Javed, Tučková & Jibril, 2020), which identified that gender is an important variable to discriminate the use of social networks. Understanding that they use these sources more to inform themselves before the trip. There is no change for males. For them, the concern for security aspects in post-Codiv-19 also increases. That's because they travel more than they do and, on many occasions, alone. Therefore, we conclude that there is a change in the intentions of females in relation to their travels.

Another relevant conclusion we reached is related to the communication and image of the tourist destination. The new tourist has demonstrated that he needs more information, not just health, to make a decision when choosing the next destination.

Therefore, the communication policies and strategies of the destinations must revolve around this function, to communicate. Efforts, therefore, must be aimed at keeping the potential tourist more informed, generating confidence in this consumer, dialoguing with him and increasing engagement through a more lasting relationship. Thus, it is increasingly necessary to use digital channels to chat directly with your potential customer.

Finally, we conclude that trips to Europe will not be affected because the image before the pandemic (of countries like Portugal, Italy, France and Spain) remains more important in the choice than the effects of covid-19. That is, after the crisis, the perception of Brazilians is that these destinations will be safe again. Thus, we can conclude that the crisis resulting from the SARS-cov-2 coronavirus pandemic does not seem to indicate a complete change in the expectative of the tourist consumer, and contrary to what was previously predicted, it is not that there will be a preference for domestic travel (Zenker & Kock, 2020). What our results have shown is that the needs of potential tourists are only more acute. That is, the need for information only shows that in tourism there remains a more relational communication between destination and tourist. Likewise, the tourist experience will not be affected according to the identified intentions. In short, hospitality and exchanges between resident and visitor remain necessary for the continuity of tourism.

The main limitation of the present investigation was the use of a non-probability sampling method. These methods do not guarantee the generalization of results for the population. Another limitation was not to differentiate the respondents' internal origin, perhaps this aspect was relevant to measure the differences in perceptions between the different areas of Brazil. In addition, the authors recommends this investigation should be conducted to other case studies.

REFERENCES

Abraham, V., Bremser, K., Carreno, M., Crowley-Cyr, L., & Moreno, M. (2020). Exploring the consequences of COVID-19 on tourist behaviors: Perceived travel risk, animosity and intentions to travel. *Tourism Review*. Advance online publication. doi:10.1108/TR-07-2020-0344

Adamuz, J. A. (2020). The keys to post-Covid-19 tourism [Las claves del turismo post Covid-19]. *National Geographic*. https://viajes. nationalgeographic. com. es/ lifestyle/turismo-despues-coronavirus_15469

Almeida, E. B. (2009). *The tourist's eating behavior and their safety in the consumption of green corn and churros by the sea* [O comportamento alimentar do turista e sua segurança no consumo de milho verde e churros à beira-mar]. Academic Press.

Bahls, A. A. D. S. M., Beleze, R. L., Pires, P. S., & Krause, R. W. (2020). Culinary Cultural Heritage vs. Hygiene and Food Safety: A possible inverse correlation. *Rev. Hosp.*, *17*, 115–139. doi:10.21714/2179-9164.2020.v17n1.007

Baloglu, S., & McCleary, K. W. (1999). A model of destination image formation. *Annals of Tourism Research*, *26*(4), 868–897. doi:10.1016/S0160-7383(99)00030-4

Beerli, A., & Martín, J. D. (2004). Tourists' characteristics and the perceived image of tourist destinations: A quantitative analysis—a case study of Lanzarote, Spain. *Tourism Management*, *25*(5), 623–636. doi:10.1016/j.tourman.2003.06.004

Botero, C. M., Mercadé, S., Cabrera, J. A., & Bombana, B. (2020). *Sun and beach tourism in the context of Covid-19; scenarios and recommendations* [El turismo de sol y playa en el contexto de la Covid-19; escenarios y recomendaciones]. Red Iberoam. Gestión Cert. Playas–PROPLAYAS.

Chen, J. S., & Uysal, M. (2002). Market positioning analysis: A hybrid approach. *Annals of Tourism Research*, *29*(4), 987–1003. doi:10.1016/S0160-7383(02)00003-8

Confederação Nacional do Comércio. (2020). *CNC Highlights Tourism Sector Effort During Brazilian Forum* [CNC Destaca Esforço do Setor de Turismo Durante Fórum Brasileiro]. Available online: http://www.cnc.org.br/editorias/turismo/noticias/cnc-destaca-esforco-do-setor-de-turismo-durante-forum-brasileiro

Couto, G., Castanho, R. A., Pimentel, P., Carvalho, C., Sousa, Á., & Santos, C. (2020). The impacts of COVID-19 crisis over the tourism expectations of the Azores Archipelago residents. *Sustainability*, *12*(18), 7612. doi:10.3390u12187612

Crosby, A. (2020). *The future is no longer what it was: Can tourism recover?* [El futuro ya no es lo que era: ¿Se podrá recuperar el turismo?]. Available online: https://www.hosteltur.com/comunidad/004373_el-futuro-ya-no-es-lo-que-era-se-podra-recuperar-el-turismo.html

Cui, F., Liu, Y., Chang, Y., Duan, J., & Li, J. (2016). An overview of tourism risk perception. *Natural Hazards*, *82*(1), 643–658. doi:10.100711069-016-2208-1

de Araújo, L. M., Martins, C., & Perinotto, A. R. C. (2021). Entrepreneurship and Innovation in Communities for Women Who Travel. In *Innovation and Entrepreneurial Opportunities in Community Tourism* (pp. 191–203). IGI Global. doi:10.4018/978-1-7998-4855-4.ch011

Echtner, C. M., & Ritchie, J. B. (1991). The meaning and measurement of destination image. *Journal of Tourism Studies*, *2*(2), 2–12.

Fakeye, P. C., & Crompton, J. L. (1991). Image differences between prospective, first-time, and repeat visitors to the Lower Rio Grande Valley. *Journal of Travel Research, 30*(2), 10–16. doi:10.1177/004728759103000202

Fuchs, G., & Pizam, A. (2011). 18 The Importance of Safety and Security for Tourism Destinations. *Destination Marketing and Management*, 300.

Fundação Getúlio Vargas. (2017). Consumer Survey: Travel Intention [Sondagem do Consumidor: Intenção de Viagem]. FGV Projetos, Ministério do Turismo.

Galo, I. (2020.) *Immunological Passport* [Pasaporte Inmunológico]. Available online: https://www.abc.es/viajar/noticias/abci-ocho-claves-como-sera-turismo-tras-covid-19-202005190148_noticia.html

George, R. (2003). Tourist's perceptions of safety and security while visiting Cape Town. *Tourism Management, 24*(5), 575–585. doi:10.1016/S0261-5177(03)00003-7

Gössling, S., Scott, D., & Hall, C. M. (2020). Pandemics, tourism and global change: A rapid assessment of COVID-19. *Journal of Sustainable Tourism, 29*(1), 1–20. doi:10.1080/09669582.2020.1758708

Hair, J. F., Black, W. C., Babin, B. J., Anderson, R. E., & Tatham, R. L. (2009). *Multivariate data analysis* [Análise multivariada de dados]. Bookman editora.

Hair, J. F. Jr, Gabriel, M. L., & Patel, V. K. (2014). Covariance-Based Structural Equation Modeling (CB-SEM) with AMOS: Guidelines on your application as a Marketing Research Tool [Modelagem de Equações Estruturais Baseada em Covariância (CB-SEM) com o AMOS: Orientações sobre a sua aplicação como uma Ferramenta de Pesquisa de Marketing]. *Revista Brasileira de Marketing, 13*(2), 44–55.

Hall, C. M., Timothy, D. J., & Duval, D. T. (2012). *Safety and security in tourism: relationships, management, and marketing*. Routledge. doi:10.4324/9780203049464

Herrera, J. M. V. (2020). *What Tourism Will Be Like After COVID-19* [Cómo Será el Turismo Después de la COVID-19]. Available online: https://www.entornoturistico.com/como-sera-el-turismo-despues-de-la-covid-19/

Hosteltur. (2020). *Hosteltur Entrevista a Erika Schamis, Head of Packages and Media at Almundo* [Head de Paquetes y Media de Almundo] [Video]. YouTube. Available online: https://youtu.be/HlxYc_6eKq8

Javed, M., Tučková, Z., & Jibril, A. B. (2020). The role of social media on tourists' behavior: An empirical analysis of millennials from the Czech Republic. *Sustainability, 12*(18), 7735. doi:10.3390u12187735

Karagöz, D., Işık, C., Dogru, T., & Zhang, L. (2021). Solo female travel risks, anxiety and travel intentions: Examining the moderating role of online psychological-social support. *Current Issues in Tourism*, *24*(11), 1595–1612. doi:10.1080/13683500.2020.1816929

Lovelock, B. (2004). New Zealand travel agent practice in the provision of advice for travel to risky destinations. *Journal of Travel & Tourism Marketing*, *15*(4), 259–279. doi:10.1300/J073v15n04_03

MacLaurin, T. L. (2004). The importance of food safety in travel planning and destination selection. *Journal of Travel & Tourism Marketing*, *15*(4), 233–257. doi:10.1300/J073v15n04_02

Rubio Gil, A. (2020). Spanish tourism after COVID-19 [El turismo español tras el COVID-19]. *Hosteltur*.

Sánchez, M. M. (2020). Tourism flows, geopolitics and COVID-19: When international tourists are vectors of transmission [Flujos turísticos, geopolítica y COVID-19: cuando los turistas internacionales son vectores de transmisión]. *Geopolítica*, *11*, 15.

Soares, J. R. R. (2015). *The Relationship between the Touristic Image and Loyalty: An Analysis of International Students in Galicia [Ph.D. Thesis]*. University of A Coruña. Available online http://hdl.handle.net/2183/14919

Tarlow, P. E. (2014). *Tourism Security: Strategies for Effectively Managing Travel Risk and Safety*. Butterworth-Heinemann.

Tomaello, F. (2020). *Tourism Experts from Around the World Analyze What It Will Be Like to Travel in the New Post-Pandemic Scenario* [Expertos Turismo de Todo el Mundo Analizan Cómo Será Viajar en el Nuevo Escenario Post Pandemia]. Available online: https://www.infobae.com/turismo/2020/06/14/expertos-turismo-de-todo-el-mundo-analizan-como-sera-viajar-en-el-nuevo-escenario-post-pandemia/

TRLV. (2020). *Pulse Tourism and Covid-19* [Pulso Turismo e Covid-19]. TRLV Lab.

Urraco, M. (2020). *What Will the Return of Tourism Be Like After the Lockdown?* [¿Cómo Será la Vuelta del Turismo Tras el Confinamiento?]. RTVE. Available online: https://www.rtve.es/noticias/20200422/como-sera-vuelta-del-turismo-tras-confinamiento/2012448.shtml

Wall, G. (2006). Recovering from SARS: the case of Toronto tourism. In Tourism, Security and Safety (pp. 143-152). Routledge. doi:10.1016/B978-0-7506-7898-8.50014-X

Zenker, S., & Kock, F. (2020). The coronavirus pandemic–A critical discussion of a tourism research agenda. *Tourism Management*, *81*, 104164. doi:10.1016/j.tourman.2020.104164 PMID:32518437

Zou, Y., & Meng, F. (2020). Chinese tourists' sense of safety: Perceptions of expected and experienced destination safety. *Current Issues in Tourism*, *23*(15), 1886–1899. doi:10.1080/13683500.2019.1681382

Chapter 9
Intersectionality Between Racism and Sexism in the Brazilian Airline Industry:
Perceptions and Strategies of Black Women Crewmembers

Natália Araújo de Oliveira
https://orcid.org/0000-0003-4815-8352
Federal University of Santa Maria, Brazil

Cassiana Gabrielli
Federal University of São Carlos, Brazil

Gabriela Nicolau dos Santos
Aveiro University, Portugal

Laiara Amorim Borges
Metropolitan College of the State of São Paulo, Brazil

ABSTRACT

This work aims to discuss the barriers of access and permanence of Black woman crewmembers in the Brazilian airline industry as well as resistance strategies faced by them. Using intersectionality in a theoretical-methodological way, this research, of qualitative nature, carried out interviews with six Black women of the aforementioned sector. The work revealed how the airline industry is an elitist environment that excludes Black bodies, making use of the domination of structural, cultural, disciplinary, and interpersonal powers in order to give white subjects the advantage. However, it was also possible to perceive strategies of affronting, which involve the union of the Black airline industry workers into a collective—the Quilombo Aéreo—helmed by women who sought to open opportunities for the insertion of more Black people into the airline industry, taking care of the mental health of the ones who already work there, and also be a beacon for support.

DOI: 10.4018/978-1-6684-4194-7.ch009

INTRODUCTION

Facing the lack of investigations that discuss tourism and racial relations in the Brazilian academic environment (Oliveira, 2021), the incipient stage of research regarding gender and tourism in Brazil (Gabrielli, 2021) and, also, due to the inexistence of debate concerning gender and race inequality in the airline industry (Calvet, Cond, Ballart, & Almela, 2021; Yu & Hyun, 2021), the following work emerges. Focusing specifically on Brazilian aviation, there is no in-depth analysis of professionals working in this area in the national academic production. Even data on the composition of the labor market in the airline industry are deficient in this context. Through this it is possible to identify only the number of licenses issued for each professional category, stratifying them by gender, while the racial issue is still neglected.

The absence of literature reported here makes it impossible (in addition to highlighting the need and urgency) an academic debate about how the national airline sector treats the black women who are there. More than that, it does not allow us to know who these women are, if they receive the same salary as men, if they have access to the most prestigious spaces in the activity, or at least, if they have the same working conditions and treatment as the other crew members. Faced with this problem, the general objective of this chapter is to investigate the barriers to access and permanence of black women crew members in the Brazilian airline sector, as well as the resistance strategies (both for access and for permanence) used by them. Using the intersectional perspective (of black feminism), the research focuses on manifestations of racism and sexism, themes linked to a critical debate on tourism.

Given the scarcity of data and production on the subject, which reflect, somehow, the lack of interest in discussing such issues on the part of official entities, research institutions and market operators, references and partnership were sought with the only identified entity, until then, which has guided racial issues in the Brazilian airline industry. The *Quilombo Aéreo* is brought to this investigation because it is a collective of black aeronauts created in 2018 with the goal of "bringing visibility to the black crewmembers of the Brazilian Civil Aviation" (Quilombo Aéreo, 2022). Through active participation in the conduction of the research presented here, ways for articulating critical thought to critical praxis is sought, according to intersectional studies. It makes possible that the academic environment and social movement influence one another, aiming towards fairer social relationships in an environment full of inequality such as the airline industry. In this sense, the collective is a co-participant in this research, from its design to the publication of its results, enabling active exchanges between theory and practice, as proposed by intersectionality.

The research, which is qualitative, was carried out through interviews with six women who are currently working or have worked in Brazilian aviation, as flight attendants or pilots. All the women interviewed recognized themselves as black and pointed to difficulties they had experienced since their intention to enter aviation and still to remain in it. The responses received were categorized and interpreted from the intersectional literature, which finds in Collins and Bilge (2021) great expression from the theory of domains of power, an important analytical tool that reveals how black female bodies are seen and treated.

This chapter is structured as follows: initially, the theoretical framework of the research is presented, centered on the discussion of intersectionality (Akotirene, 2019; Collins & Bilge, 2021) based on social markers of race and gender. Then, the methodology presents the steps followed for the construction of the work, presenting the women interviewed and the techniques used for the collection and analysis of the information obtained. Subsequently, in the results and discussions, the barriers listed by the interviewees to enter the airline industry and to remain in it are brought up, linking them to the literature used in the research, especially from the reference of the power domains of Collins and Bilge (2021). The results and discussions also reveal the strategies of counterpower, that is, of resistance, daily used by black women in the sector, with emphasis on the collective initiative of *Quilombo Aéreo*. Finally, the conclusion reflects on the inequalities encountered by black women working in Brazilian aviation.

LITERATURE REVIEW

This work has as basis the intersectionality, as such gives "(...) theoretical-methodological instrumentality to the structural inseparability of racism, capitalism and cis-hetero-patriarchy" (Akotirene, 2019, p.14), being here discussed, specifically, the intersections between gender and race. Even though the term has been coined by Crenshaw (1991) in the beginning of the 1990s, previous intellectual and activist discussions (Davis, 2016 [1981]; Gonzales, 1981; hooks, 1981) have already highlighted the necessary articulation between gender, race and class in order to perceive the specific conditions of inequality attributed to black women (Collins & Bilge, 2021).

Considering that "the goal of intersectional studies is to contribute to the social justice initiatives" as analytical tools, "the intersectionality investigates how intersectional power relations influence upon social relationships in societies marked by diversity, as well as daily individual experience" (Collins & Bilge, 2021, p.16). Thus, four distinct "domains of power" were identified - structural, cultural, disciplinary and interpersonal - which are interconnected in organizational spheres (as it is the case of the airline industry). However, in agreement with Collins and

Bilge (2021, p.52), who named critical praxis as fundamental to the understanding of intersectionality, that it can't be reduced to a solely analytical tool.

As the authors affirm:

(...) the common understandings of intersectionality underestimate the practices that make possible the intersectional knowledge, especially those which involve criticism, rejection or attempts to correct the social problems created by complex social inequalities. The critical praxis also constitutes an important characteristic of the intersectional investigation – which is attentive to the intersection of the power relationships and is vital for resisting social inequality (Collins & Bilge, 2021, p.52).

The structural domain of power makes reference to the fundamental structures of social institutions (labor market, housing, education, health). The cultural one emphasizes the growing importance of ideas and daily culture in the organization of power relationships. Disciplinary domain points out the fair or unfair application of rules and regulations based on race, sexuality, class, gender, age and similar categories. Lastly, the interpersonal domain explains how individuals experience the convergence of structural, cultural and disciplinary powers. The domains of power of Collins and Bilge (2021) bring the perspective of Grada Kilomba (2019), which points out how the combination of prejudice and power formed racism. Then, the connection about an historical, political, social and economic power comes into fruition.

Aiming to bring the condition of black women in the airline industry into the spotlight it is necessary to discuss racism – defined as systematic domination – structural, institutional, and daily – of an ethnical group upon another. Structural because as white subjects receive more privileges, such excludes the others from the majority of social and political structures. Institutional for being rooted within the institutions – such as systems and educational agendas, labor markets, criminal justice, etc., placing *white subjects* once more in an advantageous position. Daily because the "continual pattern of abuses'' is repeated ceaselessly and in several places, transforming black bodies into improper bodies (Kilomba, 2019, p.80), which leads to the question: which bodies are "fit" for occupying workplaces in the Brazilian airline industry?

In that sense, the discussion about patriarchy is also required, since "[it] structures social relationships and practices in which men dominate, exploit and oppress women" (Walby, 1990, p.20). According to the author, there are six structures of which patriarchy is composed of: the patriarchal mode of production, patriarchal relations in paid work, patriarchal relations in the state, male violence, patriarchal relations in sexuality, and, patriarchal relations in cultural institutions. The patriarchal means of production are related to domestic work, traditionally attributed to women in exchange for their subsistence, without social and economic recognition; the patriarchal relationships of paid work focus on the insertion of women in the labor market in specific areas and jobs of smaller status and remuneration. Knowing that the state is patriarchal, racist and capitalist, the patriarchal bias within state policies and actions is noticeable, even if they manifest in several ways throughout time; male violence is structural, given that it is legitimized, systematically tolerated and almost not fought against in several contexts; the patriarchal relationship in sexuality dialogue with compulsory heterosexuality and the exacerbated control of feminine sexuality. Lastly, the cultural institutions permeated by patriarchy shape the subjective gender constructions, attaching specific characteristics to the female and male that spread through different institutions, such as religions, educational, media, among others.

So, for the considerations hereby proposed, in agreement with Saffioti (1987, p. 60), when she explains that,

With the rise of capitalism, the symbiosis happened, a fusion between the three systems of domination-exploration [patriarchy, racism, capitalism]. Only to make the understanding of such phenomenon easier, one can separate these three systems from one another. In concrete reality, they are inseparable, as they have transformed, through said symbiotic process, into a single system of domination-exploration, which is here given the name of patriarchy-racism-capitalism Saffioti (1987, p. 60).

That way, focusing on this research's goal, one can notice that despite the advance in the systematization of information about gender inequalities in the touristic sector (Mooney, 2020), official data of the Brazilian airline industry that intersections race and gender does not exist, since, both regulatory agencies (such as the *Agência Nacional de Aviação Civil* [ANAC]) and union syndicates of the category do not collect data regarding race/color of their workers. Regarding gender, as pointed out on table 1, a survey carried along with ANAC shows that the number of female pilots in activity is minimal (2,3% among commercial pilots, 2,7% are helicopter pilots and 2,3% work in the airlines). On the other hand, acting as flight attendants, women represent more than 60% of workers (Quilombo Aéreo, 2022).

Estimations of the *Quilombo Aéreo* (2022) point that the participation of black people in the national civil aviation is of 5% for flight attendants, and 2% for pilots, without any black female pilot in activity within the national airlines. It's interesting to note that in the United States, where black women are 6,8% of the population, there are 20 female pilots (Zirulnik & Orbe, 2019), while in Brazil, black women comprise 28% of the national population (Bond, 2020).

Table 1. Representativity by gender in the Brazilian airline industry

Course, license or habilitation	Men	Women	Women Percentage
Commercial pilot	13.8000	3.283	2.3%
Helicopter pilot	18.147	520	2.7%
Airline pilot	41.590	992	2.3%
Flight Attendant	12.240	24.211	66%
Private pilot	6.609	1.637	19%

Source: Quilombo Aéreo (2022) from data collected from ANAC

The data in Table 1 converges towards the information of the *International Labor Organization* [ILO] (2019), which points that men are the majority among pilots, mechanics and engineers, being those the most privileged occupations (socially and economically), while women are majority among the flight attendant. The document also explains that the required long periods of time away from home, the lack of flexibility for work scales and also the requirement of several flight hours inhibit the participation of women in the sector, as the aforementioned are culturally in charge of the domestic work and care. Another topic that arose and is also relevant to the research is the fact of flight attendant being historically objectified and sexualized in airlines' advertisements, making it so that sexual harassment of passengers and workmates is frequent.

Considering the participation of white and black women in the Brazilian airline industry, in 2019, it is noted that they represented 38% of the formal workforce, while men are 62% (based on data collected from Instituto de Pesquisa Econômica Aplicada [IPEA], 2020). However, more than a quantitative difference, data from IPEA show that the inequality also reflects in the access to better salary ranges. Observing the remuneration based on gender, it is identified that as the income increases, the disproportion of men to women also increases. While among the smaller remunerations (up to 2 minimum wages), women are 43%, and among the most well-paid (above 5 minimum wages), they are only 34% (based on data collected from IPEA, 2020).

However, the data above do not reflect the particularities experienced by black women in the sector, making it harder to deepen reflections that aim at discussing not only structural sexism, but, above all, the manifestations of the aforementioned articulated to structural racism, both being strongly imprinted in Brazilian society. Thus, our focus is the black women, which are most of the time not considered in the debates about racism (Kilomba, 2019).

Table 2. Interviewed women's profiles

Characterization	Placeholder Name	Age	Former/Actual Work Area
Subject 1	Brenda Robinson	44yrs	Former flight attendant
Subject 2	Bessie Coleman	33yrs	Flight attendant /aviation student
Subject 3	Mae Jemison	35yrs	Flight attendant
Subject 4	Madeline Swegle	33yrs	Flight attendant
Subject 5	Chipo Matimba	33yrs	Pilot (non-acting)
Subject 6	Elizabeth Petros	34yrs	Pilot (non-acting)

Source: authors (2022)

METHODOLOGY

The research is of qualitative nature, which means that it is interested in the universe of meanings, motivations, aspirations, beliefs, values and people's attitudes (Minayo, 2002), privileging thus the social actors. In order to achieve such, interviews were used as a technique for data collection, seeking to allow a deep exploration of the actor's life conditions (Poupart, 2012). Those were semi-structured and composed of a script, pointing that the semi-structured interviews make it possible that information emerges in a free manner, and the answers are not conditioned to the strict pattern of alternatives (Manzini, 1990).

The first step for the research was to make contact with the *Quilombo Aéreo* collective, in order to know if there would be interest in such investigation, which was confirmed by the founders. From there, contact with black women from the airline industry was established, and interviews were scheduled and conducted virtually in the months of October and November of 2021. The criteria for the interruption of contact requests for new interviews was the qualitative saturation in the way that, at the moment that such became repetitive in a manner that would saturate the content, they were ceased (Gondim & Lima, 2006).

The questions inquired about these women's 'life stories' in the airline industry, investigating the obstacles they had to overcome in order to get in, to remain there and also about the strategies to confront racism and sexism. Table 2 shows a characterization of the interviewed subjects, bringing the field of work (or where they used to work) and their ages. As will be seen throughout the article, identities were preserved, using a fictitious name whose inspiration comes from black women pioneers in the airline industry.

A thematic analysis was used for data analysis, in which the recurrence of the collected information is verified, thus highlighting the most mentioned topics by the interviewed subjects, searching for patterns and connections that lead to a wider referential (Gaskell, 2008). The information was categorized in a manner to structuralize the discussions into three sections: obstacles faced in order to join the airline industry, obstacles faced to remain in it and strategies of resistance. As the interviewees are now formally presented, the next topic brings the results found in the research.

RESULTS AND DISCUSSIONS

The research results revealed that black women in the airline industry find obstacles to ingress into the area, to remain in it and also that they devise resistance strategies. Applying intersectionality as a tool of analysis, the domains of power (structural, cultural, interpersonal and disciplinary) of Collins and Bilge (2021) will be used here, attached to the speech of the interviewees in the research, in order to illustrate how such domains of power manifest themselves in the professional experiences of black women crew members.

Regarding the obstacles for ingress, table 3 shows them, linked to the aforementioned domains of power. The first barrier, which is the cost of professional habilitation, is a clear example of how the uneven social structure between white and black people influences the process of admission in the airline industry, being essential to analyze the lack of black women in the place from an intersectional perspective, in order to understand that the environment in question is extremely elitist, and excludes black women from the activity. Data from the Brazilian Geography and Statistics Institute (IBGE) analyzed by the Departamento Intersindical de Estatística e Estudos Socioeconômicos [Dieese] (2021) reveal that in the second trimester of 2021, black women earned 54% less than white men. That way, pointing social inequities in the analysis is essential to problematize the question, for the domain of structural power is revealed when showing that access to fundamental institutions in Brazilian society – such as education, labor market, housing, among others is different for men and women, white and black, denying the freedom of choice and socio-economic ascension to the most outsourced part of the population, in this case the black women. As one of the interviewees, which is a flight attendant, explains: "I had no money, obviously, to pay for the course, and then my boss back then, who had suggested me to take it, paid a few of the first tuition fees for me, because I had no money" (Madeline).

When talking about the pilot course, the reality is even further away, because a pilot spends, from the beginning to the achievement of the commercial piloting license, between R$100.000,00 and R$150.000,00. Throughout the research it was possible to hear about families taking loans in order to fulfill their daughters' dreams or, yet, about the delay in the training, making it harder to pay for the course, as

Table 3. Obstacles for black women to join the airline industry and domains of power

Obstacles	Domains of Power
Cost of professional training	Structural
Lack of career information	Cultural
Lack of representativity of other black women	Structural and cultural
Unequal recruitment process	Disciplinary
Non-acceptance of black bodies	Cultural and interpersonal

Source: authors (2022)

another interviewee says: "But at the time, college took all my salary, it was very expensive... So, I either studied at college or took flight hours, it wasn't possible to do both" (Bessie).

The high costs for learning explain, as well, the second obstacle found – lack of information about the career – which shows how black women didn't know they could occupy that space, as there were no references, in their social circle, of black people working in the airline industry, or women crew members. Many, also, thought that black women couldn't even work there. As one of the interviewees told: "(…) since I was little no one ever mentioned it, I have no one working in this area" (Chipo). Another interviewee also tells:

I remember once talking to my mother, like this: 'hey mom, I want to pilot a plane'. My mother replied: "But you can't, only men can" (…). The first time I flew a plane in my life (…) when I entered the airplane, I saw it then thought: the pilot is a man, but the flight attendant is a woman! So, it's possible to become one (Bessie).

Discriminated bodies, such as black women's bodies, go through what Collins (2019) calls control images – stereotypes and figurations that imprison black women in certain spaces and affect the way they are treated and also how they see themselves. It is unfitting in these stereotypes that black women occupy leadership positions or that they appear in gendered spaces – such as aviation. The domain of power (Collins & Bilge, 2021) found here, the cultural one, manifests itself by normalization of cultural attitudes and expectancies in regard to social inequality. That is, the representativeness and dissemination of information regarding work in the airline industry "traditionally" do not favor black women, causing them won't even consider themselves able to occupy such space. Thus, the lack of specific knowledge by women that now work in the area, of the possibility of following a career in the aforementioned, has been made itself present in all interviews. More than that, the images of control – which put the black women in positions of servitude, or as being less apt to certain professional positions, also operate along with those already in the market, making it so that this domain of power becomes also noticeable when discussing the lack of representativity in the area and in the unfair recruitment processes.

The next topic – lack of representativity of other black women – discusses the difficulty of the interviewees in seeing themselves in the environment, be it for the lack of female teachers (black or not) and black people (women or not) in schools, among instructors and colleagues, in the environments they are at until the end of the course. Of the six interviewees, only one had black instructors, and four only had two female instructors. One of them cited that throughout their flight attendant course, these two women instructors were responsible for teaching first aid and the other one for etiquette, which shows the sexual division of work, in which women are directed to jobs related to care and less valued.

This barrier of lack of representativity shows the interconnection between the domain of structural power, which systematically excludes black women (as explained above) with the cultural one which, despite spreading the belief that Brazil lives a racial democracy, it does not bring black women in positions of power and leadership, showing how the discourse is dissociated from daily praxis.

The reference to the uneven recruitment processes, the next analyzed obstacle, shows how even if they are well-prepared, black women have difficulties in being approved to work in the area. In that sense, it was possible to hear:

At least one of the selections I have been through, I'm sure that I was extremely well-prepared, I'm sure that it was racism that excluded me (…). But it's how it goes, we can't prove structural racism, yet. Structural racism is very strong, the institutional one too, then I still can't prove that they were the reasons (Mae).

In the same direction, another interviewee said:

In a selection I took part (…) a hundred were there, and in the end, it was divided into three groups of eight. I was among the eight, in my group, I was the only one that did not pass. And in this group, the girl [white] said this: "Dude, I'm despairing, in the English interview I didn't manage to say a thing". And I answered: "No, I managed to answer everything, I'm fine". And in that group, I was the only one who didn't pass (Chipo).

From the speeches, the domain of disciplinary power is inferred, and such presents itself when it is understood that groups and people are disciplined to fit or fight persistent disciplinary practices in order to have access to certain spaces and positions (Collins & Bilge, 2021), as it was explicit by one of the interviewees, who mentioned having heard the following advice: "Don't take the tech pilot course, join college [Aeronautical Sciences]. Because the tech course is cheaper, takes less time but you won't get a job". And followed, "women pilots who are in the airline industry today, at least the ones I know (...) every one of them have Aeronautical Sciences. And the men have the tech course" (Bessie). That is, she seeks strategies to circumvent the *status quo* which disciplines women and black people to not occupy the position of pilots, while others figure out that they were excluded by the same disciplinary practices.

It was possible to notice a non-acceptance of black bodies – last obstacle mentioned – in a way that all the interviewees, while still being candidates to a spot in the airline industry, knew that they could not arrive to the interviews with their natural haircuts. One of the pilots says: "If you get into a company with an afro, black power haircut, to an interview, no way" (Chipo). Here, the intersection between the domain of cultural and interpersonal power is reinforced. The cultural matter is evidenced with the myth of meritocracy, which preaches that the recruitment processes are neutral and that everyone would have the same opportunities, and the most dedicated and prepared would be able to be hired. To this narrative still are added the cultural constructions referring to gender and race, which was already seen here in the aforementioned speeches, aiming to demonstrate that such processes are not really fair or based only on the candidates' skills, but are permeated by cultural constructions that lead towards the non-acceptance of black bodies in certain spaces, related to positions of power, such as the airline industry.

The interpersonal domain of power highlights the personal experiences regarding the articulation of the other domains of power, aiming to ponder about the several identities of individuals and their social experiences. Here, one can notice that black women are forced to make choices concerning their appearances, which could reinforce their black or feminine identity, risking to suffer retaliations concerning the domains of structural, disciplinary and/or cultural power. Or they can opt to "camouflage" their identities of race and gender, fitting into the disciplinary and cultural norms that structure the relations of power involved in the processes of hiring flight attendants and pilots, which, according to the perceived obstacle, deny the black bodies in such space.

The difficulties for remaining in the sector were categorized in seven aspects, and can be seen in table 4, which also brings the domains of power of Collins and Bilge (2021).

The obstacle of lack of representativity points out not only the lack of other black people working, but also of other black people traveling. Thus, the report of interviewees saying that they were the only black people in the place was quite recurrent:

Table 4. Obstacles for black women to remain in the airline industry and domains of power

Obstacles for remaining	Domains of Power
Lack of representativity	Structural, cultural and interpersonal
Different level of demands	Disciplinary and cultural
Denial of the black body	Interpersonal and cultural
Non-acceptance of the afro hair	Disciplinary and interpersonal
Mental/laboral health	Disciplinary and interpersonal
Machismo	Structural and cultural
Harassment	Cultural and interpersonal

Source: authors (2022)

Look, when I fly with black people, I take pictures (laughs) to record. It's true, because it is very rare (...). Sometimes I also take pictures as well to show I am the only black person in the flight. It's because generally that's what happens. So, it is a place of great solitude (Madeline).

In this speech it is possible to notice that the domains of structural, cultural and interpersonal power make themselves present. While remembering that the domain of structural power manifests itself by denying access to parts of the population to education or dignified jobs, for example, it is understood that more than excluding back people from the labor market in the airline industry, these people are, also, systematically excluded from the higher remuneration ranges, making it so that they have little access to services with higher cost – such as air transportation. This reflects in the absence of black passengers. Along with that, it should be pointed out that culturally, black people have also not been valued, or even duly represented in the market of travel and tourism (Oliveira, 2022), distancing such groups even further away from potential consumption in the sector. Lastly, while pointing that flights are a place of "great solitude", Madeline gives us hints of an interpersonal domain of power, since she sees herself negotiating her personal solitude experience due to her racial identity so that she can remain in an elitist space that denies the presence of other black people.

The different level of demands made to them brings reflections of the racism that always demands more from black people, as the sexism demands more from women, giving the feeling that the "bar's level" is higher for the women afro-descendants. As one of the interviewed pilots points out: "The feeling I have is that I have to prove to others every time that I'm capable of doing things. (...). It's tiresome" (Elizabeth). Zirulnik and Orbe (2019), when conducting interviews with African-

American pilots, also highlighted how they feel that they need to work twice harder to prove they're good enough for the job they occupy. In the same way, one of the interviewees remembers two women pilots who graduated together and had different opportunities along their career, in a way that ten years after graduation, while one found the first job in the area, the other already was a commander outside of Brazil, both having the same graduation, same degree" (Bessie). However, one of them is a "white, blonde woman" (*id*), while the other is a black woman.

Just like in the uneven recruitment processes, after joining the labor market in the airline industry, the black women keep being demanded in a different manner, being necessary to submit or fight the disciplinary rules instituted daily. In the passage above highlighted by Bessie, it is possible to notice the intersectionality of race and gender in this domain of power which, when being challenged regarding gender, accepting a white woman as a pilot, denies the same opportunity to a black woman, keeping thus the disciplinary power instituted in the sector and reinforcing the need of interseccional view. That way, the domain of cultural power can also be noticed, as it is through the "images of control", already mentioned before, that bosses and supervisors choose people (based on social markers) which are more or less demanded from.

The category "denial of the black body" reflects about the cases of racism that occurred in the area, be it "deny to receive a glass on your hand" (Brenda), say that the pilot "looked more like a carnival dancer than a pilot" (Elizabeth), not having their leadership position acknowledged – even while using a different attire to denote their position, among other examples heard along the interviews. Zirulnik and Orbe (2019) also emphasized how African-American women pilots hear racist and sexist comments that question their abilities. In that case, both the incidence of the interpersonal and cultural domains of power are verified. Interpersonal because while putting oneself in a place that would otherwise be denied to them, more than strangeness, these women experienced daily situations of prejudice due to their racial and gender identities. Cultural because it articulates images of control, previously discussed, which reflect both in the black women themselves, and also influence the racist and sexist practices from those that do not make part of such groups.

In the same line comes the aspect of the denial of afro hair which, from its relevance, earned its own category. The afro hair, in a mixed country like Brazil, denotes afro-descendant and is the first item to be "tamed" in airlines which, also, as mentioned before, deny those right away on interviews. It is noteworthy that every airline has its own dress code, under allegation of flight security, which has to be strictly followed by the crewmembers, and which also include specifications about hairstyles. However, more than safety, racism can be seen when an interviewee affirms:

In my hair's case, it's more because of the 'scrunched nose' it causes, you know? I don't want to straighten it out, so I'd rather keep it tied (...). But they notice it, it's a fact. You have to present yourself in a more serious manner, right? Because they think afro hair is not a serious image... (Elizabeth).

Besides that, a few companies use caps – which demands that afro hair be straightened out to fit there. Thus:

The matter of caps which the [airline] sets. Man, I'll have to tie my hair, like, I won't be able to use it loose, I'll have to do brushing, I'll have to do something so that thing fits my hair, because it won't fit. So, like, I think that's where it starts, they add a few elements which certain people won't be able to put in unless they change their looks radically. It's a violence, that's what it is (Madeline).

Here, the disciplinary domain of power is evident, given that it's about codes instituted to subject the appearance of certain professionals to those accepted by the airlines, in a clear example of bodies disciplining. Such intersects with the interpersonal, as once more the interviewed women report the personal direction, as they notice "scrunched noses" or the necessity (different to desire) of straightening their hair denying their black identity.

The reflex of racism in the area comes described in the next category – mental/ laboral health – which makes black women to step away from their job and make them think about quitting – which some end doing. Brenda pointed out that: "The issue about the hair, what I did, I began cutting (...). I transformed myself into a person that turned into that just to be accepted. (...)" The speech of this former flight attendant evidences how disciplinary and interpersonal domains of power intersection leading to compromising, many times, of these women's mental health, since while they subject themselves to negotiate their identities to fit under disciplinary norms, they go through a subjective process which, in certain cases, leads to sickness, given its complexity.

As pointed out by another flight attendant, being a black woman in the airline industry is "to have your mental health being daily tested" (Mae) – a reflex of society that sickens black people, having herself, at that, stepping off for this reason. Studies show a greater prevalence of mental disturbances in non-white people and the suicide rate among young black teenagers is 45% greater than among whites (Smolen & Araújo, 2017; Ministério da Saúde, 2018). The same interviewee points out that she's always stigmatized as the "crazy person" who sees racism in everything, which reminds Kilomba (2019, p.138) when the author explains that "since racism is not seen as a social phenomenon, those who face it are always confronted with the message that their experiences come from their own excessive sensitivity and, thus, are their own responsibility".

Here, once more, it is easy to notice how disciplinary norms are imposed in a way to accept certain behavior standards of certain people and repel others, interconnecting with the interpersonal issue since the way such as black women subjectivize such norms lean directly towards their personal experiences.

The answers categorized as machismo show how female crewmembers are not respected for being women, in a way that they have their requests for passengers denied, while they see the same requests being made by male crewmembers being obeyed. Reminding that the topic at hand is security instructions, that is, women are not giving suggestions, but are giving instructions. Another point arisen by the interviewees refers to the presentation and women's dresses, since women need to paint their nails, use makeup, wear uncomfortable clothes/shoes while the male outfits do not have those obligations, which encumber only women. A pilot interviewee affirmed that she had services denied because she would be too close to the clients and their wives would be jealous. Besides that, the interviewed women also problematized the fact that using tight clothes, which are counterproductive in situations of potential or effective emergency, also hypersexualizes them. Calvet et al. (2021) also point out that there are demands for physical standards that affect especially the flight attendant.

The machismo, as patriarchal praxis, is essentially structural, once it spreads through several fundamental institutions of the contemporary society, such as family, religion, education, among others, interfering actively in inequality between men and women, stimulating these to discredit women, such as in the citation about refusing to comply to instructions given by female flight attendant, or ignoring their position of leadership. Here it can be noted that its intersection with the cultural domain of power, since the contemporary discourses still corroborate with the patriarchal structures, feeding narratives such as hypersexualizing of certain jobs or the imposition of appearance standards specifically for female bodies.

Lastly, the final category treats harassment suffered by women, which they reported as being recurrent, denouncing passengers as well as workmates. All the interviewees affirm that harassment for being a woman is "common", "normal" or "frequent". One of them even points out having lost a job opportunity for not giving in. She narrates: "I have already lost a job because the guy wanted an… exchange, see? (...), and I said no, that I was only interested in flying. Then he didn't call me anymore and started badmouthing me (…)". (Elizabeth). About harassment from passengers, it was frequent to hear that "what happens is a lot of harassment, sometimes the girl is going through the aisle and the guy spanks the girl's rear indeed, and doesn't care at all about it." (Brenda). Or, as Bessie says with emphasis: "Wow! Harassment in a plane is very common, like... more than you think, you know?".

Harassment here was understood as a manifestation of domains of cultural power intersections with the interpersonal one. Cultural because, as seen in the aforementioned speeches, there is a normalization of this type of violence, since invisibility and maintenance make it so that women themselves internalize acceptance of such behavior as something cultural, aiming to minimize, in many cases, its effects. Such allies itself to interpersonal domain, as the way women are forced to deal with daily harassment interfere in each of their personal experiences, as in the case of the loss of a job opportunity. Or, in cases revealed by other interviewees, regarding the lack of support from the airlines themselves, making them have to choose between reporting something that hits them as women, or avoid retaliation or discredit by trying to fight this type of instituted violence.

As the obstacles for entry and remaining were presented, now the work shows the strategies of resistance, with emphasis to the *Quilombo Aéreo*, whose story begins in 2018 with two black women from the airline industry meeting each other in social networks – Kenia Aquino, which discussed representativity of black crewmembers in Brazil, and Laiara Amorim, which drew attention to the lack of gender, race and class equity, in the command cabin of national airplanes.

The meeting of these two in social media show, as Collins and Bilge explain (2021, p.149), how digital media are a vibrant stage for intersectionality, facilitating the global reach of this topic, since black feminists "are not only online, as they lean onto intersectionality to analyze the fundamental importance of digital space for the reproduction of intersectional power relationships". In that sense, it's from this encounter in virtual space, that they felt the need for collective action:

The official order, repression, was called it quilombo, which is a black name that means union. So, when blacks unite, pile up, they are always forming a quilombo, eternally forming a quilombo, they are always forming a quilombo, eternally forming a quilombo, the African name is union (Nascimento, 1977, p. 126).

The perspective of union of black people, which also comes in the name of the collective, shows the tone of its creation since, if there was no internal support network before, it was created with the intention of giving visibility to black people of the area, with debates and actions which propose to mitigate the effects of racism and sexism in aviation, to develop strategies of self-care – with special attention to black aeronauts' mental health – and show companies the effects of institutional racism. Coming from different social/black movements, among them a group of black lawyers, psychologists, masters and doctors the *Quilombo* was formed, with the perspective of establishing a base of information about black people in the Brazilian aviation sector through data collection, denouncement systematization and also collection and registration of its people's path.

With the view of contributing to anti-racist agenda and to open spaces for the entrance and permanence of more black people in the airline industry, the Collective created affirmative structural actions, such as the projects *Fly like a black girl* which aims to accelerate the training of black female pilots and the *Blacks who fly*, which finances suburban black people to take the courses for flight attendant. The *Blacks who fly* was financed through a *matchfunding* which raised more than R$ 90.000,00. Such resulted in the graduation of ten black flight attendants, the first majorly black group to graduate in this course in Brazil, which happened on November 20th, 2021.

Even feeling accomplished with the deed, the founders of *Quilombo* point to the necessity of opening and opportunity in other instances of the airlines industry in order to seek racial equality, since the sector is still recognizably elitist and whit, with Eurocentric determined pattern. As Yu and Hyun (2021) clarify, the experience of multiracial groups in the airline industry results in bigger creativity and productivity. Furthermore, the authors say, ignoring diversity leads to racism.

The *Quilombo Aéreo* deems it important to act on several fronts. One of them, the academic front, seeks the collection of data that prove the area's structural racism. Another reflects upon the representativity to show society that there are black professionals acting in the area and question, along with companies and regulating entities, the violence over black bodies and its effects on air transport security. Lastly, for the training and occupation, it works the democratization of aviation and professionalization of black people to work in the airline industry.

CONCLUSION

Grada Kilomba (2019), while pondering about the reflections of racism on black people, explains that it is common to question what a person has done after having suffered the act, instead of asking what racism has done to the person. To inquire what racism has done, the author continues, is not to victimize, but to empower someone, as the black person turns into an active voice which describes their own reality. To question "what has racism done to you" is a real act of decolonization and political resistance, which allows the black person to occupy themselves with themselves and not with their white peers, explains the author. So, it is important to ask: What has racism done to Brazilian Civil Aviation? This research shows what has been done starting from racism and sexism, echoing to the strategies of resistance – which are many and need to gain space.

The chapter highlighted reflections of women who recognize the importance of black bodies occupying elitist spaces, in a way to distinguish places and have them become mirrors for other black girls that dream about being flight attendants, pilots, that is, to act in places where they, being interviewed, once did not even know that such could be occupied by black women. However, it has been made clear that their black bodies are deemed unfit for that environment, which submits black women to obedience to physical standards linked to occidental beauty standards (Calvet et al., 2021).

Five obstacles to black women entering the airline industry were identified: cost of professional training; lack of career information; lack of representativity of other black women; unequal recruitment process; non-acceptance of black bodies. As it was exposed throughout the analysis of the results, these exist specifically for black women. As well as the obstacles perceived for the permanence of those who manage to enter this system: lack of representativity; different levels of demands; denial of the black body; non-acceptance of the afro hair; mental/laboral health; machismo; harassment. It is interesting to notice that in the permanence category seven barriers were identified, that is, more than for entering. That is why research of various kinds to approach racism and sexism in the airline industry is urgent, since, in principle, this has not proven to be a democratically healthy environment for all.

In this sense, it is still worth remembering that there is no official data that offers information on race and gender in the airline industry. The data made available by Anac refer to licenses issued, however, it would be interesting, in order to deepen the intersectional debates in the sector, if the information on the profile of people in real activity, in each professional category, were systematized. Here it is important to point out that one of the strategies outlined by *Quilombo Aéreo* is precisely to analyze and give visibility to the few accessible data of gender and race in the Brazilian airline sector.

The research emphasizes the segmentation by gender and race when it reflects on the fact that there are no black women pilots in the country. As explained in the document of the ILO (2019), there are cultural constructions that influence women's disinterest in aviation. However, one cannot fail to observe that, despite such constructions, in the category of flight attendants, women account for more than 60% of professionals. Thus, it can be speculated that women may be willing to subvert the traditional roles of family care, but perhaps some positions, such as commander, are still not really available to them. In this sense, it is noteworthy that in airlines women correspond to 2.3% of pilots, while as private pilots they reach the mark of 19%. Still, concerning the placement of women in the airline industry, the clear horizontal segregation cannot be left unmentioned, where women are pushed to certain functions, while men have to fill others. Just like certain vertical segregation can be perceived, when certain conditions for professional ascension are imposed, and such affect men and women differently. When noticing that women are the majority among flight attendants, it is evidenced that their placement in the jobs of serving and care, while men are led to jobs of responsibility and command. Beyond the women's issue, the intersectional dimension shows that black women have specific conditions of social inequality when it is possible to single them out from the generic group that makes up the workforce in the sector.

Regarding such modes of segregation, horizontal and vertical, both clearly affect women crewmembers. However, after the intersectional research, one realizes that vertical segregation, that which imposes obstacles to the professional ascension of women, is even more significant when it comes to black women in the aviation sector, since, according to the estimates previously presented, black people account for only 5% of the flight attendants in Brazil (Quilombo Aéreo, 2022), while women, in general, occupy 66% of the positions. On the other hand, horizontal segregation is also perceived more emphatically when observing the reality of black women. Although underrepresented, women in general, appear in all pilot categories, however, the fact that there is no record of any black female pilot in a commercial airline operating throughout the country, highlights how the intersectionality of gender and race excludes this profile of women, even more than others.

Finally, one cannot fail to mention the importance of bringing intersectionality into the discussions of tourism studies, since tourism is an activity that involves different actors and contexts, and it is essential to deepen the mechanisms of analysis and practice necessary for sustainability in the tourism field. Pondering the dimensions of power (structural, disciplinary, cultural, and interpersonal) used here, as support for analysis, can be of great value when considering other social markers to be thought of as intersectionality in this scenario. This research also points to the need for the development of affirmative action and policies to combat racism and institutional sexism in the airline industry and in tourism, intending to foster new forms of social relations in this area.

Thus, the present work is concluded, aware of the necessity to deepen reflections regarding touristic activity starting from intersectionality, aiming to promote new forms of social relationships in this area, which was deepened here especially through analysis of the airline industry. Such intent seeks to unveil the several forms that operate the maintenance of inequalities between men and women, between blacks and whites, aiming to subside debates about social justice and to stimulate changes regarding empowerment of parts of the population that have been systematically excluded from touristic activities.

REFERENCES

Akotirene, C. (2019). *Intersectionality* [Interseccionalidade]. Pólen.

Bond, L. (2020, October 7). Black women are 28% of Brazilians, but have low political participation [Negras são 28% dos brasileiros, mas tem baixa participação política]. *Agência Brasil.* https://agenciabrasil.ebc.com.br/eleicoes-2020/noticia/2020-10/negras-sao-28-dos-brasileiros-mas-tem-baixa-participacao-politica

Calvet, N. A., Cond, C. I., Ballart, A. L., & Almela, M. S. (2021). *Gender inequalities in the tourism labour market* [Desigualdades de género en el mercado laboral turístico] (Vol. 14). https://www.albasud.org/noticia/es/1299/desigualdades-de-genero-en-el-mercado-laboral-turistico

Collins, P. H. (2019). *Black feminist thinking* [Pensamento feminista negro]. Boitempo.

Collins, P. H., & Bilge, S. (2021). *Intersectionality* [Interseccionalidade]. Boitempo.

Crenshaw, K. (1991). Demarginalizing the intersection of race and sex; a black feminist critique of discrimination doctrine, feminist theory and antiracist politics. *University of Chicago Legal Forum*, 139–167.

Davis, A. (2016). *Women, race and class* [Mulheres, raça e classe]. Boitempo.

de Oliveira, N. A. (2022). Representation and representation of blacks in a luxury tourism magazine in Brazil [Representação e representatividade dos negros em uma revista de turismo de luxo do Brasil]. *Revista Brasileira de Pesquisa em Turismo, 16*(1), 2325. doi:10.7784/rbtur.v16.2325

Departamento Intersindical de Estatística e Estudos Socioeconômicos. (2021). *Special Bulletin November 20 - Black Consciousness Day* [Boletim Especial 20 de novembro - Dia da Consciência Negra]. https://www.dieese.org.br/boletimespecial/2021/conscienciaNegra.html

Gabrielli, C. (2021). Women in the Brazilian tourism market: reflections and perspectives in the light of gender studies [Mulheres no mercado turístico brasileiro: reflexões e perspectivas à luz dos estudos de gênero]. *Rosa dos Ventos - Turismo e Hospitalidade, 13*(4), 1049–1068. http://www.ucs.br/etc/revistas/index.php/rosadosventos/article/view/9254/0

Gaskell, G. (2008). Individual and group interviews [Entrevistas individuais e grupais]. In M. Bauer & G. Gaskell (Eds.), *Pesquisa qualitativa com texto: imagem e som: um manual prático* (pp. 64–79). Vozes.

Gondim, L. M. P., & Lima, J. C. (2006). *Research as intellectual crafts: considerations about method and common sense* [A pesquisa como artesanato intelectual: considerações sobre método e bom senso]. EdUFSCar.

Gonzales, L. (1981, November 22). Black woman, that kilomba [Mulher negra, essa quilomba]. *Folhetim, 4.*

hooks, b. (1981). *Ain't I a woman: Black women and feminism.* South End Press.

Instituto de Pesquisa Econômica Aplicada. (2020). *Information system on the labour market in the tourism sector - SIMT* [Sistema de informações sobre o mercado de trabalho no setor turismo – SIMT]. Recuperado em 15 de dezembro de 2020 de: http://extrator.ipea.gov.br/

International Labor Organization. (2019). *Women and aviation: quality jobs, attraction and retention.* http://www.ilo.org/sector/Resources/publications/WCMS_740235/lang--en/index.htm

Kilomba, G. (2019). *Memories of the plantation: episodes of everyday racism* [Memórias da plantação: episódios de racismo cotidiano]. Cobogó.

Manzini, E. J. (1990). The interview in social research [A entrevista na pesquisa social]. *Didática, 26/27*, 149–158.

Minayo, M. C. de S. (2002). Science, technique and art: the challenge of social research [Ciência, técnica e arte: o desafio da pesquisa social]. In M. C. de S. Minayo (Ed.), Pesquisa social: teoria, método e criatividade (pp. 9–29). Vozes.

Ministério da Saúde. (2018). *Deaths by suicide among black adolescents and young people from 2012 to 2016* [Óbitos por suicídio entre adolescentes e jovens negros 2012 a 2016]. https://bvsms.saude.gov.br/bvs/publicacoes/obitos_suicidio_adolescentes_negros_2012_2016.pdf

Mooney, S. K. (2020). Gender research in hospitality and tourism management: Time to change the https://www.emerald.com/insight/content/doi/10.1108/IJCHM-09-2019-0780/full/html. doi:10.1108/IJCHM-09-2019-0780

Nascimento, B. (1977). *Historiography of the quilombo* [Historiografia do quilombo]. Quinzena do negro na USP. https://edisciplinas.usp.br/pluginfile.php/4934266/mod_resource/content/1/Untitled_29082019_193614.pdf

Oliveira, N. A. de. (2021). Blacks and Tourism: analysis of academic production on the subject in journals linked to graduate programs in Tourism in Brazil [Negros e turismo: análise da produção acadêmica sobre o tema em revistas vinculadas aos Programas de Pós-Graduação em Turismo no Brasil]. *Rosa dos Ventos - Turismo e Hospitalidade, 13*(1), 219–238. doi:10.18226/21789061.v13i1p219

Poupart, J. (2012). The qualitative interview: epistemological, theoretical and methodological considerations [A entrevista do tipo qualitativo: considerações epistemológicas, teóricas e metodológicas]. In A pesquisa qualitativa: enfoques epistemológicos (3rd ed., pp. 215–253). Vozes.

Quilombo aéreo. (2022). *Air Quilombo* [Quilombo Aéreo]. https://quilomboaereo.com.br/#

Saffioti, H. (1987). *The power of the male* [O poder do macho]. Moderna.

Smolen, J. R., & de Araújo, E. M. (2017). Race/skin color and mental disorders in Brazil: A systematic review [Raça/cor da pele e transtornos mentais no Brasil: uma revisão sistemática]. *Ciencia & Saude Coletiva*, *22*(12), 4021–4030. doi:10.1590/1413-812320172212.19782016 PMID:29267719

Walby, S. (1990). *Theorizing patriarchy*. Basil Blackwell.

Yu, M., & Hyun, S. S. (2021). Development of modern racism scale in global airlines: A study of asian female flight attendants. *International Journal of Environmental Research and Public Health*, *18*(5), 2688. doi:10.3390/ijerph18052688 PMID:33800093

Zirulnik, M. L., & Orbe, M. (2019). Black female pilot communicative experiences: Applications and extensions of co-cultural theory. *The Howard Journal of Communications*, *30*(1), 76–91. doi:10.1080/10646175.2018.1439422

Chapter 10
Tourism, Contradiction, and Afro-Religious (In)Visibility

Emerson Costa de Melo
https://orcid.org/0000-0002-4395-2517
Instituto Federal Fluminense, Brazil

Marina Furtado Gonçalves
Universidade Federal de Ouro Preto, Brazil

Solano de Souza Braga
Parnaíba Delta Federal University, Brazil

Aline da Fonseca Sá e Silveira
https://orcid.org/0000-0003-0690-2809
Centro Federal de Educação Tecnológica Celso Suckow da Fonseca, Brazil

Denilson Damasceno Costa
Parnaíba Delta Federal University, Brazil

ABSTRACT

Since the mid-1980s, studies on cultural heritage, whether material or immaterial, have been gaining prominence in tourism. However, there have been few debates and approaches dedicated to the understanding of socio-historical and ethnic-racial cultural peculiarities that promote the establishment of an agenda of tourist services that involve cultural heritage that recall Afro-Brazilian traditions. It is in this perspective that the authors propose a reflection elaborated from the intersection between the debate of ethnic-racial relations and tourism in Afro-religious communities, analyzing the challenges and contradictions of the promotion of tourist activities in Terreiros of Candomblé and Umbanda, in addition to gathering information that show the invisibility and prejudices in relation to these religions at the national level and valuing their tourist potential.

DOI: 10.4018/978-1-6684-4194-7.ch010

INTRODUCTION

Tourism in Brazil is a demonstrably exclusionary activity, as only a small portion of the population has the resources to travel and have access to culture and leisure (Trigo, 2020). This fact is aggravated by the country's social inequality, culminating in the disparity in income distribution. Although not all Brazilian citizens can travel to discover the heritage, including cultural manifestations from other places, culture continues to be one of the main motivations for travel around the world (Brasil, 2010).

For a long time, the cultural destinations in Brazil were exclusively built monuments of exceptional artistic and historical character, following the preservationist logic in force in the country since the 1930s. This view was only modified during the administration of Renato Soeiro in the extinct Service of National Historical and Artistic Heritage (SPHAN), between 1968 and 1979, when there was an expansion of the concept of monument following the process of internationalization of preservation (Pinheiro, 2006). Thus, the etymological sense of "monument" is interpreted as proposed by Alois Riegl in his book The Modern Cult of Monuments, that is, "as instruments of collective memory and as works of historical value that, even though they are not "works of art ", are always works that have a configuration, a conformation" (Kühl, 2006, p. 18). Monuments came to be seen as elements within a socioeconomic context and heritage preservation initiatives began to be "articulated with specific plans and policies for local and regional economic development, also aiming at social and economic goals, in addition to cultural ones" (Pinheiro, 2006, p. 12). This new economic activity, in which culture and tourism were allied, received investments, especially with the construction of roads and the promotion of tourist infrastructure in the historic centers of colonial cities built between the 16th and 18th centuries, favoring the value of antiquity of the monument.

In the mainstay of such movements, the destinations of visitors with cultural motivations in Brazil were exclusively large architectural complexes, museums and places that housed the material treasures of past cultures. Only recently, at the end of the 20th century, the concept of culture has been changing, expanding the limits of what scholars and institutions responsible for preservation initiatives understood as cultural heritage, including discussions about traditional knowledge, crafts and "ways of doing". Although the Brazilian Federal Constitution of 1988 already recognized the existence of cultural assets of a material and immaterial nature, only in 2000 the National Historical and Artistic Heritage Institute (IPHAN) instituted the Register of Cultural Assets of an Intangible Nature, in compliance with legal requirements and creating adequate instruments for the recognition and preservation of intangible assets (Sandroni, 2010). According to the United Nations Educational, Scientific and Cultural Organization (UNESCO), intangible heritage is defined by practices, representations, expressions, knowledge and techniques – with the instruments, objects, artifacts and cultural places associated with them – that communities, groups and, in some cases, individuals recognize as an integral part of their cultural heritage. Such conceptual changes and cultural protection guidelines had a direct influence on the characterization of Cultural Tourism, on the profile of cultural tourists and on the relationship between tourism and culture (Brasil, 2010).

Although this change in the understanding of cultural heritage in Brazil has been observed, there are still gaps to be filled. For example, few debates and approaches have been devoted to understanding socio-historical and ethnic-racial cultural peculiarities that promote the establishment of a tourist services agenda involving Afro-Brazilian traditions. The concept of cultural heritage based on a Eurocentric vision ignored the contributions of black-African and indigenous populations to Brazilian culture in much of the trajectory of public policies on tourism and cultural and natural heritage.

The (non) Recognition of the Cultural Heritage of Black People in Brazil

It is in this context of contradictions and denials that, in 1986, Ilê Axé Iyá Nasso Oka, the oldest candomblé ground (as known as terreiro) in Brazil, founded in 1835, was recognized and listed as the first ethnic-religious cultural heritage of black-African origin in Brazilian lands, breaking with the patrimonialization policies solely of material goods of an European background. This is an achievement arising from a long process of struggle and resistance led by the members of the terreiro with the support of civil society, highlighting the need for recognition and appreciation of other aesthetic forms (essence and appearance) in addition to those of western white origin found in the landscapes of the Brazilian colonial cities (Iphan, 2015).

The recognition of the Ilê Axé Iyá Nasso Oka terreiro of candomblé recalls the struggle of the African population that, in times of enslavement, despite being persecuted, managed to regroup and establish the cult of their ancestors, inaugurating a new religious practice in the New World. And although its foundation dates back to the beginning of the 19th century, according to the available literature and historical records safeguarded by the terreiro's oral traditions, Ilê Axé Iyá Nasso Oka would be an extension of the Candomblé da Barroquinha, the Iyá Omi Axé Airá Intilé. The Iyá Omi Axé Airá Intilé would have operated on the limits between Cidade Baixa and Alta in the city of Salvador, Bahia, at the end of the 18th century, which highlights it as a symbol of resistance by the black population and an exponent of such traditions in Brazil (Silveira, 2006).

Despite the historical nuances that enhance and elevate Ilê Axé Iyá Nasso Oka to the status of a national cultural heritage, there are still few and rare movements to insert it in the scope of religious tourism commonly explored in the city of Salvador.

It is in this sense that it is necessary and relevant to question how a religious practice of black-African origin, (re)signified in Brazilian lands, in activity for over two centuries, which has expanded throughout the national territory and even to other countries from Latin America and Europe (Melo & Correa, 2016), it is not part of a national heritage valuation plan? In addition to that, especially what are the obstacles to its exploration in the field of tourism, given that religious tourism is an ancient practice?

The signaled criticism makes us reflect on the movement of invisibility of such characters in the constitution of the national heritage and puts us in front of the need to understand how and why in Brazil, so little is known about the traditions and customs of the different peoples that make up the distinct traits of our culture, especially those of black-African origin. It is not uncommon to find in different social spaces knowledgeable characters or stories about Greek or Norse mythologies, but when it comes to the cult of Orixás – deified African ancestors – in Candomblé traditions, little or nothing is known by the majority of the Brazilian population.

In this matter, it is speculated that the population's lack of knowledge and, consequently, the prejudice against the different Afro-religious manifestations are related to the structural racism present in Brazilian society. For, according to Schwarcz (1993), racism developed in Brazil in a very specific way, present in social practices and in hegemonic discourses since colonial times, as attitude racism. However, denied by the old and recent whitening ideals of the Brazilian nation, which, by valuing and recognizing only heritages of European origin, erase the traces of culture and aesthetics that recalled black populations.

Thus, it is believed that the racism present in Brazilian society reaches the Afro-religious manifestations in a veiled way. In this way, religious prejudice would be linked to the practice of structural racism, mainly by propagating demonization and attacking the origins of these religions, "making them appear as the great enemy to be fought" (Nascimento, 2016, p. 168), excluding them from all processes that involve their valorization as Brazilian cultural heritage. This is a problem the authors intend to explore in this study, based on the intersection between the debate on ethnic-racial relations and tourism in Afro-religious communities, with the main purposeful characteristic of understanding the challenges and contradictions of promoting tourist activities in terreiros of candomblé.

Consequently, this work aims to contribute to the improvement of community-based tourism, allowing agents of public and private management to develop policies and mechanisms for the identification and inclusion of this religious practice as a guiding principle of local tourism, enabling new perspectives and nuances on tourism. Thus, it is also expected to recognize the diversity of tourist profiles, which could certainly attribute meanings and perceive a market hitherto unexplored, in view of the non-offer of religious tourism practices of Afro-religious manifestations.

Regarding the nature of the research, it is defined as qualitative, in which Appolinário (2006) defines as the one which arises from the social interactions of the researcher and the researched field, predicting different information from the field in advance. Thus, "this kind of research does not have conditions for generalization, that is, it is not possible to extract predictions or laws that can be extrapolated to phenomena other than the one being researched" (Appolinário, 2006, p.61).

Ilé Àse Ìyá Nassò Oká, History and Memory, Struggle and Resistance and the Issue of Heritage

The socio-religious formation process of the first *terreiros* of Candomblé intersected, firstly, with the colonial policies of enslavement of the population of black African origin (1530-1888). And, later, with those adopted by the Brazilian State after the Proclamation of the Republic of Brazil in 1889, when were instituted the first ideological political movements aiming at the constitution and defense of a national identity.

It is in this context of conflicts and contradictions, of the transition from the slave-like mercantile to capitalist production regime, that in the 1930s the notion of cultural heritage intertwines with the consolidation of a national identity elaborated under hegemonically white, Eurocentric and culturally Christian references used as guiding principles to forge the identity of the Brazilian people. This movement, as it became politically institutionalized by asserting itself under white Western standards and references, began the process of invisibility, marginalization and persecution of all cultural and religious practices and manifestations other than those adopted by the State.

However, it is emphasized here that the process of socio-religious organization, "legally" institutionalizing the practices of Candomblé in the 20th century, is the result of movements of struggle and resistance that began in the regime of enslavement of the black population at the end of the 18th century and the beginning of the 20th century. Such practices are still alive and active in the memory of the black Brazilian population, even those who do not practice religions of African origins.

In fact, it is not possible to specify the exact date of foundation of the first *terreiro* of Candomblé in Brazil. However, according to Afro-Brazilian religious literature, the Iyá Omi Axé Airá Intilé, or Candomblé da Barroquinha as it became known, was the first religious "temple" of African origin founded in Brazilian lands, still in the late 18th century. Based on historical records, the Iyá Omi Axé Airá Intilé would have operated for more than three decades, at the back of the Church of Nossa Senhora da Barroquinha, in the historic center of the city of Salvador, leaving the place after the strict policies to control cultural and religious manifestations of the black population. This change is an issue explored by several researchers attesting that it was at that moment, around 1835, under the leadership of Priestess Iyá Nasso, that the Iyá Omi Axé Airá Intilé was transferred to the neighborhood of Engenho Velho da Federação, receiving the name of Ilê Axé Iyá Nasso Oka, that is, The House of Mother Nasso Oka (Silveira, 2006).

In operation until the present day, it is necessary to understand the Ilê Axé Iyá Nasso Oka as a locus of cultural production with a black-African matrix that, over the last two centuries, has acted and acts as an exponent in the production and resignification of cultural elements that nourish Afro-Brazilian religious identity. In this case, the *terreiro* of Candomblé, in addition to being a religious temple, must be understood as a meeting place for different cultural matrices with peculiar ethical and philosophical values and principles, contributing to the (re)design of an Afro-religious symbolic territory constituted from elements common to black African societies.

It is, therefore, a territory organized from the movement of reterritorialization of the black population in Brazilian lands, which had been dehumanized, deterritorialized and sent to Brazil under the condition of merchandise. In other words, the *terreiro* of Candomblé as a territory assumes the condition of a space of struggle and resistance, with political, religious and symbolic characteristics – material and immaterial – allowing its members to affirm a typically black religious identity in Brazilian lands, placing it in the condition of a heritage asset to be preserved. Preservation is even more necessary when we consider the historical nuances of its contribution to the recognition of civilizing values that, even if given new meanings, are responsible for maintaining philosophical principles that strengthen the identity of the black population and, consequently, of the Brazilian people.

At the beginning of the 1980s, when Ilê Axé Iyá Nasso Oka completed its 150th anniversary of existence and functioning, its directors started with the National Historical and Artistic Heritage Service (SPHAN), corresponding to the current IPHAN, the necessary measures for the listing the terreiro as cultural heritage. On May 31, 1984, pursuant to process n°1067-T-82, IPHAN's Advisory Board accepted the request for the preservation of the Ilê Axé Iyá Nassô Oká, registering it in the two IPHAN's log books: the historical and the archaeological, ethnographic and landscape book, making its recognition effective on July 3, 1986, under numbers 504 (sheets 93-94) and 93 (sheet 42) (Iphan, 2015).

However, the listing of the Ilê Axé Iyá Nassô Oká as a national cultural heritage recognized by the Brazilian State does not include it in the valuation circuit of listed properties, nor does it bring visibility to it. One of the main reasons for the mischaracterization and/or invisibility of heritage assets linked to cultural and religious manifestations of black African origin, such as the Ilê Axé Iyá Nassô OkáNeste, point to the impacts of the imposition of philosophical and religious perspectives of white-western origin implanted, since the 16th century, in the different European colonies that extended across America. Such construction makes it impossible to understand other forms of social, cultural, political and religious organizations, as they do not recognize their mythical-philosophical principles as real and/or valid. These are fixed structures of a white, Eurocentric, culturally hegemonic model of thinking, which denies aesthetic principles and/or forms, functions, essences and appearances other than those of Judeo-Christian origin.

When reviewing the history of enslavement of the black population in Brazil, it is observed that this way of thinking about the other – the black, from its mischaracterization and marginalization, did not end with the abolition of slavery proclaimed on May 13, 1888, nor with the Proclamation of the Republic of Brazil in the following year. The black population, ex-enslaved, in this scenario of transition of political and economic ideals, was made invisible from the political and cultural scene of its time.

Not unlike that, the constitution of the "Estado Novo" (1937-1945), managed by the then president of Brazil Getúlio Vargas (1882-1954), although it brought significant changes to the direction of Brazilian society, accompanied the defense of white-hegemonic cultural values. An example of this is the defense of the "Motherland, God and Family" combined with the ideal of national identity, contributing to reinforce the movements of de-characterization and marginalization of the black population, making it invisible in debates for social rights (Schwarcz, 1993).

It is in this context that the researcher Giberto Freyre (1933), together with other thinkers of his time, defended his thesis on the contribution of the black African cultural matrix, both in the formation of identity and in the cultural and religious practices of the Brazilian people. Although Freyre presents plausible and convincing arguments about the contribution and permanence of different traits of black customs and traditions in the formation of Brazilian society, his observations clashed with the interests of the elites of the time. The elite defended the ideal of a "typically white Brazilian identity", which had followed, since the end of the 19th century, the incentive of whitening policies. Thus, the insertion of black people in Brazilian society would only be possible via the assimilation of cultural values constituted from the incentive to miscegenation in favor of the elimination of the black phenotype and culture. This reality makes the existing ethnic-racial conflicts invisible, contributing to the massification of an ideology based on the ideal of a white nation (Schwarcz, 1993).

In this way, the project of idealizing the identity of the Brazilian people took shape in political debates, which signaled the need and importance of encouraging research aimed at identifying and recognizing cultural assets for the constitution of a national identity. The defense of such interests in the political sphere contributed to the creation, in 1937, of the National Historical and Artistic Heritage Service (SPHAN) and, soon after, to the enactment of Decree-Law number 25, organizing the protection of the National Historic and Artistic Heritage (MEC/SPHAN/FNPM, 1980). Thus, the institutionalization and promotion of public policies for the recognition, organization and preservation of heritage assets serving the interests of the State can be observed. Current policies valued and prioritized a nationalist sentiment constituted from the idealization and defense of a white identity with well-defined racial ideals, which did not allow the integration of black and indigenous populations into Brazilian society.

In this context, the Brazilian State, through SPHAN's actions and through the Decree Law number 25, recognized as "national historical and artistic heritage" every work of "pure" art related to erudite, national and/or foreign knowledge, and also the set of movable and immovable property in the country, whose conservation was of public interest. For the State, the goods of interest should have some relation with memorable historical facts of the nation, using the built heritage – the colonial urban sites, squares, fountains – as fundamental elements to characterize and identify the greatness of the nation. It is noteworthy that such monuments have, in most cases, their history linked to the process of colonization of Brazilian lands and the enslavement of indigenous and African peoples.

When we think of historical heritage as a cultural reference, especially in the process of constitution of a Brazilian identity, there are several issues not only cultural, but also political involved, since they are representations of an imaginary inherent to a certain historical reality subjugated to relationships of interest. According to London (2000), the idealization and consolidation of "what should be recognized as heritage" come from the value judgment of specific groups and are not always legitimized by the general population:

The value is always attributed to them by particular subjects and according to certain criteria and historically conditioned interests. Taken to its ultimate consequences, this perspective affirms the relativity of any process of value attribution - be it historical, artistic, national, etc. - to goods, and calls into question the criteria adopted until then for the constitution of "cultural heritage", legitimized by disciplines such as history, art history, archeology, ethnography, etc. (Londres, 2000, p. 12).

In this way, with an elitist group at the forefront of defining the identity of national heritage, there was no integration of the black population into Brazilian society, nor did it make it possible to recognize their religious practices. Since religious practice and/or religiosity common to African peoples and their descendants were not considered a religion, as they did not have the same rite-liturgical structures and the same organizational and aesthetic pattern as the hegemonic religion accepted by the State, black people were not guaranteed freedom of religious manifestations. Despite the enactment of Decree N. 119-A, of January 7, 1890, prohibiting the intervention of the federal authority and the federated states in religious matters, the decree did not recognize Candomblé, for example, as a religion.

The impossibility of cultural recognition of religious manifestations of African origin was also due to the criminalization of different practices of Spiritism from the Penal Code of 1890, framing the practice of Candomblé in this scenario. From Articles number 156, 157 and 158 of the Penal Code mentioned below, it can be observed that the limitation of religiosity presents punishments to "magical practices", "to witchdoctors", "to charlatanism and to Spiritism", making anyone involved in such cults be tried for crimes against the order:

Art. 156. Practice medicine in any of its branches, dentistry or pharmacy: practice homeopathy, dosimetry, hypnotism or animal magnetism, without being authorized according to the laws and regulations.

Art. 157. Practicing spiritism, magic and their spells, using talismans and fortune-telling, to arouse feelings of hate or love, inculcate cures for curable or incurable diseases, in short, to fascinate and subjugate public credulity.

Art. 158. Administering or simply prescribing, as a curative means, for internal or external use, and in any prepared form, substance from any of the kingdoms of nature, thus performing, or exercising, the office of the so-called healer. (Brazilian Penal Code of 1890).

With the support of the Law, the use of such a code was an instrument of power legitimizing the common practice of police repression in the *terreiros* of Candomblé of Bahia, other states in the Northeast and Rio de Janeiro (Maggie, 2009), which extended from end of the 19th century to the middle of the 20th century. It was only from 1939 onwards, with the enactment of Decree of Law Number 1.202, that police attacks on the *terreiros* of Candomblé would be minimized. Despite the Decree vetoing the State and the Municipality from establishing, subsidizing or embargoing the exercise of religious cults, making the practice of Afro-religious cults "legal", even so, the persecutions did not cease. According to Oliveira (1978) the Candomblezeiros (Candomblé practitioners) were beaten, their musical instruments destroyed, the food spilled and their games prematurely ended.

This shows the great repression suffered by religious groups of African origin, making their organization and manifestations difficult. This scenario only began to change in the second half of the 20th century with the approval of Law Number 1.390 of July 3, 1951, transforming the practice of racial or color prejudice into a criminal misdemeanor. The religious issue was addressed years later, with the Federal Constitution of 1988, providing in its article number 5 the right to freedom of the exercise of faith. Finally, with the signing of Law number 7.716, transforming prejudice into an unbailable crime, the *terreiros* of Candomblé, among other Afro-religious manifestations, obtained real conditions to organize themselves. From this moment on, the process of institutionalization and regulation of the *terreiros* and other Afro-religious places of worship began. It is noteworthy that, most of the time, such spaces are located in remote and difficult to access and places on the outskirts of the city, or even camouflaged under religious models and arrangements with a peculiar aesthetic that recalls common standards to Christian doctrine. Even today, Ilê Axé Iyá Nasso Oka has in its interior remnants of altars where images of Catholic saints were displayed during their services (Silveira, 2006).

It is interesting to note that in this same period, more precisely in the late 1970s and early 1980s, IPHAN's policies signaled changes with regard to the recognition of heritage assets related to the identity of the Brazilian people. The policy hitherto concerned with the valorization of colonial historical sites and European architectural identity broadens its horizons on the notion of heritage and monument beyond the interpretations established by official history, also recognizing the contribution of different cultural matrices, as well as their material and immaterial heritage, which contributed to the formation of the identity of the Brazilian people. In this scenario of contradictions and contestations, the leaders of Ilê Axé Iyá Nasso Oka, in favor of the recognition and preservation of the *terreiro*, fall within the scope of IPHAN's heritage policy under a new perspective, highlighting the different forms of cultural and religious manifestations that contributed to the formation of national identity.

Umbanda and Candomblé: An Afro-Brazilian Religious Matrix

Umbanda in the mid-20th century promised to be the only Brazilian religion, "called 'the Brazilian religion' par excellence, Umbanda brought together white Catholicism, the tradition of the orixás of the black strand, and symbols, spirits and rituals of indigenous reference, thus being inspired by the three basic sources of mestizo Brazil" (Prandi, 2004, p. 223). Soon, Candomblé was created in the state of Bahia, being also considered a Brazilian religion of African origin, expanding and adapting throughout Brazil, through the doors opened by Umbanda.

The Umbanda and the Candomblé religion began to be persecuted in the Vargas Era (1930-1945), a government supported by the Catholic religion. Umbanda and Candomblé were taxed as mystifying and false religions, being, therefore, forced to "whiten" their cults. This fact gave rise to religious syncretism and the mixed Brazilian social construction in relation to religion. In this scenario, Rohde explains that "in the 1930s, in the midst of the elaboration of a Brazilian identity, of an imagined nationality, miscegenation is taken as the true national characteristic, recognized and exalted by the Estado Novo" (Rohde, 2009, p. 86). As stated earlier, from then on,

Umbanda and Candomblé began to suffer regular attacks against their manifestation, being forced to syncretism with the Catholic religion. In the described context, several social perceptions emerged that are impregnated in Brazilian society in relation to Umbanda and other religions of African origin, involving prejudice and religious intolerance, causing serious social problems experienced today.

With regard to the moralization of religion – which in its foundations did not exist, there was the construction of the image of a God similar to man and punisher, doing justice to Christian thought. With that, "all *terreiros*, or almost all, seem to have been somehow affected by it. The idea of a transcendent and perfect God, the conception of sin, the incorporation of Christian values and attitudes, are widely generalized" (Negrão, 1994, p. 116). Perhaps, for this reason, Nietzsche (1895) argues that Christianity ends up being like a factory of acculturation and ethnocentrism.

Regarding economic interests, Umbanda initially had as its main foundation "Love, faith and charity", as in the Bible "Give and receive". However, these ideas, while similar, can have antagonistic connotations. The words love and charity refer to the act of welcoming and offering with non-profit interest, a more altruistic and intangible thought, while giving and receiving can mean something broader, that is, "visible" and/or intangible.

In this way, giving refers to the affective or material sense; receiving, on the other hand, represents the meaning of spiritual and/or material return, such as tithes, baptisms and marriages, which in all of them have a monetary fee as an offering. Therefore, it is attested that "economic interest can lead to greed and the denial of charity, but also, in the extreme case, to the opposite, the realization of evil against the innocent" (Negrão, 1994, p. 118). This behavior can reflect both the entry and exit of believers and practitioners of different religions, beliefs and doctrines.

Religious tourism, from the Umbanda and the Candomblé perspective, can appropriate the mystical, esoteric and cultural aspects, behaving as a comprehensive activity and breaking social standards rooted by the Christian mass, for its plurality and for being holistic, giving rise to the different possibilities of doing and studying tourism, in order to be fair and common. The activities and tourist services related to religion essentially deal with pilgrimages, and, in the case of Brazil, the studied pilgrimages are mostly related to the Catholic religion. It so happens that this is not the only religious matrix in Brazilian territory (Dias & Silveira, 2003).

For this reason, religious tourism must, by obligation and ethics, provide democracy in the access to diverse religious cultures, paying attention to the very notion of cultural diversity that predominates in the country. As a result, due to its diversity and invisibility, Brazil emerges with an enormous potential for the religious exploration of tourism, in the quest to understand the various facets of each religion or belief. A form of travel in which the main motivation is religious, however, other motivations may occur, such as curiosity or cultural interest in understanding the tangible and intangible manifestations of a particular religious culture (Dias & Silveira, 2003).

The experiences offered by the phenomenon of religious tourism have several aspects, from the search for the exotic, mystical or esoteric, to faith and knowledge of culture and recognition of the other. Thus, it is highlighted that "the experience of the sacred dates back to individual and collective behaviors quite remote in the history of humanity" (Rosendahl, 2002, p. 232). The sacred, as inscribed in the origins of religious tourism, refers to the search for faith and spiritual healing.

From the pretexts of faith, penance and worship, there are meetings, shopping, entertainment, health and education exercises, etc., in addition to mystical renewal, overcoming the simple mechanism of the satisfaction of needs (Oliveira, 2005). Within the religions of African origin, there are cultural manifestations in the form of worship and celebration of saints and orixás, as well as in other religions, such as processions, pilgrimages and celebration of the gods, saints or religious entities. The hierarchy in the African pantheon of orixás, which the Umbanda and the Candomblé appropriate, is as follows:

- **Oxalá:** Supreme orixá, syncretized with Jesus Christ, he is at the top of the hierarchy being considered the father of all, representing the color white. His symbol is an Apaxorô – an aluminum staff, or the white dove.
- **Iemanjá:** Goddess of the seas, mermaid of the waters, receives several names such as Janaína, Dandaluna among other names, being the mother of all people. It is syncretized with the Virgin Mary, Our Lady of Navigators, among other saints that vary by region. Her symbol is a mirror.
- **Nanã Boruquê:** The oldest orixá of the female class, Goddess of mud and the depths of the rivers. She is the matriarch of the orixás, syncretized by Sainta Ana. Her symbol is the Ibiri – a kind of large rattle decorated with straw and whelks. Nanã's color is Lilac.
- **Obaluaê:** God of life and death, health and disease, syncretized by Saint Lazare. Its symbol is a Xaxará – an instrument similar to that of Nanã. His colors are black and white.
- **Ogun:** God of war, syncretized by Saint George. He carries a sword with him, so the ones that are guarded by Ogun say they are protected by his sword or the sword of Saint George. His color is red or light green.
- **Iansã:** Goddess of storms, lightning and thunder, syncretized by Santa Barbara. Her symbols are a sword and a ponytail. Her color is red or dark brown.
- **Xangô:** God of justice and quarries, syncretized by Saint Geronimo or Saint John the Baptist, represented by an axe. His color is brown or white and red.

- **Oxum:** Goddess of rivers and streams, syncretized by Our Lady of Aparecida. Her symbol is similar to that of Iemanjá, being that a mirror. Her color is golden yellow.
- **Oxóssi:** God of the woods, nature itself, syncretized by San Sebastian or, in some states of Brazil, Saint George. His symbols are a bow and arrow and a ponytail. His color is green or blue.
- **Ibêjis or Children:** they are the mystical deities that exist in the *terreiros* that brighten the environment, for their innocence. Syncretized by Cosmas and Damian, their symbols are an Ogun sword (kind of plant) or sweets. They are also represented by twins. Their color is blue and pink.
- **Exu:** God of virility and carnal desires responsible for the protection and opening of paths. He is syncretized by Saint Anthony. Its symbol is an Ogó (a tool similar to a male sexual organ) with garlic. His color is black and red.

The description of the symbols and Catholic saints with which the entities are syncretized, as well as the objects associated with the orixás are still unknown by a large part of the Brazilian population. The presentation of such elements, given that they are little known, has the objective of dissemination and identification.

It is important to point out that Umbanda and Candomblé are monotheistic religions, because as much as natural elements such as the orixás are created, which are represented by natural figures, such as water, earth, fire and air, Umbanda and Candombé practitioners believe in the likeness of God to man, similar to Christianity.

In the context of Umbanda and Candomblé, it is common to worship saints, such as the Iemanjá festivals held on the beaches, the Oxum festivals at the waterfalls, among other festivals for Orixás, Santos, Caboclos, Pretos Velhos, Erês and other entities. Furthermore, gastronomy is a strong point of expression and devotion to the saints, a peculiarity that each orixá has its favorite food. Hospitality, gastronomy and religious cultural diversity are the characteristic point of Umbanda and Candomblé. In the context of tourism, these characteristics are part of the necessary framework for the development of responsible tourism, which provides for the integration of cultures and the guarantee of the maintenance of Brazilian religious diversity.

TOURISM, CONTRADICTION AND AFRO-RELIGIOUS (IN) VISIBILITY

Brazil is considered one of the most religious countries in the world, if not the most Catholic, "Brazil is the largest Catholic country in the world, with a population characterized by high religiosity" (Cypriano & Lima, 2008, p. 7). According to the Brazilian Institute of Geography and Statistics (IBGE, 2022) data in absolute numbers collected in the last national census in 2010, the largest group is composed of Catholics (123,280,172 people), the second by Evangelicals (42,275,440), followed by Spiritualists (3,848,876 people). African-based religions correspond to a much smaller number with Candomblé (167,363 people), Umbanda and Candomblé (588,797 people), Umbanda (407,331 people) and other declarations of Afro-Brazilian religiosity (14,103 people). In this way, the importance of religious events in the Brazilian tourist context can be noted, being a segment with high potential for social, economic and cultural development.

In Brazil, and more specifically in tourism, racisms defined as every day, institutional and structural are present in different ways (Oliveira, 2021). In addition, racism appears in the lack of offer and promotion of cultural attractions related to the culture and history of black people. This is also reflected in studies on the subject in the country, as Afro-religious culture and manifestations are not the agenda of academic discussions in the field of tourism. A survey carried out in the seven national journals linked to the eleven Postgraduate Programs with a basic area in tourism revealed that, of the 2,618 articles published in the journals, only five give space to the theme, totaling 0.19% of everything already produced (Oliveira, 2021).

Another face of racism in tourism, but now mentioned in research, can be exemplified in the study conducted by Macena (2008). The author analyzed the African heritage existing in the Cabula neighborhood in Salvador, in the state of Bahia, and points out the unique aspect of the territory conferred by the concentration of *terreiros* of Candomblé and typical quilombola[1] food restaurants. Although the researcher gathered enough data to prove the cultural richness of the place and, in this way, to be a justification for attracting visitors, the residents of the neighborhood themselves did not identify these same elements as a potential for tourism. In other words, the community itself does not understand the cultural wealth represented there.

Seeking to give visibility to traditional communities, ethnic tourism becomes an alternative. The ethnotourism, when well planned, implemented and managed, can promote interaction between tourists and the local population, as well as the different groups of tourists among themselves, the understanding of the local context visited, the socialization of local residents among themselves, and the resignification of the relationship with tourism and tourists present in the territory. Ethnotourism "is inserted, therefore, in what is intended to be understood by democratic, pluralist, complex, multiethnic and multicultural societies" (Trigo & Panosso Netto, 2011, p. 6).

The official definition adopted by the Brazilian government and which serves as a guide for public policies in the sector defines Ethnic Tourism, or ethnotourism, as a segment of tourism formed by the set of activities based on the experience of authentic experiences arising from direct contact with the modes of life and identity of ethnic groups. In this segment, there is a search for proximity and interaction with the host community, participation in its traditional activities, participatory observation and learning about cultural expressions, lifestyles and unique customs. The official definition adopted in Brazil also highlights that in many cases ethnotourism activities are a search for the tourist's own origins, in a return to the traditions of their ancestors (Brasil, 2006).

When analyzing the definition of religious tourism it is possible to consider that the discussion about tourism in spaces and/or events related to Afro-religious culture, practiced by many Brazilians, has interfaces with both segments. This interface with the ethnic component is necessary when analyzing the relationship between Brazilians and religions from other countries and continents.

It is important to remember that Brazil is a country historically tolerant of all religious manifestations, but cults of African origin have always been, at least, marginalized. A fact that does not occur with Asian, Arab and/or European religions practiced in national territory. According to the National Human Rights Ombudsman of the Brazilian Ministry of Women, Family and Human Rights, in 2021 there were 586 complaints of violation of religious freedom regarding Afro-religious culture. It shows an increase of 141% in relation to the previous year, which had 243 complaints (Brasil, 2022). It is clear that everyday racism is reflected in the way African-based religions are seen in Brazil. And it is clear that how this is reflected in the little appreciation and demand that these spaces still have for tourists, as they are still marginalized and located on the outskirts of large urban centers.

CONCLUSION

African-based religions need to be further studied and understood in a global context. Understanding these religions is of paramount importance for tourism and other areas that are interested in religious cults. It is not possible to generate innovations and development if there are prejudice, resistance and the ability to see natural and immaterial potentialities. Through this research, it was possible to identify both the peculiarities of religions of African origin and their potential, seeking to demystify the prejudices about Umbanda and Candomblé. Tourism as a transforming and holistic activity has the role of reinventing and restructuring itself from new perspectives and perspectives of social use.

The *terreiros* still suffer prejudice and are made invisible by the public authorities. In the case of the study, it was possible to identify that despite having its historical and cultural importance recognized, it has not become a prominent tourist destination not yet bringing positive economic and social impacts to the surrounding community.

We conclude that despite the historical and cultural relevance of religions such as Candomblé and Umbanda, the Afro-religious heritage is neglected in Brazil by the government and, in general, by a large portion of the population. We believe that this fact is a reflection of the racism that exists in Brazilian society and that tourism can be a means of valuing, preserving and disseminating the great diversity and wealth of symbols, rituals and sacred places of religions of African origin.

REFERENCES

Appolinário, F. (2006). *Methodology of science: philosophy and practice of research* [Metodologia da ciência: filosofia e prática da pesquisa]. Pioneira Thomson Learning.

Brasil. (2006). *Ministry of Tourism. Tourism Segmentation: Conceptual Milestones* [Ministério do Turismo. Segmentação do Turismo: Marcos Conceituais]. Brasília: Ministério do Turismo.

Brasil. (2010). *Ministry of Tourism Cultural tourism: basic guidelines* [Ministério do Turismo Turismo cultural: orientações básicas] (3rd ed.). Brasília: Ministério do Turismo.

Brasil. (2022). *Ministry of Women, The Family and Human Rights. Panel of data of the National Ombudsman for Human Rights* [Ministério da Mulher, da Família e dos Direitos Humanos. Painel de dados da Ouvidoria Nacional de Direitos Humanos]. Brasília: Ministério da Mulher, da Família e dos Direitos Humanos.

Instituto do Patrimônio Histórico e Artístico Nacional - IPHAN. (2015). *IPHAN precautionary policies: Ilê Axé Iyá Nassô Oká: White House terreiro* [Políticas de acautelamento do IPHAN: Ilê Axé Iyá Nassô Oká: Terreiro da Casa Branca]. IPHAN.

Kühl, B. M. (2006). History and ethics in the conservation and restoration of historical monuments [História e ética na conservação e na restauração de monumentos históricos]. *Revista CPC*, (1), 16–40. doi:10.11606/issn.1980-4466.v0i1p16-40

Londres, C. (2000) Cultural references: basis for new heritage policies [Referências culturais: base para novas políticas de patrimônio]. In Inventário nacional de referências culturais: manual de aplicação. Brasília (DF): Instituto do Patrimônio Histórico e Artístico Nacional.

Macena, D. D. O. (2008). Socio-cultural tourism in the Cabula neighborhood [Turismo sócio-cultural no bairro do Cabula]. *Seminário Estudantil de Produção Acadêmica, 11*(1).

Maggie, Y. (2009) The macumba arsenal. The objects of sorcery collected by the police throughout the twentieth century [O arsenal da macumba. Os objetos da feitiçaria recolhidos pela polícia ao longo século XX]. Raízes Africanas.

MEC/SPHAN/FNPM. (1980). Protection and revitalization of cultural heritage in Brazil: a trajectory [Proteção e revitalização do patrimônio cultural no Brasil: uma trajetória]. Brasília: SPHAN/FNPM.

Melo, E., & Correa, A. M. (2016). Between flows and eflows, territorial agencies and the transnationalization of candomblé [Entre fluxos e refluxos, agenciamentos territoriais e a transnacionalização do candomblé]. In *Territorios, fiestas y paisajes peregrinos: cartografías sociales de lo sagrado.* Buenos Aires: La Imprenta Digital SRL.

Nascimento, W. F. (2016). On the candomblés as way of life: Philosophical images between Africas and Brasis [Sobre os candomblés como modo de vida: Imagens filosóficas entre Áfricas e Brasis. In: Ensaios Filosóficos]. Rio de Janeiro: UERJ.

Oliveira, A. G. d. (1978). *Candomblé sergipano.* SEC/CDFB.

Oliveira, N. A. d. (2021). Blacks and Tourism: analysis of academic production on the subject in journals linked to graduate programs in Tourism in Brazil [Negros e turismo: análise da produção acadêmica sobre o tema em revistas vinculadas aos Programas de Pós-Graduação em Turismo no Brasil]. *Rosa dos Ventos - Turismo e Hospitalidade, 13*(1), 219–238. Disponível em: http://www.ucs.br/etc/revistas/index.php/rosadosventos/article/view/8480

Pinheiro, M. L. B. (2006). Origins of the notion of preservation of cultural heritage in Brazil [Origens da noção de preservação do patrimônio cultural no Brasil]. *Risco Revista De Pesquisa Em Arquitetura E Urbanismo,* (3), 4-14. doi:10.11606/issn.1984-4506.v0i3p4-14

Sandroni, C. (2010). Samba de roda, intangible heritage of humanity [Samba de roda, patrimônio imaterial da humanidade]. *Estudos Avançados, 24*(69). Advance online publication. doi:10.1590/S0103-40142010000200023

Schwarcz, L. M. (1993). *The Spectacle of races – scientists, institutions and racial issue in Brazil 1870-1930* [O Espetáculo das Raças – cientistas, instituições e questão racial no Brasil 1870-1930]. Cia. das Letras.

Silveira, R. (2006). *The Candomblé da Barroquinha: Process of constitution of the first bahian terreiro of keto* [O Candomblé da Barroquinha: Processo de constituição do primeiro terreiro baiano de keto]. Edições Mainanga.

Trigo, L. G. G. (2020). Travel and tourism: from imagined scenarios to disruptive realities [Viagens e turismo: dos cenários imaginados às realidades disruptivas]. *Revista Brasileira de Pesquisa em Turismo (RBTUR), 14*(3), 1–13. Advance online publication. doi:10.7784/rbtur.v14i3.2107

Trigo, L. G. G., & Panosso Netto, A. (2011). *Afro ethnic tourism in Brazil. VIII Seminar of the National Association research and graduate in Tourism, Balneario Cambour* [Turismo étnico afro no Brasil. VIII Seminário da Associação Nacional Pesquisa e Pós-Graduação em Turismo, Balneário Camboriú]. https://www.anptur.org.br/anais/anais/files/8/10. pdf

ENDNOTE

1 The quilombolas are the remnants of an ethnic-racial group formed by descendants of runaway slaves during the period of slavery in Brazil, among other groups that lived in the so-called quilombos. Quilombos are spaces and communities formed by populations that were formed from situations of territorial, social and cultural resistance in Brazil.

Chapter 11
Tourism Promotion and Racism Against Indigenous People in Rio Grande do Norte (Brazil)

Marília Barbosa Gonçalves
https://orcid.org/0000-0002-1384-3301
Universidade Federal do Rio Grande do Norte, Brazil

Juanna Beatriz de Brito Gouveia
https://orcid.org/0000-0002-0707-5780
Universidade Federal do Rio Grande do Norte, Brazil

Daniel Dantas Lemos
Universidade Federal do Rio Grande do Norte, Brazil

Renata Laíze Alves Coelho Lins Paino Ribeiro
Universidade Federal do Rio Grande do Norte, Brazil

Guilherme Arnaud Lopes Nunes
Universidade Federal do Rio Grande do Norte, Brazil

ABSTRACT

Perceiving that the fields of tourism and communication are linked with a certain degree of dependence of the former on the latter, this chapter reinforces the importance of media discourse as an element to sustain the orientation of tourism production. For this reason, discursive elements that permeate this type of production, especially, in institutional and official spaces on the internet are the main goal. This text is based in studies about racism from a theoretical-methodological perspective of the critical discourse analysis based on ethics and aims to recognize the abuse of power in language in order to empower those under such oppression. From this perspective, two discursive events will be analyzed in spaces of official and institutional touristic publicity in Rio Grande do Norte on the internet.

DOI: 10.4018/978-1-6684-4194-7.ch011

INTRODUCTION

Tourism and communication go hand in hand, the former being practically dependent on the latter for success, based on the various forms of tourism promotion and dissemination that can be carried out and have already occurred long before the entire "digital revolution" that has been experienced. The work on these two themes is no longer new, but much is being done on the part of management linked to marketing metrics. In this chapter, the perspective is to bring another look, embarked on by Critical Discourse Analysis - ACD and associated with the discursive marks of racism in tourist communication, something little studied so far, seeking to recognize the discursive elements that permeate this type of production, especially in official/ institutional spaces on the Internet.

The methodology used is qualitative, based on CDA, the Analysis Çritique of this Discourse, and part of the conceptual understanding of the effects of the colonialist constitution of race, to justify a project of withdrawal of humanity from non-whites, and construction of a structural racism that permeates the discourses and builds relations of disadvantages and privileges through the use of institutions hegemonized by social groups that impose their economic and social interests. This contributes to social relations being collectively structured to reproduce the practice of denying the existence of the non-white other without, however, recognizing it, on the contrary, propagating the myth of racial democracy.

Racism against indigenous people is evident in various practices and violence, from the use of weapons, assimilation, acculturation, the appeal to national unity, but especially the historiographical erasure of the protagonism of indigenous resistance to European colonization. The precepts worked here on race and racism are based on Almeida (2019), Nascimento (1978;2016) and Milanez (2020). Then, it addresses more specifically how the relationship between communication in tourism and destination marketing takes place as an informer of the characteristics of places, recognizing that the lexical choices of the discourse designed to produce the imaginary through signs, most of the times of institutional form, reflecting social relations governed by power relations; in this sense, Coriolano (2005), Tomazzoni (2006), Falco (2011), Hintze & Almeida Júnior (2012), Oliveira (2021).

The idea of publicity on the internet and in wide-ranging social networks, of institutional advertising campaigns, while reflecting an expansion of access to information on tourist destinations, generating a democratization of information for the public, also concentrates on the part of broadcasters, thus developing tourism marketing, understanding the destination as a product. In view of this contextualization of the presupposed frameworks, this work aims to recognize the discursive elements on structural racism that permeate tourism communication, as well as to present the methodology of Critical Discourse Analysis as a tool that is interested in identifying the discursive reproduction of situations of abuse. of power, which result in inequality and social injustice based on the concept of power in its linguistic conception, discursive and communication. Van Dijk (2015), starting from a concrete context, understood as situated social practice, the perspectives of critical discourse analysis are explained, moving on to the analysis of the corpus, starting with the choice of the name "Everything Begins Here", on the page of the Rio Grande do Norte Tourism Office.

BACKGROUND

Race and Racism

Silvio Almeida (2019, p. 22) highlights, since the beginning of the last century, that anthropology and biology have shown that there are no cultural or biological differences that justify discrimination between human beings, yet, the idea of race still naturalizes and it legitimizes inequality, segregation and the genocide of sociological minority groups. It is thus essential to understand the origin of this concept, which today is an important political factor.

The concept of race emerges as the populations of these primitive places seek for themselves the benefits of liberal revolutions, opposing colonial forces, says Almeida (2019, p. 19-20).

With nineteenth-century positivism, philosophical questions about human differences were transformed into scientific questions. The thought classified as scientific racism was embraced by academic and political circles.

Biology and physics served as explanatory models of human diversity: the idea was born that biological characteristics - biological determinism - or climatic and/or environmental conditions - geographic determinism - would be able to explain the moral, psychological and intellectual differences between different races. In this way, non-white skin and the tropical climate would favor the emergence of immoral, lascivious and violent behaviors, besides to indicate little intelligence (Almeida, 2019, p. 21).

From the historical perspective of the concept, race operates from two basic registers that intersect and complement each other: 1) as a biological characteristic, in which race is attributed by physical trait, such as skin color; 2) as an ethnic-cultural characteristic, where racial identity is associated with geographic origin, religion, language or other customs, a certain way of existing.

Then, Almeida (2019) goes on to address racism, which he defines as: a systematic form of discrimination based on race, and which is manifested through conscious or unconscious practices that culminate in disadvantages or privileges for individuals, depending on the racial group to which they belong (Almeida, 2019, p. 22).

The author (2019) reiterates that racism has a systemic character, not being an act or a set of discriminatory acts, but a process, which can be a) individualistic; b) institutional; c) structural.

In the first conception, racism would be an ethical or psychological phenomenon of an individual or collective nature, attributed to isolated groups; or, still, racism would be an "irrationality" to be fought in the legal field through the application of civil or criminal sanctions, says Almeida (2019, p.26). This classification covers only individual or collective attitudes and fails to consider racism in the functioning of society, through its institutions.

These institutions, where the second manifestation of racism operates, promote stability by establishing norms and standards of action for conflicts and the antagonisms that are inherent to social life, in addition to themselves carrying these conflicts. In other words, racial inequality does not occur only in the isolated action of racist groups or individuals, but because institutions are hegemonized by racial groups that mechanize the functioning of society to impose their political and economic interests, making culture, standards aesthetics and power practices of a given group are the civilizing pattern of society. Therefore, institutions can act within this conflict, treating racial inequality as a problem to not reproduce racist practices considered "normal" in society.

The third conception, the structural one, addresses institutions as the materialization of the social structure, that is, institutions are racist because society is racist (Almeida, 2019, p.33). In this way, racism is not a social pathology or an institutional breakdown, but a factor arising from the structure of society, in political, economic, legal and family relationships.

A fundamental element for understanding how racism, against black people, indigenous peoples and other non-whites, are structural elements in Brazilian society is the myth of racial democracy, which we will address in the next session.

The Myth of Racial Democracy

For a long time the idea that Brazil would be a "racial democracy" was part of the Brazilian imagination. Thereof, Guimarães (1994) states that any study of racism in Brazil must begin by noting that racism in Brazil is a taboo, due to this notion that the country would be provided with an "institutional antiracism". Such a perception originates in history as well as in anthropological and sociological literature. In general, specialized research, such as the studies of Gilberto Freyre in the early 1930s, followed by Donald Pierson between the 1940s and 1970s, re-affirmed a relative harmony in race relations in Brazil. Yet, as Abdias Nascimento (1978) points out, the historical truth is quite the opposite and dissects this historical truth, dissecting the diverse violence motivated by racism in Brazil, from symbolic ways of suppressing culture and spirituality to the extermination of non-white peoples.

The dominating society in Brazil has destroyed the indigenous populations that were once the majorities in the country; this same society is on the edge of completing the crushing of the descendants of Africans. The techniques used have been manifold, depending on the circumstances, from the mere use of weapons to indirect and subtle manipulations that are sometimes called assimilation, other times acculturation or miscegenation; other times it is the appeal to national unity, civilizing action, etc. (Nascimento, 1978, p.101).

Thus, the idea of racial democracy not only ignores motivated violence in Brazil, but is also a tool to manipulate, through the appeal to national unity, the legacy of groups that have been victims of racism throughout the country's history.

For the creators of this racial democracy, Brazilian civilization would be open to all contributions, without any distinction, whether European, Amerindian or African, as stated by Pierre Verger (*apud* Nascimento, 2016, p. 99). Though, the defenders of this concept have in common the emphasis on the surreptitious survival characteristic of the cultural traits of non-whites in Brazil. According to Gilberto Freyre, these cultural traits that "infiltrate" into religion, cuisine, music, sculpture and painting of European origin represent not the degradation, but the enrichment of these values (*apud* Nascimento, 2016, p. 99-100).

In this sense, at the same time that they consider the integration of these cultural traits into the dominant culture the demonstration of a supposed harmonious acceptance, they state that these values have illicit and marginal origins, having infiltration as the means for this integration. Focusing on the presence of enslaved Africans in Brazil, Nascimento says that for [...] beneath the abundant generosity granted to African values, the implications of the concept of infiltration emerge, also obvious: they denounce the subterranean nature and the marginal condition, outside the law, of what infiltrates (NASCIMENTO, 1978, p. 106).

Finally, Guimarães (1994) points out that the mythical nature of racial democracy, a concept that would be the "founding myth of Brazilian nationality", is the reason why this ideal must denounce as an unfulfilled promise.

Racism Against Indigenous

In the 18th century, the Dutch ethnologist Cornelius de Pauw wrote that Native Americans have no history, are unhappy, degenerate, irrational animals whose temperit is as humid as the air and land where they grow, points out Almeida (2019). Such a definition of the original peoples of the "new world" demonstrates the dichotomous perception of civilized-primitives between Europeans and indigenous people present in the colonialist imagination. This vision reverberates to the present day in the racism of the social structure and institutions, which normalize the erasure of the history of these peoples, for example.

Little attention has been paid by traditional historiography to the protagonism of indigenous resistance to European colonization, too addressing the "transition" from indigenous to black slavery in a way that reinforces the narrative of extinction, placing indigenous people in a past time. It also disregards the violent system of exploitation, dispossession and genocide from the early colonial period that remains until today. A new historiography of Brazil illuminates this reality of indigenous peoples, venting their protagonism in history and denying mythical perspectives of a heroic colonization.

Darcy Ribeiro (1970) revealed the violence of the "integration" of indigenous peoples to settlers, in an investigation of the relationship between indigenous and whites. While he hoped that the result would be assimilation through miscegenation, research has revealed that the majority of the indigenous population has been wiped out, while the survivors remain self-identified indigenous. The main reason for this ethnic transfiguration (Ribeiro, 1970, p. 17), it was the conflict between settlers and indigenous peoples that barred European expansion.

The work by Milanez et al. (2020) considers that the multiple experiences narrated help us to realize that talking about racism against indigenous peoples means entering an amalgam of practices and discourses whose common element has been the structural violence that marks indigenous daily lives from North to South of Brazil. At innumerable facets of violence that have been a striking and foundational feature of indigenous history in societies like ours, characterized by colonialism, need to be face seriousness and commitment (Milanez et al., 2020).

Next, we will reflect on elements of communication and tourism, and then present Critical Discourse Analysis as a theoretical-methodological perspective that will help us in the task of observing the corpus highlighted in this work with the goal of verifying the discursive marks of racism present in tourist dissemination materials[1]. That erase the indigenous peoples of Rio Grande do Norte and silence them.

Communication, Marketing and Discourse in Tourism

The junction of tourism and communication already happens naturally, since the first depends on the second to promote itself, reach the public, attract demand, build success or embitter the crisis. Zardo (2003) reminds us that for a good development of the activity, tourism and communication need to be inseparable, since it is only through communication that the tourist will reach the product, he wants to consume, in addition to obtaining varied information and news. Thus, the media discourse facilitates the consumer's understanding of tourist information and promotions.

Tomazzoni (2006, p. 340) states that one of the elements that most support the orientation of tourism production towards the market economy is the media discourse, which also influences the ideology of tourism consumption, justifies the satisfaction of customers' needs, to the detriment of the social demands of the host communities. The author still reinforces that this discourse contributes significantly to the existence of tourism, as it is not simply a factor in the visibility of destinations and attractions, and can be more seductive and more touristy than the attraction itself that it advertises.

For Coriolano (2005, p. 51), tourism has its own discourse. It is the representatives of governments, entrepreneurs and communities that formulate it. Discourses are produced for the control of society or the subjects themselves. The author also recalls that the discourse around places and tourism is a controversial repertoire, in which the referent is disputed by those interested, in a tense relationship of changes in meanings, configuring itself as a practice of resistance and confrontation.

Cooper et al. (1998) sees that the tourism discourse contributes to sustaining and preserving cultures, and can also institute acculturation processes that transform and destroy cultures. In this analysis, we will see more. The forward like the lexical choices for promotional campaigns and institutional texts of the destination Rio Grande do Norte were made destroying part of its history and culture, in favor of the European people. In this sense Coriolano (2006, p. 52) states that the analysis of discourse, the imaginary, the signs, the images are produced in a way related to the way in which social relations are inscribed in history and are governed by power relations.

The internet has fostered the discourse of tourism, through new forms of communication, dissemination and marketing of tourism. According to Buhalis & Law (2008), it has reformulated the way information related to tourism is distributed, the way people consume and plan trips. Falco (2011, p. 25) says that marked by the emergence of new technologies and by the resurgence of old human needs, the means of communication and travel also started to be seen from new paradigms of social understanding. To influence and persuade people to travel, arousing the desire to discover a new place, in addition to maintaining or improving the destination's image, attracting new consumers, providing information on supply, encourage joint efforts and correct distortions (Marujo, 2008; Heath & Wall, 1991).

It can be said that we are facing a great paradox, because if on the one hand we have the technological evolution of the media and the bombardment of information to which we are subjected daily, we also have a proliferation of specialized media, generating a democratization of the public and a concentration on the part of issuers (Wenzel & John, 2012). This democratization also allowed greater access of tourist. The detailed information over the tourist destination, such as its history, curiosities, infrastructure, services, among others. Thus, keeping official information channels active on tourist destinations with institutional texts and news is essential.

According to Falco (2011), in this context, tourist destinations increasingly need specialized media to reach tourists' imagination and plans. For this reason, websites and official profiles of destinations on social networks are so necessary, so that the tourist has security when looking for information. With this advancement of technologies in the media, we sought to create a sense of presence and participation for the reader/tourist, a fact that could lead to the formatting of texts, reports or materials to take the reader to undertake a kind of journey imaginary at the time of reading or viewing, instigating the presence physics of individuals and the interaction with space and its population (Falco, 2011, p. 37). From this perspective, tourism marketing comes in with the focus of increasing the attractiveness of the public, whether internal or external, considering the development of positioning strategies. According to Seaton (1996), destination marketing is the nerve center of tourism marketing, as it is the destination that concentrates and supports the different interests involved in the tourist activity.

For Pearce (1992), Destination Marketing Organizations (DMOs) play an important role in marketing and promoting a tourist destination. They are, consequently, considered the best providers of information about the attractions of destinations.

According to Cooper et al. (2007), destination marketing is still a relatively new process for many places, particularly at the regional and local levels, where those responsible tend to be the public sector, which ends up generating a series of implications for the marketing process that are rooted in inability of this sector to control the product. But, in general, the communication process is maintained.

Since the destination is a product that cannot be known a priori and the experience can only live on the spot, communication makes it possible to generate these expectations in the consumer about the destination (Ladeiro, 2012, p. 23). When creating a slogan, devising a new marketing positioning or a promotional campaign, the destination and those planning its communication need to be ware of the message they want to deliver to the tourist, and how it will be interpreted.

Any statement carries intentions, including marketing aimed at tourism, whose goal, eventually, in the case of promoting tourist destinations, is to lead to commercial behavior.

For Ladeiro (2012, p. 26), it is in the strategic marketing phase that the identity of the tourist destination is defined, and its positioning, that is, the part of the identity that is decided to communicate to the target audience. In turn, in the operational marketing phase, the identity is communicated through its signs - logo and slogan.

Analyzing tourism communication from the critical discourse brings this conversation to a new field, full of new information based on media precepts and, for referring to the discursive marks of structural racism. To have an idea, the theme of racism is still rarely dealt with in Tourism in Brazil, so perchance bringing it to the media field is more plausible, in search of a more sensitive look. The work closest to the theme of this project is aligned with the article "Estudos críticos em turismo: A comunicação turística e o mito da democracia racial no Brasil", by Hintze and Almeida Jr. (2012), in which they analyze, from the perspective of the discourse critic, images from Viagem e Turismo magazine. This research, on the other hand, aims to analyze the discourses of official channels of tourist destinations on the Internet.

The research carried out by Oliveira (2021, p. 233) is also an example, which brings an investigation into the scientific knowledge produced in national journals linked to Post Graduate Tourism Programs, and found that, of 2,618 articles by them, already published, only five (0.19%) present discussions that analyze the theme black people and tourism. In the same vein, we also have the database on Tourism and Ethnic-Racial Relations, from UNIRIO, which presents the production of articles, dissertations and theses, books and book chapters, news, podcasts, lives, IGs and TVs about Tourism and Ethnic-Racial Relations, and demonstrates the very few productions on the subject.

These data are reinforced when we look at the annals of the National Association of Research and Post Graduate Studies in Tourism – Anptur, among the publications from 2005 to 2020. Of the 2,839 published works, (0.39%) 11 deal with the Indigenous theme, while (0 .32%) 9 deal with Blacks, but not all publications envisage the context of racism, including articles with the word racism in the title were not found. Milanez et al. (2020), when addressing racism against indigenous people in Brazil, points to the scarcity of literature on the subject and brings testimonies and practical and theoretical reflections of indigenous authors on racism.

It is noteworthy how low the frequency of the theme is, however, as Hudson et al. (2018), the academic literature on Tourism pays little attention to the relationship between racial discrimination and tourism. According to Oliveira (2021, p.233) the few results found reveal a silencing in the academy in Tourism in Brazil, of themes that discuss racism and tourism, which turns out to be symptomatic of how they appear in the activity, or worse, do not appear, which further reinforces the idea of bringing the discussion to the media field.

Since the official communication of destinations is managed by public bodies, governments, at their municipal, state or national level, must be aware of the agendas discussed and defended in contemporary times, bringing this context into tourist marketing.

It is from this communication that the potential consumer will form an image of the tourist destination. In this way, what image would you form of a destiny that tells you: "It all starts here?"

MAIN FOCUS OF THE CHAPTER

The Critical Discourse Analysis

Talking about Critical Discourse Analysis, Van Dijk (2015, p. 9) lists several fundamental aspects for the understanding of works in this area. Critical Discourse Analysis (CDA) is interested in the discursive reproduction of situations of abuse of power. So, the examination of the concept of power is a central task, from the linguistic, discursive and communicational dimensions. In this way, CDAs are concerned with analyzing how a specific intonation, a pronoun, a journalistic headline, a topic, a lexical item, a metaphor, a color or a camera angle, among a range of other semiotic properties of the discourse, relate to something as abstract and general as power relations in society.

This theoretical-methodological perspective uses any method that is relevant to the objectives of its research projects, and such methods are those used in discourse studies in general. Thus, we understand that Critical Discourse Analysis is not a method, but a set of academic, transdisciplinary practices that can be adopted and relate to all human and social sciences.

This is how we can say that ACD is not just interested in the any type of power, but focuses on the abuse of power, that is, on forms of domination that result in social inequalities and injustices.

This theoretical-methodological perspective is based on applied ethics and a moral philosophy to be able to define that abuse is bad - which leads the analyst to be concerned, for example, with the critical analysis of discursive practices manifested in prejudice, racism and in sexism. This analysis assumes that these forms of social abuse are wrong because they are inconsistent with social equality.

ACD cannot be neutral. As Batista Jr, Sato & Melo (2018, p. 13) say, it always takes a critical stand. Criticism, the authors recall, walks, in this way, in a double sense - both normative, (applying value judgments) in its starting point, and explanatory, when revealing the mechanisms and social articulations that perpetuate power relations (Batista Jr, Sato & Melo, 2018, p. 13).

Critical Discourse Studies

In CDA, discourse is not only analyzed as an autonomous "verbal" object, but also as a situated interaction, as a social practice or as a type of communication.in asocial, cultural, historical or controversial situation. Yet, about the special analytical focus of critical discourse studies, CDA methods do not infringe on the rights of the people studied and are compatible with the interests of the social groups that are the focus of research, that is, they are chosen so that research can contribute to the social empowerment of dominated groups, especially in the domain of discourse and communication.

It is in this way that discursive situations of abuse of power are analyzed that, in the perspective of ACD, can only manifest itself in the language in circumstances where there is the possibility of variation or choice, such as calling the Portuguese occupation at the time of the colony "discovery" or "invasion", depending on the speaker's position and ideology.

This makes it clear that CDA focuses on the properties of discourse that are commonly associated with the expression, confirmation, reproduction, or confrontation of the speaker's or writer's social power as a member of the dominant group – as a white man when referring to Brazilian indigenous peoples in a racist way. This racist discourse emphasizes, in various discursive ways, the positive characteristics of our own group and its members, and the (alleged) negative characteristics of the Others, the outside group, playing a key role in expression, acquisition, confirmation, and so, in the reproduction of social inequality.

Therefore, a CDA will have as its goals the study of the discursive reproduction of the abuse of power; the relations of domination from the perspective of the dominated group and its interest; from the experiences of members of dominated groups, used as evidence to assess dominant discourse; what can be shown of the discursive actions of the dominant group as illegitimate; of how viable alternatives to dominant discourses that are compatible with the interests of dominated groups can be formulated. Such research is committed to an engagement in favor of dominated groups in society: they take a position and do so explicitly.

In Critical Discourse Studies, the notion of power, which in itself does not need to be abusive, is understood, according to Van Dijk (2015), as the control of a group over other groups and their members. Thus, abuse of power occurs when control is in the exclusive interest of those who exercise power and against the interests of those who are controlled.

The first step towards the abusive exercise of control and power is to control the discourse and its contexts. For example, elite or powerful organizations can decide who can and cannot take part in some communicative event, when, where and with what purposes – it can define who can be news in the newspapers and in what way, or who will appear in the history books or not.

For years, the official discourse defined that there were no indigenous peoples remaining in Rio Grande do Norte and, by establishing this, excluded any members of this ethnic group from participating, in this condition, in any communicative event.

Methodology

This work is based on the understanding that CDA is says as being textually oriented, which means that its discursive analysis is done on the material basis of concrete texts. The ACD is also says as socially oriented, since it observes themes related to inequalities, oppression, violence, abuse of power with the purpose of promoting change in the asymmetric situation and social change. It is for this reason, as stated above, that CDA recognizes itself as compromised and biased. In Fairclough's perspective on CDA, one of the fundamental theoretical-methodological elements for the method of a Criticism of Discourse is the three-dimensional conception of discourse, which is cited by us from Gonçalves-Segundo (2018). In this conception, it is understood, first, that all discourse manifests itself in a text Gonçalves-Segundo (2018, p. 80), constituting a discursive event. Second, Gonçalves-Segundo (2018, p. 80) says that all discourse is processed by a discursive practice of production, distribution, consumption and interpretation textual. And in the third dimension, the model understands that all discourse fits into a social/sociocultural practice.

The discourse, then, manifests itself in the discursive event, in the text. When describing the manifestation of discourse in the text, which can be presented in different semiosis, the analyst must be able to state from the text the discursive and social practices that are involved there. In this it is possible to perceive the embedding that texts and discursive practices have within social practice - what a text manifests are a discourse that circulates in the form of power relations that fit from social practices and discursive processes.

Batista Jr; Sato & Melo (2018, p. 16-17) present the script that we assumed, at least in part, in this work: (a) identify a problem in social practice that needs to be uncovered; (b) identify the networks of practices in which the problem is inserted. In these representations are power and ideology; (c) perceive the action of discourse and the order of discourse; (d) apply the categories of textual analysis to text analysis (discursive genre) to confront in the discursive instance what was observed in the analysis of practices; (e) reflect on the role of practices in relation to the configurations of the text, discriminating the participation of practices in the problem studied; (f) check possible ways of overcoming in the midst of social practices and discourses; (g) to reflect, explaining the relationships between the elements of practice with a view to unveiling the problem, explaining the hegemonic articulations for possible overcoming the observed reality.

Discourse analysis in a critical perspective starts from an ethical position, as we said above, so it needs to be careful when it comes to defining what is right and wrong, fair and unfair, so that the problem under analysis must be inserted into the analysis in a way that can result in reflexivity and agency for those who remain subjugated and/or socially disadvantaged. By revealing the order of the speech, research it reveals at the same time the position of the participants in the face of power and the modes of relationships that are established between the subjects and that regulate this order of parley.

SOLUTIONS AND RECOMMENDATIONS

The publicity material of Rio Grande do Norte as a destination, officially published by the state government and its tourism company, will be taken here as a corpus for analysis, since they are relevant discursive events in the official discourse of the public power in the social sphere. of tourism promotion.

This is how we will focus on highlighting, at first, the website Visit Rio Grande do Norte[2], which was called, until recently, "Everything starts here"[3]. Dantas (2012) clarifies, based on what Charaudeau (2006) and Foucault (2007) thought, about the naming process in the scope of discourse. When Charaudeau (2006) describes the workings of the machinery that operates the media discourse and its production of sense and states that the first of its steps is the identification of the beings of the world, naming them Dantas (2012, p. 104). Dantas (2012, p. 104) goes on to quote Foucault (2007, p. 166) when defines the naming as sovereign act, the place where things and words are linked in their common essence, and which allows you to give them a name. Thus, says Dantas (2012, p. 166), the word and naming are based on an arbitrary relationship that, in the field of discourse, is essential for the organization of meanings. Naming implies a certain form of ideological framing, placing things in the world and their meaning in the midst of the process that Charaudeau (2006) calls the transformation of the world to be signified into a signified world. Giving a name positions the type of meaning that the enunciator intends to be established in the instance of meaning of the discourse which, in the case of a tourist promotion website, is the target audience of potential visitors to the locality in question.

The name, therefore, is neither accidental nor irrelevant. He communicates and does so through a discursive and ideological process. So, the analysis in our article will focus on this work stage, in the old name of that official website, that is, "Everything starts here", which still remains unchanged on the equal Facebook page and which is referred to on institutional Instagram. He communicates and does so full of ideological charge.

The naming of these virtual spaces is a reference to Professor Lenine Pinto's thesis that Cabral's fleet would have initially arrived in Rio Grande do Norte in 1500, instead of Bahia (citation). On Facebook, the page[4] still goes by the name of "Everything starts here", as it was also called on Instagram[5].

Critical Discourse Analysis indicates that discursive situations of abuse of power are manifested, in language, in circumstances in which exist the possibility

Figure 1. Home screen of the "everything starts here" page on Facebook
Source: https://www.facebook.com/tudocomecaaquirn(AccessedonMay13,2021)

of variation or choice. In the discursive event under analysis, we can point out that the lexical choices indicate the understanding that everything only begins in RN with the arrival of the Portuguese, since this was the historical landmark dated for "everything begins", nullifying the presence and history of indigenous peoples both before the European conquest and throughout our history from the Portuguese conquest.

It is possible to apprehend this event on official state government websites, discursive practices that signal the historical erasure and silencing of indigenous peoples in Rio Grande do Norte. Dantas (2012, p. 98) talks about the actions of silencing the subjects, based on of nomination processes. Citing Orlandi (*apud* Dantas, 2012, p. 98), Dantas explains that silencing is the action of, by asserting a meaning, erasing other possible but undesirable meanings. Who orders these speeches is who silences words, discourses and meanings that need to be excluded? In this way, we can say that by stating that "Everything starts here", the institutional texts of the state government silence and exclude the historical presence of the native peoples of our land, part of the authoritarian characteristics of the discourse, as stated by Dantas (2012, p. 98), silencing, the conscious path towards monosemy,

Figure 2. Screen print visit Rio Grande do Norte on Instagram, with emphasis on the "everything starts here" campaign
Source: https://www.instagram.com/visiteriograndedonorte/(AccessedonMay13,2021)

towards consensus, is indispensable in authoritarian and religious discourse, being an expression of the power of discursive agents or mediators.

The discursive practices analyzed so far indicate the social practice in which they are embedded together with the discursive event. These are manifestations of a racist ideology that makes the indigenous peoples of the land invisible and the genocide to which they were victims throughout the country's history since the landing of Europeans. The manifest racism in this case refers to what Nascimento (2016) describes when referring to the racism against African peoples in Brazil and the genocide under which they also suffered. Nascimento (2016, p. 38) refers to the work of Gilberto Freyre as he uses do a of racial euphemisms in order to rationalize race relations in the country, as exemplified by his emphasis and insistence on the term "morenidade". The defense of the thesis of "morenidade" is, in fact, an attempt to promote the disappearance of non-white peoples[6], both physically and spiritually, through the malicious process of whiten (Nascimento, 2016, p. 38), ideas that became intrinsic to the intellectuality of the white Brazilian elite.

The promotion of the historical erasure and discursive silencing of non-white peoples in Brazil, particularly in our case, indigenous peoples correspond to the concretization in the form of genocide of the ideology of racism. Discourse erases so that history does not exist. With no presence in history, or with history only beginning with the Portuguese arrival, it would not be possible to speak of indigenous peoples, in their presence, erased, silenced, exterminated. The logical consequence of the racist ideology of Europeanized whitening note is the legitimation of the policy of historic genocide against indigenous populations. Therefore, it is understandable for the official historiography of Rio Grande do Norte to state, for a long time, that there were no more indigenous people in the state. If they no longer existed at the level of discourse and ideology, they could be eliminated from real life without major problems. This is one of the points that are addressed by Moura (2019) in her master's thesis. According to the author,

The attempt to silence indigenous populations in the Northeast was a long and continuous process, mainly due to a historiography written outside academic contexts and, essentially, by local elites who tried to erase, at all costs, ethnic specificities over the centuries. (Cavignac, 2010; Pacheco de Oliveira, 1999; 2011); (Moura, 2019, p. 15).

Moura (2019, p. 15-16) further explains that the belief that there would be no more indigenous people in Rio Grande do Norte was promoted in the writings of historians, such as Câmara Cascudo, who affirmed that the indigenous populations of the state would have been physically exterminated or - supported by theories of acculturation - that they had been assimilated to the way of life of non-indigenous Brazil. In common sense and in textbooks, the so-called "Guerra dos Bárbaros" (1650 - 1720), which followed the departure of the Dutch from "Potiguar" lands, is seen as the milestone of this indigenous extermination in Rio Grande do Norte (Moura, 2019, p. 16).

Inversely, Moura (2019, p. 16) cites several researchers who question the notion of total extermination and have been reviewing traditional historiography, pointing out the need to understand the agency of indigenous peoples and their resistance strategies. against the historical erasure and discursive silencing of this racist ideology emerging in the academic sphere, Moura (2019, p. 16) highlights that various groups have reorganized themselves in search of their history and memory, claiming indigenous identity. Thus, in recent decades indigenous peoples considered to have disappeared have organized themselves in the struggle for their rights, which has also produced a population growth through people who acquired the courage to declare themselves indigenous.

At this point, it is worth bringing to analysis the other discursive event selected as a corpus for this work. This is an institutional text about the state of Rio Grande do Norte published on the official website of the Secretary of Tourism of the State[7]. We will only highlight the section text whose title is "History", reproduced below:

História

Os originais habitantes da região são os índios potiguares, que em língua tupi quer dizer "comedor de camarão". O nome do Estado, porém, faz alusão ao Rio Potengi que tem sua nascente no município de Cerro Corá e sua foz na Praia do Meio, em Natal.

As primeiras expedições portuguesas e espanholas passaram pela região entre 1499 e 1501. Durante as primeiras décadas do séc. XVI, no entanto, a área foi dominada pelos corsários franceses que estabeleceram comércio de pau-brasil e outras riquezas com os índios e permaneceram dominando a região até meados de 1530 quando foram expulsos pelos portugueses. Durante os vinte anos que se seguiram os donatários portugueses, oficiais donos das terras doadas pela Coroa Portuguesa, travaram intensa batalha com as tribos de índios da região, na tentativa de colonizar a Capitania do Rio Grande. A vitória chegou em 1598 e foi coroada com a construção do Fortaleza dos Reis Magos.

A região sofreria outro turbulento momento na história, com a invasão holandesa, que mantiveram um primeiro contato com a região em 1625. Sem encontrar muita resistência e tendo os índios como grandes aliados, os holandeses tomaram o controle da região entre 1633 e a ocupação durou cerca de 21 anos. Em 1654, os holandeses foram expulsos definitivamente pelos portugueses que finalmente colonizaram a região[8].

The text begins by talking about the native peoples of the region, the "Indians from Potiguar", but indicates that, according to the discourse that circulates through this text and its discursive practices, indigenous peoples cannot be seen as owners of the land. through the possession of land is always among white Europeans (French, Portuguese, Spanish, Dutch)—in this land, the only role for indigenous people is to resist. Their resistance to the oppression of the invader is nearly silenced, but their defeat is celebrated: "The victory arrived in 1598 and was crowned with the construction of the [sic] Fortaleza dos Reis Magos". The victory of the white invader against indigenous peoples, a mark of a racist ideology, of an imperialist and genocidal policy against these communities, is celebrated as a milestone in the history of the state.

Associated with this, in the discursive event under analysis, discursive practices are perceived that, in addition to erasing indigenous peoples, dehumanize and disqualify their culture, existence, history, social and communal life - after all, if the original peoples of the land are the indigenous, the owners are the Portuguese who, finally, after the defeat of the Dutch and the indigenous, were able to colonize the region. The story begins, then, at that moment, because there is no history, people, people, culture with the indigenous people, these barbarians.

Once again, that the discursive practices of this event point to the racist ideology and practice of historical erasure and discursive silencing against indigenous peoples, a form of realization and perpetuation of racist genocide, which makes in discourse, in history and in fact, the indigenous does not exist. Even in the tourist promotion of the state, which goes so far as to celebrate the "victory" that represents the subjection and historical erasure of native peoples.

The websites of the Rio Grande do Norte state government officials promote tourism with racist discursive practices against indigenous peoples. It is the role of Critical Discourse Analysis, in addition to state relations of abuse of power like this, to point out the possibility of solving the problem which, in this case, involves the recognition and assumption of the ethnic diversity of the state, rejecting all the historical and discursive perspectives that silence the indigenous. As offer to all communities in the state the prerogative of signaling how the history of Rio Grande do Norte can refers to and appear on tourist promotion websites without perpetuating the silencing of indigenous peoples, their historical erasure and the policy of extermination-genocide to which they were historically subjected by European whites.

CONCLUSION

At the beginning of this work, we proposed, based on the ACD, to analyze discursive events published on the Internet by official profiles of the tourism agencies of the state government of Rio Grande do Norte in search of discursive manifestations of racism.

In the corpus we selected, both on Facebook and Instagram and on websites institutes is, we were able to identify discursive marks of historical erasure and discursive silencing of indigenous peoples in the state of Rio Grande do Norte, which is in line with the historical thesis reinforced for so long that there were no more indigenous people in this state.

As highlighted above, Critical Discourse Analysis is concerned how empowerment of victims of abuse of power, both demonstrating the relationships in which such abuse is manifest, as suggesting possibilities for the solution of the discursive problem. In the case on which this work focuses, the solution of the problem passes through the historical recognition and by the assumption of the ethnic diversity of the state, rejecting in the official discourse of the state apparatus all historical and discursive perspectives that silence the indigenous people, offering to all communities in the state the prerogative of signaling how the history of the Rio Grande do Norte can be referred, denouncing all genocide of which indigenous peoples were victims in the history of the country and how the massacre is perpetuated when their history is erased and their voice is silenced by the State and white society.

The study will be in-depth, taking ACD into tourist communication, not only in digital media, but also in print. It is necessary to identify which discursive marks are present in the dissemination of these destinations, being able to go beyond racism, seeking all forms of evident abuse of power. The selection of the corpus of analysis can bases on the information made available on the official channels of dissemination of the destination, and its analysis will understand the intentions of the discourse in the dissemination of the destination. What story does he want to tell us? What to hide or disguise? Who is he selling himself to? All the elements present in tourism promotion campaigns for destinations answer questions like these, whether through texts or images, and everything that composes these *corpuses* in a qualitative and in-depth way, going beyond metric questions.

REFERENCES

Almeida, S. (2019). Structural Racism [Racismo estrutural]. São Paulo: Sueli Carneiro; Pólen.

Batista, J. R. L., Jr., Sato, D. T. B., & de Melo, I. F. (Org.). (2018). Critical discourse analysis for linguists and non-linguists [Análise de discurso crítica para linguistas e não linguistas]. Gonçalves. São Paulo: Parábola.

Buhalis, D., & Law, R. (2008). Progress in Information Technology and Tourism Management: 20 years on and 10 years after the internet — The State Of E-Tourism Research. *Tourism Management, 29*(4), 609–623. doi:10.1016/j.tourman.2008.01.005

Cavignac, J. A. (2010). The hidden ethnicity: 'Indians' and 'Blacks' in Rio Grande do Norte [A etnicidade encoberta: 'índios' e 'negros' no Rio Grande do Norte]. *Mneme - Revista De Humanidades, 4*(8). Recuperado de https://periodicos.ufrn.br/mneme/article/view/167

Charaudeau, P. (2006). Media Speech [Discurso das mídias]. São Paulo: Contexto.

Cooper, C. (2007). Tourism: Principles and practices [Turismo: Princípios e práticas] (3rd ed.). Porto Alegre: Bookman.

Cooper, C., Fletcher, J., Wanhill, S., Gilbert, D., & Shepeherd, R. (1998). *Tourism, principles and practice* [Turismo, princípios e prática]. Artmed.

Coriolano, L. N. M. T. (2005). Epistemology of discourse analysis in tourism [Epistemologia da análise do discurso no turismo]. *Caderno virtual de turismo.*

Dantas, D. (2012). *Argumentation as a discursive element in digital media: A study on the blog "Fatos e Dados"* [A argumentação como elemento discursivo na mídia digital: Um estudo sobre o blog "Fatos e Dados"] [Thesis]. Federal University of Rio Grande do Norte. Graduate Program in Language Studies, Natal.

de Oliveira, N. A. (2021). Blacks and tourism: Analysis of the academic production on the theme in journals linked to Post-Graduate Programs in Tourism in Brazil [Negros e turismo: Análise da produção acadêmica sobre o tema em revistas vinculadas aos Programas de Pós-Graduação em Turismo no Brasil]. *Rosa dos Ventos - Turismo e Hospitalidade, 13*(1), 219–238. doi:10.18226/21789061.v13i1p219

Falco, D., & De, P. (2011). Tourist narratives: Imaginary and media in the urban experience of tourism [Narrativas turísticas: Imaginário e mídia na experiência urbana do turismo]. *Rosa dos Ventos, 1*(3), 24-38.

Foucault, M. (2007). Words and Things: An Archeology of the Human Sciences [As palavras e as coisas: Uma arqueologia das ciências humanas] (9th ed.). São Paulo: Martins Fontes.

Gonçalves-Segundo, P. R. (2018). Discourse and social practice [Discurso e prática social]. In *Análise de discurso crítica para linguistas e não linguistas*. Parábola.

Guimarães, A. S. A. (1995). Racism and anti-racism in Brazil [Rascismo e anti-racismo no Brasil]. *Novos Estudos, 3*(43), 26-44. Available in http://Novosestudos.Com.Br/Produto/Edicao-43/

Heath, E. E., & Wall, G. (1991). *Marketing tourism destinations* [Marketing tourism destinations]. John Wiley & Sons.

Hintze, H., & Almeida Júnior, A. R. de. (2012). Critical studies of tourism: Tourism communication and the myth of racial democracy in Brazil [Estudos críticos do turismo: A comunicação turística e o mito da democracia racial no Brasil]. *Revista turismo e desenvolvimento*, (17-18), 57-72.

Hudson, S., So, K. K. F., Meng, F., Cárdenas, D., & Li, J. (2018). Racial discrimination in tourism: The case of African-American travellers in South Carolina. *Current Issues in Tourism, 23*(4), 438–451. doi:10.1080/13683500.2018.1516743

Ladeiro, M. M. L. (2012). *The effectiveness of tourist sites case study: Lisbon and the main competitors* [A eficácia dos sites turísticos estudo de caso: Lisboa e os principais concorrentes] [Dissertação de Mestrado]. Escola Superior de Hotelaria e Turismo do Estoril.

Marujo, M. N. N. V. (2008). *The internet as a new means of communication for tourist destinations: The case of Madeira Island* [A internet como novo meio de comunicação para os destinos turísticos: o caso da Ilha da Madeira]. São Paulo: Revista turismo em análise.

Milanez, F. (2020). Existence and difference: Racism against indigenous peoples [Existência e diferença: O racismo contra os povos indígenas]. *Rev. Direito Práx, 10*(3), 2161-2181. Http://Www.Scielo.Br/Scielo.Php?Script=Sci_Arttext&Pid=S2179-89662019000302161&Lng=En&Nrm=Iso

Moura, A. D. M. D. E. (2019). *"Here is the blood and sweat of an Indian": Resistance, ethnicity and political struggle of the Tapuias of Lagoa do Tapará – RN* ["Aqui tem sangue e suor de índio": Resistência, etnicidade e luta política dos Tapuias da Lagoa do Tapará – RN] [Dissertação de Mestrado]. Universidade Federal do Rio Grande do Norte, Natal, RN, Brasil.

Nascimento, A. (1978). *The Brazilian Black Genocide: Process of a Masked Racism* [O genocídio do negro brasileiro: Processo de um racismo mascarado]. Paz e Terra.

Nascimento, A. (2016). *The Brazilian Black Genocide: Process of a Masked Racism* [O genocídio do negro brasileiro: Processo de um racismo mascarado]. Perspectivas.

Pacheco de Oliveira, J. (Org.). (2011). The indigenous presence in the Northeast: Process of territorialization territorialization process, modes of recognition and memory regimes [A presença indígena no Nordeste: processo de territorialização, modos de reconhecimento e regimes de memória]. Rio de Janeiro: Contra Capa.

Pacheco de Oliveira, J. (1999). *Essays in Historical Anthropology* [Ensaios em Antropologia histórica]. Editora da UFRJ.

Pearce, D. (1992). *Tourist organizations*. John Wiley & Sons.

Ribeiro, D. (1970). *Indians and Civilization* [Os índios e a civilização]. Civilização Brasileira.

Seaton, A. V. (1996). Destination marketing. In Marketing tourism products. Thomson Business Press.

Tomazzoni, E. L. (2006). Analysis of tourist discourse in the Serra Gaucha [Análise do discurso turístico da serra gaúcha]. *Em questão*, *12*(2), 339-365.

Van, D. T. A. (2015). Speech and power [Discurso e poder] (2nd ed.). São Paulo: Contexto.

Wenzel, K., & John, V. M. (2012). Travel Journalism: An analysis of the main Brazilian magazines [Jornalismo de viagens: Análise das principais revistas brasileiras]. *Estudos em Comunicação*, (11), 291–311.

Zardo, E. F. (2003). *Tourism Marketing* [Marketing aplicado ao turismo]. Roca.

ENDNOTES

1. The Communication, Culture and Media research group, through one of the authors of this article, is involved in a doctoral research project whose theme "Discursive marks of structural racism in the digital media of tourist destinations" also intends to describe how the method and its procedures can be used in future studies on communication in tourist destinations, an initial proposal in the field of research in Brazil.
2. Available inhttp://visiteriograndedonorte.com.br,accessed on May 13, 2021.
3. In portuguese, "Tudo começa aqui".
4. Available at https://www.facebook.com/tudocomecaaquirn,accessed on May 13, 2021.
5. Available at https://www.instagram.com/visiteriograndedonorte/,accessed on May 13, 2021.

6 Nascimento (2016, p. 38) highlights black Africans, but the same idea can be extrapolated to indigenous peoples and other non-whites, such as gypsies, for example.

7 Available in:http://setur.rn.gov.br/?page_id=4050,access on: 13 May. 2021.

8 Translate - History: The original inhabitants of the region are the Potiguar Indians, which in the Tupi language means "shrimp eater". The name of the State, however, alludes to the Potengi River, which has its source in the municipality of Cerro Corá and its mouth at Praia do Meio, in Natal. The first Portuguese and Spanish expeditions passed through the region between 1499 and 1501. During the first decades of the 19th century. In the 16th century, however, the area was dominated by French corsairs who established trade in pau-brasil and other riches with the Indians and remained dominating the region until the mid-1530s when they were expelled by the Portuguese. During the twenty years that followed, the Portuguese grantees, officials who owned the lands donated by the Portuguese Crown, fought an intense battle with the Indian tribes of the region, in an attempt to colonize the Captaincy of Rio Grande. Victory came in 1598 and was crowned with the construction of the fortress of the Magi. The region would suffer another turbulent moment in history, with the Dutch invasion, which kept first contact with the region in 1625. Without encountering much resistance and having the Indians as great allies, the Dutch took the control of region between 1633 and the occupation lasted about 21 years. In 1654, the Dutch were definitively expelled by the Portuguese who finally colonized the region. (Translated by the authors)

Chapter 12
Essay on the Appropriation of Tourism in LGBT+ Elderly Communities:
A Look at the Book *The Shining of LGBT+ Old Ages*

Adriano Carlos Nunes
https://orcid.org/0000-0002-7338-5402
Escola de Artes, Ciências e Humanidades, Universidade de São Paulo, Brazil

Ademílson Damasceno
https://orcid.org/0000-0002-3387-0948
São Paulo State University, Brazil

ABSTRACT

The chapter aims at studying the inclusion of these groups in a consumer market, especially in the tourism industry, and it is a continuation of a master study carried out by one of the authors of the text in the Graduate Program in Tourism at the University of São Paulo. To this end, the authors focus their attention on the NGO Eternamente SOU, a reference in welcoming LGBT+ elderly people in Brazil, and on the life stories of its participants, recently published in the book Os Brilhos das Velhices LGBT+ and as a supporting text, the book Introduction to Elderly LGBTI+.

INTRODUCTION

When looking at the studies of the elderly, there is a concentration of scientific

DOI: 10.4018/978-1-6684-4194-7.ch012

productions in the field of health and well-being. According to Debert (1998), the production of knowledge related to the aging process comprises multiple dimensions; from demographics and increased life expectancy, to physiological wear and associated costs of social policies. The studies, in the literature of LGBT+ old age, have a tendency to portray men and women who identify themselves as homosexuals, cisgender, white, middle classes, residents of large metropolises and generally people who are in the early stages of aging, but recently have emerged studies that addressed bisexual, transsexual, and Queers old ages. (Henning, 2017).

LGBT tourism has become attractive and shows itself as a growing niche in the travel industry as we have seen in studies in Brazil, where it has been found that tourists in this segment spend 30% more than other travelers, seek more specialized agencies (87% against 42% of the national average) and move 10% of the tourism sector, according to studies of Azevedo et al (2012) and Hahn et al (2021). It is a demanding audience regarding tourism services/products and that requires focus on specific campaigns. The United Nations (UN, 2020[1]) predicts that the planet will have more than 2 billion people over 60 by 2050, with an estimated annual movement of US$ 7.1 trillion.

However, this essay aims at analyzing the LGBTQIA+ elderly from their reports, whose parameters are proposed in the Oral History method in the scope of the Master's research in Tourism in association with those presented in the book "The sparkles of LGBT old age", which covered elderly people between 47 and 72 years old. Associated with this approach, we propose content analysis and bibliographic review in a database on the scientific production on the subject and, through content analysis, observe its territorial dynamics, its specificities in the choices of destinations, and what fears and amides are present in its relationships with the sector.

In a scenario in which identity struggles gain visibility in society, including with great global repercussion of their actions in search of greater equality of rights, we propose to study the insertion of LGBT+ elderly communities (Lesbians, Gays, Bisexuals, Transsexuals and more possibilities of Genders) in the Tourism market, and what are the social dynamics involved in this journey. It should be noted that the acronym is in constant dispute and recent changes in its name aim to include a wider range of identities and greater plurality.

The present essay aims at studying the inclusion of these groups in a consumer market, especially in the Tourism industry, and is a continuation of a Master's study carried out by one of the authors of the text in the Graduate Program in Tourism at the University of São Paulo. To this end, we turned our attention to the NGO Eternamente SOU, a reference in welcoming LGBT+ elderly people in Brazil, and the life stories of its participants, recently published in the book Os Brilhos das Velhices LGBT+ and, as a supporting text, the book Introduction to Elderly LGBTI+, also organized by its members, through content analysis.

But why analyze the insertion of a historically peripheral group in a consumer market? More than a movement of people in search of satisfaction, leisure or knowledge in tourist centers, Tourism implies a wide range of forms of displacement that give rise to the mobilization of ideas and social models, resources, workers and specific or shared infrastructure, in a way to better serve this group.(Archer, 1982; Beauvoir,1990; Cleaver&Muller, 2002; Dann, 2002). As it is a powerful industry with a strong movement of capital, it causes changes in the urban fabric of the destination hubs, in addition to bringing a series of behavioral issues and discussions to the communities involved.

The forms of mobility associated with contemporary tourism are illustrative of the new dynamics of existing displacement as well as reflecting a whole set of socioeconomic and psychosocial issues present in society. The inequality in access to this consumer good is also representative of the existing social conditions and the accumulation of issues in which the subjects were involved. According to Rios (2009), in many cases, inequalities form processes of stigmatization: the transformation of differences into social inequalities, actions that are configured as a deterioration of humanity and, therefore, discrimination and oppression.

It is worth mentioning that, although the market seems to reach a younger part of the population or with greater access to capital goods, the growth of the tourism industry is dynamic and changes according to a myriad of variables such as tourist income, the type of tourism attraction, the price of tourist goods and services. These variables influence the demand that will compose the market, according Tadini, RF & Melquiades T.(2008). A greater offer of destinations, as well as the economic rise of once marginalized groups, brought a new social set with peculiarities that mass tourism was not ready to meet, generating new discussions about their participation in this industry. On the relationship between Tourism and Society, Ricco comments:

Due to its fundamentally cultural nature, it reveals itself in a process of continuous interactions between different communities that occupy different socially constructed spaces and that, by presenting this diversity, become attractive for the knowledge of the other. Today, tourism can be considered one of the main mechanisms through which the approach of different world cultures occurs, resulting from the globalization process that affects the entire planet. (Ricco, 2012, pp. 167)

The displacements cited by the author reconfigure existing landscapes and the relationship between indigenous groups and tourists. But this is not just a discussion about global movements with an impact on Tourism, nor about young people. The core of the text seeks to observe the dynamics of inclusion of new groups in this economic segment, which are their confluences and specificities.

The increase in the elderly population is due to the social advances obtained in the post-war period, through the expansion of health services, vaccination coverage, basic sanitation, expansion of the State of Social Welfare, greater income distribution, access to the labor market, and expansion of Social Security services, among others. Measures that allowed a rapid population growth, whose children were nicknamed baby boomers, according Doll (2007), Fernandes & Soares (2012), Felix (2019) Neves & Brambatti (2019) and Vidal da Rocha et al (2021). That ended up changing the shape of the age pyramid, as in the example of Brazil, formerly composed mostly of young people. This generation is now reaching retirement or retirement age, with a gradual increase in life expectancy, de according to the Institutes INATEL(2005), IBGE (2012) and EUROSTAT (2012), which, associated to the reduction of birth rates, provided the inversion of the age pyramid in the European continent and some Asian countries such as Japan and South Korea, and that is also beginning to be observed in other continents. On a global scale, it is estimated that the number of people over 60 years old, will be more than double to constitute 22% of the world population by 2050 (Magnus, 2009). Aging is a reality that has repercussions on various social levels and generates different impacts. Thus, it is urgent the need of development of studies on the subject, both to clarify and equip the productive system, as well as for the greater knowledge of this public for the elaboration of policies.

The expectation of population growth in the segment should affect the senior tourism market in the coming decades substantially, with a population increasingly stimulated to travel, with less and less limitations, and with reduced travel time and increased duration of stays, according Nimrod & Rotem (2010). These, in association to a broad program of restructuring pension and retirement programs, would allow increasing occupancy rates in the low tourist season.

It is also worth remembering that studies on the elderly population are quite recent, emerging in a post-war context in which the numerous achievements in the field of health provided an increase in population and greater longevity, which ended up changing the shape of the age pyramid, as in the example of Brazil, formerly composed mainly of young people. Aging is a reality that has repercussions on various social levels and generates different impacts. Thus, it is urgent that studies on the subject are developed, whether to clarify and equip the productive system, or for a greater knowledge of this public for the elaboration of policies.

Such a movement will have an effect on the consumer market, which, as it grows older, has introduced new tastes and priorities, in addition to promoting social mobilization in the sense of offering products and services that are more appropriate to the needs of the group. And the discussion is not just about the capitalist mode of production, as historian Theodore Zeldin declares:

All human beings are, by their origin, escapists, all descend from ancestors who migrated from Africa and Asia... Industrial society began as an escape from poverty. Now it has become an escape from work to leisure, to favorite pastimes and sport. However, even a civilization devoted to leisure has enemies, so the art of escape has been further refined. (Zeldin, 2008, pp. 273).

When looking at studies of the elderly, there is a concentration of scientific production in the field of health and well-being. For Debert (1998), the production of knowledge related to the aging process involves multiple dimensions, from demography and the increase in life expectancy, to the physiological wear and tear and costs associated with social policies. Studies in the literature of LGBT+ old age (Lesbian, gay, bisexual and transsexual and more gender possibilities) tend to portray men and women who identify as homosexual, cisgender, white, middle-class, residents of large metropolises, and generally of people who are in the initial phase of aging, but recently there has been research that addressed bisexual, transsexual, queer old age, according Henning (2017).

The previous paragraphs demonstrate the importance of establishing specific public policies for the sector, as social tourism programs play an important role in tourism accessibility as well as serve the market with actions that guide investments. The initiatives to promote social tourism among the elderly are generally supported by public funding, and most of them, take the form of low-cost domestic holidays, according to the studies of Minnaert, Maitland, & Miller (2009), Almeida (2011), Felix (2019) and Dantas (2021), with tourism programs aimed at the elderly, stimulating the economies of the destination areas, particularly in the low season. According Almeida (2011), Diekmann & McCabe (2011), McCabe & Johnson(2009;2013) Minnaert et al. (2011) Fernandes & Soares (2012) Eusébio et al. (2013a) and Rougemont (2016) in a complementary way, public policies should also interfere positively in host regions, allowing vulnerable groups in these places to have greater access to consumer goods and to be able to take advantage of the equipment in the low season for their own leisure. In addition to heating up the local economy during the rest of the season, according Debert (1998), Trigo (2009) and Vidal da Rocha et al (2021).

On the subject, Kripendorf (2001) states that Tourism is part of the modern industrial society and the dynamics of travel cannot be distinguished from the understanding of leisure and well-being, as its reason for selling was directly linked to the idea of escaping from the place of work and housing. These are, therefore, social achievements, directly linked to the social protection of work and reduced working hours. And Tourism as an industry is created by seizing free time and better income distribution on account of these achievements.

Kripendorf's brilliant interpretation of the emergence of Tourism in an industrial society makes us think beyond, when analyzing groups that historically were on the sidelines of the process, or their access to the best jobs were for a long time fraught with blockages and obstacles, when reaching consumption potential, have the need to remedy their ancestors frustrations. Given this starting point, we intend to analyze how LGBT+ elderly communities were inserted in this context and how they reoriented their modes of consumption with a view to tourism.

However, the current economic situation has inspired the debate in many countries about the size and role of the State in the supply of goods and services, as well as its ability to formulate effective policies in economic areas, calling for a more active involvement of private agents in solving societal problems. Associated with this movement, there is greater pressure on social security and pension budgets, which directly affects income transfers to the elderly, according Minnaert et al.(2011) and Eusebio & Carneiro (2012). Given the above, offering public policies to the tourism sector in order to include groups to which they normally do not have access, requires arguments that demonstrate concrete impacts of these programs and their prioritization in access to public funds. Therefore, part of the advancement of policies is also associated with better social communication that can crystallize in public opinion the evident gains of the policy, especially in times of scarcity of resources.

The Future is Old...and Full of Diversity

LGBT+ tourism has become attractive and is showing itself as a growing niche in the travel industry, as we have seen in studies in Brazil, where it was found that tourists in this segment spend 30% more than other travelers, seeking more specialized agencies (87% against 42% of the national average) and move 10% of the tourism sector, according Azevedo et al (2012) and Hahn et al. (2021). This is a demanding public in terms of tourism services/products and demands focus on specific campaigns. The World Tourism Organization (WTO) released a report in 2016, which pointed to the worldwide interest in the growth of this segment, as an example of the Open For All Campaign, reinforcing the idea that everyone is welcome.

The United Nations (UN, 2020) predicts that the planet will have more than 2 billion people over the age of 60 by 2050, with an estimated annual turnover of US$ 7.1 trillion. Thinking specifically about the elderly public, the Ministry of Tourism in Brazil launched in 2010 the "Viaja Mais Melhor Idade" program, with the aim of promoting the social inclusion of people aged 60 and over, providing them with opportunities to enjoy the benefits of the touristic activity. However, such action did not encompass policies for the LGBT segment, whose term was removed from the National Tourism Plan 2018-2022 (MTur, 2018). In disagreement with the Brazilian counterpart, in 2017, the Ministry of Tourism in Portugal established in the Tourism Strategy 2027 document the promotion of the country as an LGBTI destination among its priorities, with wide participation of LGBT elderly people in the promotional video of Proudly Portugal; Fort Lauderdale, Florida (USA) was the first tourist destination in the world to include transgender people in its "Celebrate You" campaign.

The verified increase in the tourist activity of the elderly brings to light new studies on the spatial mobility of the group and the possibilities of conceptualizing the phenomenon, according of Aboim (2014), Ashton et al.(2015) and Vidal da Rocha et al.(2021). Many of these studies discuss the definition of what is elderly and how they can be defined as a tourist. In general terms, "elderly travelers" are understood as people over 55 years old, generally retired, according Almeida (2011), Araujo&Carlos (2018) and Felix (2019). This characteristic can also be highlighted in studies related to leisure, which emphasize changes in working conditions and the transition to retirement as a relevant factor for changes in the group's lifestyle, according Doll (2007) and Nimrod (2008). The classification and establishment of a starting point for this phase is of vital importance for the tourism industry, in order to better offer the later tourist preferences of the elderly.

In Brazil, the aging of the LGBT+ population needs to be contextualized in a scenario where there is an expectation of an increase in the segment (IBGE, 2012). For the Brazilian Ministry of Health, a person is considered elderly from the age of 60, even if internationally, some countries establish 65 years as a marker for this age group, according Brasil (2011), Azevedo et al (2012) and Hahn et al. (2021). The understanding of LGBT+ old age is questioned, anticipating the minimum age of elderly in this group to 50 years, given the lower life expectancy, resulting from greater exposure to violence, due to prejudice. Corroborating this point, it appears that Brazil ranks first in murders of the Trans population, both in absolute and relative numbers (ANTRA, 2020). Brazil thus tends to follow the conditions verified in the central countries of the capitalist mode of production. In the United States, for example, the workforce of retired people exceeded by 20%, this biggest jump was observed among college graduates, according to a new study by United Income Resource Manager. By BLS estimates, the Baby Boomer generation (born between 1946 and 1964) will account for the greatest growth in labor force participation at least until 2024.[1]" But statistics on the growth of the elderly population do not reflect in all groups, which leads to the question presented above about the anticipation of the minimum age of this specific group. In the United States, there is also an increase in cases of violence against the Trans population, especially after the coronavirus pandemic, which affected basic rights and raised unemployment rates. Added to this is the growth of anti-trans bills in the US.[2]" Although it is not a question of tourism governance, safety and respect for diversity compromise the choice of destination.

When talking about the elderly, we must also understand that age can often be subjective. Not infrequently, age classifications start at 60 years old, but in the case of LGBTQIAP+ groups they are often classified from 55 years old onwards due to greater exposure to violence and lower life expectancy [2], according Gomes (2005), Couto et al. (2009), Aboim (2014), Henning (2017), Neves & Brambatti (2019) and Kishigami (2020). This perception of age can contribute to the understanding of how the elderly see themselves and behave, and how they understand the life cycle, according Wilkes (1992), and how they use it as a reference for their behaviors (Neugarten & Neugarten 1986: pp. 42). Social factors are predominant in this age perception, but psychological factors also contribute to subjective age differences, according Debert (1998), Doll (2007), Green (2018) and Felix (2019).

Although the United Nations in its Universal Declaration of Humanity's Rights (1948) included the enjoyment of leisure and vacations in this list, tourism is still an activity that excludes a number of people for several reasons. For the elderly, it would be appropriate to observe which economic and health peculiarities are impediments to the enjoyment of leisure, according Fleischer & Pizam (2002), Nimrod (2008), Paixão (2008), BITS (2011) and Ashton et al. (2015), but also to understand that deficiencies motor skills are an additional constraint common to the group, which should increase with advancing age. (Carneiro, Kastenholz and Alvelos, 2016).

The elderly tourist segment presents itself, therefore, as a sector in constant expansion, which is reflected in the increase in research to understand the phenomenon (Amaral et al. 2020). The group has proven to be an increasingly important source of income for the tourism sector, not only because of its population growth, but also because of its greater availability of time and its travel characteristics. A greater volume of research by the group may reveal their motivations.

But how is it possible for us to know and learn more about who the LGBT+ elderly are, given that, in a significant part of their existence, they were passed over in the formulation of public policies or research that could demonstrate which yearnings were present in their consumption desires? And how much of these analyzes can be based on traditional methodologies alone? Given the scenario presented, it becomes relevant to discuss the formulation of tourism policies aimed at this group.

METHODOLOGY

Adapting research methods to categories that, due to less access to the consumer market in the past, have a lesser theoretical legacy is the challenge that this chapter proposes. How to provide the historicity necessary for the understanding of this group without directing the study to a merely economic bias? In line with the above, Panosso Netto & Trigo (2009) emphasize the indispensability of peripheral classes and populations to question power relations and appropriate their own discourses in the production of knowledge in tourism, from a philosophical basis that favors action with a critical view.

Researching historically marginalized groups also requires attention to the tools to be used, as their lower political power also reflects a lower availability of public data arising from collection policies. Therefore, the option for an exploratory/experimental approach with the help of content analysis proves to be capable of capturing the information necessary for the understanding of this new social dynamics.

The researcher, at this point, needs to make use of a set of methods capable of producing the necessary data for the analysis of this phenomenon.

To achieve this objective, we propose the use of interviews with members of the NGO Eternamente Sou, whose parameters are proposed by Oral History, associated with the content analysis of the book "O Brilho das Velhices LGBT+" recently released by the NGO itself, in partnership with the Universidade São Judas Tadeu, with Editora HUCITEC, which brings together a total of twenty interviews with LGBT+ elderly people between 47 and 72 years old. The collection of testimonials for the book was conducted in a relaxed and informal way, following a semi-structured script with guiding questions, all respondents signed a free consent form during the year 2020. Associated with this approach, we propose content analysis and bibliographic review in a database on the scientific production on the subject.

In the first stage of the research, a search was carried out in the database of publications on Tourism at USP, considered the main specific database on Tourism in Brazil according Silva et al. (2021), the result of the university extension project of the University of São Paulo. EACH USP Tourism Graduate Program, with a total of 11748 indexed articles from 40 Ibero-American scientific journals.

Data collection carried out in May 2021 through search engines considered all fields using the terms "LGBT" and "elderly" to select the articles that make up the object of study of this research, and it was found that there were no publications related to the theme, reinforcing the relevance and urgency in the discussion of the subject.

Pink Money and the Danger of Social Group Generalizations

The greater insertion of the LGBTQIA+ public in the consumer market, in addition to bringing relevance to that public, also attracted the eyes of companies to the public. Although controversial, estimates indicate that the group's consumption potential varies between US$884 and US$3.6 trillion, according Gomes (2005), Green (2018) and Alves&Aguiar (2020) and an estimated wealth of US$18 trillion (LGBT Capital, 2018). According to recent data from the LGBT Travel Market survey, carried out by the consultancy Out Now/WTM, in 2018 alone, LGBT tourism generated about US$ 218.7 billion (about R$ 859.49 billion) in the world (Alves & Aguiar, 2020).

In Brazil, the group's financial potential is estimated at 133 billion dollars, in a universe of 20 million inhabitants and about 67,400 families (Scrivano & Sorima

Neto (2015) and Alves & Aguiar (2020[3]) and, according to the 2010 census, family income was around R$5,200. By way of comparison, heterosexual couples presented an average of R$ 2.8 thousand (IBGE, 2010). In a survey conducted by InSearch Tendências e Estudos de Mercado, 36% of the LGBT population belong to class "A" and 47% belong to class "B" (Nascimento, 2018).

This public represents 10% of those who travel the most in the world, moving around 15% of the sector's revenue, according to data from the World Tourism Organization (WTO, 2019), with Brazil being one of the countries with the greatest growth potential among countries in Latin America, according to the Brazilian LGBT Tourism Association (ABTLGBT).

The LGBT+ niche becomes attractive the moment it looks at its economic potential. The expression "pink money" appears in the heating of the consumer market. An example of the good use of this resource is the State of Israel, which, despite boycott proposals by pro-Palestinian communities, has consolidated itself as a tourist destination in this segment. In this regard, Oliveira (2016) comments:

However, stronger evidence of the importance of the LGBT segment is the volume of money it moves. It should be noted that the World Tourism Organization already deals with this segment officially and publishes annual reports together with the International Gay & Lesbian Travel Association (IGLTA). In the report published in 2012, these two organizations estimated the annual impact of LGBT tourism on the world tourism market at US$140 billion. In 2015, the result of a survey carried out by the consulting firm Out Now Global, reported by The Economist magazine (2016) on its Twitter account, and by organizations in the hospitality sector, gives the exact dimension of the economic importance that LGBT tourists have: they spent about 202 billion dollars worldwide in 2014. Of that amount, 25.3 billion dollars were spent in Brazil. (Oliveira, 2016, p.48)

According to surveys carried out in the US, of the 4 million elderly LGBT+ Americans, 80% are single, 90% do not have children and 75% of this group live in individual housing. Such results are very different from those observed in the general population, whose percentages are, respectively, 40%, 20% and 33%, according Kama et al (2012) and Rebelato, C. et al (2021). This result demonstrates a need to understand this group in order to better direct projects and policies.

In this context, for Trigo (2009, p.153) "gay people with greater purchasing power, evidently, have a significant impact on spending on sophisticated and superfluous products and services". According to Nunan (2015), LGBT groups present individualistic behaviors, with a greater need to group together, avoiding routines, stress and assistance. The acronym DINKS (double income, no kids, and professional couples without children) is a representation of how the group is seen in the market. On the subject, Zeldin comments:

Coming out of the closet, proclaiming the independence of the Gay Nation, was the culmination of this phase. This makes it seem, on the surface, that homosexuals were necessarily interested only in their own group. However, those who were able to delve into their innermost motives often wanted more than just being themselves, with the ultimate goal of escaping from themselves, looking for partners from other cultures, from another generation, from a different social class. .Desire was the magic that made transitions into uncharted territory possible. Desire allowed the normally snobbish wealthy classes to see those considered inferior, and themselves, in a different light (Zeldin, 2008, page 156).

Tadioto, Moreira&Campos (2016) refers to the appropriation of the LGBT+ by economic power, in what he calls the Consumer Discursive Place. According to the author, there was a process of marketing appropriation of the acronym GLS, also as a response to their struggles and a form of recognition of the agenda with its insertion in the capitalist mode of production. There is a generalization of consumption in this group by the media and the market.

For Neves & Brambatti (2019), such behavior ends up generating studies in the area of Tourism focused only on the economic character of the segmentation of the group, highlighting the financial returns above the others. For the author, such studies reproduce an exacerbated stereotype, not always according to the totality of this group, as if sexuality determined the income and education of this population. A significant portion of the LGBT+ population is on the sidelines of the services offered to the general population and inhabits the outskirts of cities, as well as presenting greater school dropout due to prejudice. Their spaces were constituted where sexualities could be experienced, far from social pressures. Ferreira & Aguinsky (2013) complete:

It is also understood that the inscription of these subjects as such will only be possible when there are no spaces, public or private, delimited for the different non-normative forms of expression of sexuality and gender. (Ferreira & Aguinsky, 2013)

Thus, for LGBT+ tourists, especially the elderly, tourism must include security, well-being and the right to diversity and freedom to live their own identities. In the words of Krippendorf (2001), leisure and tourism must constitute acquired rights for the entire population through policies and actions that enable social inclusion and, consequently, the pleasure and social, personal and critical social development of individuals. For the author, giving tourism a more human face is a way of awakening and promoting the potential that remains dormant in each individual, regardless of their gender identity or age.

Despite the expansion of mass tourism, world tourism indicators propose a greater growth in the so-called "niche tourism", in which the tourist requires much more than basic structures. About this, Oliveira (2016) comments:

When talking about LGBT tourism, many people ask if tourism differs depending on who the audience is or ask why the need for tourism specifically aimed at lesbian, gay, bisexual and transgender people. Strictly speaking, tourism practiced by members of the LGBT community is no different from tourism practiced by members of the heterosexual community with regard to the infrastructure and attractions of tourist destinations. After all, any tourist needs to stay, eat, and get around. However, due to the homophobic behaviors existing in many societies, it is necessary for the LGBT tourist to have a minimum guarantee that he will not be spending his money in a destination whose residents have a history of morally harassing and discriminating against lesbians, gays, bisexuals and the transgender. In this sense, tourism specifically aimed at the LGBT community is justified, as it presupposes a certain attitude of the receiving community and, consequently, a more specific marketing work.

Concerning this, Trevisan (2006) states that homosexual travel was a constant in the lives of thousands of people, in different countries and times. The same author asks: Why do homosexuals travel so much? In response to the feeling of exile in their own country, common among large numbers of homosexuals, there is a pressing need to know the world. The tendency is for homosexuals to leave the most inhospitable and aggressive places, including their hometowns, to "look for their place", driven by the desire to free themselves.

Identities and Desires: A Look at the Eternamente Sou Community

In a recent survey developed by the Perseu Abramo Foundation in 2020, it was revealed that 57% of the elderly would like to carry out activities outside the home, highlighting the desire to travel or go for a walk, pointed out by 32% of respondents. Doll (2007) agrees, pointing out that tourism occupies the top of the wish list of the elderly, especially the younger ones, and its greater evidence loses space as health concerns emerge among their priorities.

But what does research into this behavior say? In a previous survey by the NGO Eternamente Sou, carried out in 2020 and involving its participants, there was a huge appreciation among the elderly for travel. Among the group's favorite activities are, in order: Accessing the internet (76%), Traveling: (69%), Watching TV (61%), Cinema (55%) and Theater (55%). Among their greatest desires are: Traveling (35%), Getting married (8%), staying healthy (6%), helping people (6%) and Social Justice (6%). Among the greatest desires of the researched group are Travel (49%), live elsewhere (10%), Lose weight (10%), Retire (10%) and have a love (8%). In addition to travel, we noticed that a good part of the desires of this group are directly linked to the construction of new memories as well as the construction of some social legacies.

Therefore, it is considered that the aspiration to travel is representative during old age and, perhaps, this ambition is related to the social motivations of Tourism, not only as a recovery from the wear and tear resulting from work, but, above all, as a constituent of a planning that involves physical, economic, mental and social aspects. Its practice would even alleviate the pathologies, especially the psychological ones, typical of age, in addition to removing the fear of death.

Tourism, in this way, does not present itself only as a means of escaping from a reality or allowing the creation of spaces of refuge to new forms of social expatriation. It also involves creating emotional connections with the group's desires and creating connections with the spaces they occupy. Creating specific public policies also allows the group to meet their consumption frustrations and repressed demands, which directly affect their well-being. But capturing these frustrations and demanding specific actions requires the exercise of a human capacity: listening.

RESULT ANALYSIS

In a society that is fully interconnected and with informed citizens, it is not enough to treat the individual as a client or economic potential, since he/she needs legal security for displacements and real enjoyment of his/her condition as a being. The LGBT+ public has wide relevance both in the social and economic fields. And this relevance should be reflected in public policies to promote and prospect business in the sector.

When looking at the behavior studies of LGBTQIA+ elderly people, we noticed that part of their relationship with Tourism is directly linked to the social formation of the being. To understand how the choice of tourist destinations occurs, it is first necessary to understand how the individual sees himself and which group he relates or identifies with. To set a benchmark for product formation for the group, many companies set the senior age at 55 years old. According to this perspective, consumers begin to feel different needs, and begin to predict and plan for aging at this age.

Existing studies in the field of travel motivations for seniors, which seek to answer which external factors attract a tourist to a certain place, according Iso-Ahola (1982), Doll (1998), Paixão (2008), Couto et al (2009), Trigo (2009), Nunan (2015),

Aboim, (2014), Eusebio et al (2015), (Felix, 2019), Dantas (2021) and Hahn et al (2021), indicate that in the context of the elderly, the main attributes of a destination that attracts them are; good weather conditions, safety, travel cost, and natural and cultural attractions (Paixão, 2008; Trigo, 2009; Eusebio et al, 2015; Felix, 2019). Other relevant factors mentioned are; places of historical interest, medical service (facilities) and weather conditions (Couto et al, 2009; Eusebio et al, 2015; Dantas, 2021). Their values, experiences and desires are also taken into account, such as sentimentality, desire to escape the hustle and bustle of the city, etc. (Paixão, 2008; Trigo, 2009; Couto et al, 2009; Moraes et al, 2011; Eusebio et al, 2015; Hahn et al, 2021).

In Brazil, Tourism has the PNT's, National Tourism Plans, whose purpose is to direct energy to growing segments. In the previous government's plan, the strategies to promote the LGBT+ tourism segment were intended to "raise awareness in the sector for the inclusion of the elderly and the LGBT public in tourism". The initiative was aborted in the elaboration of a new plan, keeping only the elderly in its text.

Motivations to travel encompass a wide range of human behaviors and experiences, and the typical list of these motivations might include relaxation, excitement, social interactions with friends or family, adventure, status, and escape from routine or stress, according Paixão (2008), Wheat (2009), and Eusebio et al. (2015). Income and health-related restrictions were identified as two of the most important groups of restrictions for the elderly, according Fleischer & Pizam (2002), Paixão (2008), Trigo (2009), Almeida (2011) and Eusebio et al (2015). However, health deterioration, widowhood or other events that influence emotional state also represent an important travel constraint at the intrapersonal level, as they can influence confidence to travel (Couto et al, 2009; Moraes et al., 2011; Eusebio et al, 2015; Nunan, 2015; Rougemont, 2016; Henning, 2017)

In the United States, SAGE - Advocacy and Services for LGBT Elders, is the oldest organization dedicated to the rights and improvement of the quality of life of LGBT+ older people, playing the role of dialogue between activism and multidisciplinary academic fields. (Baron, L. Henning, L.E. & Ortiz, S. Brilhos da velhices LGBT, 2020, pg 35). However, the same path seen in Brazil after the rise of a conservative group to power took place in the United States, which, during the administration of President Barack Obama, in 2012, issued a national strategic order for tourism that aimed to facilitate the release of visas for an increase of 40%, mainly from tourists from China and Brazil. This policy underwent a setback in the Donald Trump administration, which in 2017 began to require a personal interview again for the granting of tourist visas to Brazilians, making the process difficult.

Understanding leisure travel restrictions and the various dimensions of these restrictions is critical for different stakeholders – tourism marketers and destination management organizations – in order to suggest strategies that can be used to overcome restrictions and help non-travelers negotiate (Eusebio et al, 2015). Social tourism as a phenomenon can be understood as a tool to overcome financial or other difficulties (e.g. health, mobility or disability problems) faced by social tourism users, according Debert (1998), McCabe, Joldersma & Li(2010), Almeida, (2011), Diekmann & McCabe (2013) and Felix (2019) within which the elderly are an important group. Participation in travel is specifically encouraged through the provision of different financial schemes and specific provisions (e.g. selection of specific accommodation and provision of support services) available to economically disadvantaged individuals and other users (Minnaert et al. al., 2011; Eusebio et al, 2015; Minnaert et al., 2015).

Historically, Brazilian Tourism internationalization projects provided for the dissemination of our landscape advantages, as well as selling the idea of a sunny country with a predominance of young and healthy bodies with a clear intention of attracting a male external audience.

Because of this, in the international imagination, Brazil is seen as a welcoming country, with excellent natural landscapes, an annual calendar of festive activities of its own, Latin culture, also, it is where the second largest Diversity Parade in the world takes place, in São Paulo. Part of this movement towards the internationalization of our tourism, has also had an effect on the way individuals see the sector.

Therefore, social tourism initiatives are generally sensitive to individual financial circumstances, and strategies for providing (public/charitable) funds should be identified as a key factor in encouraging the tourist participation of economically disadvantaged people, according Almeida (2011), Minnaert, Maitland & Miller(2011), Diekmann & McCabe (2013), Eusebio et al (2015) and Hahn et al. (2021). The private sector can benefit from additional revenues during the low season (Minnaert, Maitland & Miller, 2009). According to the study by Minnaert (2014), in order to increase the willingness to participate and the potential results of the vacation, social tourism providers must also offer the tourism products most adapted to each beneficiary, carefully considering the travel experience and levels of uncertainty before departure. Minnaert (2014, pp. 288) states that "reducing uncertainty is often a crucial gateway to participation in tourism: inexperienced tourists may refuse to participate in tourism even when financial barriers are overcome, if the levels of uncertainty met are considered "high".

When analyzing the interviews collected for the book, we realized that part of the anguish and frustrations of the participants is due to the invisibilities of each one with regard to the recognition of their sexualities, races and genders, and their fears and uncertainties for having gone through the Aids pandemic. Fueled by the idea of their own community, as well as their families and projected in dreams.

That said, it reminds us that the LGBT+ elderly of today lived a historical period of sexuality control, where the norm was oppressive, fostering this invisibility of their identities, where the fear of assuming their sexual orientation was greater. (page 19).

In the book, we highlight the interview of a transsexual man who declares himself as a heterosexual binary, Raicarlos Coelho Durans who declares:

...I lived in the period of the military dictatorship and was afraid of all kinds of violence. Of being arrested, tortured and raped. It ended up being me stuck with myself. (Raicarlos, trans-man).

This prison in which he refers denotes his understanding of his concept of family and that in fact imprisoned him:

...Furthermore, I also dislike the term ``family"., but I had a small childhood, because I was deprived of everything! But I was deprived for security reasons. My mother realized that I was a boy, that I had always been a boy, and she didn't know how to deal with it. Not knowing how to deal with it, she kept me, but it wasn't anything like that chained in a dark room. Look, girl, stay there, when you grow up, when you're old enough, then you'll understand everything I'm doing today! Everything I do is for your own good, but you'll have your whole life to go out and have fun. (Raicarlos, trans-man, binary, heterosexual).

The LGBT+ theme brings up many discussions about their bodies and in the most recent studies they have added more identity letters about the acronym, which is constantly changing. This is mainly due to discussions about Queer bodies. On the subject, the writer Guacira Lopes Louro (2000) collaborates with its definition: "Queer can be translated as strange, perhaps ridiculous, eccentric, rare, and extraordinary. But the expression also constitutes the pejorative way in which homosexual men and women are designated..." (Louro, 2000, pp. 60).

Still on this subject, the writer Berenice Bento comments: "the colors are the metaphor of a conception of gender and sexuality that denies fundamental rights to those who diverge from the position of the ideologists of "gender ideology". We are therefore facing a political dispute over which gender identities and sexuality have the right to exist." (Bento, B., 2019 apud Almeida Filho, J. M. M., preface, in: Genealogia Queer, 2021, pag.18).

That said, we come to understand these issues in the testimony of Denise Taynáh:

"Society defines me as a trans woman, but I perceive myself as a non-genetic woman..." she continues,

...I was never gay; I was a male being for many years. I had many children, each with a wife. I was a samba dancer, who really liked dancing, music with orchestras, in short, a busy male life, but I denied that female being that was inside me.

In gender studies, a discussion of intersectionality goes beyond, where it is not intended to homogenize the different populations, a good contribution to this discourse"... what is undeniable is that the use of the term intersectionality today in Brazil has gained popularity in discussions about gender. and race and points to an expansion of theoretical productions regarding this concept in the near future. All of us who have ventured to study black feminist thought, no doubt at some point, come across the concept of intersectionality. (Nzinga Nbandi, 2019, apud Santos, E. C. M.dos, 2021, p.51).

In the book, the account of José Carlos Kerua, 54 years old, bisexual, opens with his testimony about his race:

I'm black, peripheral, the son of a poor man, understand? I'm a survivor, a victor, just because I'm black and I'm alive at this age, going through everything that nero goes through. (José Carlos Kerua, 54 years old, bisexual, black).

The generation over 50 years old today lived through the AIDS pandemic, a milestone in their lives, as we analyzed in the interview with Ary Dálmeida, 66, who has been HIV positive for 29 years:

There are people who know about HIV because they read it, they know it because they found out about it, but not because they experienced it, and this experience has a great weight on me (Gay man, 66 years old, HIV positive).

In her report, where we learned the way she learned about her diagnosis, we noticed fear and the word family again:

The biggest impact, however, was when the disease started to hit my closest, closest friends - and it turned out that I was already HIV positive too. Manoel got sick and started having a series of problems. When he was hospitalized, my brother-in-law, who was a doctor and had a great deal of dialogue with me, showed that they tried everything to find out why he was ill. Then, he said; "Look, the only thing left to do is the HIV test, do you allow it?" Asked him and asked me. Then you see... It was between me and him, neither my family got into it, nor his family. I was responsible for it and allowed it. "You know your test is going to come out too. If it's positive for him, you're bound to go..." I replied: 'No problem'. (gay man, 66 years old, HIV positive).

The above reports bring a series of nuances difficult to be raised in cold statistics. By focusing on the exploratory study on these individuals, who report issues related to a generational culture to which they were subjected, we come to understand a historical path whose reports shed light on a discussion that should be addressed to develop demands for this public, and in view of this scenario establish the guidelines that tourism should cover in order to serve this specific public.

CONCLUSION

Culturally, men and women's bodies locate places, images and powers attributed to gender (Butler, 2015). They experience different relationships and social representations in relation to their bodies, regardless of age. The sociocultural meanings attributed to the body begin to influence directly on the relationship between subjects and their bodies and the way in which they will be recognized by the other's gaze (Louro, 2000, pp. 11). Aging, in this way, becomes the place where the individual starts to be judged by his aesthetics and, not infrequently, the social architecture begins to limit the circulation of specific groups. According to Louro (2000) and Butler (2015), the body is judged by its condition and capacity in society. For Tourism, such observation is important to define and categorize this group, whose personal interests also involve the extensive use of travel as a way of escaping this judgment.

Part of this interpretation of tourism by minority groups reflects the logic of Brazil's insertion in the world market, whose relevance is still very recent, as well as bringing to light the discussion on the World stage. As stated by Zeldin earlier, tourism, seen as an escape strategy for various societies, transfers to individuals the need to search for realities that meet expectations and desires different from their daily lives.

Furthermore, considering the LGBT+ civil rights agenda as a premise that also crosses tourism as a practice of freedom, it demands investigations beyond the economistic bias of this phenomenon. In this context, it is necessary to understand new forms of participation and production of leisure and tourism specific to this group, bringing together contributions to the field of Leisure and Tourism, Gerontology, Anthropology and Social Psychology. In this sense, it appears the relevance of building multi/inter/transdisciplinary research, above all, for the understanding of complex issues, such as the aging of LGBT+ people, allowing crossings that dialogue in favor of a more inclusive tourism in Brazilian scientific production.

Therefore, thinking of the group as a market advantage strategy without considering the specificities and difficulties of this segment in accessing the labor market and consumer goods becomes a complicating factor in the formulation of content and promotion plans, as well as generating dissatisfaction with the consumer for not having been met in their desires.

In view of the current national political scenario, whose perspective of public policies to encourage LGBT+ tourism was restricted due to its withdrawal from the current National Tourism Plan (Brasil, 2015), we are in favor of a contrary position, mainly because: 1) it is a historically oppressed and violated group. There are prerequisites that need to be met to generate a competitive advantage in choosing a tourist destination. 2) Despite the expansion of mass tourism, global tourism indicators suggest a greater growth of the so-called "niche tourism", in which the tourist needs much more than basic structures. 3) The importance of recording the memories of LGBT+ elderly people to foster future research.

When thinking about the group in question, one must consider that part of their experience and existence was determined by fears and anxieties that reflected their insertion in society, whose appropriation by the tourism market is beyond generalities. Therefore, choosing a destination is directly linked to a series of requirements linked to survival itself and a specific way of reading the world.

Thus, it provides the demand for research for and on the subject, an unexplored field, which needs to be brought to light for the theoretical knowledge of tourism, as well as for managers who intend to format new policies to meet this group increasingly inserted in the logic of tourism consumption.

The LGBT+ elderly are increasingly an expressive cut that find their spaces to conquer a more active and sociable life, and for that it is necessary to be recognized and welcomed, with Tourism, in its greatest characteristic, the sector in the economy that can foster new public policies to provide more leisure and utility in the lives of the oldest.

REFERENCES

Aboim, S. (2014). Narratives of aging: Being old in contemporary society [Narrativas do envelhecimento: ser velho na sociedade contemporânea]. *Tempo Social, São Paulo, 26*(1), 207–232.

Almeida, M. V. (2011). The development of social tourism in Brazil. *Current Issues in Tourism, 14*(5), 483–489. doi:10.1080/13683500.2011.568057

Alves, R. F., & de Aguiar, R. G. (2020). *The Pink Money market and the positioning of brands: a study on the perception of consumers in Fortaleza/CE* [O mercado Pink Money e o posicionamento das marcas: um estudo sobre a percepção dos consumidores de Fortaleza/CE]. Artigo (Graduação em Administração) – Centro Universitário Fametro. http://repositorio.unifametro.edu.br/handle/123456789/934

Amaral, M., Rodrigues, A. I., Diniz, A., Oliveira, S., & Leal, S. (2020). Designing and evaluating tourism experiences in senior mobility: An application of the OEC framework. *Tourism & Management Studies, 16*(4), 59–72. doi:10.18089/tms.2020.160405

ANTRA. (2020). *Dossier on Murders and Violence Against Brazilian Trans Persons Trans Brasileiras* [Dossiê dos Assassinatos e da Violência Contra Pessoas]. https://antrabrasil.files.wordpress.com/2021/01/dossie-trans-2021-29jan2021.pdf

Araujo, L. F. de; Carlos, K. P. T. (2018). Sexuality in old age: a study on LGBT aging [Sexualidade na velhice: um estudo sobre o envelhecimento LGBT]. *Psicol. Conoc. Soc., 8*(1), 188-205.

Archer, B. H. (1982). The value of multipliers and their policy implications. *Tourism Management, 3*(4), 236–241. doi:10.1016/0261-5177(82)90044-9

Ashton, S. G. M., Cabral, S., Santos, G. A. dos, & Kroetz, J. (2015). The relationship between tourism and Quality of Life in the Aging Process [A relação do turismo e da Qualidade de Vida no Processo de Envelhecimento]. *Revista Hospitalidade, 12*(2), 547 – 566.

Australian Bureau of Statistics. (1993). Disability, Ageing and Carers Australia. Commonwealth of Australia.

Azevedo, M. S., Martins, C. B., Pizzinatto, N. K., & Farah, O. E. (2012). Segmentation in the tourism sector: LGBT tourists from São Paulo [Segmentação no setor turístico: turistas LGBT de São Paulo]. *Revista de Administração da UFSM, 5*(3), 493–506. doi:10.5902/198346593852

BITS. (2011). http://www.bits-int.org/

Brasil. (1988). *Constitution of the Federative Republic of Brazil* [Constituição da República Federativa do Brasil]. http://www.planalto.gov.br/ccivil_03/constituicao/constituicaocompilado.htmBrasil

Brasil. (2012). *Instituto Brasileiro de Geografia e Estatística.2010 Demographic Census: General sample results* [Censo demográfico de 2010: Resultados gerais da amostra]. IBGE.

Brasil. (2015). *Ministério do Turismo. National Tourism Plan 2013/2016* [Plano Nacional do Turismo 2013/2016]. Brasília.

Brasil. Ministério da Saúde. (2011). *Health Portal. What is the Pact for Health?* [Portal da Saúde. O que é o Pacto pela Saúde?]. http://portal.saude.gov.br/portal/saude/ profissional/area.cfm?id_area=1021

Butler, J. (2015). Self-report: Critique of ethical violence [Relatar a si mesmo: crítica da violência ética]. Belo Horizonte: Autêntica.

Cleaver, M., & Muller, T. E. (2002). I want to pretend I'm eleven years younger: Subjective age and seniors' motives for vacation travel. *Social Indicators Research, 60*(1-3), 227–241. doi:10.1023/A:1021217232446

Couto, M. C. de P. (2009). Assessment of discrimination against the elderly in a Brazilian context - ageism [Avaliação de discriminação contra idosos em contexto brasileiro - ageismo]. *Psic.: teor. e pesq., 25*(4), 509-518.

Dann, G. (2002). Senior Tourism and Quality of Life. *Journal of Hospitality & Leisure Marketing, 9*(1-2), 5–19. doi:10.1300/J150v09n01_02

Dantas, A. J. L. (2021). *Life story narratives of elderly lesbians: intersectionality between old age, gender and sexuality* [Narrativas de histórias de vida de idosas lésbicas: interseccionalidade entre velhice, gênero e sexualidade] [Dissertation]. Universidade Federal do Ceará, Fortaleza. Disponível em https://repositorio.ufc.br/handle/riufc/57519

de Beauvoir, S. (1990). *Old age: the most important contemporary essay on the living conditions of the elderly* [A velhice: o mais importante ensaio contemporâneo sobre as condições de vida dos idosos]. Nova Fronteira.

Debert, G. G. (1998). The reinvention of old age. Socialization and aging reprivatization processes [A reinvenção da velhice. Socialização e processos de reprivatização do envelhecimento]. São Paulo: Edusp, Fapesp.

Diekmann, A., & McCabe, S. (2011). Systems of social tourism in the European Union: A critical review. *Current Issues in Tourism, 14*(5), 417–430. doi:10.1080/13683500.2011.568052

Doll, J. (2007). Education, culture and leisure: Prospects of successful old age [Educação, cultura e lazer: Perspectivas de velhice bem-sucedida]. In *Elderly people in Brazil: Experiences, challenges and expectations in the elderly* [Idosos no Brasil: Vivências, desafios e expectativas na terceira idade] (pp. 109–123). Abramo.

dos Santos, E. C. M. (2021). Can a good Creole survive racism? [Pode um bom crioulo sobreviver ao racismo?]. In Queer genealogy [Genealogia Queer]. Devires.

EESC. (2006). Opinion of the European Economic and Social Committee on social tourism in Europe. *EESC- Official Journal of the European Union.*

EUROSTAT. (2012). *Population projections.* http://epp.eurostat.ec.europa.eu/statistics_explained/index.php/Population_projections

Eusébio, C., & Carneiro, M. J. (2012). Socio- cultural impacts of tourism in urban destinations. *Revista Portuguesa de Estudos Regionais*, *30*(1), 65–76.

Eusebio, C., Carneiro, M. J., Kastenholz, E., & Alvelos, H. (2013). The Economic Impact of Health Tourism Programmes. In Quantitative Methods in Tourism Economics. Lisbon: Physica-Verlag. doi:10.1007/978-3-7908-2879-5_9

Eusebio, C., Carneiro, M. J., Kastenholz, E., & Alvelos, H. (2015). The impact of social tourism for seniors on the economic development of tourism destinations. *European Journal of Tourism Research*, *12*, 5–24. doi:10.54055/ejtr.v12i.210

Félix, J. de O. (2019). *Tourism for the elderly: leisure in nature, in Sergipe* [Turismo da terceira idade: lazer na natureza, em Sergipe] [Dissertation]. Universidade Federal de Sergipe: São Cristóvão.

Fernandes, M. T. O., & Soares, S. M. (2012). The development of public policies for elderly care in Brazil. *Revista da Escola de Enfermagem da USP*. https://www.scielo.br/pdf/reeusp/v46n6/en_29.pdf

Ferreira, G. G., & Aguinsky, B. G. (2013). Social movements of sexuality and gender: analysis of access to public policies [Movimentos sociais de sexualidade e gênero: análise do acesso às políticas públicas]. *Revista Katálysis, 16*(2), 223-232. doi:10.1590/S1414-49802013000200008

Fleischer, A., & Pizam, A. (2002). Tourism constraints among Israeli seniors. *Annals of Tourism Research*, *29*(1), 106–123. doi:10.1016/S0160-7383(01)00026-3

Fundação Perseu Abramo &Serviço Social do Comércio. (2020). *Elderly in Brazil: Experiences, Challenges and Expectations in the Third Age* [Idosos no Brasil: Vivências, Desafios e Expectativas na Terceira Idade]. Disponível em: https://fpabramo.org.br/publicacoes/wp-content/uploads/sites/5/2020/08/Pesquisa-Idosos-II-Completa-v2.pdf

Gee, S., & Baillie, J. (1999). Happily Ever After? An Exploration of Retirement Expectations. *Educational Gerontology*, *25*(2), 109–128. doi:10.1080/036012799267909

Gomes, F. G. de V. (2005). *The Perception of the GLBT Segment About the Service of the Brazilian Tourism Sector* [A Percepção do Segmento GLBT Sobre o Atendimento do Setor Turístico Brasileiro]. UniCEUB.

Gonçalves, M. E. (2021). *Murder of trans people grows in the US in 2021* [Assassinato de pessoas trans cresce nos EUA em 2021]. https://revistahibrida.com.br/2021/04/26/assassinato-de-pessoas-trans-cresce-nos-eua-em-2021/

Green, J. N. (2018). *History of the LGBT movement in Brazil* [História do movimento LGBT no Brasil] (1st ed.). Alameda.

Hahn, I. S., Bianchi, J., Baldissarelli, J. M., & Martins, A. A. M. (2021). Destination choice for LGBT+ tourists: Relationship between psychological motivations and destination images [Escolha do destino de turistas LGBT+: Relação entre motivações psicológicas e imagens de destino]. *Revista de Administração da UFSM, 14*(spe1), 1086-1100. doi:10.5902/1983465965024

Henning, C. E. (2017). *LGBT Gerontology: Old Age, Gender, Sexuality and the Constitution of "LGBT Elders"* [Gerontologia LGBT: Velhice, Gênero, Sexualidade e a Constituição dos "idosos LGBT"] [Dissertação de Mestrado]. UFGO: Goiânia.

INATEL. (2005). *Execution Report of the Programa Turismo Sénior 2005*. INATEL.

Iso-Ahola, S. E. (1982). Toward a social psychological theory of tourism motivation: A rejoinder. *Annals of Tourism Research, 9*(2), 256–262. doi:10.1016/0160-7383(82)90049-4

Kama, A., Ram, Y., Hall, C., & Mizrachi, I. (2019). The benefits of an LGBT-inclusive tourist destination. *Journal of Destination Marketing & Management, 14*, 100374. Advance online publication. doi:10.1016/j.jdmm.2019.100374

Kishigami, F. D. (2020). Public policies: leisure and tourism as an instrument for the social insertion of transvestites and transsexuals in social vulnerability [Políticas públicas: lazer e turismo como instrumento de inserção social de travestis e transexuais em vulnerabilidade social] [Master's Dissertation]. Escola de Artes, Ciências e Humanidades, University of São Paulo. www.teses.usp.br doi:10.11606/D.100.2020.tde-10012020-173305

Krippendorf, J. (2009). *Sociology of Tourism. For a new understanding of leisure and travel* [Sociologia do turismo. Para uma nova compreensão do lazer e das viagens]. Aleph.

Louro, G. L. (2000). Body pedagogies [Pedagogias do corpo]. In *LOURO, Guacira Lopes (org.). The educated body* [O corpo educado] (pp. 7–21). Autêntica.

Luiz, K., & Henz, A. (2018). LGBT tourism: a study about initiatives in Brazil [Turismo LGBT: um estudo acerca das iniciativas no Brasil]. 12º Fórum Internacional de Turismo do Iguassu,, Foz do Iguaçu, Brasil.

Magnus, G. (2009). *The Age of Ageing*. John Wiley.

McCabe, S. (2009). Who needs a holiday? Evaluating social tourism. *Annals of Tourism Research, 36*(4), 667–688. doi:10.1016/j.annals.2009.06.005

McCabe, S., Joldersma, T., & Li, C. (2010). Understanding the benefits of social tourism: Linking participation to subjective well-being and quality of life. *International Journal of Tourism Research, 12*(6), 761–773. doi:10.1002/jtr.791

McCabe, S. S., & Johnson, S. (2013). The happiness factor in tourism: Subjective well-being and social tourism. *Annals of Tourism Research, 41*, 42–65. doi:10.1016/j.annals.2012.12.001

Miller, R. E., & Blair, P. D. (1985). *Input-Output Analysis: Foundations and Extensions*. Prentice Hall.

Minnaert, L., Maitland, R., & Miller, G. (2009). Tourism and social policy: The value of social tourism. *Annals of Tourism Research, 36*(2), 316–334. doi:10.1016/j.annals.2009.01.002

Minnaert, L., Maitland, R., & Miller, G. (2011). What is social tourism? *Current Issues in Tourism, 14*(5), 403–415. doi:10.1080/13683500.2011.568051

Moraes, K. M. (2011). Companionship and sexuality of couples at the best age: caring for the elderly couple [Companheirismo e sexualidade de casais na melhor idade: cuidando do casal idoso]. *Rev. Bras. Geriatr. Gerontol., 14*(4), 787-798.

Moreira, M. G.; Hallal, D. R. (2017). Travels and Border Experiences in the Transgression of the Gay Closet [As Viagens e as Experiências de Fronteira na Transgressão do Armário Gay]. *Revista Rosa dos Ventos – Turismo e Hospitalidade, 9*, 133-155.

Neri, A. L. (1993). Quality of life and mature age [Qualidade de vida e idade madura] (7th ed.). Campinas: São Paulo: Papirus Editora.

Neugarten, B. L., & Neugarten, D. A. (1986). Changing meanings of age in the aging society. In A. Pifer & L. Bronte (Eds.), *Our Aging Society: Paradox and Promise* (pp. 33–51). W. W. Norton.

Neves, C.S.B. & Brambatti, L.E. (2019). The behavior of LGBT tourists in relation to consumption on leisure trips [O comportamento do turista LGBT com relação ao consumo em viagens de lazer]. *Rosa dos Ventos – Turismo e Hospitalidade, 11*(4), 832-846.

Nimrod, G. (2008). Retirement and tourism – Themes in retirees' narratives. *Annals of Tourism Research, 35*(4), 859–878. doi:10.1016/j.annals.2008.06.001

Nimrod, G., & Rotem, A. (2010). Between relaxation and excitement: Activities and benefits in retireeś tourism. *International Journal of Tourism Research, 12*(1), 65–78. doi:10.1002/jtr.739

Nunan, A. (2015). *Homosexuality of Prejudice to Consumption Patterns* [Homossexualidade do Preconceito aos Padrões de Consumo]. Caravansarai Editora Ltda.

Oliveira, L. A. (2016). *Post Modern Tourism: The LGBT segment in Brazil* [Turismo Pós Moderno: O segmento LGBT no Brasil] [Dissertação de Mestrado]. UFRN:Mossoró – RN.

Paixão, D. L. D. (2008). *Hedonistic tourism: a post-modern segment of travel combined with pleasure* [Turismo hedonista: um segmento pós-moderno de viagens aliadas ao prazer]. Anais do V Seminário da Associação Nacional de Pesquisa e Pós-Graduação em Turismo.

Panosso Neto, A., & Trigo, L. G. G. (2009). *Brazilian tourism scenarios* [Cenários do turismo brasileiro]. Aleph.

Rebelato, C. (2021). *Introduction to LGBTI+ old age* [Introdução às velhices LGBTI+]. SBGG.

Ricco, A. S. (2012). Tourism as a social and anthropological phenomenon [O Turismo como fenômeno social e antropológico]. In Tourism, space and local development strategies [Turismo, espaço e estratégias de desenvolvimento local]. UFPB.

Rios, L. F. (2009). Homosexuality in the plural of genders: reflections to implement the debate on sexual diversity in schools [Homossexualidade no plural dos gêneros: reflexões para implementar o debate sobre diversidade sexual nas escolas]. In Gender, diversity and inequalities in education: interpretations and reflections for teacher training [Gênero, diversidade e desigualdades na educação: interpretações e reflexões para formação docente]. UFPE.

Rougemont, F. dos R. (2016). The longevity of youth [A longevidade da juventude]. In Velho é lindo! Rio de Janeiro: Civilização Brasileira.

Scrivano&Sorima Neto. (2015). Potential for LGBT purchases is estimated at R$ 419 billion in Brazil [Potencial de compras LGBT é estimado em R$ 419 bilhões no Brasil]. *O Globo, Caderno de Economia.* https://oglobo.globo.com/economia/potencial-de-compras-lgbt-estimado-em-419-bilhoes-no-brasil-15785227

Tadini, R.F., & Melquiades, T. (2008). Analysis of the performance of service volunteers to the National Olympic and Paralympic Committees in the scope of the Pan and Parapan American Games Rio 2007 [Análise da atuação dos voluntariados de serviço aos Comitês Olímpicos e Paraolímpicos Nacionais no âmbito dos Jogos Pan e Parapanamericanos Rio 2007]. In V Seminário de Pesquisa em Turismo do MERCOSUL – SeminTUR, 2008. Universidade de Caxias do Sul.

Tadioto, M. V., Moreira, M. G., & Jung de Campos, L. (2016). Discourse Analysis: A theoretical-analytical device to problematize Tourism [Análise do Discurso: um dispositivo teórico - analítico para problematizar o Turismo]. In Anais... XIII Seminário da Associação Nacional de Pesquisa e Pós-Graduação em Turismo - ANPTUR. São Paulo, Brasil: Anptur.

Trevisan, J. S. (2006). Tourism and sexual orientation [Turismo e orientação sexual]. In *Ministério do Turismo do Brasil. Social tourism. Tourism dialogues: a journey of inclusion* [Turismo social. Diálogos do turismo: uma viagem de inclusão] (pp. 139–171). Instituto Brasileiro de Administração Municipal.

Trigo, L. G. G. (2009). Rise of pleasure in today's society: GLS Tourism [Ascensão do prazer na sociedade atual: Turismo GLS]. In Tourism market segmentation: studies, products and perspectives [Segmentação do mercado turístico: estudos, produtos e perspectivas]. Manole.

UN. (2020). *Aging* [Envelhecimento]. https://www.who.int/health-topics/ageing#tab=tab_1

United Nations. (1948). *General Assembly Resolution 217 A*. United Nations.

Vidal da Rocha, M. C., Luis da Silva, R., Gabrig Oliveira, I., & Faria Duarte, A. L. (2021). Benefícios da Atividade Turística na Manutenção da Saúde da Terceira Idade. *Revista Estudos E Pesquisas Em Administração, 5*(1). doi:10.30781/repad.v5i1.11634

WHO. (2015). *World Report on Aging and Health* [Relatório Mundial de Envelhecimento e Saúde]. Brasília, DF: OMS. Disponível em: https://sbgg.org.br/wpcontent/uploads/2015/10/OMS-ENVELHECIMENTO-2015-port.pdf

Wilkes, R. E. (1992). A structural modeling approach to the measurement and meaning of cognitive age. *The Journal of Consumer Research, 19*, 292–301.

Zeldin, T. (2008). *Uma História Intima da Humanidade*. Bestbolso.

ENDNOTES

1. https://www.who.int/health-topics/ageing#tab=tab_1
2. A survey of 356 elderly Australians aged between 56 and 93 years, produced data on their subjective age measured in terms of: (a) how old they felt, (b) the activities they would choose to experience or enjoy while on vacation, and (c) the age at which they wanted to be treated and recognized, as well as, their

psychological reasons for vacation travel, personal values, and self-rated health. The results of the multivariate analyzes indicate that the difference between the real age and the subjective age is a function of the particular motives of the elderly to travel and what they value in life and, for certain aspects of the subjective age, how healthy they feel and their genre. In: Australian Bureau of Statistics: 1993, Disability, Aging and Cares Australia.

3 In Scrivano & Sorima Neto. (2015) Potencial de compras LGBT é estimado em R$ 419 bilhões no Brasil. https://oglobo.globo.com/economia/potencial-de-compras-lgbt-estimado-em-419-bilhoes-no-brasil-15785227

Chapter 13
Transcreation in Digital Tourism Information:
An Inclusive Language Approach

Juncal Gutiérrez-Artacho
https://orcid.org/0000-0002-0275-600X
University of Granada, Spain

María-Dolores Olvera Olvera-Lobo
https://orcid.org/0000-0002-0489-7674
University of Granada, Spain

ABSTRACT

This chapter tackles the need to incorporate strategies of linguistic and cultural accessibility that guarantee respect for diversity and equality in processes of dissemination and access to tourism information in the web environment. The proposal focuses on transcreation as a fundamental tool from the perspective, furthermore, of inclusive language. These reflections will contribute to establishing recommendations aimed at facilitating the creation of contents adapted to the characteristics of the new media. These guidelines may be of great use both for professionals in the tourism sector and for those in the field of communication or translation, amongst others. In addition, the contribution aims to favour the development of teaching resources linked to aspects of the specific language of communication and marketing, encouraging more holistic training for students of tourism and related areas. This rejuvenated professional profile will also require knowledge in post-digital communication to undertake this task in a global manner.

DOI: 10.4018/978-1-6684-4194-7.ch013

INTRODUCTION

Language is one of the main persuasive instruments when developing informative resources and marketing tools aimed at potential clients. In the context of the modern digital society, one aspect to arouse considerable interest refers to the importance of facilitating access to information adopting a multilingual and translingual perspective. The need to favor communication and the dissemination of information from the sector, along with interaction with potential consumers, makes it essential for tourism companies and professionals to achieve an internet presence that is solid, professional and adapted to target markets. This aspect is even more important in the case of small and medium sized enterprises, for which the use of the internet and Web 2.0 tools offers numerous opportunities in exchange for reduced cost (Ferreira; Gutiérrez-Artacho & Bernardino, 2017).

Essentially, from the professional, enterprise and human perspective it is necessary that companies adapt their corporate websites to different languages and cultures if they seek to reach greater success and bigger audiences. It is necessary, however, to take into account that the information destined towards dissemination on the web is comprised of different semiotic sources –linguistic elements, images, color, design, animations, voices, music, etc. For these multi-mode texts, language is no longer the dominant semiotic source, rather, another resource that interacts with the rest, creating meaning (Munday, 2004). Therefore, the mere translation of a website into other languages is often insufficient for contributing to a satisfactory experience on the part of its users. Transcreation, which consists of the intra or interlinguistic reinterpretation of a text to adapt it to the target public (Gaballo, 2012), constitutes a growing trend in the sphere of translation. This is reflected in the fact that standards such as Spanish ISO 17100 (Aenor, 2016) have recognized transcreation as an added value service within the language services industry. In the case of interlinguistic reinterpretation (which implies at least two communication languages), transcreation leads to a type of translation wherein both the words and the meaning of the original texts can be susceptible to serious modification with the aim of producing the same effect in the target receivers as in the source audience –taking into account the possible existence not only of language differences, but also cultural differences between both publics.

Given its nature, the fields where transcreation has reached a greater development are precisely those related to marketing, communication and advertising (Díaz-Millón & Olvera-Lobo, 2021; Olvera-Lobo *et al.*, 2019), due to the need to adapt advertising campaigns and marketing actions to other globalized markets. In this regard, the aim is for an advertising text to achieve the desired effect in all target markets but always conserving the creative intention of the original campaign, the message that it intended to transmit and specific aspects of the marketing language such as the so-called brand voice (Pedersen, 2014). Thus, transcreation seeks interlinguistic adaptation to different audiences and markets, to which it does not constitute a mere translation subtype, rather, it involves complex processes that require translation methods and skills up to a certain point or in some phases (Katan, 2016; Pedersen, 2016). The transcreation approach can therefore be described as a creative, subjective and emotive process via which some parts of the message are translated and others adapted to the target market. For all of the above, it is perfectly possible, even recommendable, to apply transcreation processes to certain digital products, such as corporate websites, given that they include diverse elements specific to the language of advertising (Morón & Calvo, 2018; Rike, 2013). A characteristic of these products is that they present numerous translation problems arising from cultural components, humor, poetry, neologisms, plays on words and other evocative resources. In these cases, translation professionals approach jobs from clients (companies or individuals) creatively, to which the process becomes transcreative.

The adequate use of language is a fundamental ingredient in plural contexts –multilingual, multiethnic, multicultural, multigender– such as those in which transcreation processes occur. Therefore, so-called inclusive language must consider speakers of any origin, nationality, sexual orientation, gender identity, race or religion. Specifically, from a gender perspective, translation –and, hence, also transcreation– may be a powerful tool for social change and for promoting the visibility of the role of women in society (De Marco, 2012). Attention might be drawn to the initiatives that have given rise to guides for the use of inclusive, non-sexist language such as those proposed by the European Parliament (2009) translated into 22 languages, and by numerous public and private bodies and institutions from very different geographical points. Certain publications also include guidelines on how to use images in a non-sexist way. In this way, given the creative freedom enjoyed by transcreation specialists, which allows them to have an influence over the contents they adapt and modify, it is essential that these professionals acquire a gender perspective that permits them identify the way in which social inequalities are reflected in texts, and how to reduce the impact thereof.

This chapter talk to the need to incorporate strategies of linguistic and cultural accessibility that guarantee respect for diversity and equality in processes of dissemination and access to tourism information in the web environment. Our proposal focuses on transcreation as a fundamental tool from the perspective, furthermore, of inclusive language. These reflections will contribute to establishing recommendations aimed at facilitating the creation of contents adapted to the characteristics of the new media. These guidelines may be of great use both for professionals in the tourism sector and for those in the field of communication or translation, amongst others. In addition, our contribution tries to favor the development of teaching resources linked to aspects of the specific language of communication and marketing, encouraging more holistic training for students of tourism and related areas. This rejuvenated professional profile will also require knowledge in post-digital communication to undertake this task in a global manner.

From the gender perspective, transcreation professionals may constitute social and cultural change agents by means of identifying and modifying those aspects of the product target to interlinguistic adaptation that present gender, race, or age discrimination, among other. Due to the multi-modal nature of the texts that are transcreated, this may appear in different elements of the product being transcreated; for instance, in the visual components or the content of the text. In this context, it is vital the integration of a gender perspective, and inclusive language on the whole, the training and the performance of transcreation. For this task, special emphasis will be placed on the importance of using inclusive language that reflects the role and presence of women and men in today's society.

Background

Digital marketing comprises all of enterprise's efforts for communicating, promoting, and selling products or services through the Internet (Kotler et al., 2007). Alternative proposals suggest digital marketing covers –besides social media, search engines or mobile applications– various channels that do not involve Internet usage, such as mobile messaging. Chaffey and Smith (2013) understand digital marketing as the application of digital technologies for contributing to marketing activities which aim to achieve profitability and customer retention. To this end, it is essential to recognize the strategic importance of digital technologies and to develop a planned approach directed toward improving knowledge about customers, reaching effective communication and providing online services tailored to individual needs.

Digital marketing facilitates the interactions between enterprises and consumers throughout communities, thus promoting loyalty (Urrutikoetxea-Arrieta, Polo-Peña & Martínez-Medina, 2017). Hence, the first step for the companies to delve into digital marketing must be designing an attractive website that ensures engagement with users while serving the objectives and interests of the company (Alcaide *et al.*, 2013; Gutiérrez-Artacho & Olvera-Lobo, 2018).

Furthermore, a fundamental aspect that arouses huge interest and has become very popular in the context of the information society is the importance of facilitating the access to multilingual and translingual information. It is necessary to reflect on transcreation as a useful mean to achieve specific objectives in marketing, communication and advertising (Gutiérrez-Artacho *et al.*, 2019).

MAIN FOCUS OF THE CHAPTER

Practical Guidelines of Exclusive Communication

Nowadays, within any transcreation project, it is essential to mainstream the gender issue from the beginning, in other words, incorporating the gender transversality in the different intervention areas of the project. Because transcreation is a reinterpretation of the original text in another language, specialized materials are key to ensure an appropriate intervention. Inclusive language represents a communication code that considers reality as it is, sexed. This code enables women and men to name the world from their gender and to be named taking into account their sex, without subordination or invisibilization of any of either sex. Or, as far as images are concerned, that they reflect a balanced presence of men and women far from gender stereotypes (Igualdad en las empresas, 2022). Practical guidelines for inclusive communication are aimed to provide touristic SMEs with a useful instrument for their digital marketing.

There are currently no specific guidelines in Spanish for the tourism sector, although given the characteristics of the area, the good practices of others can be applied. Therefore, all available guides have been analyzed for this article, according to data from the Ministry of Equality of Spain (Ministerio de Igualdad, 2022).

Methodology

There is a rising interest in an inclusive scope and the use of the language as a vehicle for social awareness, which has led multiple organisms to develop their own guides for inclusive language. In Díaz-Millón et al. (2021), a comprehensive analysis is carried out on all non-sexist language guidelines published by Spanish universities, emphasizing that it is therefore evident that there is a lack of consensus among the Spanish public universities concerning their guides for inclusive language and there is a need to delve deeper into the keys to inclusive language and to develop tools specifically designed to assess gender-inclusive language.

For the purpose of this study, and in order to compile institutionally validated criteria and indications for inclusive language, we have analyzed all the guides included in the official list of the Spanish Ministry of Equality. Although we assume that there are other guides available on the Web, we have focused only on those of the Ministry since they are all from official organizations or institutions (a total of 120 guides). The last intention of these papers are, on one hand, to make a theoretical approach to a reality in which language, the basic tool for communication, and hence for conveying information throughout mass media, continues to be used with little certainty when it comes to consolidating practices and dynamics that favor equality and diversity in our citizenship. On the other hand, these guides pursue the

Figure 1. Practical guidelines for inclusive communication by sectors

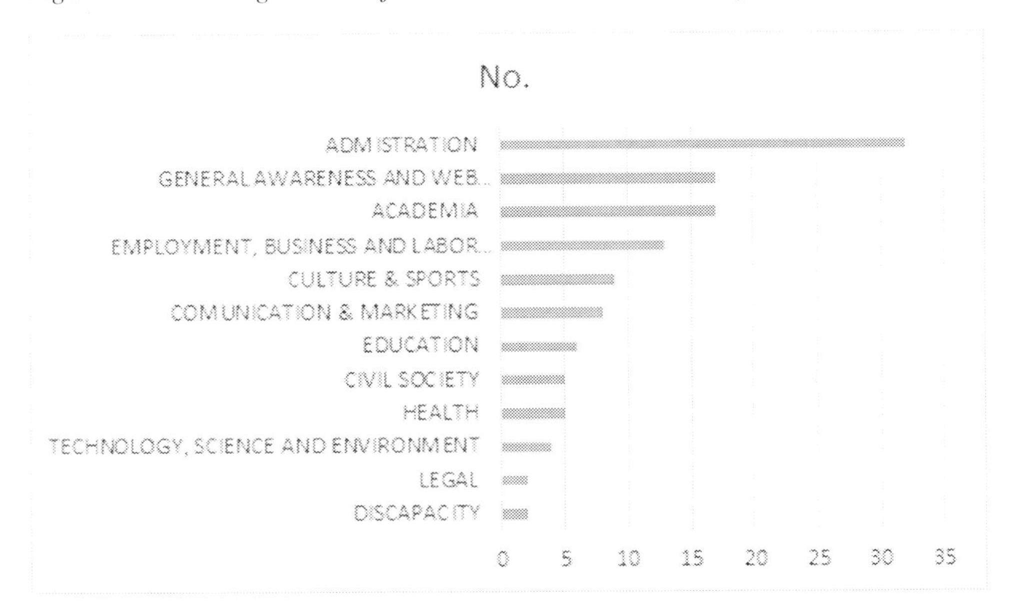

establishment of standards of action within the media that promotes an ethical and equal treatment of the image of both genders. In addition, these guides intend to become into tools for effective consultation, agile and practical for all people who work for companies or organizations, both public or private, in order to complement and reinforce existing handbooks on the non-sexist use of language.

This collection is organized around various aspects such as Administration (32 guides), General Awareness and Web Resources (17), Academia (17) or Employment, Business and Labor Relations (13), among others (Figure 1). Although all these guides may be used in many different contexts, some of them may be particularly useful in the field to which this study refers, i.e., for tourism-oriented transcreation. These are those related to Communication and Marketing (8), General Awareness and Web Resources (17) and Civil Society (5).

These guides are written in Spanish, Catalan and Basque (the last two ones are co-official Spanish languages).

They are oriented to the use of language in written documents and their purpose is twofold. On one hand, helping to understand that there is an intimate connection between our usage of the language and the situation of inequality that women suffer in society. On the other hand, it aims to provide sufficient tools to identify sexism and androcentrism in texts, suggesting at the same time different alternatives for the use of non-discriminatory formulas and terms.

The analysis of the guidelines contained in these guides has allowed us to extract some recommendations that may be useful for the creators of multilingual websites oriented to diverse audiences, i.e. transcreated, in the tourism sector.

SOLUTIONS AND RECOMMENDATIONS

Practical guides for inclusive communication are good tools for development of professionals to create attractive products for the target audience in the tourism sector. Below, we highlight some of the specific recommendations of these guides that can be applied to the transcreation of tourism products:

1. As a general rule, perform the investment test. That is, replace the questionable word with its corresponding word of the opposite gender. If the phrase is inappropriate and is offensive to one of the two sexes, the first word is sure to be as well.
2. It is necessary to establish self-regulatory mechanisms in the media, as well as to devise methods to eradicate programs in which there is gender bias.
3. It is desirable to have guidelines and resources that support the use of inclusive and non-sexist communication in a systematic way.
4. Do not confuse social sexism with linguistic sexism, although they are related to each other.
5. A plural, non-sexist and inclusive iconography is one that makes all people visible on an equal basis; however, there is still a tendency to use the heteropatriarchal male figure as a generic model of representation of the entire population.
6. Appropriate use of language and iconography, requiring a careful and conscious examination of the implication of digital media in the maintenance or elimination of inequalities among all people.

The guides for the use of inclusive language are useful tools to evaluate the presence of (gender-)inclusive language features in texts, including multimodal texts (which incorporate audio-visual elements). Given its broad scope, these tools could be used to evaluate inclusive language not just in educational or institutional texts, but also in other types of texts, such as websites, information materials, etc.

CONCLUSION

As shown in previous sections of this work, public Spanish institutions have produced a significant amount of guides for the use of inclusive language, accounting for the increasing interest raised in recent years by this issue: producing respectful texts towards the gender.

For that reason, the main objective of this work was to tackle the need to incorporate strategies of linguistic and cultural accessibility that guarantee respect for diversity and equality in processes of dissemination and access to tourism information in the web environment. Our proposal has focused on transcreation as a fundamental tool from the perspective, furthermore, of inclusive language. These reflections have contributed to establishing recommendations aimed at facilitating the creation of contents adapted to the characteristics of the new media. These guidelines may be of great use both for professionals in the tourism sector and for those in the field of communication or translation, among others.

ACKNOWLEDGMENT

This research is part of the project "Transcreación y Marketing Digital Para la Difusión Web de la Información Corporativa de Pymes Andaluzas del Sector Turístico", funded by the Consejería de Transformación económica, industria, comercio y universidades, Junta de Andalucía (Spain). Reference: B-SEJ-402-UGR20 (PROYECTOS DE I+D+I EN EL MARCO DEL PROGRAMA OPERATIVO FEDER ANDALUCÍA 2014-2020).

REFERENCES

Aenor. (2016). *UNE EN ISO 17100:2015. Standard for translation agencies* [Norma para agencias de traducción]. Retrieved from https://normadecalidad.iso17100.com/

Alcaide, J. C., Bernués, S., Díaz-Aroca, E., Espinosa, R., Muñiz, R., & Smith, C. (2013). *Marketing and SMEs. The main marketing keys in small and medium-sized companies* [Marketing y Pymes. Las principales claves de marketing en la pequeña y mediana empresa]. Retrieved from https://bit.ly/38AowiG

Chaffey, D., & Smith, P. R. (2013). *EMarketing eXcellence : planning and optimizing your digital marketing*. Routledge. doi:10.4324/9780203082812

De Marco, M. (2012). *Audiovisual Translation through a Gender Lens*. Rodopi. doi:10.1163/9789401207881

Díaz-Millón, M., & Gutiérrez-Artacho, J. (2019). New professional profiles in translation: Skills necessary for transcreation [Nuevos perfiles profesionales en traducción: Competencias necesarias para la transcreación]. *1st International Conference On Digital Linguistics – CILiDi´19.*

Díaz-Millón, M., & Olvera-Lobo, M. D. (2019). Transcreation in Higher Education. Strengths and shortcomings of the Degree in Translation and Interpreting [La transcreación en Educación Superior. Fortalezas y carencias del Grado en Traducción e Interpretación]. *XIII Congreso Internacional de Educación e Innovación (IEI 2019).*

Díaz-Millón, M. & Olvera-Lobo, M. D. (2021). Towards a Definition of Transcreation: A Systematic Literature Review. *Perspectives: Studies in Translation Theory and Practice*. doi:10.1080/0907676X.2021.2004177

Díaz-Millón, M., Rivera Trigueros, I., & Gutiérrez-Artacho, J. (2019). Creativity as a core competency in transcreation training: a case study [La creatividad como una competencia básica en la formación en transcreación: un estudio de caso.]. *VII Congreso Internacional de Traducción e Interpretación Entreculturas.*

Díaz-Millón, M., Rivera-Trigueros, I., Olvera-Lobo, M. D., & Gutiérrez-Artacho, J. (2021). Disruptive Methodologies and Cross-curricular Competences for a Training Adapted to the New Professional Profiles in the undergraduate degree programme in Translation and Interpreting Studies. In S. Palahicky (Ed.), *Enhancing Learning Design for Innovative Teaching in Higher Education*. IGI Global.

Díaz-Millón, M., Rivera-Trigueros, I., & Pérez-Contreras, Á. (2021). Development of and Evaluation Tool for Assessing the Use of Inclusive Language: An Institutional Perspective. In *Proceedings of ICERI2021 Conference*. IATED Academy. 10.21125/iceri.2021.0492

European Parlament. (2009). *Gender-neutral language in the European Parliament*. Retrieved from: https://www.europarl.europa.eu/RegData/publications/2009/0001/P6_PUB(2009)0001_EN.pdf

Ferreira, T., Gutiérrez-Artacho, J., & Bernardino, J. (2018). Freemium Project Management Tools: Asana, Freedcamp and Ace Project. In Á. Rocha, H. Adeli, L. P. Reis, & S. Costanzo (Eds.), *Trends and Advances in Information Systems and Technologies. WorldCIST'18 2018. Advances in Intelligent Systems and Computing* (Vol. 745). Springer. doi:10.1007/978-3-319-77703-0_100

Gaballo, V. (2012). Exploring the Boundaries of Transcreation in Specialized Translation. *ESP Across Cultures*, 9. Retrieved from: www.badlanguage.net/translation-vs

Gutiérrez-Artacho, J., & Olvera-Lobo, M. D. (2018). Identification and adaptation of the cultural references of the web localization of Spanish SMEs [Identificación y adecuación de los referentes culturales de la localización web de las pymes españolas]. *36º Congreso Internacional de AESLA: «Lingüística aplicada y transferencia del conocimiento: empleabilidad, internacionalización y retos sociales»*.

Gutiérrez-Artacho, J., Olvera-Lobo, M. D., & Rivera-Trigueros, I. (2019). Communicative competence and new technologies in the web localization process: MDPT model for the training of professionals in localization [Competencia comunicativa y nuevas tecnologías en el proceso de localización web: modelo MDPT para la formación de profesionales en localización]. *Revista Fuentes*, *21*(1), 73–84. doi:10.12795/revistafuentes.2018.v21.i1.05

Katan, D. (2016). Translation at the cross-roads: Time for the transcreational turn? *Perspectives*, *24*(3), 365–381. doi:10.1080/0907676X.2015.1016049

Kotler, P., Wong, V., Saunders, J., & Armstrong, G. (2007). *Modern marketing*. Grada.

Ministerio de Igualdad. (2022). *Guide to the non-sexist use of language* [Guía para el uso no sexista del lenguaje]. Retrieved: https://www.inmujeres.gob.es/servRecursos/formacion/GuiasLengNoSexista/docs/Guiaslenguajenosexista_.pdf

Morón, M., & Calvo, E. (2018). Introducing transcreation skills in translator training contexts: A situated project-based approach. *The Journal of Specialised Translation*, 29. Recuperado de: https://www.jostrans.org/issue29/art_moron.pdf

Munday, J. (2004). Advertising: Some Challenges to Translation Theory. *The Translator*, *10*(2), 199–219. doi:10.1080/13556509.2004.10799177

Olvera-Lobo, M. D., Gutiérrez-Artacho, J., & Díaz-Millón, M. (2019). Web transcreation in the Spanish business context: the case of healthcare SMEs. In *5th International Conference on Communication and Management (ICCM2019)*. Athens: Communications Institute of Greece.

Pedersen, D. (2014). Exploring the concept of transcreation - transcreation as 'more than translation'? *The Journal of Intercultural Mediation and Communication*, 7. Retrieved from: https://iris.unipa.it/retrieve/handle/10447/130535/197987/cultus%20_7_2014.pdf#page=57

Pedersen, D. (2016). *Transcreation in Marketing and Advertising*. Aarhus University.

Rike, S. M. (2013). Bilingual corporate websites-from translation to transcreation? *Journal of Specialised Translation*, 20. Retrieved from: https://www.jostrans.org/issue20/art_rike.pdf

Urrutikoetxea-Arrieta, B., Polo-Peña, A. I., & Martínez-Medina, C. (2017). The Moderating Effect of Blogger Social Influence on Loyalty Toward the Blog and the Brands Featured. In *Marketing at the Confluence between Entertainment and Analytics* (pp. 885–898). Springer. doi:10.1007/978-3-319-47331-4_180

ADDITIONAL READING

Benetello, C. (2018). When translation is not enough: Transcreation as a convention defying practice. A practitioner's perspective. *The Journal of Specialised Translation*, 29. Retrieved from: https://www.jostrans.org/issue29/art_benetello.pdf

Díaz-Millón, M., Gutiérrez-Artacho, J., & Olvera-Lobo, M. D. (2022). Transcreation and Creativity in Higher Education: A Task-Based Learning Experience in the Undergraduate Programme of Translation & Interpreting. In *I. Rivera-Trigueros et al. Using Disruptive Methodologies and Game-Based Learning to Foster Transversal Skills* (pp. 68–86). IGI Global., doi:10.4018/978-1-7998-8645-7.ch004

Díaz-Millón, M., & Rivera-Trigueros, I. (2022). Can We Assess Creativity? The Use of Rubrics for Evaluating Transcreation in the Undergraduate Program of Translation and Interpreting. In A. Mesquita, A. Abreu, & J. V. Carvalho (Eds.), *Perspectives and Trends in Education and Technology. Smart Innovation, Systems and Technologies* (Vol. 256). Springer., doi:10.1007/978-981-16-5063-5_13

Grand, A., Holliman, R., Collins, T., & Adams, A. (2016). We muddle our way through: Shared and distributed expertise in digital engagement with research. *Journal Science Communication*, *15*(4), 1–23. doi:10.22323/2.15040205

Gutiérrez-Artacho, J., Olvera-Lobo, M. D., & Rivera-Trigueros, I. (2019). Hybrid Machine Translation Oriented to Cross-Language Information Retrieval: English-Spanish Error Analysis. In WorldCIST'19 2019: New Knowledge in Information Systems and Technologies (pp. 185–194). Springer International Publishing. doi:10.1007/978-3-030-16181-1_18

Linguasoft, M. T. M. (2015). *Transcreate. The transcreation process.* Retrieved from: https://www.mtmlinguasoft.com/wp-content/uploads/MTM-LinguaSoft-transcreation-process.pdf

Malenkina, N., & Ivanov, S. (2018). A linguistic analysis of the official tourism websites of the seventeen Spanish Autonomous Communities. *Journal of Destination Marketing & Management*, *9*, 204–233. doi:10.1016/j.jdmm.2018.01.007

Muñoz-Leiva, F., Hernández-Méndez, J., Liébana-Cabanillas, F., & Marchitto, M. (2016). Analysis of advertising effectiveness and usability in Travel 2.0 tools. An experimental study through eye-tracking technique. *Tourism & Management Studies*, *12*(2), 7–17. doi:10.18089/tms.2016.12202

Rivera-Trigueros, I., Olvera-Lobo, M. D., & Gutiérrez-Artacho, J. (2020). Overview of Machine Translation Development. In *Encyclopedia of Organizational Knowledge, Administration, and Technologies*. IGI Global.

Sulaiman, M. Z. (2016). The misunderstood concept of translation in tourism promotion. *Translation & Interpreting*, *8*(1), 53. doi:10.12807/ti.108201.2016.a04

Zhu, P. (2015). Translation Criteria: How they may affect international business. *Journal of Technical Writing and Communication*, *45*(3), 285–298. doi:10.1177/0047281615578850

KEY TERMS AND DEFINITIONS

Digital Marketing: It involves the use of the Internet and ICTs technologies on the part on the companies to reach customers.

Digitalization: It involves the use of digital technologies by business. In some cases, the digitalization can imply moving to a complete digital business model.

Inclusive Language: It represents a communication code that considers reality as it is, sexed. This code enables women and men to name the world from their gender and to be named taking into account their sex, without subordination or invisibilization of any of either sex.

Linguistic Management: Linguistic management is understood as the application of communicative management strategies in response to business internationalization processes.

Tourism: It is a social, cultural and economic phenomenon which entails the movement of people to countries or places outside their usual environment for personal or business/professional purposes.

Transcreation Strategy: Transcreation strategy is understood as a tactic or method of creative interlingual reinterpretation of a text by which it is adapted with variant levels of similarity to the original.

Web 2.0: It is the term used to make reference to the second stage of the Internet development. Web 2.0 is characterized by user-generated content, ease of use and the development of social media.

Compilation of References

Aboim, S. (2014). Narratives of aging: Being old in contemporary society [Narrativas do envelhecimento: ser velho na sociedade contemporânea]. *Tempo Social, São Paulo, 26*(1), 207–232.

Abraham, V., Bremser, K., Carreno, M., Crowley-Cyr, L., & Moreno, M. (2020). Exploring the consequences of COVID-19 on tourist behaviors: Perceived travel risk, animosity and intentions to travel. *Tourism Review*. Advance online publication. doi:10.1108/TR-07-2020-0344

Acerenza, M. Á. (2002). Tourism administration: Conceptualization and organization [Administração do turismo: Conceituação e organização]. *Tradução de G. R. Hendges, 1*.

Adamuz, J. A. (2020). The keys to post-Covid-19 tourism [Las claves del turismo post Covid-19]. *National Geographic*. https://viajes. nationalgeographic. com. es/lifestyle/turismo-despues-coronavirus_15469

Adshead, D., Thacker, S., Fuldauer, L. I., & Hall, J. W. (2019). Delivering on the Sustainable Development Goals through long-term infrastructure planning. *Global Environmental Change, 59*, 101975. doi:10.1016/j.gloenvcha.2019.101975

Aenor. (2016). *UNE EN ISO 17100:2015. Standard for translation agencies* [Norma para agencias de traducción]. Retrieved from https://normadecalidad.iso17100.com/

Ageeva, E., & Foroudi, P. (2019). Tourists' destination image through regional tourism: From supply and demand sides perspectives. *Journal of Business Research, 101*, 334–348. doi:10.1016/j.jbusres.2019.04.034

Agyeiwaah, E., Otoo, F. E., Suntikul, W., & Huang, W.-J. (2019). Understanding culinary tourist motivation, experience, satisfaction, and loyalty using a structural approach. *Journal of Travel & Tourism Marketing, 36*(3), 295–313. doi:10.1080/10548408.2018.1541775

Akay, H., & Baduna Koçyiğit, M. (2020). Flash flood potential prioritization of sub-basins in an ungauged basin in Turkey using traditional multi-criteria decision-making methods. *Soft Computing, 24*(18), 14251–14263. doi:10.100700500-020-04792-0

Akotirene, C. (2019). *Intersectionality* [Interseccionalidade]. Pólen.

Alarcón & Cañada. (2018). *Gender dimensions in tourism.* Alba Sud Publishing Informes en Contraste Series, no. 4. Retrieved from: http://www.albasud.org/publ/docs/81.en.pdf

Alarcón, D. M., & Cole, S. (2019). No sustainability for tourism without gender equality. *Journal of Sustainable Tourism, 27*(7), 903–919. doi:10.1080/09669582.2019.1588283

Alcaide, J. C., Bernués, S., Díaz-Aroca, E., Espinosa, R., Muñiz, R., & Smith, C. (2013). *Marketing and SMEs. The main marketing keys in small and medium-sized companies* [Marketing y Pymes. Las principales claves de marketing en la pequeña y mediana empresa]. Retrieved from https://bit.ly/38AowiG

Al-Dajani, H., & Marlow, S. (2013). Empowerment and entrepreneurship: A theoretical framework. *International Journal of Entrepreneurial Behaviour & Research, 19*(5), 503–524. doi:10.1108/IJEBR-10-2011-0138

Almeida, E. B. (2009). *The tourist's eating behavior and their safety in the consumption of green corn and churros by the sea* [O comportamento alimentar do turista e sua segurança no consumo de milho verde e churros à beira-mar]. Academic Press.

Almeida, S. (2019). Structural Racism [Racismo estrutural]. São Paulo: Sueli Carneiro; Pólen.

Almeida, M. V. (2011). The development of social tourism in Brazil. *Current Issues in Tourism, 14*(5), 483–489. doi:10.1080/13683500.2011.568057

Alshareef, F. M., & AlGassim, A. A. (2021). Women empowerment in tourism and hospitality sector in Saudi Arabia. *International Journal on Recent Trends in Business and Tourism, 5*(4), 11–20. doi:10.31674/ijrtbt.2021.v05i04.003

Alves, R. F., & de Aguiar, R. G. (2020). *The Pink Money market and the positioning of brands: a study on the perception of consumers in Fortaleza/CE* [O mercado Pink Money e o posicionamento das marcas: um estudo sobre a percepção dos consumidores de Fortaleza/CE]. Artigo (Graduação em Administração) – Centro Universitário Fametro. http://repositorio.unifametro.edu.br/handle/123456789/934

Amaral, M., Rodrigues, A. I., Diniz, A., Oliveira, S., & Leal, S. (2020). Designing and evaluating tourism experiences in senior mobility: An application of the OEC framework. *Tourism & Management Studies, 16*(4), 59–72. doi:10.18089/tms.2020.160405

Ampumuza, C. (2021). *Batwa, gorillas and the Ruhija road: a relational perspective on controversies at Bwindi Impenetrable National Park, Uganda* [Doctoral Dissertation]. Wageningen University and Research.

Anbalagan, K., & Lovelock, B. (2014). The potential for coffee tourism development in Rwanda–Neither black nor white. *Tourism and Hospitality Research, 14*(1-2), 81–96. doi:10.1177/1467358414529579

ANTRA. (2020). *Dossier on Murders and Violence Against Brazilian Trans Persons Trans Brasileiras* [Dossiê dos Assassinatos e da Violência Contra Pessoas]. https://antrabrasil.files.wordpress.com/2021/01/dossie-trans-2021-29jan2021.pdf

Appolinário, F. (2006). *Methodology of science: philosophy and practice of research* [Metodologia da ciência: filosofia e prática da pesquisa]. Pioneira Thomson Learning.

Araujo, L. F. de; Carlos, K. P. T. (2018). Sexuality in old age: a study on LGBT aging [Sexualidade na velhice: um estudo sobre o envelhecimento LGBT]. *Psicol. Conoc. Soc., 8*(1), 188-205.

Araújo-Vila, N., Otegui-Carles, A., & Fraiz-Brea, J. A. (2021). Seeking Gender Equality in the Tourism Sector: A Systematic Bibliometric Review. *Knowledge (Beverly Hills, Calif.), 1*(1), 12–24. doi:10.3390/knowledge1010003

Archer, B. H. (1982). The value of multipliers and their policy implications. *Tourism Management, 3*(4), 236–241. doi:10.1016/0261-5177(82)90044-9

Ashton, S. G. M., Cabral, S., Santos, G. A. dos, & Kroetz, J. (2015). The relationship between tourism and Quality of Life in the Aging Process [A relação do turismo e da Qualidade de Vida no Processo de Envelhecimento]. *Revista Hospitalidade, 12*(2), 547 – 566.

Aslam & Jolliffe. (2015). Repurposing colonial tea heritage through historic lodging. *Journal of Heritage Tourism, 10*(2), 111-128.

Australian Bureau of Statistics. (1993). Disability, Ageing and Carers Australia. Commonwealth of Australia.

Ayorekire, J., Mugizi, F., Obua, J., & Ampaire, G. (2021). Community-Based Tourism and Local People's Perceptions Towards Conservation: The Case of Queen Elizabeth Conservation Area, Uganda. In *Prospects and Challenges of Community-based Tourism and Changing Demographics* (pp. 56–82). IGI Global Publishers.

Azevedo, M. S., Martins, C. B., Pizzinatto, N. K., & Farah, O. E. (2012). Segmentation in the tourism sector: LGBT tourists from São Paulo [Segmentação no setor turístico: turistas LGBT de São Paulo]. *Revista de Administração da UFSM, 5*(3), 493–506. doi:10.5902/198346593852

Bahls, A. A. D. S. M., Beleze, R. L., Pires, P. S., & Krause, R. W. (2020). Culinary Cultural Heritage vs. Hygiene and Food Safety: A possible inverse correlation. *Rev. Hosp., 17*, 115–139. doi:10.21714/2179-9164.2020.v17n1.007

Baloglu, S., & McCleary, K. W. (1999). A model of destination image formation. *Annals of Tourism Research, 26*(4), 868–897. doi:10.1016/S0160-7383(99)00030-4

Balsalobre, D., Sinha, A., Driha, O. M., & Mubarik, S. (2021). Assessing the Impacts of Ageing and Natural Resource Extraction on Carbon Emissions: A proposed Policy Framework for European Economies. *Journal of Cleaner Production, 296*, 126470. doi:10.1016/j.jclepro.2021.126470

Barbosa, L. G., Coelho, A. M., & Motta, F. do A., & Guimarães, I. L. (2020). Economic Impact of Covid-19 Proposals for Brazilian Tourism [Impacto Econômico do Covid-19 Propostas para o Turismo Brasileiro]. *Fundação Getúlio Vargas, 1*, 1–24.

Batista, J. R. L., Jr., Sato, D. T. B., & de Melo, I. F. (Org.). (2018). Critical discourse analysis for linguists and non-linguists [Análise de discurso crítica para linguistas e não linguistas]. Gonçalves. São Paulo: Parábola.

Baum, T. (2013). *International perspectives on women and work in hotels, catering and tourism. Bureau for Gender Equality*. Working Paper No. 1/2013, Sectoral Activities. Department Working Paper No. 289. International Labour Organization: Geneva

Baum, T., & Hai, N. T. T. (2020). Hospitality, tourism, human rights, and the impact of COVID-19. *International Journal of Contemporary Hospitality Management*, *32*(7), 2397–2407. doi:10.1108/IJCHM-03-2020-0242

Bedford, E. (2020). *Value of the global tea market from 2018 to 2026*. Retrieved on November 8th, 2021, available at: www.statista.com/ statistics/326384/global-tea-beverage-market-size

Beerli, A., & Martín, J. D. (2004). Tourists' characteristics and the perceived image of tourist destinations: A quantitative analysis—a case study of Lanzarote, Spain. *Tourism Management*, *25*(5), 623–636. doi:10.1016/j.tourman.2003.06.004

Behl, A., Jayawardena, N., Pereira, V., Islam, N., Del Giudice, M., & Choudrie, J. (2022). Gamification and e-learning for young learners: A systematic literature review, bibliometric analysis, and future research agenda. *Technological Forecasting and Social Change*, *176*, 1–24. doi:10.1016/j.techfore.2021.121445

Beni, M. C. (1998). Structural analysis of tourism [Análise estrutural do turismo] (2nd ed.). SENAC.

Beni, M. C. (2020). Tourism and COVID-19: some reflections. *Revista Rosa Dos Ventos - Turismo e Hospitalidade*, *12*, 1–23. . doi:10.18226/21789061.v12i3a02

Benjamin, S., & Dillette, A. K. (2021). Black travel movement: Systemic racism informing tourism. *Annals of Tourism Research*, *88*, 103169. doi:10.1016/j.annals.2021.103169

Besky, S. (2014). The labor of terroir and the terroir of labor: Geographical indication and darjeeling tea plantations. *Agriculture and Human Values*, *31*(1), 83–96. doi:10.100710460-013-9452-8

Bigoditourism. (2021, December 7). *Bigodi tourism*. Bigodi Tourism. Retrieved from https://bigoditourism.com/

BITS. (2011). http://www.bits-int.org/

Biz, A. A. (2020). Initial Perspectives of Covid-19 Impacts on Tourism in the State of Santa Catarina – Brazil [Perspectivas Iniciais Dos Impactos Da Covid-19 No Turismo Do Estado De Santa Catarina –Brasil]. *Revista Turismo & Cidades*, *2*, 139–152.

Boluk, K. A., Cavaliere, T., & Higgins-Desbiolles, F. (2017). A critical framework for interrogating the United Nations Sustainable Development Goals 2030 Agenda in tourism. *Journal of Sustainable Tourism*, *27*(7), 847–864. doi:10.1080/09669582.2019.1619748

Bond, L. (2020, October 7). Black women are 28% of Brazilians, but have low political participation [Negras são 28% dos brasileiros, mas tem baixa participação política]. *Agência Brasil*. https://agenciabrasil.ebc.com.br/eleicoes-2020/noticia/2020-10/negras-sao-28-dos-brasileiros-mas-tem-baixa-participacao-politica

Boonabaana, B. (2012). *Community-based Tourism and Gender Relations in Uganda* [Doctoral Dissertation]. University of Otago, Dunedin, New Zealand.

Boonabaana, B. (2014). Negotiating gender and tourism work: Women's lived experiences in Uganda. *Tourism and Hospitality Research, 14*(1–2), 27–36. doi:10.1177/1467358414529578

Botero, C. M., Mercadé, S., Cabrera, J. A., & Bombana, B. (2020). *Sun and beach tourism in the context of Covid-19; scenarios and recommendations* [El turismo de sol y playa en el contexto de la Covid-19; escenarios y recomendaciones]. Red Iberoam. Gestión Cert. Playas–PROPLAYAS.

Brain, L. (2018). *Uganda chooses coffee tourism to boost its revenues*. Retrieved on December 9th 2021, available at: www. tourism-review.com/coffee-tourism-in-uganda-to-boost-profits-news10856

Brain, L. (2018). *Uganda chooses coffee tourism to boost its revenues?* Retrieved on 3rd December 2021. www. tourism-review.com/coffee-tourism-in-uganda-to-boost-profits-news10856

Brasil, O. N. U. (2015). *SGD 5: Gender equality: Achieving gender equality and empowering all women and girls* [SGD 5: Igualdade de gênero: Alcançar a igualdade de gênero e empoderar todas as mulheres e meninas]. Retrieved from: https://brasil.un.org/pt-br/sdgs/5

Brasil. (1988). *Constitution of the Federative Republic of Brazil* [Constituição da República Federativa do Brasil]. http://www.planalto.gov.br/ccivil_03/constituicao/constituicaocompilado.htmBrasil

Brasil. (2006). *Ministry of Tourism. Tourism Segmentation: Conceptual Milestones* [Ministério do Turismo. Segmentação do Turismo: Marcos Conceituais]. Brasília: Ministério do Turismo.

Brasil. (2010). *Ministry of Tourism Cultural tourism: basic guidelines* [Ministério do Turismo Turismo cultural: orientações básicas] (3rd ed.). Brasília: Ministério do Turismo.

Brasil. (2012). *Instituto Brasileiro de Geografia e Estatística.2010 Demographic Census: General sample results* [Censo demográfico de 2010: Resultados gerais da amostra]. IBGE.

Brasil. (2015). *Ministério do Turismo. National Tourism Plan 2013/2016* [Plano Nacional do Turismo 2013/2016]. Brasília.

Brasil. (2022). *Ministry of Women, The Family and Human Rights. Panel of data of the National Ombudsman for Human Rights* [Ministério da Mulher, da Família e dos Direitos Humanos. Painel de dados da Ouvidoria Nacional de Direitos Humanos]. Brasília: Ministério da Mulher, da Família e dos Direitos Humanos.

Brasil. Ministério da Saúde. (2011). *Health Portal. What is the Pact for Health?* [Portal da Saúde. O que é o Pacto pela Saúde?]. http://portal.saude.gov.br/portal/saude/ profissional/area.cfm?id_area=1021

Buhalis, D., & Law, R. (2008). Progress in Information Technology and Tourism Management: 20 years on and 10 years after the internet — The State Of E-Tourism Research. *Tourism Management, 29*(4), 609–623. doi:10.1016/j.tourman.2008.01.005

Butler, J. (2015). Self-report: Critique of ethical violence [Relatar a si mesmo: crítica da violência ética]. Belo Horizonte: Autêntica.

Buzinde, C., Shockley, G., Andereck, K., Dee, E., & Frank, P. (2017). Theorizing Social Entrepreneurship within Tourism Studies. In P. J. Sheldon & R. Daniele (Eds.), *Social Entrepreneurship and Tourism, Philosophy and Practice* (pp. 21–34). Springer International Publishing. doi:10.1007/978-3-319-46518-0_2

Calvet, N. A., Cond, C. I., Ballart, A. L., & Almela, M. S. (2021). *Gender inequalities in the tourism labour market* [Desigualdades de género en el mercado laboral turístico] (Vol. 14). https://www.albasud.org/noticia/es/1299/desigualdades-de-genero-en-el-mercado-laboral-turistico

Campos, V. F. (1992). TQC - Total quality control [TQC – Controle de qualidade total] (2nd ed.). São Paulo: Bloch Editores.

Candelo, E., Casalegno, C., Civera, C., & Büchi, G. (2019). A ticket to coffee: Stakeholder view and theoretical framework of coffee tourism benefits. *Tourism Analysis, 24*(3), 329–340. doi:10.3727/108354219X15511864843830

Castelli, G. (2001). *Hotel Administration* [Administração Hoteleira] (8th ed.). EDUSC.

Cavignac, J. A. (2010). The hidden ethnicity: 'Indians' and 'Blacks' in Rio Grande do Norte [A etnicidade encoberta: 'índios' e 'negros' no Rio Grande do Norte]. *Mneme - Revista De Humanidades, 4*(8). Recuperado de https://periodicos.ufrn.br/mneme/article/view/167

Chaffey, D., & Smith, P. R. (2013). *EMarketing eXcellence : planning and optimizing your digital marketing*. Routledge. doi:10.4324/9780203082812

Chambers, D. (2021). Are we all in this together? Gender intersectionality and sustainable tourism. *Journal of Sustainable Tourism*, 1–16.

Chambers, D., & Airey, D. (2001). Tourism Policy in Jamaica: A Tale of Two Governments. *Current Issues in Tourism, 4*(2–4), 94–120. doi:10.1080/13683500108667884

Chan. (2007). Film-induced tourism in Asia: A case study of Korean television drama and female viewers' motivation to visit Korea. *Tourism Culture Communication, 7*(3), 207-224.

Charaudeau, P. (2006). Media Speech [Discurso das mídias]. São Paulo: Contexto.

Chavarria, & Phakdee-auksorn. (2017). Understanding international tourists' attitudes towards street food in Phuket, Thailand. *Tourism Management Perspectives, 21*, 66-73.

Chen & Huang. (2018). Local food in China: A viable destination attraction. *British Food Journal, 120*(1), 146-157.

Chen, G., Cheng, M., Edwards, D., & Xu, L. (2021). COVID-19 pandemic exposes the vulnerability of the sharing economy: A novel accounting framework. *Journal of Sustainable Tourism*. Advance online publication. doi:10.1080/09669582.2020.1868484

Chen, J. S., & Uysal, M. (2002). Market positioning analysis: A hybrid approach. *Annals of Tourism Research, 29*(4), 987–1003. doi:10.1016/S0160-7383(02)00003-8

Cherrington, E. A., Griffin, R. E., Anderson, E. R., Hernandez Sandoval, B. E., Flores-Anderson, A. I., Muench, R. E., Markert, K. N., Adams, E. C., Limaye, A. S., & Irwin, D. E. (2020). Use of public Earth observation data for tracking progress in sustainable management of coastal forest ecosystems in Belize, Central America. *Remote Sensing of Environment, 245*, 111798. doi:10.1016/j.rse.2020.111798

Chio, J., Gill, T., Gonzalez, V. V., Harp, S. L., McDonald, K., Rosenbaum, A. T., Rugh, S. S., & Thomas, L. L. (2020). Discussion: Tourism and race. *Journal of Tourism History, 12*(2), 173–197. doi:10.1080/1755182X.2020.1756465

Cleaver, M., & Muller, T. E. (2002). I want to pretend I'm eleven years younger: Subjective age and seniors' motives for vacation travel. *Social Indicators Research, 60*(1-3), 227–241. doi:10.1023/A:1021217232446

Cohen, E., & Avieli, N. (2004). Food in tourism. *Annals of Tourism Research, 31*(4), 755–778. doi:10.1016/j.annals.2004.02.003

Cole. (2006). Qualitative research: a challenging paradigm for infection control. *British Journal of Infection Control, 7*(6), 25-29.

Collins, P. H. (2019). *Black feminist thinking* [Pensamento feminista negro]. Boitempo.

Confederação Nacional do Comércio. (2020). *CNC Highlights Tourism Sector Effort During Brazilian Forum* [CNC Destaca Esforço do Setor de Turismo Durante Fórum Brasileiro]. Available online: http://www.cnc.org.br/editorias/turismo/noticias/cnc-destaca-esforco-do-setor-de-turismo-durante-forum-brasileiro

Cooper, C. (2007). Tourism: Principles and practices [Turismo: Princípios e práticas] (3rd ed.). Porto Alegre: Bookman.

Cooper, C., Fletcher, J., Wanhill, S., Gilbert, D., & Shepeherd, R. (1998). *Tourism, principles and practice* [Turismo, princípios e prática]. Artmed.

Corbari, S. D., & Grimm, I. J. (2020). The COVID-19 pandemic and the impacts on the tourism sector in Curitiba (PR): A preliminary analysis [A pandemia de COVID-19 e os impactos no setor do turismo em Curitiba (PR): uma análise preliminar]. *Ateliê Do Turismo, 4*(2), 1–26.

Coriolano, L. N. M. T. (2005). Epistemology of discourse analysis in tourism [Epistemologia da análise do discurso no turismo]. *Caderno virtual de turismo.*

Costa, C., Carvalho, I., & Breda, Z. (2011). Gender inequalities in tourism employment: The portuguese case. *Revista Turismo& Desenvolvimento, 15*, 37–52.

Couto, M. C. de P. (2009). Assessment of discrimination against the elderly in a Brazilian context - ageism [Avaliação de discriminação contra idosos em contexto brasileiro - ageismo]. *Psic.: teor. e pesq., 25*(4), 509-518.

Couto, G., Castanho, R. A., Pimentel, P., Carvalho, C., Sousa, Á., & Santos, C. (2020). The Impacts of COVID-19 Crisis over the Tourism Expectations of the Azores Archipelago Residents. *Sustainability, 12*(18), 7612. doi:10.3390u12187612

Crenshaw, K. (1991). Demarginalizing the intersection of race and sex; a black feminist critique of discrimination doctrine, feminist theory and antiracist politics. *University of Chicago Legal Forum*, 139–167.

Crosby, A. (2020). *The future is no longer what it was: Can tourism recover?* [El futuro ya no es lo que era: ¿Se podrá recuperar el turismo?]. Available online: https://www.hosteltur.com/comunidad/004373_el-futuro-ya-no-es-lo-que-era-se-podra-recuperar-el-turismo.html

Cui, F., Liu, Y., Chang, Y., Duan, J., & Li, J. (2016). An overview of tourism risk perception. *Natural Hazards, 82*(1), 643–658. doi:10.100711069-016-2208-1

Dann, G. (2002). Senior Tourism and Quality of Life. *Journal of Hospitality & Leisure Marketing, 9*(1-2), 5–19. doi:10.1300/J150v09n01_02

Dantas, A. J. L. (2021). *Life story narratives of elderly lesbians: intersectionality between old age, gender and sexuality* [Narrativas de histórias de vida de idosas lésbicas: interseccionalidade entre velhice, gênero e sexualidade] [Dissertation]. Universidade Federal do Ceará, Fortaleza. Disponível em https://repositorio.ufc.br/handle/riufc/57519

Dantas, D. (2012). *Argumentation as a discursive element in digital media: A study on the blog "Fatos e Dados"* [A argumentação como elemento discursivo na mídia digital: Um estudo sobre o blog "Fatos e Dados"] [Thesis]. Federal University of Rio Grande do Norte. Graduate Program in Language Studies, Natal.

Davis, A. (2016). *Women, race and class* [Mulheres, raça e classe]. Boitempo.

de Araújo, L. M., Martins, C., & Perinotto, A. R. C. (2021). Entrepreneurship and Innovation in Communities for Women Who Travel. In *Innovation and Entrepreneurial Opportunities in Community Tourism* (pp. 191–203). IGI Global. doi:10.4018/978-1-7998-4855-4.ch011

de Beauvoir, S. (1990). *Old age: the most important contemporary essay on the living conditions of the elderly* [A velhice: o mais importante ensaio contemporâneo sobre as condições de vida dos idosos]. Nova Fronteira.

De Marco, M. (2012). *Audiovisual Translation through a Gender Lens*. Rodopi. doi:10.1163/9789401207881

de Oliveira, N. A. (2021). Precisamos falar sobre racismo no turismo. *RITUR: Revista Iberoamericana de Turismo, 11*(2), 267–280.

de Oliveira, N. A. (2022). Representation and representation of blacks in a luxury tourism magazine in Brazil [Representação e representatividade dos negros em uma revista de turismo de luxo do Brasil]. *Revista Brasileira de Pesquisa em Turismo, 16*(1), 2325. doi:10.7784/rbtur.v16.2325

Debert, G. G. (1998). The reinvention of old age. Socialization and aging reprivatization processes [A reinvenção da velhice. Socialização e processos de reprivatização do envelhecimento]. São Paulo: Edusp, Fapesp.

Departamento Intersindical de Estatística e Estudos Socioeconômicos. (2021). *Special Bulletin November 20 - Black Consciousness Day* [Boletim Especial 20 de novembro - Dia da Consciência Negra]. https://www.dieese.org.br/boletimespecial/2021/conscienciaNegra.html

Díaz-Millón, M. & Olvera-Lobo, M. D. (2021). Towards a Definition of Transcreation: A Systematic Literature Review. *Perspectives: Studies in Translation Theory and Practice*. doi:10.1080/0907676X.2021.2004177

Díaz-Millón, M., & Olvera-Lobo, M. D. (2019). Transcreation in Higher Education. Strengths and shortcomings of the Degree in Translation and Interpreting [La transcreación en Educación Superior. Fortalezas y carencias del Grado en Traducción e Interpretación]. *XIII Congreso Internacional de Educación e Innovación (IEI 2019).*

Díaz-Millón, M., & Gutiérrez-Artacho, J. (2019). New professional profiles in translation: Skills necessary for transcreation [Nuevos perfiles profesionales en traducción: Competencias necesarias para la transcreación]. *1st International Conference On Digital Linguistics – CILiDi´19.*

Díaz-Millón, M., Rivera Trigueros, I., & Gutiérrez-Artacho, J. (2019). Creativity as a core competency in transcreation training: a case study [La creatividad como una competencia básica en la formación en transcreación: un estudio de caso.]. *VII Congreso Internacional de Traducción e Interpretación Entreculturas.*

Díaz-Millón, M., Rivera-Trigueros, I., Olvera-Lobo, M. D., & Gutiérrez-Artacho, J. (2021). Disruptive Methodologies and Cross-curricular Competences for a Training Adapted to the New Professional Profiles in the undergraduate degree programme in Translation and Interpreting Studies. In S. Palahicky (Ed.), *Enhancing Learning Design for Innovative Teaching in Higher Education*. IGI Global.

Díaz-Millón, M., Rivera-Trigueros, I., & Pérez-Contreras, Á. (2021). Development of and Evaluation Tool for Assessing the Use of Inclusive Language: An Institutional Perspective. In *Proceedings of ICERI2021 Conference*. IATED Academy. 10.21125/iceri.2021.0492

Diekmann, A., & McCabe, S. (2011). Systems of social tourism in the European Union: A critical review. *Current Issues in Tourism*, *14*(5), 417–430. doi:10.1080/13683500.2011.568052

Doll, J. (2007). Education, culture and leisure: Prospects of successful old age [Educação, cultura e lazer: Perspectivas de velhice bem-sucedida]. In *Elderly people in Brazil: Experiences, challenges and expectations in the elderly* [Idosos no Brasil: Vivências, desafios e expectativas na terceira idade] (pp. 109–123). Abramo.

dos Santos, E. C. M. (2021). Can a good Creole survive racism? [Pode um bom crioulo sobreviver ao racismo?]. In Queer genealogy [Genealogia Queer]. Devires.

Dos Santos, S., & Bomfim, C. (2021). *Mechanisms of trust in indigenous tourism: a study of the Pataxó Jaqueira community in Porto Seguro, Brazil* (Doctoral dissertation). Oxford Brookes University.

Echtner, C. M., & Ritchie, J. B. (1991). The meaning and measurement of destination image. *Journal of Tourism Studies*, *2*(2), 2–12.

EESC. (2006). Opinion of the European Economic and Social Committee on social tourism in Europe. *EESC- Official Journal of the European Union.*

Esquivel, V., & Sweetman, C. (2016). *Gender and the Sustainable Development*. Academic Press.

European Parlament. (2009). *Gender-neutral language in the European Parliament*. Retrieved from: https://www.europarl.europa.eu/RegData/publications/2009/0001/P6_PUB(2009)0001_EN.pdf

EUROSTAT. (2012). *Population projections*. http://epp.eurostat.ec.europa.eu/ statistics_explained/ index.php/Population_projections

Eusebio, C., Carneiro, M. J., Kastenholz, E., & Alvelos, H. (2013). The Economic Impact of Health Tourism Programmes. In Quantitative Methods in Tourism Economics. Lisbon: Physica-Verlag. doi:10.1007/978-3-7908-2879-5_9

Eusébio, C., & Carneiro, M. J. (2012). Socio- cultural impacts of tourism in urban destinations. *Revista Portuguesa de Estudos Regionais*, *30*(1), 65–76.

Eusebio, C., Carneiro, M. J., Kastenholz, E., & Alvelos, H. (2015). The impact of social tourism for seniors on the economic development of tourism destinations. *European Journal of Tourism Research*, *12*, 5–24. doi:10.54055/ejtr.v12i.210

Fakeye, P. C., & Crompton, J. L. (1991). Image differences between prospective, first-time, and repeat visitors to the Lower Rio Grande Valley. *Journal of Travel Research*, *30*(2), 10–16. doi:10.1177/004728759103000202

Falco, D., & De, P. (2011). Tourist narratives: Imaginary and media in the urban experience of tourism [Narrativas turísticas: Imaginário e mídia na experiência urbana do turismo]. *Rosa dos Ventos*, *1*(3), 24-38.

Farsani, N. T., Ghotbabadi, S. S., & Altafi, M. (2019). Agricultural heritage as a creative tourism attraction. *Asia Pacific Journal of Tourism Research*, *24*(6), 541–549. doi:10.1080/10941665.2019.1593205

Farsani, T. (2018). Food heritage and promoting herbal medicine-based niche tourism in Isfahan, Iran. *Journal of Heritage Tourism*, *13*(1), 77–87. doi:10.1080/1743873X.2016.1263307

Félix, J. de O. (2019). *Tourism for the elderly: leisure in nature, in Sergipe* [Turismo da terceira idade: lazer na natureza, em Sergipe] [Dissertation]. Universidade Federal de Sergipe: São Cristóvão.

Ferguson, L., Boonabaana, B., Lattimore, C. K., & Alarcon, D. M. (2021, December). *Global Report on Women in Tourism* (No. 2). UNWTO.

Fernandes, M. T. O., & Soares, S. M. (2012). The development of public policies for elderly care in Brazil. *Revista da Escola de Enfermagem da USP*. https://www.scielo.br/pdf/reeusp/v46n6/en_29.pdf

Fernando, Rajapaksha, & Kumari. (2017). Tea tourism as a marketing tool: a strategy to develop the image of Sri Lanka as an attractive tourism destination. *Kelaniya Journal of Management, 5*(2).

Ferreira, G. G., & Aguinsky, B. G. (2013). Social movements of sexuality and gender: analysis of access to public policies [Movimentos sociais de sexualidade e gênero: análise do acesso às políticas públicas]. *Revista Katálysis, 16*(2), 223-232. doi:10.1590/S1414-49802013000200008

Ferreira, T., Gutiérrez-Artacho, J., & Bernardino, J. (2018). Freemium Project Management Tools: Asana, Freedcamp and Ace Project. In Á. Rocha, H. Adeli, L. P. Reis, & S. Costanzo (Eds.), *Trends and Advances in Information Systems and Technologies. WorldCIST'18 2018. Advances in Intelligent Systems and Computing* (Vol. 745). Springer. doi:10.1007/978-3-319-77703-0_100

Ferreras-Garcia, R., Sales-Zaguirre, J., & Serradell-López, E. (2021). Competency assessment and learning results in tourism internships: is gender a relevant factor? Higher Education, Skills and Work-Based Learning. doi:10.1108/HESWBL-05-2021-0096

Ferreras-Garcia, R., Sales-Zaguirre, J., & Serradell-López, E. (2021). Sustainable Innovation in Higher Education: The Impact of Gender on Innovation Competences. *Sustainability, 13*(9), 5004. doi:10.3390u13095004

Figueroa-Domecq, C., Palomo, J., Flecha-Barrio, M., & Segovia-Perez, M. (2020). Technology double gender gap in tourism business leadership. *Information Technology & Tourism, 22*(1), 75–106. doi:10.100740558-020-00168-0

Figueroa-Domecq, C., & Segovia-Perez, M. (2020). Application of a gender perspective in tourism research: A theoretical and practical approach. *Journal of Tourism Analysis: Revista de Análisis Turístico, 27*(2), 251–270. doi:10.1108/JTA-02-2019-0009

Fleischer, A., & Pizam, A. (2002). Tourism constraints among Israeli seniors. *Annals of Tourism Research, 29*(1), 106–123. doi:10.1016/S0160-7383(01)00026-3

Foucault, M. (2007). Words and Things: An Archeology of the Human Sciences [As palavras e as coisas: Uma arqueologia das ciências humanas] (9th ed.). São Paulo: Martins Fontes.

Fuchs, G., & Pizam, A. (2011). 18 The Importance of Safety and Security for Tourism Destinations. *Destination Marketing and Management*, 300.

Fundação Getúlio Vargas. (2017). Consumer Survey: Travel Intention [Sondagem do Consumidor: Intenção de Viagem]. FGV Projetos, Ministério do Turismo.

Fundação Perseu Abramo &Serviço Social do Comércio. (2020). *Elderly in Brazil: Experiences, Challenges and Expectations in the Third Age* [Idosos no Brasil: Vivências, Desafios e Expectativas na Terceira Idade]. Disponível em: https://fpabramo.org.br/publicacoes/wp-content/uploads/sites/5/2020/08/Pesquisa-Idosos-II-Completa-v2.pdf

Gaballo, V. (2012). Exploring the Boundaries of Transcreation in Specialized Translation. *ESP Across Cultures*, 9. Retrieved from: www.badlanguage.net/translation-vs

Gabrielli, C. (2021). Women in the Brazilian tourism market: reflections and perspectives in the light of gender studies [Mulheres no mercado turístico brasileiro: reflexões e perspectivas à luz dos estudos de gênero]. *Rosa dos Ventos - Turismo e Hospitalidade*, *13*(4), 1049–1068. http://www.ucs.br/etc/revistas/index.php/rosadosventos/article/view/9254/0

Galo, I. (2020.) *Immunological Passport* [Pasaporte Inmunológico]. Available online: https://www.abc.es/viajar/noticias/abci-ocho-claves-como-sera-turismo-tras-covid-19-202005190148_noticia.html

Garcia-Ramon, M., Canoves, G., & Valdovinos, N. (1995). Farm tourism, gender, and the environment in Spain. *Annals of Tourism Research*, *22*(2), 267–282. doi:10.1016/0160-7383(94)00096-4

Gaskell, G. (2008). Individual and group interviews [Entrevistas individuais e grupais]. In M. Bauer & G. Gaskell (Eds.), *Pesquisa qualitativa com texto: imagem e som: um manual prático* (pp. 64–79). Vozes.

Gee, S., & Baillie, J. (1999). Happily Ever After? An Exploration of Retirement Expectations. *Educational Gerontology*, *25*(2), 109–128. doi:10.1080/036012799267909

George, R. (2003). Tourist's perceptions of safety and security while visiting Cape Town. *Tourism Management*, *24*(5), 575–585. doi:10.1016/S0261-5177(03)00003-7

Gesimba, Langat, Liu, & Wolukau. (2005). The tea industry in Kenya; The challenges and positive developments. *Journal of Applied Sciences*, *5*(2), 334–336. doi:10.3923/jas.2005.334.336

Gianesi, I. G. N., & Corrêa, H. L. (1996). *Strategic service management* [Administração estratégica de serviços]. Atlas.

Gibson, L., Lynch, P. A., & Morrison, A. (2005). The local destination tourism network: Development issues. *Tourism Hospitality Planning Development*, *2*(2), 87–99. doi:10.1080/14790530500171708

Gil, G. D. E. S., Noel, M., & Hirschfeld, C. (2020). Border in disenchantment notes on the state, tourism and Covid-19 in Foz do Iguaçu-BR. [Fronteira em desencanto notas sobre o estado, turismo e Covid-19 em Foz do Iguaçu-BR]. *Revista SURES*, *15*, 22–42.

Gomes, F. G. de V. (2005). *The Perception of the GLBT Segment About the Service of the Brazilian Tourism Sector* [A Percepção do Segmento GLBT Sobre o Atendimento do Setor Turístico Brasileiro]. UniCEUB.

Gonçalves, M. E. (2021). *Murder of trans people grows in the US in 2021* [Assassinato de pessoas trans cresce nos EUA em 2021]. https://revistahibrida.com.br/2021/04/26/assassinato-de-pessoas-trans-cresce-nos-eua-em-2021/

Gonçalves-Segundo, P. R. (2018). Discourse and social practice [Discurso e prática social]. In *Análise de discurso crítica para linguistas e não linguistas*. Parábola.

Gondim, L. M. P., & Lima, J. C. (2006). *Research as intellectual crafts: considerations about method and common sense* [A pesquisa como artesanato intelectual: considerações sobre método e bom senso]. EdUFSCar.

Gonzales, L. (1981, November 22). Black woman, that kilomba [Mulher negra, essa quilomba]. *Folhetim, 4.*

Gössling, S., Scott, D., & Hall, C. M. (2021). Pandemics, tourism and global change: A rapid assessment of COVID-19. *Journal of Sustainable Tourism, 29*(1), 1–20. doi:10.1080/09669582.2020.1758708

Green, J. N. (2018). *History of the LGBT movement in Brazil* [História do movimento LGBT no Brasil] (1st ed.). Alameda.

Guimarães, A. S. A. (1995). Racism and anti-racism in Brazil [Rascismo e anti-racismo no Brasil]. *Novos Estudos, 3*(43), 26-44. Available in http://Novosestudos.Com.Br/Produto/Edicao-43/

Guimarães, V. L., Catramby, T., Moraes, C. C. de A., & Soares, C. A. L. (2020). Covid-19 pandemic and higher education in tourism in the state of Rio De Janeiro (Brazil): Preliminary research notes. *Revista Rosa Dos Ventos - Turismo e Hospitalidade, 12*, 1–18. . doi:10.18226/21789061.v12i3a09

Gullo, M. C. R. (2020). The Economy in the Covid-19 Pandemic: Some Considerations [A Economia na Pandemia Covid-19: Algumas Considerações]. *Rosa Dos Ventos*, *12*(3), 1–8. doi:10.18226/21789061.v12i3a05

Guloba, M., Ssewanyana, S., & Birabwa, E. (2017). Rural Women Entrepreneurship in Uganda: A Synthesis Report on Policies, Evidence, and Stakeholder. Research Series No. 134, Economic Policy Research Centre (EPRC).

Gupta, K., Khanna, K., & Gupta, R. K. (2019). Preferential analysis of street food amongst the foreign tourists: A case of Delhi region. *International Journal of Tourism Cities*, *6*(3), 511–528. doi:10.1108/IJTC-07-2018-0054

Gutiérrez-Artacho, J., & Olvera-Lobo, M. D. (2018). Identification and adaptation of the cultural references of the web localization of Spanish SMEs [Identificación y adecuación de los referentes culturales de la localización web de las pymes españolas]. *36º Congreso Internacional de AESLA: «Lingüística aplicada y transferencia del conocimiento: empleabilidad, internacionalización y retos sociales».*

Gutiérrez-Artacho, J., Olvera-Lobo, M. D., & Rivera-Trigueros, I. (2019). Communicative competence and new technologies in the web localization process: MDPT model for the training of professionals in localization [Competencia comunicativa y nuevas tecnologías en el proceso de localización web: modelo MDPT para la formación de profesionales en localización]. *Revista Fuentes*, *21*(1), 73–84. doi:10.12795/revistafuentes.2018.v21.i1.05

Haddaway, N. R., Collins, A. M., Coughlin, D., & Kirk, S. (2015). The role of Google Scholar in evidence reviews and its applicability to grey literature searching. *PLoS One*, *10*(9), 138–237. doi:10.1371/journal.pone.0138237 PMID:26379270

Hahn, I. S., Bianchi, J., Baldissarelli, J. M., & Martins, A. A. M. (2021). Destination choice for LGBT+ tourists: Relationship between psychological motivations and destination images [Escolha do destino de turistas LGBT+: Relação entre motivações psicológicas e imagens de destino]. *Revista de Administração da UFSM, 14*(spe1), 1086-1100. doi:10.5902/1983465965024

Hair, J. F., Black, W. C., Babin, B. J., Anderson, R. E., & Tatham, R. L. (2009). *Multivariate data analysis* [Análise multivariada de dados]. Bookman editora.

Hair, J. F. Jr, Gabriel, M. L., & Patel, V. K. (2014). Covariance-Based Structural Equation Modeling (CB-SEM) with AMOS: Guidelines on your application as a Marketing Research Tool [Modelagem de Equações Estruturais Baseada em Covariância (CB-SEM) com o AMOS: Orientações sobre a sua aplicação como uma Ferramenta de Pesquisa de Marketing]. *Revista Brasileira de Marketing, 13*(2), 44–55.

Hall, C. M. (2019). Constructing sustainable tourism development: The 2030 agenda and the managerial ecology of sustainable tourism. *Journal of Sustainable Tourism, 27*(7), 1044–1060. doi:10.1080/09669582.2018.1560456

Hall, C. M., & Sharples, L. (2003). The consumption of experiences or the experience of consumption? An introduction to the tourism of taste. In C. M. Hall, L. Sharples, R. Mitchell, N. Macionis, & B. Cambourne (Eds.), *Food Tourism around the World*. Butterworth Heinemann. doi:10.1016/B978-0-7506-5503-3.50004-X

Hall, C. M., Timothy, D. J., & Duval, D. T. (2012). *Safety and security in tourism: relationships, management, and marketing*. Routledge. doi:10.4324/9780203049464

Hall, M., Sharples, L., Mitchell, R., Macionis, N., & Cambourne, B. (2004). *Food tourism around the world*. Routledge. doi:10.4324/9780080477862

Handaragama, S., & Kusakabe, K. (2021). Participation of women in business associations: A case of small-scale tourism enterprises in Sri Lanka. *Heliyon, 7*(11), e08303. doi:10.1016/j.heliyon.2021.e08303 PMID:34778588

Hasanat, O., Alhelalat, J. A., & Valeri, M. (2021). Women Leadership in the Jordanian Hospitality Sector: Obstacles and Future Opportunities. In M. Valeri & V. Katsoni (Eds.), *Gender and Tourism: Challenges and Entrepreneurial Opportunities* (1st ed., pp. 149–158). Emerald Publishing. doi:10.1108/978-1-80117-322-320211009

Heath, E. E., & Wall, G. (1991). *Marketing tourism destinations* [Marketing tourism destinations]. John Wiley & Sons.

Hedrick, J., Yeiser, M., Harris, C. L., Wampler, J. L., London, H. E., Patterson, A. C., & Wu, S. S. (2021). Infant Formula with Added Bovine Milk Fat Globule Membrane and Modified Iron Supports Growth and Normal Iron Status at One Year of Age: A Randomized Controlled Trial. *Nutrients, 13*(12), 4541. doi:10.3390/nu13124541 PMID:34960093

Hedrick, V. E., Comber, D. L., Estabrooks, P. A., Savla, J., & Davy, B. M. (2010). The beverage intake questionnaire: Determining initial validity and reliability. *Journal of the American Dietetic Association, 110*(8), 1227–1232. doi:10.1016/j.jada.2010.05.005 PMID:20656099

Henning, C. E. (2017). *LGBT Gerontology: Old Age, Gender, Sexuality and the Constitution of "LGBT Elders"* [Gerontologia LGBT: Velhice, Gênero, Sexualidade e a Constituição dos "idosos LGBT"] [Dissertação de Mestrado]. UFGO: Goiânia.

Herrera, J. M. V. (2020). *What Tourism Will Be Like After COVID-19* [Cómo Será el Turismo Después de la COVID-19]. Available online: https://www.entornoturistico.com/como-sera-el-turismo-despues-de-la-covid-19/

Hintze, H., & Almeida Júnior, A. R. de. (2012). Critical studies of tourism: Tourism communication and the myth of racial democracy in Brazil [Estudos críticos do turismo: A comunicação turística e o mito da democracia racial no Brasil]. *Revista turismo e desenvolvimento*, (17-18), 57-72.

hooks, b. (1981). *Ain't I a woman: Black women and feminism.* South End Press.

Hosteltur. (2020). *Hosteltur Entrevista a Erika Schamis, Head of Packages and Media at Almundo* [Head de Paquetes y Media de Almundo] [Video]. YouTube. Available online: https://youtu.be/HlxYc_6eKq8

Hudson, S., So, K. K. F., Meng, F., Cárdenas, D., & Li, J. (2018). Racial discrimination in tourism: The case of African-American travellers in South Carolina. *Current Issues in Tourism, 23*(4), 438–451. doi:10.1080/13683500.2018.1516743

Hutchings, K., Moyle, C. L., Chai, A., Garofano, N., & Moore, S. (2020). Segregation of women in tourism employment in the APEC region. *Tourism Management Perspectives, 34*, 1–15. doi:10.1016/j.tmp.2020.100655

IBGE, Instituto Brasileiro de Geografia e Estatística. (2017). *Gross Domestic Product of Municipalities* [Produto Interno Bruto dos Municípios]. Avalaible online: https://cidades.ibge.gov.br/brasil/sc/joinville/pesquisa/38/47001?tipo=ranking

IBGE, Instituto Brasileiro de Geografia e Estatística. (2020). *Cities and States* [Cidades e Estados]. Avalaible online: https://www.ibge.gov.br/cidades-e-estados/sc/joinville.html

Ignatov, E., & Smith, S. (2006). Segmenting Canadian culinary tourists. *Current Issues in Tourism, 9*(3), 235–255. doi:10.2167/cit/229.0

INATEL. (2005). *Execution Report of the Programa Turismo Sénior 2005*. INATEL.

Indra Munshi. (2006, October). *Tourism Processes and Gender Relations: Issues for Exploration and Intervention* (No. 42). Economic and Political Weekly. https://www.jstor.org/stable/4418837

Instituto de Pesquisa Econômica Aplicada. (2020). *Information system on the labour market in the tourism sector - SIMT* [Sistema de informações sobre o mercado de trabalho no setor turismo – SIMT]. Recuperado em 15 de dezembro de 2020 de: http://extrator.ipea.gov.br/

Instituto do Patrimônio Histórico e Artístico Nacional - IPHAN. (2015). *IPHAN precautionary policies: Ilê Axé Iyá Nassô Oká: White House terreiro* [Políticas de acautelamento do IPHAN: Ilê Axé Iyá Nassô Oká: Terreiro da Casa Branca]. IPHAN.

International Labor Organization. (2019). *Women and aviation: quality jobs, attraction and retention*. http://www.ilo.org/sector/Resources/publications/WCMS_740235/lang--en/index.htm

Islam, T., Ahmed, I., Ali, G., & Ahmer, Z. (2019). Emerging trend of coffee cafe in Pakistan: Factors affecting revisit intention. *British Food Journal*, *121*(9), 2132–2147. doi:10.1108/BFJ-12-2018-0805

Iso-Ahola, S. E. (1982). Toward a social psychological theory of tourism motivation: A rejoinder. *Annals of Tourism Research*, *9*(2), 256–262. doi:10.1016/0160-7383(82)90049-4

Jarquin, W., Wiggins, L. D., Schieve, L. A., & Van Naarden-Braun, K. (2011). Racial disparities in community identification of autism spectrum disorders over time; Metropolitan Atlanta, Georgia, 2000–2006. *Journal of Developmental and Behavioral Pediatrics*, *32*(3), 179–187. doi:10.1097/DBP.0b013e31820b4260 PMID:21293294

Javed, M., Tučková, Z., & Jibril, A. B. (2020). The role of social media on tourists' behavior: An empirical analysis of millennials from the Czech Republic. *Sustainability*, *12*(18), 7735. doi:10.3390u12187735

Jayasooriya, S. S. W. (2019). Exploring the potentials, issues, and challenges for community-based tea tourism development (with reference to hanthana mountains). *International Journal of Advance Research, Ideas and Innovations in Technology*, *5*(2), 475–480.

Jayawardena, N. S. (2020). The e-learning persuasion through gamification: An elaboration likelihood model perspective. *Young Consumers*, *22*(3), 480–502. doi:10.1108/YC-08-2020-1201

Jayawardena, N. S. (2021). The role of culture in student discipline of secondary schools in cross-cultural context: A systematic literature review and future research agenda. *International Journal of Educational Management*, *35*(6), 1099–1123. doi:10.1108/IJEM-06-2020-0325

Jayawardena, N. S., Ross, M., & Grace, D. (2020). Exploring the relationship between Australian university websites and international student enrolments. *International Journal of Educational Management*, *34*(10), 1527–1557. doi:10.1108/IJEM-02-2019-0068

Jayawardena, N. S., Ross, M., Quach, S., Behl, A., Gupta, M., & Lang, D. (2021). Effective online engagement strategies through gamification: A systematic literature review and a future research agenda. *Journal of Global Information Management*, *30*(5), 1–25. doi:10.4018/JGIM.290370

Jia, Z., Wu, M., Niu, Z., Tang, B., & Mu, Y. (2020). Monitoring of UN sustainable development goal SDG-9.1.1: Study of Algerian "Belt and Road" expressways constructed by China. *PeerJ*, *8*, e8953. doi:10.7717/peerj.8953 PMID:32547851

Jordan, J. (2018). Global goods away from global trading points? Tea and coffee in early modern Bern. *History of Retailing Consumption*, *4*(3), 217–234. doi:10.1080/2373518X.2018.1549401

JUCESC. Junta Comercial do Estado de Santa Catarina. (2020). *Statistics 2020* [Estatísticas 2020]. Avalaible online: http://www.jucesc.sc.gov.br/index.php/informacoes/estatisticas/503-estatisticas-2020

Juran, J. M. (1994). The Next Century of Quality [O Próximo Século da Qualidade]. Congresso Anual de Qualidade da ASQC.

Kabeer, N. (1999). Resources, agency, achievements: Reflections on the measurement of women's empowerment. *Development and Change*, *30*(3), 435–464. doi:10.1111/1467-7660.00125

Kama, A., Ram, Y., Hall, C., & Mizrachi, I. (2019). The benefits of an LGBT-inclusive tourist destination. *Journal of Destination Marketing & Management*, *14*, 100374. Advance online publication. doi:10.1016/j.jdmm.2019.100374

Kaplan, U. (2017). From the tea to the coffee ceremony: Modernizing buddhist material culture in contemporary korea. *Material Religion: the Journal of Objects, Art and Belief*, *13*(1), 1–22. doi:10.1080/17432200.2016.1271969

Karagöz, D., Işık, C., Dogru, T., & Zhang, L. (2021). Solo female travel risks, anxiety and travel intentions: Examining the moderating role of online psychological-social support. *Current Issues in Tourism*, *24*(11), 1595–1612. doi:10.1080/13683500.2020.1816929

Katan, D. (2016). Translation at the cross-roads: Time for the transcreational turn? *Perspectives*, *24*(3), 365–381. doi:10.1080/0907676X.2015.1016049

Kilomba, G. (2019). *Memories of the plantation: episodes of everyday racism* [Memórias da plantação: episódios de racismo cotidiano]. Cobogó.

Kilomba, G. (2021). *Plantation memories: episodes of everyday racism*. Between the Lines.

Kim & Lee. (2017). Promoting customers' involvement with service brands: evidence from coffee shop customers. *Journal of Services Marketing*.

Kimbu, A. N., & Ngoasong, M. Z. (2016). Women as vectors of social entrepreneurship. *Annals of Tourism Research*, *60*, 63–79. doi:10.1016/j.annals.2016.06.002

Kim, E. H., & Choi, C. (2012). Men's talk: A Korean American view of South Korean constructions of women, gender, and masculinity. In *Dangerous Women* (pp. 75–126). Routledge. doi:10.4324/9780203379424-7

Kinnaird, V., & Hall, D. (1996). Understanding tourism processes: A gender-aware framework. *Tourism Management*, *17*(2), 95–102. doi:10.1016/0261-5177(95)00112-3

Kishigami, F. D. (2020). Public policies: leisure and tourism as an instrument for the social insertion of transvestites and transsexuals in social vulnerability [Políticas públicas: lazer e turismo como instrumento de inserção social de travestis e transexuais em vulnerabilidade social] [Master's Dissertation]. Escola de Artes, Ciências e Humanidades, University of São Paulo. www.teses.usp.br doi:10.11606/D.100.2020.tde-10012020-173305

Kladeen, M. (2020). Women and Tourism: Hindering Factors of Women Employment in the Hotel Sector in Sri Lanka. *International Journal of Psychosocial Rehabilitation, 24*(03), 2005–2013. doi:10.37200/IJPR/V24I3/PR200947

Knollenberg, D., Duffy, L. N., Kline, C., & Kim, G. (2021). Creating competitive advantage for food tourism destinations through food and beverage experiences. *Tourism Planning & Development, 18*(4), 379–397. doi:10.1080/21568316.2020.1798687

Koc, E. (2019). Do Women Make Better in Tourism and Hospitality? A Conceptual Review from A Customer Satisfaction and Service Quality Perspective. *Journal of Quality Assurance in Hospitality & Tourism, 21*(4), 402–429. doi:10.1080/1528008X.2019.1672234

Koide, R., & Akenji, L. (2017). Assessment of Policy Integration of Sustainable Consumption and Production into National Policies. *Resources, 6*(4), 48. doi:10.3390/resources6040048

Kotler, P., Wong, V., Saunders, J., & Armstrong, G. (2007). *Modern marketing*. Grada.

Kourtesopoulou, A., & Chatzigianni, E. (2021). Gender Equality and Women's Entrepreneurial Leadership in Tourism: A Systematic Review. In M. Valeri & V. Katsoni (Eds.), *Gender and Tourism: Challenges and Entrepreneurial Opportunities* (1st ed., pp. 11–36). Emerald Publishing. doi:10.1108/978-1-80117-322-320211002

Kourtesopoulou, A., & Chatzigianni, E. E. (2021). *Gender Equality and Women's Entrepreneurial Leadership in Tourism: A Systematic Review*. Gender and Tourism.

Krippendorf, J. (1989). *Sociology of Tourism: For a new understanding of leisure and travel* [Sociologia do Turismo: para uma nova compreensão do lazer e das viagens]. Civilização Brasileira.

Krippendorf, J. (2009). *Sociology of Tourism. For a new understanding of leisure and travel* [Sociologia do turismo. Para uma nova compreensão do lazer e das viagens]. Aleph.

Kühl, B. M. (2006). History and ethics in the conservation and restoration of historical monuments [História e ética na conservação e na restauração de monumentos históricos]. *Revista CPC*, (1), 16–40. doi:10.11606/issn.1980-4466.v0i1p16-40

Kuniyal, J. C., Maiti, P., Kumar, S., Kumar, A., Bisht, N., Sekar, K. C., Arya, S. C., Rai, S., & Nand, M. (2021). Dayara bugyal restoration model in the alpine and subalpine region of the Central Himalaya: A step toward minimizing the impacts. *Scientific Reports, 11*(1), 16547. doi:10.103841598-021-95472-y PMID:34400660

Kwanya, T. (2015). *Indigenous knowledge and socioeconomic development: indigenous tourism in Kenya.* Paper presented at the International Conference on Knowledge Management in Organizations. 10.1007/978-3-319-21009-4_26

Ladeiro, M. M. L. (2012). *The effectiveness of tourist sites case study: Lisbon and the main competitors* [A eficácia dos sites turísticos estudo de caso: Lisboa e os principais concorrentes] [Dissertação de Mestrado]. Escola Superior de Hotelaria e Turismo do Estoril.

Larsen, B., Brun, W., & Øgaard, T. (2009). What tourists worry about–Construction of a scale measuring tourist worries. *Tourism Management*, *30*(2), 260–265. doi:10.1016/j.tourman.2008.06.004

Laverack G, & Wallerstein, N. (2001). Measuring community empowerment: A fresh look at organizational domains. *Health Promotion International*, *16*(2).

Lee. (2017). The Agriculture-Food-Tourism Industry Cluster in the Republic of Korea: The Formation and Growth Factors of Clusters in Regional Agriculture. In*A Multi-Industrial Linkages Approach to Cluster Building in East Asia* (pp. 55-71). Springer.

Lee, W., Wall, G., & Kovacs, J. F. (2015). Creative food clusters and rural development through place branding: Culinary tourism initiatives in Stratford and Muskoka, Ontario, Canada. *Journal of Rural Studies*, *39*, 133–144. doi:10.1016/j.jrurstud.2015.05.001

Lin, Q., & Wen, J. J. (2018). Tea tourism and its impacts on ethnic marriage and labor division. *Journal of China Tourism Research*, *14*(4), 461–483. doi:10.1080/19388160.2018.1511490

Liu, Y. (2019). Study on the Development of Tea Culture Tourism in Xinyang City. *World Scientific Research Journal*, *5*(7), 17–22.

Li, W., Wen, T., & Leung, A. (2011). An Exploratory Study of the Travel Motivation of Chinese Female Outbound Tourists. *Journal of China Tourism Research*, *7*(4), 411–424. doi:10.1080/19388160.2011.627020

Loh, W. (2020). Japanese tourists in Victorian Britain: Japanese women and the British heritage industry. *Textual Practice*, *34*(1), 87–106. doi:10.1080/0950236X.2018.1539031

Londres, C. (2000) Cultural references: basis for new heritage policies [Referências culturais: base para novas políticas de patrimônio]. In Inventário nacional de referências culturais: manual de aplicação. Brasília (DF): Instituto do Patrimônio Histórico e Artístico Nacional.

Louro, G. L. (2000). Body pedagogies [Pedagogias do corpo]. In *LOURO, Guacira Lopes (org.). The educated body* [O corpo educado] (pp. 7–21). Autêntica.

Lovelock, B. (2004). New Zealand travel agent practice in the provision of advice for travel to risky destinations. *Journal of Travel & Tourism Marketing*, *15*(4), 259–279. doi:10.1300/J073v15n04_03

Luchiari, M. T. (1997). Tourism and culture fell on the north coast of São Paulo [Turismo e cultura caiçara no litoral norte paulista]. In Turismo Modernidade e Globalização. HUCITEC.

Luiz, K., & Henz, A. (2018). LGBT tourism: a study about initiatives in Brazil [Turismo LGBT: um estudo acerca das iniciativas no Brasil]. 12° Fórum Internacional de Turismo do Iguassu,, Foz do Iguaçu, Brasil.

Lützkendorf, T., & Balouktsi, M. (2019). On net zero GHG emission targets for climate protection in cities: More questions than answers? *IOP Conference Series: Earth and Environmental Science*, 323. 10.1088/1755-1315/323/1/012073

Macena, D. D. O. (2008). Socio-cultural tourism in the Cabula neighborhood [Turismo sócio-cultural no bairro do Cabula]. *Seminário Estudantil de Produção Acadêmica, 11*(1).

MacLaurin, T. L. (2004). The importance of food safety in travel planning and destination selection. *Journal of Travel & Tourism Marketing, 15*(4), 233–257. doi:10.1300/J073v15n04_02

Maggie, Y. (2009) The macumba arsenal. The objects of sorcery collected by the police throughout the twentieth century [O arsenal da macumba. Os objetos da feitiçaria recolhidos pela polícia ao longo século XX]. Raízes Africanas.

Magnus, G. (2009). *The Age of Ageing*. John Wiley.

Mahaliyanaarachchi, R. (2016). Agri Tourism as a Risk Management Strategy in Rural Agriculture Sector: With Special Reference to Developing Countries. *Journal of Agricultural Sciences–Sri Lanka, 11*(1), 1. doi:10.4038/jas.v11i1.8075

Mahendra, I.W., Sumantra, I.K., Widnyana, I.K., & Vipriyanti, N.U. (2020). Identification of potentials and community perceptions in tourism village planning based on potential resources. *International Journal of Research-GRANTHAALAYAH, 8*(4), 13-22.

Makandwa, G., de Klerk, S., & Saayman, A. (2021). Understanding the Experiences of Rural Women in Sustaining Tourism Enterprises. In M. Valeri & V. Katsoni (Eds.), *Gender and Tourism: Challenges and Entrepreneurial Opportunities* (1st ed., pp. 93–112). Emerald Publishing. doi:10.1108/978-1-80117-322-320211006

Malapit, H. J., Quisumbing, A. R., Meinzen-Dick, R. S., Seymour, G., Martinez, E. M., Heckert, J., Rubin, D., Vaz, A., & Yount, K. M. (2019). *Development of the project-level Women's empowerment in agriculture index (pro-WEAI)*. https://ebrary.ifpri.org/utils/getfile/collection/p15738coll2/id/133061/filename/133271.pdf

Manzini, E. J. (1990). The interview in social research [A entrevista na pesquisa social]. *Didática, 26/27*, 149–158.

Marujo, M. N. N. V. (2008). *The internet as a new means of communication for tourist destinations: The case of Madeira Island* [A internet como novo meio de comunicação para os destinos turísticos: o caso da Ilha da Madeira]. São Paulo: Revista turismo em análise.

McCabe, S. (2009). Who needs a holiday? Evaluating social tourism. *Annals of Tourism Research, 36*(4), 667–688. doi:10.1016/j.annals.2009.06.005

McCabe, S. S., & Johnson, S. (2013). The happiness factor in tourism: Subjective well- being and social tourism. *Annals of Tourism Research, 41*, 42–65. doi:10.1016/j.annals.2012.12.001

McCabe, S., Joldersma, T., & Li, C. (2010). Understanding the benefits of social tourism: Linking participation to subjective well-being and quality of life. *International Journal of Tourism Research, 12*(6), 761–773. doi:10.1002/jtr.791

McCall, C. E., & Mearns, K. F. (2021). Empowering Women Through Community-Based Tourism in the Western Cape, South Africa. *Tourism Review International, 25*(2), 157–171. doi:10.3727/154427221X16098837279967

MEC/SPHAN/FNPM. (1980). Protection and revitalization of cultural heritage in Brazil: a trajectory [Proteção e revitalização do patrimônio cultural no Brasil: uma trajetória]. Brasília: SPHAN/FNPM.

Mecca, M. S., Gorete, M., & Amaral, D. O. (2020). Covid-19: Reflexos no Turismo. *Rosa Dos Ventos, 12*(3), 1–5. doi:10.18226/21789061.v12i3a06

Melo, E., & Correa, A. M. (2016). Between flows and eflows, territorial agencies and the transnationalization of candomblé [Entre fluxos e refluxos, agenciamentos territoriais e a transnacionalização do candomblé]. In *Territorios, fiestas y paisajes peregrinos: cartografías sociales de lo sagrado.* Buenos Aires: La Imprenta Digital SRL.

Menke, A. (2018). *The global coffee industry.* Retrieved on November 8th, 2021, available at: https://globaledge.msu.edu/blog/post/ 55607/the-global-coffee-industry

Milanez, F. (2020). Existence and difference: Racism against indigenous peoples [Existência e diferença: O racismo contra os povos indígenas]. *Rev. Direito Práx, 10*(3), 2161-2181. Http://Www.Scielo.Br/Scielo.Php?Script=Sci_Arttext&Pid=S2179-89662019000302161&Lng=En&Nrm=Iso

Miller, R. E., & Blair, P. D. (1985). *Input-Output Analysis: Foundations and Extensions.* Prentice Hall.

Minayo, M. C. de S. (2002). Science, technique and art: the challenge of social research [Ciência, técnica e arte: o desafio da pesquisa social]. In M. C. de S. Minayo (Ed.), Pesquisa social: teoria, método e criatividade (pp. 9–29). Vozes.

Ministério da Saúde. (2018). *Deaths by suicide among black adolescents and young people from 2012 to 2016* [Óbitos por suicídio entre adolescentes e jovens negros 2012 a 2016]. https://bvsms.saude.gov.br/bvs/publicacoes/obitos_suicidio_adolescentes_negros_2012_2016.pdf

Ministerio de Igualdad. (2022). *Guide to the non-sexist use of language* [Guía para el uso no sexista del lenguaje]. Retrieved: https://www.inmujeres.gob.es/servRecursos/formacion/GuiasLengNoSexista/docs/Guiaslenguajenosexista_.pdf

Ministry of Tourism, Wildlife, and Antiquities [MOTWA]. (2014). *Uganda Tourism Development Master Plan (2014-2024).* Author.

Ministry of Tourism, Wildlife, and Antiquities [MoTWA]. (2020). *The impact of COVID-19 on the tourism sector in Uganda.* Government of Uganda.

Minnaert, L., Maitland, R., & Miller, G. (2009). Tourism and social policy: The value of social tourism. *Annals of Tourism Research, 36*(2), 316–334. doi:10.1016/j.annals.2009.01.002

Minnaert, L., Maitland, R., & Miller, G. (2011). What is social tourism? *Current Issues in Tourism, 14*(5), 403–415. doi:10.1080/13683500.2011.568051

Mitra, S. (2019). What Works in Girls' Education: Evidence for the World's Best Investment? *Social Change, 49*(3), 556–558. doi:10.1177/0049085719863903

Mooney, S. K. (2020). Gender research in hospitality and tourism management: Time to change the https://www.emerald.com/insight/content/doi/10.1108/IJCHM-09-2019-0780/full/html. doi:10.1108/IJCHM-09-2019-0780

Moraes, K. M. (2011). Companionship and sexuality of couples at the best age: caring for the elderly couple [Companheirismo e sexualidade de casais na melhor idade: cuidando do casal idoso]. *Rev. Bras. Geriatr. Gerontol., 14*(4), 787-798.

Moreira, M. G.; Hallal, D. R. (2017). Travels and Border Experiences in the Transgression of the Gay Closet [As Viagens e as Experiências de Fronteira na Transgressão do Armário Gay]. *Revista Rosa dos Ventos – Turismo e Hospitalidade, 9*, 133-155.

Moreira, M. G., & Campos, L. J. D. (2019). The ritual of ideological interpellation in LGBT Tourism and the impossibility of the desire that moves. *Revista Brasileira de Pesquisa em Turismo, 13*(2), 54–68. doi:10.7784/rbtur.v13i2.1542

Morón, M., & Calvo, E. (2018). Introducing transcreation skills in translator training contexts: A situated project-based approach. *The Journal of Specialised Translation*, 29. Recuperado de: https://www.jostrans.org/issue29/art_moron.pdf

Moura, A. D. M. D. E. (2019). *"Here is the blood and sweat of an Indian": Resistance, ethnicity and political struggle of the Tapuias of Lagoa do Tapará – RN* ["Aqui tem sangue e suor de índio": Resistência, etnicidade e luta política dos Tapuias da Lagoa do Tapará – RN] [Dissertação de Mestrado]. Universidade Federal do Rio Grande do Norte, Natal, RN, Brasil.

Mu, L., Chen, Q., & Liang, F. (2019). *Research on the Combination Path of Tea Culture Experience and Urban Leisure Tourism.* Paper presented at the 2019 International Conference on Management, Education Technology and Economics (ICMETE 2019). 10.2991/icmete-19.2019.141

Munday, J. (2004). Advertising: Some Challenges to Translation Theory. *The Translator, 10*(2), 199–219. doi:10.1080/13556509.2004.10799177

Murphy, C., & Halstead, L. (2003). *The person with the idea for the campsite is a hero: Institutional arrangements and livelihood change regarding community-owned tourism enterprises in Namibia.* Directorate of Environmental Affairs, Research Discussion Paper 61, Government of Namibia, Ministry of Environment and Tourism, Windhoek, Namibia.

Nair, L. R., & Dhanuraj, D. (2018). *Kerala Tourism - The Role of the Government and Economic Impacts.* Centre for Public Policy Research.

Nascimento, B. (1977). *Historiography of the quilombo* [Historiografia do quilombo]. Quinzena do negro na USP. https://edisciplinas.usp.br/pluginfile.php/4934266/mod_resource/content/1/Untitled_29082019_193614.pdf

Nascimento, W. F. (2016). On the candomblés as way of life: Philosophical images between Africas and Brasis [Sobre os candomblés como modo de vida: Imagens filosóficas entre Áfricas e Brasis. In: Ensaios Filosóficos]. Rio de Janeiro: UERJ.

Nascimento, A. (1978). *The Brazilian Black Genocide: Process of a Masked Racism* [O genocídio do negro brasileiro: Processo de um racismo mascarado]. Paz e Terra.

Nassani, A. A., Aldakhil, A. M., Abro, M. M. Q., Islam, T., & Zaman, K. (2019). The impact of tourism and finance on women empowerment. *Journal of Policy Modeling*, *41*(2), 234–254. doi:10.1016/j.jpolmod.2018.12.001

National Planning Authority [NPA]. (2020). *Third National Development Plan (NDPIII), 2020/2021-2024-2025.* The Republic of Uganda.

Neri, A. L. (1993). Quality of life and mature age [Qualidade de vida e idade madura] (7th ed.). Campinas: São Paulo: Papirus Editora.

Neugarten, B. L., & Neugarten, D. A. (1986). Changing meanings of age in the aging society. In A. Pifer & L. Bronte (Eds.), *Our Aging Society: Paradox and Promise* (pp. 33–51). W. W. Norton.

Neves, C.S.B. & Brambatti, L.E. (2019). The behavior of LGBT tourists in relation to consumption on leisure trips [O comportamento do turista LGBT com relação ao consumo em viagens de lazer]. *Rosa dos Ventos – Turismo e Hospitalidade, 11*(4), 832-846.

Nguyen, C. P. (2022). Tourism and gender (in)equality: Global evidence. *Tourism Management Perspectives*, *41*, 100933. doi:10.1016/j.tmp.2021.100933

Nimrod, G. (2008). Retirement and tourism – Themes in retirees' narratives. *Annals of Tourism Research*, *35*(4), 859–878. doi:10.1016/j.annals.2008.06.001

Nimrod, G., & Rotem, A. (2010). Between relaxation and excitement: Activities and benefits in retirees´ tourism. *International Journal of Tourism Research*, *12*(1), 65–78. doi:10.1002/jtr.739

Noguer-Juncà, E., & Crespi-Vallbona, M. (2021). Gender Perspective in University Education: The Case of Bachelor's Degrees in Tourism in Catalonia. *International and Multidisciplinary Journal of Social Sciences*, *10*(2), 81–111. doi:10.17583/rimcis.8156

Nomnga, V. J. (2021). Empowering Rural Women in the Hospitality Industry through Small, Medium and Micro Enterprises. *International Journal of Innovation, Creativity and Change, 15*(8).

Nomnga, V. J. (2017). Unlocking the Potential of Women Entrepreneurs in the Tourism and Hospitality Industry in the Eastern Cape Province, South Africa. *Journal of Economics and Behavioral Studies*, *9*(4), 6–13. doi:10.22610/jebs.v9i4.1817

NSC TV. (2020). *SC tourism sector adds losses with cancelled events and fears impact in high season* [Setor turístico de SC soma prejuízos com eventos cancelados e teme impacto na alta temporada]. Avalaible online: https://www.nsctotal.com.br/noticias/os-impactos-da-pandemia-no-setor-turistico-de-sc

Nunan, A. (2015). *Homosexuality of Prejudice to Consumption Patterns* [Homossexualidade do Preconceito aos Padrões de Consumo]. Caravansarai Editora Ltda.

Ochieng, A., Ahebwa, W. M., & Twinomuhangi, R. (forthcoming). *Nexus between biodiversity, climate change and tourism: implications for sustainable tourism in Uganda*. Academic Press.

Okumus, B., & Cetin, G. (2018). Marketing Istanbul as a culinary destination. *Journal of Destination Marketing & Management, 9*, 340–346. doi:10.1016/j.jdmm.2018.03.008

Oliveira, A. G. d. (1978). *Candomblé sergipano*. SEC/CDFB.

Oliveira, L. A. (2016). *Post Modern Tourism: The LGBT segment in Brazil* [Turismo Pós Moderno: O segmento LGBT no Brasil] [Dissertação de Mestrado]. UFRN:Mossoró – RN.

Oliveira, L. O. (2003). Endogenous elements of regional development: considerations about the role of local society in the development process [Elementos endógenos do desenvolvimento regional: considerações sobre o papel da sociedade local no processo de desenvolvimento]. *Revista FAE, 6*(2).

Oliveira, N. A. d. (2021). Blacks and Tourism: analysis of academic production on the subject in journals linked to graduate programs in Tourism in Brazil [Negros e turismo: análise da produção acadêmica sobre o tema em revistas vinculadas aos Programas de Pós-Graduação em Turismo no Brasil]. *Rosa dos Ventos - Turismo e Hospitalidade, 13*(1), 219–238. Disponível em: http://www.ucs.br/etc/revistas/index.php/rosadosventos/article/view/8480

Oliveira, N. A. de. (2021). Blacks and Tourism: analysis of academic production on the subject in journals linked to graduate programs in Tourism in Brazil [Negros e turismo: análise da produção acadêmica sobre o tema em revistas vinculadas aos Programas de Pós-Graduação em Turismo no Brasil]. *Rosa dos Ventos - Turismo e Hospitalidade, 13*(1), 219–238. doi:10.18226/21789061.v13i1p219

Olvera-Lobo, M. D., Gutiérrez-Artacho, J., & Díaz-Millón, M. (2019). Web transcreation in the Spanish business context: the case of healthcare SMEs. In *5th International Conference on Communication and Management (ICCM2019)*. Athens: Communications Institute of Greece.

ONU Women. (2018). *Turning promises into action: Gender equality in the 2030*. Author.

Out Now. (2012). *Better LGBT* Retrieved from: http://www.outnowbusinessclass.com/learn/

Pacheco de Oliveira, J. (Org.). (2011). The indigenous presence in the Northeast: Process of territorialization territorialization process, modes of recognition and memory regimes [A presença indígena no Nordeste: processo de territorialização, modos de reconhecimento e regimes de memória]. Rio de Janeiro: Contra Capa.

Pacheco de Oliveira, J. (1999). *Essays in Historical Anthropology* [Ensaios em Antropologia histórica]. Editora da UFRJ.

Paixão, D. L. D. (2008). *Hedonistic tourism: a post-modern segment of travel combined with pleasure* [Turismo hedonista: um segmento pós-moderno de viagens aliadas ao prazer]. Anais do V Seminário da Associação Nacional de Pesquisa e Pós-Graduação em Turismo.

Paixão, W., Cordeiro, I., & Körössy, N. (2021). Effects of the COVID-19 pandemic on tourism in Fernando de Noronha during the first half of 2020 [Efeitos da pandemia do COVID-19 sobre o turismo em Fernando de Noronha ao longo do primeiro semestre de 2020]. *Revista Brasileira de Pesquisa em Turismo, 15*(1), 2128. doi:10.7784/rbtur.v15i1.2128

Paladini, E. P. (1995). *Quality Management in the Process; quality in the production of goods and services* [Gestão da Qualidade no Processo; a qualidade na produção de bens e serviços]. Atlas.

Panosso Neto, A., & Trigo, L. G. G. (2009). *Brazilian tourism scenarios* [Cenários do turismo brasileiro]. Aleph.

Parashar, S. (2014). Marginalized by race and place: A multilevel analysis of occupational sex segregation in post-apartheid South Africa. *The International Journal of Sociology and Social Policy, 34*(11/12), 747–770. doi:10.1108/IJSSP-01-2014-0003

Park, Satoh, Miki, Urushihara, & Sawada. (2015). Medications associated with falls in older people: systematic review of publications from a recent 5-year period. *European Journal of Clinical Pharmacology, 71*(12), 1429-1440.

Passer, A., Lützkendorf, T., Habert, G., Kromp-Kolb, H., Monsberger, M., Eder, M., & Truger, B. (2020). Sustainable built environment: Transition towards a net zero carbon built environment. *The International Journal of Life Cycle Assessment, 25*(6), 1160–1167. doi:10.100711367-020-01754-4

Pearce, D. (1992). *Tourist organizations*. John Wiley & Sons.

Pedersen, D. (2014). Exploring the concept of transcreation - transcreation as 'more than translation'? *The Journal of Intercultural Mediation and Communication*, 7. Retrieved from: https://iris.unipa.it/retrieve/handle/10447/130535/197987/cultus%20_7_2014.pdf#page=57

Pedersen, D. (2016). *Transcreation in Marketing and Advertising*. Aarhus University.

Peña-Sánchez, A. R., Ruiz-Chico, J., Jiménez-García, M., & López-Sánchez, J. A. (2020). Tourism and the SDGs: An Analysis of Economic Growth, Decent Employment, and Gender Equality in the European Union (2009–2018). *Sustainability, 12*(13), 5480. doi:10.3390u12135480

Petit, N. (2007). Ethiopia's coffee sector: A bitter or better future? *Journal of Agrarian Change, 7*(2), 225–263. doi:10.1111/j.1471-0366.2007.00145.x

Pinheiro, M. L. B. (2006). Origins of the notion of preservation of cultural heritage in Brazil [Origens da noção de preservação do patrimônio cultural no Brasil]. *Risco Revista De Pesquisa Em Arquitetura E Urbanismo,* (3), 4-14. doi:10.11606/issn.1984-4506.v0i3p4-14

Poon, A. (1993). *Tourism, Technology and Competitive Strategies*. CAB International.

Poupart, J. (2012). The qualitative interview: epistemological, theoretical and methodological considerations [A entrevista do tipo qualitativo: considerações epistemológicas, teóricas e metodológicas]. In A pesquisa qualitativa: enfoques epistemológicos (3rd ed., pp. 215–253). Vozes.

Power, K. (2020). The COVID-19 Pandemic Has Increased the Care Burden of Women and Families. *Sustain. Sci. Pract. Policy*, *2020*(16), 67–73. doi:10.1080/15487733.2020.1776561

Qi, J., Li, J., Lu, Y., & Pu, Y. (2019). *A Study on the Tourism Development of Tea Mountain in Yunnan Province—Take Baiying Mountain in Lincang City as an example.* Paper presented at the 2019 2nd International Conference on Education, Economics and Social Science (ICEESS 2019).

Qiu, R. T. R., Park, J., Li, S., & Song, H. (2020). Social costs of tourism during the COVID-19 pandemic. *Annals of Tourism Research*, *84*, 102994. doi:10.1016/j.annals.2020.102994 PMID:32834228

Quan, S., & Wang, N. (2003). Towards a structural model of the tourist experience: An illustration from food experiences in tourism. *Tourism Management*, *25*(3), 297–305. doi:10.1016/S0261-5177(03)00130-4

Quilombo aéreo. (2022). *Air Quilombo* [Quilombo Aéreo]. https://quilomboaereo.com.br/#

Rachão, S., Breda, Z., Fernandes, C., & Joukes, V. (2019). Food tourism and regional development: A systematic literature review. *European Journal of Tourism Research*, *21*, 33–49. doi:10.54055/ejtr.v21i.357

Rachão, S., Breda, Z., Fernandes, C., & Joukes, V. (2020). Cocreation of tourism experiences: Are food-related activities being explored? *British Food Journal*, *122*(3), 910–928. doi:10.1108/BFJ-10-2019-0769

Ramsey, D., Thimm, T., & Hehn, L. (2019). Cross-border Shopping Tourism: A Switzerland-Germany Case Study. European Journal of Tourism. *Hospitality Recreation*, *9*(1), 3–17. doi:10.2478/ejthr-2019-0002

Rebelato, C. (2021). *Introduction to LGBTI+ old age* [Introdução às velhices LGBTI+]. SBGG.

Remoaldo, P. (2020). Creativity in tourism in pandemic period COVID-19 - the ambition and role of the local in the global [Criatividade em turismo em período de pandemia COVID-19 - a ambição e o papel do local no global]. doi:10.21814/uminho.ed.25.13

Republic of Uganda. (2007). *The Uganda Gender Policy*. Ministry of Gender, Labour and Social Development.

Ribeiro, D. (1970). *Indians and Civilization* [Os índios e a civilização]. Civilização Brasileira.

Ricco, A. S. (2012). Tourism as a social and anthropological phenomenon [O Turismo como fenômeno social e antropológico]. In Tourism, space and local development strategies [Turismo, espaço e estratégias de desenvolvimento local]. UFPB.

Richards, G. (2020). Tourism and Resilience: From "overtourism" to no tourism. *Conference: Summer School on the Management of Creativity Organized by HEC Montreal and the University of Barcelona.*

Ridgeway, C. L., & Correll, S. J. (2004). Unpacking the Gender System: A Theoretical Perspective on Gender Beliefs and Social Relations. *Sage Publication, 18*(4), 510–531. doi:10.1177/0891243204265269

Rike, S. M. (2013). Bilingual corporate websites-from translation to transcreation? *Journal of Specialised Translation,* 20. Retrieved from: https://www.jostrans.org/issue20/art_rike.pdf

Rios, L. F. (2009). Homosexuality in the plural of genders: reflections to implement the debate on sexual diversity in schools [Homossexualidade no plural dos gêneros: reflexões para implementar o debate sobre diversidade sexual nas escolas]. In Gender, diversity and inequalities in education: interpretations and reflections for teacher training [Gênero, diversidade e desigualdades na educação: interpretações e reflexões para formação docente]. UFPE.

Ritchie, J. R. B., & Crouch, G. I. (2000). The competitive destination: A sustainability perspective. *Tourism Management, 21,* 1–7.

Robinson & Getz. (2014). Profiling potential food tourists: An Australian study. *British Food Journal, 116*(4), 690-706.

Rougemont, F. dos R. (2016). The longevity of youth [A longevidade da juventude]. In Velho é lindo! Rio de Janeiro: Civilização Brasileira.

Rousta & Jamshidi. (2020). Food tourism value: Investigating the factors that influence tourists to revisit. *Journal of Vacation Marketing, 26*(1), 73-95.

Rubio Gil, A. (2020). Spanish tourism after COVID-19 [El turismo español tras el COVID-19]. *Hosteltur.*

Ruiz Estrada, M. A., Park, D., & Lee, M. (2020). The Evaluation of the Final Impact of Wuhan COVID-19 on Trade, Tourism, Transport, and Electricity Consumption of China. SSRN *Electronic Journal.* doi:10.2139/ssrn.3551093

Sabina, J. M., & Nicolae, J. C. (2013, October). Gender Trends in Tourism Destination. *Procedia: Social and Behavioral Sciences, 92,* 437–444. doi:10.1016/j.sbspro.2013.08.698

Saffioti, H. (1987). *The power of the male* [O poder do macho]. Moderna.

Samoggia, A., & Riedel, B. (2018). Coffee consumption and purchasing behavior review: Insights for further research. *Appetite, 129,* 70–81. doi:10.1016/j.appet.2018.07.002 PMID:29991442

Sánchez, M. M. (2020). Tourism flows, geopolitics and COVID-19: When international tourists are vectors of transmission [Flujos turísticos, geopolítica y COVID-19: cuando los turistas internacionales son vectores de transmisión]. *Geopolítica, 11,* 15.

Sandroni, C. (2010). Samba de roda, intangible heritage of humanity [Samba de roda, patrimônio imaterial da humanidade]. *Estudos Avançados, 24*(69). Advance online publication. doi:10.1590/S0103-40142010000200023

Sarkar, R., & Sinha, A. (2015). The village as a social entrepreneur: Balancing conservation and livelihoods. *Tourism Management Perspectives, 16*, 100–106. doi:10.1016/j.tmp.2015.07.006

Saufi, A., O'Brien, D., & Wilkins, H. (2014). Inhibitors to host community participation in sustainable tourism development in developing countries. *Journal of Sustainable Tourism, 22*(5), 801–820. doi:10.1080/09669582.2013.861468

Scalabrini, E. C.B., & Dalonso, Y. (2018). Impacts Of Events On Tourist Destinations: a case study in the city of Joinville, SC, Brazil [Impactos Dos Eventos Em Destinos Turísticos: um estudo de caso na cidade de Joinville, SC, Brasil]. *Revista Turismo Em Análise, 29*(2), 332–348.

Scheyvens, R. (2000). Promoting women's empowerment through involvement in ecotourism: Experiences from the third world. *Journal of Sustainable Tourism, 8*(3), 232–249. doi:10.1080/09669580008667360

Scheyvens, R. (2002). *Tourism for development: Empowering communities*. Pearson Education Limited.

Schwarcz, L. M. (1993). *The Spectacle of races – scientists, institutions and racial issue in Brazil 1870-1930* [O Espetáculo das Raças – cientistas, instituições e questão racial no Brasil 1870-1930]. Cia. das Letras.

Scott, C., Cooper, C., & Baggio, R. (2008). Destination networks: Four Australian cases. *Annals of Tourism Research, 35*(1), 169–188. doi:10.1016/j.annals.2007.07.004

Scrivano&Sorima Neto. (2015). Potential for LGBT purchases is estimated at R$ 419 billion in Brazil [Potencial de compras LGBT é estimado em R$ 419 bilhões no Brasil]. *O Globo, Caderno de Economia*. https://oglobo.globo.com/economia/potencial-de-compras-lgbt-estimado-em-419-bilhoes-no-brasil-15785227

Seaton, A. V. (1996). Destination marketing. In Marketing tourism products. Thomson Business Press.

Sebrae. (2016). Study on Business Survival in Brazil 2016 [Estudo Sobre Sobrevivencia das Empresas no Brasil 2016]. *Sebrae*. http://www.sebrae.com.br/Sebrae/Portal Sebrae/Anexos/sobrevivencia-das-empresas-no-brasil-102016.pdf

Sengel, K., & Cetin, D. (2015). Tourists' approach to local food. *Procedia: Social and Behavioral Sciences, 195*, 429–437. doi:10.1016/j.sbspro.2015.06.485

Setati, Chitera, & Essien. (2009). Research on multilingualism in mathematics education in South Africa: 2000–2007. *African Journal of Research in Mathematics, Science Technology Education, 13*(1), 65-80.

Shin, C.-S., Hwang, G.-S., Lee, H.-W., & Cho, S.-R. (2015). The impact of Korean franchise coffee shop service quality and atmosphere on customer satisfaction and loyalty. *The Journal of Business Economics Environmental Studies*, *5*(4), 47–57. doi:10.13106/eajbm.2015.vol5.no4.47.

Silva, S., & Vareiro, L. (2020, October). Residents' Perceived Impacts of LGBT Tourism: A Cluster Analysis. In *International Conference on Tourism, Technology and Systems* (pp. 207-222). Springer.

Silveira, R. (2006). *The Candomblé da Barroquinha: Process of constitution of the first bahian terreiro of keto* [O Candomblé da Barroquinha: Processo de constituição do primeiro terreiro baiano de keto]. Edições Mainanga.

Sirigunna. (2015). Food safety in Thailand: A comparison between inbound senior and non-senior tourists. *Procedia-Social Behavioral Sciences, 197*, 2115-2119.

Siston, T. G., Camara, J., Federal, U., Grande, R., Com, I. R., & Federal, G. (2020). Impacts of Covid-19 on tocantins tourism [Impactos da Covid-19 no turismo do Tocantins]. *Revista Espaço e Tempo Midiáticos*, *3*(2), 1–12.

Skalpe, O. (2007). The CEO gender pay gap in the tourism industry—Evidence from Norway. *Tourism Management*, *28*(3), 845–853. doi:10.1016/j.tourman.2006.06.005

Škare, M., Soriano, D. R., & Porada-Rochoń, M. (2021). Impact of COVID-19 on the travel and tourism industry. *Technological Forecasting and Social Change*, *163*, 120469. doi:10.1016/j.techfore.2020.120469 PMID:35721368

Smith. (2015). A sense of place: Place, culture and tourism. *Tourism Recreation Research, 40*(2), 220-233.

Smith, N., Suthitakon, N., Gulthawatvichai, T., & Karnjanakit, S. (2019b). "Creating a coffee tourism network in the North of Thailand", Local Economy. *The Journal of the Local Economy Policy Unit*, *34*(7), 718–729. doi:10.1177/0269094219893272

Smith, W. E., Kimbu, A. N., de Jong, A., & Cohen, S. (2021). Gendered Instagram representations in the aviation industry. *Journal of Sustainable Tourism*. Advance online publication. doi:10.1080/09669582.2021.1932933

Smolen, J. R., & de Araújo, E. M. (2017). Race/skin color and mental disorders in Brazil: A systematic review [Raça/cor da pele e transtornos mentais no Brasil: uma revisão sistemática]. *Ciencia & Saude Coletiva*, *22*(12), 4021–4030. doi:10.1590/1413-812320172212.19782016 PMID:29267719

Soares, J. R. R. (2015). *The Relationship between the Touristic Image and Loyalty: An Analysis of International Students in Galicia [Ph.D. Thesis]*. University of A Coruña. Available online http://hdl.handle.net/2183/14919

Soltani, A., Pieters, J., Young, J., & Sun, Z. (2018). Exploring city branding strategies and their impacts on local tourism success, the case study of Kumamoto Prefecture, Japan. *Asia Pacific Journal of Tourism Research*, *23*(2), 158–169. doi:10.1080/10941665.2017.1410195

Statista. (2021). Retrieved on 2nd December 2021. https://www.statista.com/statisticsshare-of-subscribers-to-travel-programs-worldwide-by-gender

Su & Zhang. (2020). Tea drinking and the tastescapes of wellbeing in tourism. *Tourism Geographies*, 1-21.

Sultana, A. (2012). Patriarchy and Women's Subordination: A Theoretical Analysis. *Arts Faculty Journal*, *4*, 1–18. doi:10.3329/afj.v4i0.12929

Su, M. M., Sun, Y., Wall, G., & Min, Q. (2020). Agricultural heritage conservation, tourism and community livelihood in the process of urbanization – Xuanhua grape garden, Hebei province, China. *Asia Pacific Journal of Tourism Research*, *25*(3), 205–222. doi:10.1080/10941665.2019.1688366

Su, W., Wall, G., & Wang, Y. (2019). Integrating tea and tourism: A sustainable livelihoods approach. *Journal of Sustainable Tourism*, *27*(10), 1591–1608. doi:10.1080/09669582.2019.1648482

Tadini, R.F., & Melquiades, T. (2008). Analysis of the performance of service volunteers to the National Olympic and Paralympic Committees in the scope of the Pan and Parapan American Games Rio 2007 [Análise da atuação dos voluntariados de serviço aos Comitês Olímpicos e Paraolímpicos Nacionais no âmbito dos Jogos Pan e Parapanamericanos Rio 2007]. In V Seminário de Pesquisa em Turismo do MERCOSUL – SeminTUR, 2008. Universidade de Caxias do Sul.

Tadioto, M. V., Moreira, M. G., & Jung de Campos, L. (2016). Discourse Analysis: A theoretical-analytical device to problematize Tourism [Análise do Discurso: um dispositivo teórico - analítico para problematizar o Turismo]. In Anais... XIII Seminário da Associação Nacional de Pesquisa e Pós-Graduação em Turismo - ANPTUR. São Paulo, Brasil: Anptur.

Tan, E., & Bakar, B. A. (2016). The Asian Female Tourist Gaze: A Conceptual Framework. In Asian genders in tourism (pp. 65-87). Channel View Publications.

Tarlow, P. E. (2014). *Tourism Security: Strategies for Effectively Managing Travel Risk and Safety*. Butterworth-Heinemann.

Tayibnapis, A. Z., & Sundari, M. S. (2020). Boosting indonesia's tourism sector to be competitive. *International Journal of Management & Business Studies*, *10*(1), 9–14.

Ting, H., De Run, E. C., Cheah, J.-H., & Chuah, F. (2016). Food neophobia and ethnic food consumption intention. *British Food Journal*, *118*(11), 2781–2797. doi:10.1108/BFJ-12-2015-0492

Ting, H., Fam, K.-S., Hwa, J. C. J., Richard, J. E., & Xing, N. (2019). Ethnic food consumption intention at the touring destination: The national and regional perspectives using multi-group analysis. *Tourism Management*, *71*, 518–529. doi:10.1016/j.tourman.2018.11.001

To, W. M. (2020). *How Big is the Impact of COVID-19 (and Social Unrest) on the Number of Passengers of the Hong Kong International Airport? Sustainability analysis View project Soundscape View project How Big is the Impact of COVID-19 (and Social Unrest) on the Number of P.* Working Paper. doi:10.13140/RG.2.2.12999.04002

Tomaello, F. (2020). *Tourism Experts from Around the World Analyze What It Will Be Like to Travel in the New Post-Pandemic Scenario* [Expertos Turismo de Todo el Mundo Analizan Cómo Será Viajar en el Nuevo Escenario Post Pandemia]. Available online: https://www.infobae.com/turismo/2020/06/14/expertos-turismo-de-todo-el-mundo-analizan-como-sera-viajar-en-el-nuevo-escenario-post-pandemia/

Tomazzoni, E. L. (2006). Analysis of tourist discourse in the Serra Gaucha [Análise do discurso turístico da serra gaúcha]. *Em questão, 12*(2), 339-365.

Trevisan, J. S. (2006). Tourism and sexual orientation [Turismo e orientação sexual]. In *Ministério do Turismo do Brasil. Social tourism. Tourism dialogues: a journey of inclusion* [Turismo social. Diálogos do turismo: uma viagem de inclusão] (pp. 139–171). Instituto Brasileiro de Administração Municipal.

Trigo, L. G. G. (1993). Tourism and Quality; Contemporary Trends [Turismo e Qualidade; Tendências Contemporâneas] (5th ed.). Academic Press.

Trigo, L. G. G. (2009). Rise of pleasure in today's society: GLS Tourism [Ascensão do prazer na sociedade atual: Turismo GLS]. In Tourism market segmentation: studies, products and perspectives [Segmentação do mercado turístico: estudos, produtos e perspectivas]. Manole.

Trigo, L. G. G., & Panosso Netto, A. (2011). *Afro ethnic tourism in Brazil. VIII Seminar of the National Association research and graduate in Tourism, Balneario Cambour* [Turismo étnico afro no Brasil. VIII Seminário da Associação Nacional Pesquisa e Pós-Graduação em Turismo, Balneário Camboriú]. https://www.anptur. org.br/anais/anais/files/8/10. pdf

Trigo, L. G. G. (2020). Travel and tourism: from imagined scenarios to disruptive realities [Viagens e turismo: dos cenários imaginados às realidades disruptivas]. *Revista Brasileira de Pesquisa em Turismo (RBTUR), 14*(3), 1–13. Advance online publication. doi:10.7784/rbtur.v14i3.2107

TRLV. (2020). *Pulse Tourism and Covid-19* [Pulso Turismo e Covid-19]. TRLV Lab.

Tshabalala, S. P., & Ezeuduji, I. O. (2016). Women Tourism Entrepreneurs in KwaZulu-Natal, South Africa: Any Way Forward? Acta Universitatis Danubius, 12(5).

Tucker, H., & Boonabaana, B. (2012). A critical analysis of tourism, gender and poverty reduction. *Journal of Sustainable Tourism, 20*(3), 437–455. doi:10.1080/09669582.2011.622769

Tumusiime, D. M., & Vedeld, P. (2015). Can Biodiversity Conservation Benefit Local People? Costs and Benefits at a Strict Protected Area in Uganda. *Journal of Sustainable Forestry, 34*(8), 761–786. doi:10.1080/10549811.2015.1038395

Uganda Wildlife Authority. (2018). *Bwindi Impenetrable National Park.* https://ugandawildlife.org/wp-content/uploads/2022/01/Bwindi-cc-2018-2.pdf

Uğur, N. G., & Akbıyık, A. (2020). Impacts of COVID-19 on global tourism industry: A cross-regional comparison. *Tourism Management Perspectives, 36*, 100744. doi:10.1016/j.tmp.2020.100744 PMID:32923356

Ummiroh, I. R., & Hardiyani, R. (2013). Agro-ecotourism management through cooperative based coffee plantation commodity to increase welfare of coffee farmer. *Journal of Economics, Business and Management, 1*(4), 347–349. doi:10.7763/JOEBM.2013.V1.75

UN. (2020). *Aging* [Envelhecimento]. https://www.who.int/health-topics/ageing#tab=tab_1

UNDP. (n.d.). *Sustainable development goals: United Nations Development Programme.* Retrieved from https://www.undp.org/sustainable-development-goals

United Nations Conference on Trade and development [UNCTAD]. (2017). *Economic development in Africa Report, Tourism for Transformative and Inclusive Growth.* The United Nations.

United Nations. (1948). *General Assembly Resolution 217 A.* United Nations.

United Nations. (2020). *World's Women 2020: Trends and Statistics.* Retrieved from: https://worlds-women-2020-data-undesa.hub.arcgis.com/

United Nations. (2021). *Transforming Our World: The 2030 Agenda for Sustainable Development.* A/RES/70/1. 2015. Available online: https://sdgs.un.org/2030agenda

United Nations. (n.d.). *The 17 goals | sustainable development.* United Nations. Retrieved from https://sdgs.un.org/goals

UNWTO - World Tourism Organization. (2015). *Tourism in the 2030 Agenda.* Available at: https://www.unwto.org/tourism-in-2030-agenda

Urraco, M. (2020). *What Will the Return of Tourism Be Like After the Lockdown?* [¿Cómo Será la Vuelta del Turismo Tras el Confinamiento?]. RTVE. Available online: https://www.rtve.es/noticias/20200422/como-sera-vuelta-del-turismo-tras-confinamiento/2012448.shtml

Urrutikoetxea-Arrieta, B., Polo-Peña, A. I., & Martínez-Medina, C. (2017). The Moderating Effect of Blogger Social Influence on Loyalty Toward the Blog and the Brands Featured. In *Marketing at the Confluence between Entertainment and Analytics* (pp. 885–898). Springer. doi:10.1007/978-3-319-47331-4_180

Usai, R., Cai, W., & Wassler, P. (2022). A queer perspective on heteronormativity for LGBT travelers. *Journal of Travel Research, 61*(1), 3–15. doi:10.1177/0047287520967763

van Eerdewijk, A., Wong, F., Vaast, C., Newton, J., Tyszler, M., & Pennington, A. (2017). *White paper: A conceptual model of women and girls' empowerment.* https://www.kit.nl/wp-content/uploads/2018/10/BMGF_KIT_WhitePaper_web-1.pdf

Van, D. T. A. (2015). Speech and power [Discurso e poder] (2nd ed.). São Paulo: Contexto.

Vasudevan, S. (2008). The Role of Internal Stakeholders in Destination Branding: Observations from Kerala Tourism. *Place Branding and Public Diplomacy, 4*(4), 331–335. doi:10.1057/pb.2008.24

Vidal da Rocha, M. C., Luis da Silva, R., Gabrig Oliveira, I., & Faria Duarte, A. L. (2021). Benefícios da Atividade Turística na Manutenção da Saúde da Terceira Idade. *Revista Estudos E Pesquisas Em Administração, 5*(1). doi:10.30781/repad.v5i1.11634

Vukovic, D.B., Petrovic, M., Maiti, M. & Vujko, A. (2021). Tourism development, entrepreneurship and women's empowerment – Focus on Serbian countryside. *Journal of Tourism Futures*. doi:10.1108/JTF-10-2020-0167

Walby, S. (1990). *Theorizing patriarchy*. Basil Blackwell.

Walker, J. R. (2002). *Introduction to hospitality* [Introdução à hospitalidade]. Manole.

Wall, G. (2006). Recovering from SARS: the case of Toronto tourism. In Tourism, Security and Safety (pp. 143-152). Routledge. doi:10.1016/B978-0-7506-7898-8.50014-X

Wang, C., Chen, L.-H., Su, P., & Morrison, A. M. (2019). The right brew? An analysis of the tourism experiences in rural Taiwan's coffee estates. *Tourism Management Perspectives*, *30*, 147–158. doi:10.1016/j.tmp.2019.02.009

Wang, F., Filimonau, V., & Li, Y. (2021). Exploring the patterns of food waste generation by tourists in a popular destination. *Journal of Cleaner Production*, *279*, 1–16. doi:10.1016/j.jclepro.2020.123890

Wang, L., Lehto, X., & Cai, L. (2019). Creature of habit or embracer of change? Contrasting consumer daily food behavior with the tourism scenario. *Journal of Hospitality & Tourism Research (Washington, D.C.)*, *43*(4), 595–616. doi:10.1177/1096348018817586

Weed. (2005). *"Meta interpretation": A method for the interpretive synthesis of qualitative research.* Paper presented at the Forum Qualitative Sozialforschung/Forum: Qualitative Social Research, Forum Qualitative Sozialforschung.

Wenzel, K., & John, V. M. (2012). Travel Journalism: An analysis of the main Brazilian magazines [Jornalismo de viagens: Análise das principais revistas brasileiras]. *Estudos em Comunicação*, (11), 291–311.

WHO. (2015). *World Report on Aging and Health* [Relatório Mundial de Envelhecimento e Saúde]. Brasília, DF: OMS. Disponível em: https://sbgg.org.br/wpcontent/uploads/2015/10/OMS-ENVELHECIMENTO-2015-port.pdf

Wijaya, S. (2019). Indonesian food culture mapping: A starter contribution to promote Indonesian culinary tourism. *Journal of Ethnic Foods*, *6*(1), 9. doi:10.118642779-019-0009-3

Wilkes, R. E. (1992). A structural modeling approach to the measurement and meaning of cognitive age. *The Journal of Consumer Research*, *19*, 292–301.

Wilson, T. D., & Ypeij, A. (2012). *Introduction: Tourism, Gender, and Ethnicity*. Sage Publications, Inc. https://www.jstor.org/stable/41702290?seq=1&cid=pdf

Wipulasena, A. (2020). *Tea tourism: Beyond just a cup of tea*. Retrieved on 2nd December 2021. www.dailynews.lk/2020/08/ 25/features/226821/tea-tourism-beyond-just-cup-tea

Wojtowicz, E. (2021). Stereotypes in management-Does leadership have a gender? *Humanities and Social Sciences Quarterly*, *28*(1), 125–134. doi:10.7862/rz.2021.hss.10

World Bank. (2013). *Case Studies of the Horticulture, Tourism, and Call Center Industries*. The World Bank Group.

World Food Travel Association. (2020). *What is food tourism?* Retrieved on 3rd November 2021. https://worldfoodtravel.org/what-is-food-tourism-definition-food-tourism

World Tourism Organization. (2019). *Global Report on Women in Tourism* (2nd ed.). UNWTO. doi:10.18111/9789284420384

World Tourism Organization. (2019). *Global Report on Women in Tourism* (2nd ed.). UNWTO. doi:10.18111/9789284420384

World Travel and Tourism Council. (2020). *Crisis readiness: Are you prepared and resilient to safeguard your people & destinations?* Global Rescue Report.

Woyesa, T., & Kumar, S. (2020). Potential of coffee tourism for rural development in Ethiopia: a sustainable livelihood approach. *Environment, Development and Sustainability*. doi: 2Fs10668-020-00610-7 doi:10.1007%

Xu & Ye. (2016). Tourist Experience in Lijiang—The Capital of Yanyu. *Journal of China Tourism Research, 12*(1), 108-125.

Xu, H. (2018). Moving toward gender and tourism geographies studies. *Tourism Geographies, 20*(4), 721–727. doi:10.1080/14616688.2018.1486878

Yanes, A., Zielinski, S., Diaz Cano, M., & Kim, S. I. (2019). Community-based tourism in developing countries: A framework for policy evaluation. *Sustainability, 11*(9), 2506. doi:10.3390u11092506

Yeh, S. C., Chiou, H. J., Wu, A. W., Lee, H. C., & Wu, H. C. (2019). Diverged Preferences towards Sustainable Development Goals? A Comparison between Academia and the Communication Industry. *International Journal of Environmental Research and Public Health, 16*(22), 4577. doi:10.3390/ijerph16224577 PMID:31752324

Yeh, S.-S. (2020). Tourism recovery strategy against COVID-19 pandemic. *Tourism Recreation Research*, 1–7. doi:10.1080/02508281.2020.1805933

Ying, W., & Law, W. (2018). Examining the efficacy of self-classification approach in segmenting special-interest tourists: Food tourism case. *Asia Pacific Journal of Tourism Research, 23*(10), 961–974. doi:10.1080/10941665.2018.1513048

Yousaf, S., & Xiucheng, F. (2018). Halal culinary and tourism marketing strategies on government websites: A preliminary analysis. *Tourism Management, 68*(1), 423–443. doi:10.1016/j.tourman.2018.04.006

Yu, M., & Hyun, S. S. (2021). Development of modern racism scale in global airlines: A study of asian female flight attendants. *International Journal of Environmental Research and Public Health, 18*(5), 2688. doi:10.3390/ijerph18052688 PMID:33800093

Zardo, E. F. (2003). *Tourism Marketing* [Marketing aplicado ao turismo]. Roca.

Zeldin, T. (2008). *Uma História Intima da Humanidade*. Bestbolso.

Zenker, S., & Kock, F. (2020). The coronavirus pandemic–A critical discussion of a tourism research agenda. *Tourism Management, 81*, 104164. doi:10.1016/j.tourman.2020.104164 PMID:32518437

Zhang & Hitchcock. (2017). The Chinese female tourist gaze: A netnography of young women's blogs on Macao. *Current Issues in Tourism, 20*(3), 315-330.

Zhang, J., & Zhang, Y. (2020). Tourism and gender equality: An Asian perspective. *Annals of Tourism Research, 85*, 103067. doi:10.1016/j.annals.2020.103067

Zhang, J., & Zhang, Y. A. (2021). Qualitative Comparative Analysis of Tourism and Gender Equality in Emerging Economies. *Journal of Hospitality and Tourism Management, 46*, 284–292. doi:10.1016/j.jhtm.2021.01.009

Zhou, M., Hsieh, Y. J., & Canziani, B. (2016). *Tea Tourism: Examining University Faculty Members' Expectations*. Academic Press.

Zirulnik, M. L., & Orbe, M. (2019). Black female pilot communicative experiences: Applications and extensions of co-cultural theory. *The Howard Journal of Communications, 30*(1), 76–91. doi:10.1080/10646175.2018.1439422

Zou, Y., & Meng, F. (2020). Chinese tourists' sense of safety: Perceptions of expected and experienced destination safety. *Current Issues in Tourism, 23*(15), 1886–1899. doi:10.1080/13683500.2019.1681382

About the Contributors

Priscila Cembranel is a professor at Universidade Sociedade Educacional Santa Catarina (UNISOCIESC-Brazil). Post-doctoral scholarship in Business Admonistration (Universidade Federal do Paraná).

Jakson Renner Rodrigues Soares has a degree in Business Administration, Universidade Federal do Ceará [2008]. International Ph.D. in Planning and Management of Tourism, Universidade da Coruña [2015]; Title of Ph.D. Dissertation: "Relationship between tourist image and loyalty built: Analysis of international students in Galicia", supervised by José Manuel Santos Solla, Anton Alvarez Sousa and José María Suárez Andrade (Cum Laude). Currently an Interim Professor in the Department of Management and Marketing at USC and Professor at the University School of Tourism CENP-UDC. His research interests include Competitiveness of the tourist destination, Tourism's Impacts on heritage destinations, and Gender studies and Tourism.

André Riani Costa Perinotto is a Ph.D. in Communication Sciences (Mediatic Processes) - UNISINOS/RS-Brazil. Master's degree in Geography (Organization of Space) - UNESP/Rio Claro/SP-Brazil; Specialist in Teaching for Higher Education in Tourism and Hospitality by SENAC/SP-Brazil; and Graduated in Tourism by UNIMEP/SP-Brazil. Full Professor of the Bachelor's Degree in Tourism at the Parnaiba Delta Federal University - UFDPar. Professor of the Professional Master's degree in Tourism at the Federal University of Paraná (UFPR). Professor of the Professional Master's degree in Tourism Business Management at the UECE (State University of Ceará). Former Head of the Bachelor's Degree in Tourism of the UFDPar (Head of Department and Coordination of Course); Ex-Coordinator of EITUR - Center for Interdisciplinary Studies and Research in Tourism at UFDPar.

* * *

Marília Barbosa Gonçalves is a Doctoral student in Media Studies at PPGEM/UFRN and student of Journalism/UFRN. Master in Tourism, Tourismologist and Administrator from UFRN. He has an MBA in Strategic Marketing and People Management from UNI-RN. Partner and consultant at Start Consultoria Técnica Ltda.

Brenda Boonabaana is a Lecturer at Makerere University, Uganda. She is also an Early Career Provost Fellow at the University of Texas, Austin, USA. Her research areas focus on Gender and Tourism; Gender, Women empowerment and Agriculture.

Marcelo Borba holds a PhD in Engineering and Knowledge Management from UFSC (2017), a Master's degree in Administration from FURB (2006), he is a professor at the Universityof The University of Joinville, working in the undergraduate and graduate studies, mainly on the following topics: entrepreneurship, innovation, knowledge management, information systems, strategic planning, innovation habitats and marketing. He is a professor at the Instituto Superior e Centro Educacional Luterano Bom Jesus, working in the undergraduate course. Executive Director of the Innovation Park in Joinville and Regiãinova parq. Coordinator of the C â mara de Inovação of ACAFE. Member of the Inova parq Advisory Board. Member of the Comitis Manager of Inova parq. Local Coordinator of the Postgraduate Program the Stricto Sensu Master's Degree In Productive Systems - PPGSP, (UNIPLAC / UNESC / UNIVILLE / UnC). Member of the Board of Directors of the Joinville Church Educational Foundation - FURJ. Member of the University Council at the Univille River. Member of the Municipal Council of Science, Technology and Innovation of Joinville. Univille representative in the Technology and Innovation Department of ACIJ. Member of the Joinville City Council for Sustainable Development.

Laiara Borges has a bachelor's in Aeronautics Science FTC (Faculty of Technology and Science), postgraduate student in Social Project Management. Creator of the Quilombo Aereo, instructor in the project Pretos que voam and Voe como uma garota. Leadership of the Marielle Franco Baobá project for racial and gender equity.

Solano Braga is a professor in the Bachelor's Degree in Tourism at the Federal University of Delta do Parnaíba (UFDPar), with a work regime in D.E. permanent professor of the professional master's degree in arts, heritage and museology at UFDPar. Doctor in Development and Environment - PRODEMA/Federal University of Piauí (2021), Master in Geography - Institute of Geosciences of the Federal University of Minas Gerais - IGC/UFMG (2011); Degree in Geography - UNIVERSO (2014); Degree in Tourism and Hospitality by the Teacher Training Program - Federal Center for Technological Education of Minas Gerais - CEFET/MG (2008), Bachelor's Degree in Tourism - IGC/UFMG (2006).

Fernanda Dalonso is a professor and a psychodramatist psychologist. Master´s degree in Cultural Heritage and Society from the University of the Region of Joinville, Brazil. She has academic experience and is the author of publications involving various topics related to heritage and society such as socio-environmental, shared heritage management and cultural landscape areas. Currently, she develops research in the fields of psychology, psychodrama, culture and environment.

Yoná da Silva Dalonso graduated in Tourism and Hospitality (Univali), Master in Communication Sciences (USP), and PhD in Geography (UMINHO, Portugal). Professor and Researcher in the field of Tourism and leader of the CNPq Tourism and Territory Research Group at the University of the Region of Joinville, Univille. Its publications include articles in academic journals, chapters in books, and other scientific productions on tourism, gastronomy, public policies, events, tourism planning, and regional planning.

Ademílson Damasceno graduated with a Degree in Geography from the State University of São Paulo Júlio de Mesquita Filho (2005). He is currently a Researcher at the State University of São PauloJ úlio de Mesquita Filho. He has experience in the area of Geosciences, with a phase in Geography. Acting mainly on the following topics: Baixada Santista, dengue, Serra do Mar, Coastal Zone, Public health and Metropolitan Planning.

Giselle Domingos is a Master's student in Administration at Unisul, graduated in Financial Management from the Faculty of Technology of Santa Catarina (2009). He is currently campus manager of the Sociesc College of Jaraguto the South. Experience in the area of Administration, with a degree in Management. With twelve years of activity in the commercial area, in the segments: technology, education and service. Experience in the form of teams, strategic planning, management of sales channels and KPIS, budget management and headcount, relationship with the market and other stakeholders. Educator passionate about education and its transforming power. Motivated by the challenges and opportunities to always be able to do the best, through is effective and high performance management, teams carried out and recognized, healthy and productive environments, which impossible to reach the success of organizations through is the best practice social responsibility and sustainable growth.

Jani Floriano is a PhD in Education- Psychology of Education(PUC-SP), Master in Economics - Industrial Economics (UFSC),Bachelor's Degree in Economics (Univille), Undergraduate in Dirieto (Univille) and specializing in Finance, Investments and Banking (PUC-RS). She is currently a full professor at the University of the Region of Joinville. He has experience in the area of Economics, with a phase in Macroeconomic Theory, Monet Economics and Industrial Economy, working mainly on the following topics: Macroecon Aggregates, Monet's Policy and Tax, Industrial Economy and Competitiveness of the Indú Brazilian striae. Do you act as Planning and Institutional Evaluation Advisor at the University of The University of Joinville? Univille and specializes in Quality Indicators (SINAES). Draftsman of BNI items and the SINAES Evaluators Bank.

Ana Paula Xavier Fonseca is a Business Administration student at Santa Catarina Educational Society University.

Cassiana Gabrielli is a Brazilian woman Professor at the Department of Geography, Tourism and Humanities (DGTH) at the Federal University of São Carlos (UFSCar). PhD in Interdisciplinary Studies on Women, Gender and Feminism at the Federal University of Bahia (UFBA); Master in Culture and Tourism at Santa Cruz State University (UESC/UFBA); Bachelor of Tourism at the Federal University of Paraná (UFPR). Actually is leader of the research group FRONT - Intersectional-border dimensions of sustainability -, certified by National Council for Scientific and Technological Development (CNPQ).

Marina Gonçalves is a PhD in History, Master in Arts. Holds a degree in Conservation and Restoration of Mobile Cultural Assets and a degree in Tourism.

Juanna Beatriz Gouveia is a Master's student in Media Studies (PPgEM/UFRN), holds a degree in Portuguese/English Languages from the Catholic University of Pernambuco (2019.1) and has already worked in the PIBIC program at the Catholic University of Pernambuco (2017/2018). Self-employed teacher of English and special student of the Professional Master's in Letters at the State University of Mato Grosso do Sul (UEMS). Interested in research lines: Discourse analysis. Language acquisition, development and disorders in their various manifestations.

Juncal Gutiérrez-Artacho holds a Ph.D. in Translation and Interpreting from the University in Granada, Spain, in 2015. She is lecturer in Translation and Interpreting at the FTI, University of Granada. She is also the Assistant Head of the Department on Translation and Interpreting. Her main research interest are Multilingual Information Retrieval, Human Post Editing of Machine Translations and Localization.

Nirma Sadamali Jayawardena is a PhD student of Griffith Business School, attached to Marketing Department. She completed BSc in Business Management with a first-class Honors from National School of Business Management, Green

University, Sri Lanka, and completed MBA in international business from University of Colombo, Sri Lanka. Her research interests include social cognition, consumer visual memory, and advertising.

Emilda K. Joseph is an Assistant Professor with the Department of Commerce at Christ College, MG University, Kerala, India. She received her Ph.D. from Christ (Deemed to be University), Bangalore, India in June 2020. She has six years of academic experience teaching postgraduate and undergraduate programs and research in the fields of tourism and management. She has presented papers at conferences and published articles in various journals. Her research interest is towards Sustainable tourism.

Tomy K. Kallarakal is a professor and Dean, School of commerce, Finance and Accountancy, Christ University, Bangalore. He has over 35 years of academic experience and has widely published papers in reputed refereed journals and has contributed chapters to edited volumes. Dr. Tomy has handled several prestigious roles in the university as a part of his academic career. His research interests are in the area of Human Resource Development and Organizational Behavior.

Sanjeewa Kumara Karunarathna is a final year undergraduate student in BSc (Hons) in Business Management at Cardiff Metropolitan University, UK. He has more than 15 years of work experience as a manager in CIC Holdings PLC, Sri Lanka.

Daniel Lemos holds a degree in Social Communication - Journalism from the Federal University of Rio Grande do Norte (2000), a master's degree (2006) and a doctorate (2012) in Language Studies from the Federal University of Rio Grande do Norte. Class D Professor - Associate 1 at the Department of Social Communication and at the Graduate Program in Media Studies at the Federal University of Rio Grande do Norte. Daniel coordinates the Communication, Culture and Media Research Group and the Discourse Analysis Atelier's research projects. His topics of interest are ethics, journalistic ethics, media discourse analysis, organizational communication.

Cintia Martins is a PhD in Molecular and Cell Biology at UNESP; Full Professor of Biological Sciences at the Parnaiba Delta Federal University – UFDPar.

Emerson Melo is a Doctor in Geography from the State University of Rio de Janeiro (2019), Master in Geography from the Federal University of Minas Gerais (2014), Bachelor, Degree in Geography from the Pontifical Catholic University of São Paulo (2007). He worked as Professor of Geography in public and private schools and as an educator/researcher at the Museu Afro Brasil (MAB-SP).

Adriano Nunes is a Master's student in Science with a concentration in Tourism Development at the University of São Paulo; Postgraduate in Customer Relationship Management; with an emphasis on personal training, behavioral analyst and Ombudsman/Ombudsman.

Guilherme Arnaud Nunes has experience in the field of Communication, with an emphasis on Journalism. Computer skills, internet access, e-mail, office package (Word, Power Point, Excel), good writing and typing. High ability to meet deadlines.

Natália Oliveira is a Brazilian woman Professor at the Department of Social Science at the Federal University of Santa Maria (UFSM). PhD in Sociology (Federal University of Rio Grande do Sul). Master in Social Science (University of Vale do Rio dos Sinos), Bachelor in Tourism (Mato Grosso State University).

María-Dolores Olvera-Lobo is a Doctor in Documentation, Full Professor at the Department of Information and Communication at the University of Granada (Spain) and teacher at the Faculties of Communication and Documentation, and Translation and Interpreting. She is a member of the "Scientific Information: Access and Evaluation Research Group ". Principal Investigator in national R&D&I projects financed by the Ministry of Economy, Industry and Competitiveness, and in numerous teaching innovation projects at the University of Granada.Her research lines are focused on Information Retrieval, Multilingual Information Access, Translators Training and Public Communication of Science.

Renata Laize Paino Ribeiro graduated in Law - UNI-RN (2004). Postgraduate (Specialist) in Civil Law and Civil Procedure (UFRN) 2008, Incomplete Specialization in Project Management and Public Policies (UNP-2010) Incomplete Specialization in Letters: Studies on Language Theories and Teaching. (UFRN - 2014), lawyer - Renata Laize Law Firm. Professional experience in Teaching in the field of Law, having taught in Higher Education at IES in Natal teaching the subjects Individual Labor Law, Civil Law (General Theory, Real Rights, Family Law, Succession Law), Civil Procedural Law (General Theory, Knowledge Process, General Theory of Resources), General and Professional Ethics, Legal Hermeneutics, Legal Philosophy and Sociology, and Children's and Adolescents' Law.

Raissa Mariana Rita is a Business Administration student at Santa Catarina Educational Society University.

Raquel Santiago Romo has a Master's degree in Tourism Management and Planning from the University of A Coruña and member of the GTES research team. Her main lines of research focus on the gender perspective in the tourism sector.

Gabriela Santos is a postdoctoral fellow at the Center for Languages, Literatures and Cultures (CLLC) of the University of Aveiro (Portugal). PhD in Advanced Studies in Social Anthropology from the University of Barcelona, Master in Anthropology and Ethnography from the University of Barcelona and Master in Culture and Tourism from the State University of Santa Cruz, Bahia. Bachelor in Tourism from the Pontifical Catholic University of Campinas, São Paulo.

Elaine Scalabrini is a Researcher in TurnOut Project in Instituto Politécnico de Bragança. She is a Post-doctorate at Social Sciences Institute, University of Minho and she investigated about the residents' perception toward creative tourism, more specifically in Encontrarte, an event in Amares - Portugal. She got her PhD in Geography, in 2017 at University of Minho. She got her Master in Regional Development at Fundação Regional de Blumenau (Brazil, 2009). She is member of Lab2PT (Laboratory of Landscape, Heritage and Territory) at University of Minho and Turismo e Território Group in Universidade da Região de Joinville - Univille. She was coordinator of Departament of Gastronomy in Univille (Brazil) from 2014 to 2018 and was professor in this University, teaching tourism, research methods and entrepreneurship. From 2016-2018 was President of City Council Tourism from Joinville (Brazil).

Aline Silveira is a PhD in Geography from the State University of Rio de Janeiro, Brazil (2019) EBTT Professor at the Federal Center for Technological Education Celso Suckow da Fonseca, Brazil.

Gamze Temizel was born in 1979, in Konya/Türkiye. She completed her undergraduate education in 2002, in Tourism Management, in Dokuz Eylül University in İzmir/Türkiye. She completed her postgraduate education in 2006, in Management and Organization, in Selçuk University in Konya/Türkiye. She finally get her PhD degree in 2012, in Production Management and Marketing, in Selçuk University in Konya/Türkiye. She has been working in Selçuk Üniversity since 2005. Her final position is in the faculty of Tourism as a lecturer. Her research area is social sciences and she is interested in multidisciplinary studies in tourism management.

Bindi Varghese is a Doctorate in Commerce, specializing in tourism. As an academician and tourism professional, she has over 19 years of academic and Industrial experience. Currently, she is affiliated with Christ University, as an Associate Professor. Her research interest is towards Destination Marketing and Impact assessment studies.

Manoela Veras is a gender equality researcher at GREENS (Research Group on Energy Efficiency and Sustainability).

Index

G

H

I

J

L

M

P

Q

R

S

T

Printed in the United States
by Baker & Taylor Publisher Services